REVELATION

REVELATION

The Education of a Priest

DALE COLEMAN

Foreword by Randall Balmer

RESOURCE *Publications* · Eugene, Oregon

REVELATION
The Education of a Priest

Resource Publications
An Imprint of Wipf and Stock Publishers
199 W. 8th Ave., Suite 3
Eugene, OR 97401

www.wipfandstock.com

PAPERBACK ISBN: 978-1-5326-6438-0
HARDCOVER ISBN: 978-1-5326-6439-7
EBOOK ISBN: 978-1-5326-6440-3

Manufactured in the U.S.A.   FEBRUARY 2, 2019

To Cheetah
Who is rarely happy with anything
unless it's her idea,
and who is marginally happy with this
Sine Qua Non

THE COLLAR

I struck the board, and cried, 'No more!
I will abroad.
What? shall I ever sigh and pine?
My lines and life are free; free as the road,
Loose as the wind, as large as store.
Shall I be still in suit?
Have I no harvest but a thorn
To let me blood, and not restore
What I have lost with cordial fruit?
Sure there was wine
Before my sighs did dry it : there was corn
Before my tears did drown it.
Is the year only lost to me?
Have I no bays to crown it?
No flowers, no garlands gay? all blasted?
All wasted?
Not so, my heart: but there is fruit,
And thou hast hands.
Recover all thy sigh-blown age
On double pleasures: leave thy cold dispute
Of what is fit, and not. Forsake thy cage,
Thy rope of sands,
Which petty thoughts have made, and made to thee
Good cable, to enforce and draw,
And be thy law,
While thou didst wink and did not see.
Away; take heed:
I will abroad.
Call in thy death's head there: tie up thy fears.
He that forbears
To suit and serve his need,
Deserves his load.'
But as I raved and grew more fierce and wild
At every word,
Me thoughts I heard one calling, 'Child!'
And I replied, 'My Lord!'

GEORGE HERBERT

Contents

Permissions

Foreword

HAD CIRCUMSTANCES UNFOLDED SLIGHTLY differently—or, in theological nomenclature, had *providence* allowed—my path might have crossed with Dale Coleman's far earlier in life than it did. We were both born the same year (1954) and spent our childhoods steeped (mired?) in what I have called the evangelical subculture, this vast and interlocking network of institutions contrived in the middle decades of the twentieth century to keep children like us from being tainted by the larger culture, which our parents regarded as both corrupt and corrupting.

Both Dale and I are preacher's kids—"PKs," in the lingo of the subculture—my father in the Evangelical Free Church of America and Dale's parents, both of them, in the Salvation Army. It's very likely that Dale and I unknowingly squared off on opposing teams in junior high football in Bay City, Michigan, in the mid-1960s—flag football, it turns out, because the school system could not afford pads or helmets. In any case, we both cheered our beloved Detroit Tigers to victory in the 1968 World Series against the St. Louis Cardinals. Our paths might have crossed again in Iowa thereafter, where our families moved after Michigan, but neither of us recalls such a meeting. The evangelical subculture often feels constricting to those on the inside, but it is also, as I said, vast.

Something far more consequential than coincidence was unfolding in both of us in ensuing years, something that would eventually bring us together. We were growing impatient with the barren sacramentalism within evangelicalism, yearning, sometimes without words to express it at the time, for a more substantial, historically connected expression of the Christian faith, one uncorrupted by the cult of personality that so often afflicts evangelical congregations.

Albeit through slightly different routes, both Dale and I found our way to the Episcopal Church. When I'm asked how an evangelical like me became an Episcopalian, I typically respond with two semi-flippant answers. It was, I say, a reaction to the aesthetic deprivation of my childhood. I also grew tired of the evangelical cult of novelty.

Dale Coleman's response to that question is far more nuanced and sophisticated than mine, and the details of his pilgrimage are found in these pages. It is a wonderful and engaging story, told with honesty, intelligence, and humor.

The narrative that follows is also discursive, and therein lies its real merit. Readers will chortle at the dead-on descriptions of pretentious prelates and their sartorial excesses, but they will also be instructed by the author's learned reflections about liturgy, music, and theology.

How and when did our paths finally cross? After much prayer, deliberation, and discernment, I decided late in middle age, to pursue ordination in my adopted Episcopal Church. The parish that sponsored me was Church of the Holy Faith, in Santa Fe, New Mexico. Its rector was the irrepressible Dale Coleman. We've been friends, kindred spirits, and fellow travelers ever since.

RANDALL BALMER
Feast of the Holy Name
January 1, 2019

Preface

NEAR THE END OF my senior year at Nashotah House, Dean John Samuel Ruef glared at me during lunch in the refectory, and said with some disdain, "Coleman, I imagine you will write about your time here. You're just the kind boorish person to do it." He had a point with his premonition. I have wanted to write about growing up in the Salvation Army and seminary days for years. I have wished for forty years as a priest the day would come to do this, and serve the Christian church by reminding us who we are. There are two and a half billion Christians around the world today, not including snake-handlers, who set themselves on the credal tradition of the Nicene Creed, something almost totally forgotten in the United States. In fact, much of what passes as the Christian faith would go unrecognizable to the huge majority of baptized Christians who have handed down to our age generation to generation. The Episcopal Church, in which I serve, has been undergoing an enormous doctrinal amnesia, even strangely forgetting the one who said to us, "Do this in Remembrance of me." This church is my church, my people, my heritage. When I needed our Lord's presence in my life, this is the Church He showed me in which to grow and serve. Reading through what I have written, it was crystal clear to me that God used several remarkable devout Christians to lead me to where I am today, most of them Episcopalian. I will be ever grateful for this Church taking me in, and revealing to me that I was called by the Lord Himself to be a priest in His Church.

Martin Luther once said that the first evangelist in our lives, was our mother. So it was for me. I learned the name of Jesus from my mother, Eva Roberts Coleman. But the church she knew, and in which I was reared was weird. The Salvation Army is one of the strangest of churches which call themselves Christian. They wear faux Victorian British Military Band uniforms. And they all march around with a finger up in the air pronouncing they're number one. "Lift up the Army banner, Blood and Fire" is one of their songs. I grew up in this sect, knowing all along since about age nine, something was wrong. My mind, my questioning, my asking obvious questions about what the hell we were doing playing E flat tenor horns, were all suppressed. (I was made to play one for a couple years, and gave up. My parents then decided I would take accordion lessons. I kid you not. To them, the Holy Spirit loves oom pah pah.) I handled this emotionally, actually in my very self, my soul, by developing such a strange sense of humor, that the only company in which I can think where it is understood, is Jewish. And one other.

I am grateful to the messengers God sent to guide me to the full, sacramental Christian faith, which I hold dear: Professor Jim Moody, Professor George Anastaplo, Senator John Sherman Cooper, Professor Stan Henning, Professor Robert Booth Fowler, Fr. Wayne Smith, Fr. Joseph Hunt, Fr. Bob Cooper, Preacher Will Campbell, Archbishop Michael Ramsey, Archbishop Joseph Augustine DiNoia, Professor Stanley Hauerwas, Bishop Tom Wright, Pastor Ron Neustadt. I call them saints. Siri Hustvedt in *The Sorrows of an American* calls them ghosts. But enough about her.

Several friends have assisted me in my own Christian life: Fr. Aiden (Al) Kimel, Professor David Bentley Hart, Fr. Ralph McMichael, Sr. Grace Mueller.

It was after being turned down by several publishing houses, Fr. Randall Balmer, whose friendship I treasure, urged me to send my typescript to Wipf and Stock. Matthew Wimer, Jim Tedrick, and George Callihan have been wonderful, courteous, thoughtful gentlemen, and I am happy Wipf and Stock is bringing out this memoir. Randy's "Foreword" is as generous and wonderful and articulate as his work. I am deeply thankful for his kindness. He could have told me this before I had been subjected to some horrific rejections. Just saying.

Two wonderful young women in my life have encouraged me for years to write. They are intelligent, thoughtful, talented, loving. They are my two daughters, Jacquelyn Grace Coleman, and Gillian Michal Coleman. They are as loyal and caring and independently minded as any father would wish for.

The parish I have served for nearly twelve years, St. George's Episcopal Church, welcomed me to serve as their rector, at a very low point in my life. They took me in, and helped heal me, most especially in expecting me to be a priest in the Church of Christ. They occasionally inform me of my sins, which I don't like, but desperately need, in this reconciling community. We are sinners saved by God's grace. They gave me the opportunity to write. Mostly.

I have dedicated this book to a smart, droll, intelligent lady, with a mind as quick as a flash. She is a totally beautiful person, with healing in her wings. I had begun to write first eighty pages, and then nearly two hundred, in order to settle scores. She let me know bluntly how foolish that would be, and what about being called as a priest? What about expressing my faith in God? What about allowing this to be a teaching opportunity about the beliefs and life in the Church Catholic? What about proclaiming my faith in Christ Jesus which at an increasingly dark time in our nation's and church's lives needs hope? I resisted for awhile. I thought what planet is she from? At least 95% of life is score settling. And that's in the church. On several occasions she challenged what I had written, and told me to go to hell. She has been a lovely and bracing muse, and this is very much her book as mine. But I am responsible for the final product. As a follower of Heidegger once said, "What I have written, I have written." It's even better in Heidegger's German, "*Was ich geschrieben habe, das habe ich geschrieben.*" It sounds a lot like John Macquarrie, even Ayn Rand. But no.

This is more an "out of my life and thought." It is a confession as St. Augustine used the word, as St. Paul, John Henry Newman, Albert Schweitzer, Garry Wills have written. Not Rousseau or Ben Franklin. It was coincidental to my muse's strictures, while reading Stanley Hauerwas' *Hannah's Child*, I came to the realization I did want to write about my vocation to which I had been called. I am like him in being more Aristotelian than Platonist about the Church for which our Lord gave His life. I attempted to reach Stanley, and one morning out of the blue I got a phone call with a voice that I thought was Ross Perot's. Yikes! After ten minutes or so, I said, "Jesus Christ, you're Stanley Hauerwas!". "That's what I said", offered Mr. Perot. He had read half of what I had written and he was calling me a short time before knee surgery to tell me he liked the story. "Stick with it. Get an editor. Professional. I got an editor and he cut 25% out of my memoir." I'm quite sure this is not what this brusque erudite backwoods Texas Methodist had in mind. But he made my day. He's wonderful! And *Time* magazine thinks so! Who am I to argue with *Time* magazine? But I want to see what was cut out of his book.

Last thing. There is a passage in Newman's last of his *University Sermons* which I find scintillating about the Catholic Church's development of doctrine based on responding to heresy. It is to me a wise and intricately thought out view, which may be revealing about this One, Holy, Catholic, and Apostolic Church, Christ's Body, which I love. Newman wrote about the Arian heresy:

> What a remarkable sight it is, almost all unprejudiced persons will admit, to trace the course of the controversy, from its first disorders to its exact and determinate issue. Full of deep interest, to see how the great idea takes hold of a thousand minds by its living force, and will not be ruled or stinted, but is 'like a burning fire', as the Prophet speaks, 'shut up' within them, till they are 'weary of forbearing, and cannot stay', and grows in them, and at length is born through them, perhaps in a long course of years, and even successive generations; so that the doctrine may rather be said to use the minds of Christians, than to be used by them. Wonderful it is to see with what effort, hesitation, suspense, interruption—with how many swayings to the right and to the left—with how many reverses, yet with what certainty of advance, with what precision in its march, and with what ultimate completeness, it has been evolved; till the whole truth 'self—balanced on its centre hung', part answering to part, one absolute, integral, indissoluble, while the whole world lasts! Wonderful, to see how heresy has but thrown that idea into fresh forms, and drawn out from it farther developments, with an exuberance which exceeded all questioning, and a harmony which baffled all criticisms, like Him, its Divine Author, who, when put on trial by the Evil One, was but fortified by the assault, and is ever justified in His sayings, and overcomes when He is judged.
>
> And this world of thought is the expansion of a few words, uttered, as if casually, by the fishermen of Galilee . . .

DALE COLEMAN
Feast of the Holy Name
January 1, 2019

Acknowledgments

I WISH TO THANK the following:

For the excerpt from T. S. Eliot's "Little Gidding", in *T. S. Eliot: The Complete Poems and Plays, 1909—1950*: To Harcourt, Brace and World;

For the excerpts from John Betjeman's poems "House of Rest", and "Christmas", from *John Betjeman's Collected Poems*, To John Murray Publishing House;

For the excerpts from John Henry Newman, To Penguin Random House; To Longman Publishing;

For the poem, "Adam's Curse" in *The Collected Poems of W. B. Yeats,* To MacMillan;

For The poem "Revelation" in *The Poetry of Robert Frost : All Eleven of his Books—Complete,* to Holt, Rinehart and Winston;

For the excerpt from Theodore Roethke's "The Waking", in *Words for the Wind,* to Indiana University Press.

For "The Collar", and "Love", by George Herbert, in *The New Oxford Book of English Verse*, ed. Helen Gardner, To Oxford University Press.

For "The General Prologue" to Geoffrey Chaucer's *The Canterbury Tales*, I am grateful to W. W. Norton and Company, Inc., Copyright © 1993.

All Scriptural passages are taken from The NRSV, The New Revised Standard Version Bible, copyright ©1989, Division of Christian Education of the National Council of the Churches of Christ in the United States of America. I am grateful to them. I use NRSV as an abbreviation for this Bible.

All portions of the Book Of Common Prayer, are taken from Prayer Book and Hymnal : Containing The Book of Common Prayer and The Hymnal 1982, according to the use of The Episcopal Church. Church Publishing Incorporated, New York. Copyright © by the Church Pension Fund. All rights reserve. I am grateful to them, my church. I use BCP as an abbreviation for the *Book of Common Prayer*.

Part One

MATINS

REVELATION

We make ourselves a place apart
Behind light words that tease and flout,
But oh, the agitated heart
Till someone find us really out.
'Tis pity if the case require
(Or so we say) that in the end
We speak the literal to inspire
The understanding of a friend.
But so with all, from babes that play
At hide-and-seek to God afar,
So all who hide too well away
Must speak and tell us where they are.

ROBERT FROST

I

I was 22 in early February, 1977 as I was making my way through the various hurdles set up by the Episcopal Diocese of Milwaukee for those in the process of becoming a priest, in accord with the Canons of the Episcopal Church. It was a Saturday and precisely 9:00 am as I entered the rather nondescript solid grey institutional Milwaukee hospital. My new Church mandated that any men (later women-the Milwaukee Diocese was one of the fiercest opponents of woman's ordination to the priesthood and episcopate) seeking holy orders of transitional diaconate and priesthood meet the medical, emotional and intellectual requirements set, as well as find a sponsoring Parish Church and Diocese. Normally all these requirements would have to be met before applying and one hoped, being received by a certified Episcopal Seminary. Of the ten seminaries, my sponsoring Bishop, Charles T. Gaskell, had laid down the law of my attending Nashotah House and only Nashotah House. He had stated in his dark, dank Episcopal office in his rather strained reedy voice, "Coleman, you have no background in the Church. All you know is the Salvation Army, and you're not yet confirmed. Therefore Nashotah it will be." End of discussion. Where the Bishop lurked in the old offices on East Juneau Avenue, Milwaukee, always struck me as gloomy. So when I thought well of the bishop, from time to time, I referred to him as gloomy gus. On other occasions, when he caught me by surprise in the diocesan hallway or Cathedral of All Saints', and called me "Caldwell", I thought his get up, his costume looked like that of Dracula. (I imagined he spent the day hanging upside down in the closet with his wings over his eyes.) He normally wore a purple cassock with red piping, a purple cape or *mozzetta*, black dress shoes, and a purple skullcap or *zucchetto*. The Bishop and the Diocese were styled as Anglo-Catholic, that is, Episcopalians who expressed their identity in haberdashery and excessive ritual. Early on, I learned that priests and bishops "dressed like mother and wanted to be called father". I generally found the sartorial expressions among the more extreme Anglo-Catholic clergy (who might wear "lace up the wazoo"—as certain of my more showy gay seminary friends would say) a little "dandified", even "precious". I had therefore begun referring to these extra bits as "mozzarellas", and "zucchinis" while complimenting the wearers: as in "My, I love your mozzarella, Archdeacon", or "No one can wear a zucchini as you do your grace". Most Anglo-Catholic clergy, especially the "thicky thick" ones, would be quite taken with being complimented, and hardly offer a protest over nomenclature. Christopher Buckley has an anecdote about the down side of this describing the antics of George

Brown, Prime Minister Harold Wilson's Foreign Secretary in 1966. At a state dinner in Vienna, and in his cups, Brown turned to confront his table mate:

> He had enjoyed his wine, and upon hearing the orchestra strike up a tune, turned to an exquisite creature in violet beside him and said, "Madam, you look ravishing. May we dance?" "No, Mr. Brown, for three reasons. First, this is a state dinner, not a ball. Second, that is the Austrian state anthem, not a waltz. And third, I am the cardinal archbishop of Vienna."[1]

Bishop Gaskell was a tall, dark and handsome man, who loved his job, and fully believed he and only he knew what the Lord wanted from him, which was an almost megalomaniac notion to build up the Episcopal Church in the Anglo-Catholic way, especially by shaping up young smart ass seminarian wannabees like me. And I was a "special case" for the Bishop.

I had grown up in an extreme holiness minded "church", the Salvation Army, begun in 1865 by a raving loony Methodist minister in the East end of London, William Booth, who in the best pietistic fashion felt called by God to start yet one more church, to enable the salvation of all the terrible drunks, sinners, single women, women of the streets, chain smoking, drug addicted, slack, pan handling, low living, starving, sick, toothless, raving mad, broke, handicapped. So, he reckoned, he needed absolute order and authority-his!—and insisted on this by declaring his ministers officers, and lay folk soldiers, to make up a vast army. He commissioned them, along with providing each one a British Victorian military looking uniform—and even more—a British Victorian military band instrument. Soldiers and officers wore these uniforms with either a big shiny blue or red S—on their lapels. These weird costumes are still worn today and proudly! William Booth looks like long bearded Jehovah of old—as they would say—in photographs. And he forced everyone within hearing of a Salvationist "corps"—not church—to play or listen to loud dreadful "martial" sounding music, played or sung by folks who looked "saved" or "spiritual" by their constant smiling throughout the worship services. Salvation Army music and preaching provokes strong emotion among the folks drawn to this kind of worship. It is this strong emotional commitment to Jesus (mostly) which identifies the truly saved. And William Booth, at his wife Catherine's order, nixed anything like the Sacraments as commanded by the Lord, (I'm thinking especially of the Dominical Sacraments of Baptism and Holy Communion) because Booth (or specifically his wife) knew better than the Lord how to get people saved. It was Catherine Booth's decided view that one could never trust the "sacraments" to be salvific, because of how so many nominal Christians were openly hypocritical. How could one be saved by baptism and think oneself a Christian, and then turn around and drink, smoke, cuss, be a pub habitué, watch the cinema, divorce, dance, wear nylons and lipstick? These strictures would obviously rule out any Anglican clergy, as well as most popes and cardinals. So the

---

1. Christopher Buckley, *But Enough About You*, 387

heavy lifting of being Christian was tied entirely to one's emotional decision(s) at the "altar rail", following an altar call. (It was actually called the Holiness Table, or even Mercy Seat.) Altar calls occurred at Sunday morning and evening services, as well as Wednesday evening services. An officer advanced in rank after the first few years of being a Lieutenant and then Captain, by three factors: 1) how well one could kiss his or her commanding officer's usually ample derriere; 2) how many statistical times one had saved anyone; and 3) how much money one could raise. These last two numbers were registered with some solemnity every week. The first was a little more beyond an officer's ability to classify (even as holy as he or she could be) by data, statistics, graphs, or pie charts. One could perhaps see that without the sacraments of Baptism and Communion, a Salvationist's total "security" of being saved and in the hands of Jesus, was in accord with one's feelings of being saved. And as most human beings might know if they are even vaguely emotionally aware, feelings are fleeting, and not difficult to evoke. (The Nazis did this, e.g., with the instrumental martial playing of the "*Horst Wessel Lied*". And the Volk loved this, for a while at least.) So having the same folks Sunday by Sunday respond to an emotionally powerful and manipulative Corps Officer's anguished pleadings to come to Jesus and get your warm fuzzy positive feelings back, assisted by the singing to band music of say "Almost Persuaded", or "Throw out the life line", or "Rescue the Perishing", or "Just as I am", would produce a win/win all around.

Of course, with this being my background—and frankly—a slightly omniscient sense he worked to project—Bishop Gaskell saw me as his special spiritual mission in 1977.

II

So THERE I WAS at this decidedly institutional looking Hospital having moved some
distance towards becoming a priest in the Diocese of Milwaukee. I was to spend the
next eight hours with an entire team of medical, psychological, and psychiatric spe-
cialists to determine if I could be judged within a range of normality in human physical and emotional health so as not to be unleashed on unsuspecting congregations
in order to play out what might otherwise be the rather unsavory agendas of a great
number of religious leaders in America.

I met first with a nurse and then medical doctor to undergo a physical. I endured
a number of needles and being prodded from these nurse ratchet types. Then as I
could still walk, I met with a psychiatrist who sat very close to me and asked lots of
questions very similar to the ones Will Stockdale had to endure in the film version of
"No Time For Sergeants". I remember this doctor smelling of a malodorous cologne,
and shuffling into the room in some dishevelment while dragging one foot behind the
other—his hair pomaded because he was a doctor after all. Yes, I loved my mother and
father, yes they had lots of faults, and yes I differentiated from their need to shelter my
siblings and me from the wickedness of the world, and would I say more about that.

Yes, as a matter of fact I would. I grew up in a very close knit family, all centered on
the Salvation Army. Both my parents had grown up under very difficult circumstances
in utter poverty. My dad had been farmed out along with his slightly older brother to
their mother's aunt and uncle when he was two months old. He and his brother were
the second and third children of four, all boys, and all having been born to a high
strung loud teenage mother, and an abusive alcoholic father. His parents had divorced
very early in their marriage, and so Dale and Jack went to live with Uncle Gilbert and
Aunt Rill in Hay Creek (pronounced crick) Michigan. Uncle Gilbert George McKee
was born in the late 1890s, and had been gassed in the war to end all wars. (My brother
Bill and I discovered his uniform, boots, helmet, bayonet and gas mask, and found
these useful in our war games.) Coming back from the war (not quite right as Aunt
Rill said) he married Orillia Davila Cook and settled down to try and pull themselves
out of desperate poverty. They did not succeed. Uncle Gilbert tried his hand at owning a country general store in northern Ohio, failed and ended up owning a farm just
outside of Hillsdale, Michigan. He was a bitter old man when I got to know him in the

1950s, an attitude changed only for the worse following a stroke in the early '60s. He resembled Walter Brennan, whom we all watched on television, in the "Real McCoys", except that he was taller and slurred all his words. Once when I yelled at him what baseball team the Tigers were playing on television, this in 1962, and a matter of deep concern to me, he looked at me and hollered "Mithhianplith". "What?" I said. Now with more volume-not helping the pronunciation, "Mithhianplith". What? "Jeeth, the fucking Thwinth". I corrected him with, "Uncle Gilbert, they're called the Minnesota Twins", not of course winning any points with my stupid response. It interested me how clear his swearing was. And we hardly ever heard any cussing at Aunt Rill's and Uncle Gilbert's house, because of the prudish ways of my mother. He died in 1965.

Aunt Rill, born in 1900, her age so easy to remember, was the most loving kind even saintly Christian woman anyone could have as a "grandmother". She worked hard on the farm with her husband, and took on another job as a janitor at Hillsdale College. She did this primarily to have the money needed to provide Christmas and Birthday gifts for my siblings and me. Aunt Rill was short and slight, and a fantastic cook. To this day I remember the joy my family felt when we arrived at Aunt Rill's house for Thanksgiving or Christmas. She loved us to death and showed it in the amazing turkey, mashed potatoes, yams, green beans, cranberry sauce, gravy, rolls, and two or three homemade pies, usually cherry, apple and mincemeat on display. She was true to her name. She loved us, and always hugged, kissed, touched, and smoothed my notorious cowlick with Aunt Rill special spit. My hair received a lot in those days. We attended a Wesleyan church with Aunt Rill and Uncle Gilbert, which could be enjoyable for its novelty. My entire family, including my three siblings, all enjoyed singing, and we belted out "I'll Fly Away", "Leaning on the Everlasting Arms", "Blessed Assurance", "It is Well with my Soul", "Is your Name Written there?", "For I know Whom I have Believed", among many others. Aunt Rill always gave my siblings and me a taste of what the love of Jesus was incarnate.

When my family visited the Hillsdale farm, everything was delightful. We explored acres and acres of countryside, romped in the hay lofts, stayed for hours in the barn, and, at least my brother and I, played Cowboys and Indians. (I don't know why the Indians were led by Geronimo and Cochise, except for television movies.)

So my dad grew up with his "Mama" Rill and Uncle Gilbert. He was born in 1931, in Hillsdale. He had an unfortunate sense of coarse humor about women, which might include Joanne Castle as she played "Wabash Cannonball" in her honky-tonk style on the Lawrence Welk Show, or Dolly Parton on The Porter Wagner show.) His name was Dale Duane Coleman, the kind of backwoods, rural, moonshine drinking, snake handling dumb farm boy name usually associated with a hick who reports during testimony time at Sunday night church having had several encounters of being probed for hours in every orifice by a Goober looking alien twice dumber than Floyd the Barber on Andy Griffith Show—leading the minister of music to change the next hymn to "He Touched Me". (This is the name my parents proudly blessed me with, adding Junior to it.) He was handsome-as my brother Bill is now—a jack of all trades, who could tear apart and put back together a Ford engine. He was a short order cook, his specialties usually involving venison or spam. Education was not a strong suit for my dad; he had little aptitude for it, and wasn't generally encouraged by his growing up with Aunt Rill and Uncle Gilbert, who had finished their own schooling with the 6th grade. He and my Uncle Jack were very close, both natural salesmen, athletes, and singers. They played ball together in High School, Uncle Jack a singles hitter while my dad hit for power. In High School and afterwards, they sang in a men's Gospel quartet, with two Wesleyan Methodist ministers and twins, Vernon and Verdon Dunkle out of Spring Arbor, Michigan. Some of my earliest memories were of hearing their singing as recorded on old 78 records, my dad the high tenor and Uncle Jack the bass. The quartet had a fine clear sound, and all had perfect pitch. The Dunkle—Coleman Quartet became well—known singing at church services, revivals, and live on the radio. I listened to "On the Jericho Road", "He'll Understand and Say Well Done", and "This World is Not My Home".

My dad had kept old posters announcing their concerts. What one noticed about my dad was the enjoyment he took in singing, and his handsome features, including Jerry Lee Lewis wavy hair. His was a fine physique, which he kept in shape through a discipline of lifting weights. He also had the Dale Carnegie confidence in himself, which enabled him to be a natural salesman. I was not like my dad.

My mother was seven years older than dad, and a city slicker. She was the youngest of three, born in Detroit to William Henry Roberts from Cornwall, England, and Lillian Sampson, a member of the Lumbee Tribe which had a very colorful past from Robeson County, North Carolina, many living in and around Pembroke. No one has yet discovered their origins with five or so competing notions of whence they came. A favorite myth was they were aboriginals who intermarried with the Lost Colony of Roanoke, and therefore "Croatans". This was my mother's working theory—and my mother was never very keen on history. The Lumbees were loyal to the United States during the time of the "Trail of Tears" or better the "Trail of Tears and Death" in 1830–8. This was the infamous forced march of the Five Indian Nations living in the Southeastern States of the US, the Cherokee, Chickasaw, Muskogee, Choctaw, Creek, to which was added the Seminole, for good measure. Congress passed in 1830 the Indian Relocation Act under the aggressive prodding of President Andrew Jackson. Approximately 45,000 Native Americans were marched at gunpoint away from the houses and lands they had successfully farmed in rich soil for many generations because of the greed of immigrant whites desiring their very productive land. The President was one himself who engaged in land speculation and bought a great many acres and farms. Meanwhile the Indian peoples were placed in crowded internment camps, to await their removal to lands west of the Mississippi, in the Oklahoma territory. Men, women and children succumbed to disease and freezing temperatures, unprepared for the harsh conditions to which they were subjected. Nearly a third of the people died during this relocation.

The Lumbees were allowed to stay because of their sworn loyalty to the United States and moved to less productive land in the areas around the Lumberton River. Their reward was to be hated by all other Native tribes, to be castigated as mulattos or "half-breeds" throughout the 19th century, as well as to be enslaved to assist the Confederate cause during the War of Northern Aggression (as they said in North Carolina). In the twentieth century, everyone held them in contempt, as their lot could be compared to the Untouchables in India. Many fought in WWII, and received North Carolina's gratitude by finally being officially named a State tribe in the 1950s. In 1958, a famous event occurred when the KKK Grand dragon James W. "Catfish" Cole decided to call a Rally near Hayes Pond on farmland he rented for the purpose, to end the "mongrelization" of the races which he on this occasion associated with the Lumbee. On January 13, three crosses were burned in Robeson County, one in front of a Lumbee woman's house in St. Paul's, because she was dating a white man, another on the property of a Lumbee family in Maxton, and a third near a bar which was a favorite of the Lumbee men. Cole called the rally for January 18th. About a hundred or so Klansmen showed and shouted their approval of ridding the county of "kinky haired mongrels", who were destroying the purity of the white race. They were then startled to find a large number of Lumbees surrounding them, many WWII vets who were known as fierce fighters, and not easily intimidated. When the light bulbs above Cole were shot out, five hundred or so Lumbees charged them from all sides and the Klansmen fled in terror, Cole leading them into the woods. The Lumbees had been well organized by Charlie Warriax and Simon Oxendine, both Lumbee veterans of the War. The incident became a popular *Life* magazine article with pictures of Warriax and Oxendine depicted with the KKK banner they had recovered draped around them.[1]

My mother hardly knew her own mother who died in a Diphtheria epidemic in 1927, my mother barely two and a half years old. She was deeply affected by the love she received and expressed for her mother's family, favorites being her Uncle Claude and Aunt Mary Sampson. We traveled a number of times when I was young to visit our relatives on a large tobacco farm. (The irony of this was my mother's deep antipathy towards cigarette smoking, believing it to be sinful.) Uncle Claude was an upstanding, dignified gentleman and widely known as a fine family man. He exemplified the devout Christian faith a great many Lumbees shared. Around Pembroke, there were two large Denominations, the strict Baptists, and the Holiness Methodists. Uncle Claude and his large family were Methodists. I remember when I was eight or nine, the solemnity of attending church with my relatives, and the seriousness with which the service was conducted. Men and boys sat on one side, women and girls on the other. The Hymns were lined out in an almost "sacred harp" way of singing. To this day the Lumbees-now one of the largest Indian tribes in the United States of nearly

---

1. "Lumbee Indians Break Up KKK Rally", *Life* ,28

55,000—are known for their devout Christian way of life and hardworking culture. A couple of my cousins graduated from college, and one spent most of his life with the FBI. I remember the day in 1962 when mother sat us all down for the grim news that Uncle Claude's and Aunt Mary's oldest son, Linwood, had died tragically in his teen years, by sledding in a snow storm down a hill which ended in a highway. Someone missed spotting the car coming around a bend. Years later my Sampson relatives journeyed to Flint, Michigan for my dad's funeral, and to Madison, Wisconsin for my ordination to the Episcopal Church's priesthood.

My parents frequently recited a story about me when I was around two years old. My breathing became much labored, and after ten days of finding it hard to swallow, I had lost significant weight. Mother told me she had come to think I might die. I was taken to a doctor, who immediately sent me to the hospital for the removal of my tonsils and adenoids. The surgery was successful, and I became healthy again almost overnight. I'm glad my parents were not Christian Scientists.

My earliest memories are of chasing a chicken on Uncle Claude's farm, and smelling the wonderful aroma of tobacco leaves drying in the barn. Uncle Claude's was a spacious, enjoyable, loving place, and gives me a glimpse of what is meant in our Lord's teaching about Heaven. Food was always plentiful and delicious, and on Sunday afternoons, relatives would come from miles to partake in Sunday dinner. Chickens were caught, killed with a sure blow of an axe, plucked and Southern fried. There would be gallons of ice tea, potatoes and corn on the cob. These events would bring all sorts of relatives for the social gabbing and enjoyment of being together, including WWII vets like Uncle Joe Lowry. He was a jovial, shoeless, tobacco chewing, loud, storytelling, overall wearing fun guy to be around. He and several others enjoyed joshing mother because of her being a church lady type, who never got humor of any kind, but expressed a constant nervous ha. If there were harmless hecks, or darns, gee's said, she would have an immediate loud intake of breath. For a good old Anglo—Saxon Teutonic four letter word, like "shit", she would commence lecturing the violator of her rigid rules. For myself I am feeling more and more "On Golden Pond" with Henry Fonda confronting his young charge Billy, who's letting a string of bullshits fly.

Norman Thayer:" You like that word don't cha? Bullshit."

Billy: "Yeah, Norman".

Norman: "It's a good word."

There was never a good party or fun time that my mother couldn't kill. She did not believe we were placed on this earth to have fun. As I got older I got a little wiser about her. After her mother died, she was cared for by her older sister, Lillian, five years her senior, and her brother, William, spitting image of her father, and placed almost exactly halfway between the two of the girls in age. Also, her half-sister Muriel (pronounced mur-il), would help on occasion. Mother's daddy (as she referred to him) had been a Victorian Cornishman, born in 1874 not far from Bodmin, in a hamlet called Withiel (not Lostwithiel). He was worshipped by my mother, who saw him as a very loving, moral, intelligent, deeply devout Methodist parent. He had been brought up a miner with his brothers, and family pig. Cornishmen are by and large short, as William Henry Roberts was, no taller than 5'1". He had a quick clipped way of speaking, and could quote vast passages from the King James Bible, Shakespeare, Tennyson, Kipling, and the 1662 Book of Common Prayer's Psalms; all of them. Growing up without a mother, affected mother deeply, particularly in not showing love very physically. Hers were hurried pecks on the cheek, and a quick formal embrace. Second, she showed her love by worrying. "How are you doing?" with heavy anxious emphasis, or too careful checking on some ailment, or opposing some choice my older sister Dawn or I would make in a knee jerk reaction, was how she showed her care. And she tended to smother us with her anxious presence. She had learned this of course growing up, with never remembering her mother, and never enjoying life or an intimate relationship with someone her age. From the time she was a teenager in the mid-1930s, she was her father's caretaker and companion. Even with Frank Sinatra "bobby soxer" music, she was a daddy's girl. Pictures of her from her early twenties reveal a happy young woman, with lovely black hair, and a prepossessing look. She was engaged three times, but only got married at 28 when her father's health was failing. She was affected by the dreadful circumstances of the Great Depression, which left her emotionally and spiritually exhausted. Luckily, however it was during those times that she finally found a mother figure—the Salvation Army. She lived and died with "The Army". Once she began attending at the behest of her brother, who had discovered the church in Detroit from listening to the Salvationists' band music at an open air service, she heard the sirens' call. In fact, during the early 1930s, my mother, her two siblings and their father all became Salvationists. They listened to lengthy sermons by officers with hardly any education beyond high school, impressing upon hearers to get saved, get saved, get saved. All officers, men and women (again Catherine Booth's influence), went for two years to one of the Salvation Army's Training Colleges. In the Midwest, this was located in Chicago. Officers were prepared for an active ministry on the streets, or in bars, or in some of the most depressing squalid, filthy living spaces anyone could imagine. They then repaired to the Salvation Army "Hall" or a Corps building, for encouragement, witnessing to what they had seen and accomplished at the grace of Jesus, singing rousing songs (not hymns), and praying with one another. At Christmas time, they rang bells for donations collected in kettles, distributed food and gifts to those in need, and (outside of Prohibition) year round went to the very devil's dens which served demon rum, generally in working class or poor neighborhoods of large cities, and collected money from selling the "War Cry" to mostly men, but occasionally women, who smoked and drank and caroused, looking for some way to make it through the night. There they confronted evils that put human beings beyond any recognizable hope of a productive life, many who had experienced lives of addictions, suffering, tragedy, loss of families, divorces, deaths, poverty, traumas, physical and emotional abuses, neglect, and conscious that the "good" people of society, the do-gooders, the religious folk, lower middle and middle and upper middle class members, despised these losers, if they ever saw them or heard of them especially in the crime sections of newspapers. This was my mother's life after she was commissioned (or ordained) an officer in 1948. She and her family members, firmly and without any doubt, believed with firm conviction, what Jesus had said in *St. Matthew's Gospel*, chapter 25:31–40: As you did it unto the least of these, you did it unto me.

> When the Son of Man comes in his glory, and all the
> Angels with him, then he will sit on the throne of his
> glory. All the Nations will be gathered before him, and
> he will separate people one from another as a shepherd
> separates the sheep from the goats, and he will put the
> sheep at his right hand and the goats at his left. Then the
> king will say to those at his right hand, 'Come you that
> are blessed by my Father, inherit the kingdom prepared
> for you from the foundation of the world; for I was
> hungry and you gave me food, I was thirsty and you gave
> me something to drink, I was a stranger and you
> welcomed me, I was naked and you gave me clothing, I
> was sick and you took care of me, I was in prison and
> you visited me.' Then the righteous will answer
> him, 'Lord, when was it that we saw you hungry and
> gave you food, or thirsty and gave you something to
> drink? And when was it that we saw you a stranger and
> welcomed you, or naked and gave you clothing? And
> when was it that we saw you sick or in prison and visited
> you?'And the king will answer them, 'Truly (*Amen*—
> introduces a solemn pronouncement by our Lord)
> I tell you just as you did it to one of the least of these
> who are members of my family, you did it to me.'[2]

Since the Salvation Army eschewed the Sacraments of Baptism and Holy Communion arbitrarily in the 1880s, the sacraments commanded by our Lord, making us His

2. All Scriptural quotations from *NRSV*

people through His Body the Church, I would identify these verses as the Salvation Army understanding of "Real Presence". My mother, and officers like her, believed that Christ is really and truly present in the most straitened, horrible, wretched, draggled, criminal (as Josephine Butler said), tragic of human circumstances, as they imagine this, and they have vowed before God and one another to show this presence by their ministrations. And as they believe along with all Christians that there are no limits to God's mercy and compassion, they will stay constant in calling, inveighing, preaching, caring, for all sinners, as they see them, and never flag in their zeal until one has been saved, in their own image and fashion, or gets beyond their reach.

There is a downside. C. S. Lewis once said that do-gooders quite often leave their worked over prey with a haunted, frightened look. There is an oppressive factor in do-goodism. In Christian theology, it is an overbearing Pelagianism, a heresy, with the underlying belief that God is an underachiever and needs our help. Pride, self-righteousness, sanctimony, and even a tyranny unloosed on one's victims come into play. "Throw a nickel on the drum, save another drunken bum", despite being sung derisively at Salvationists, has I think a kernel of truth. Lewis writes lucidly and with a depth of psychological awareness about this:

> Of all tyrannies, a tyranny sincerely exercised for the good of its victims may be the most oppressive. It may be better to live under robber barons than under omnipotent moral busybodies. The robber baron's cruelty may sometimes sleep, his cupidity may at some point be satiated; but those who torment us for their own good will torment us without end for they do so with the approval of their own conscience. They be more likely to go to Heaven yet at the same time likelier to make a Hell of earth. Their very kindness stings with intolerable insult. To be "cured" against one's will and be cured of states which we may not regard as disease is to be put on a level with those who have not yet reached the age of reason or those who never will; to be classed with infants, imbeciles, and domestic animals.[3]

Pelagianism (saving oneself through works or feeling) is very prevalent in our Christian churches today, among Fundamentalists, Evangelicals, Roman Catholics, and the "mainline Protestant Churches", and many of the mega Churches. With Americans' anti-intellectualism and little understanding of the central truths of Christianity, of Salvation by the Grace of God, God's initiative, God's work, they overemphasize and overcompensate with emotional feeling, provide little or no theological undergirding or doctrinal substance, and articulate a view of God and the world understandable only in accord with their own rationality, and experience, but especially feeling. Hamlet said : "There are more things in Heaven and earth, Horatio, than are dreamt of in your philosophy". (And many of these folks are far from being philosophers.) In addition, this was and is especially true of Salvation Army officers whose approach to

---

3. Lewis, *God in the Dock*, 292

the Christian faith is anti-intellectual, nonhistorical, ignorant, even obscurantist. (The chorus sung almost every Sunday night during altar calls was "Into my heart, into my heart; come into my heart Lord Jesus. Come in today, Come in to stay. Come into my heart Lord Jesus".) When people innocently or smugly testify that they have nothing to do with "book learning", only with the religion of the heart (as Catherine Booth once said), and prove it to themselves with "feeling", one is approving of Charlie Brown's comment, "How can I be wrong when I feel it so sincerely?" (George MacDonald's favorite text: "Those who would do the will of God, must know of the doctrine". *St. John* 7:17.)

Thus, the Salvation Army is a completely ersatz religion, thought up by the Booths in the 1860s, and one more 19th century attempt to "fix" God's Church, with the means of projecting one's own psychological needs on God, as Ludwig Feuerbach critiqued so much religion in 1841. It was contemporaneous with so many other new denominations like the Mormons, Plymouth Brethren, Swedenborgians, Jehovah's Witnesses, Seventh Day Adventist, and Christian Scientists, all with their founders' claims of being a unique channel to the Holy Spirit, before H. Ron Hubbard broke the mold by not resorting to a transcendent divine power at all, but making himself god in his Scientology. Be the first on your block.

My mother was overly strict morally with her holiness views. She had a rigid code of behavior: no playing on Sundays, attend Sunday School and Sunday Morning worship, attend Sunday evening worship, attend Wednesday evening service, no swearing—especially the biggies, no taking the Lord's name in vain (naively supposing this meant the word God, when the Lord's name was the tetragrammaton YHVH or JHVH in Hebrew), no smoking (one's body is a temple—used by St. Paul in a quite different context in *First Corinthians*), no dancing (stirs one up which is dirty, to be saved for the one you love), no alcohol (ditto—usually causes pregnancy when combined as it always seemed to be with "sex"), no bowling (always found with "lounges" or deceptively innocent looking bars where alcohol is served—see alcohol above), no looking at or desiring a girl's or woman's attractions; of course "good girls or good women of the Lord" never feel these ways, but only fallen women, or whores or Catholics); no masturbation (so disgustingly filthy dirty that one was never to mention this but use euphemisms, or point, as this would lead to blindness or strange psychological problems making one "crazy"), no dirty talking (penis and vagina were words used by "high falutin'" over-educated people, otherwise this meant the great variety of slang words, well known and used by boys or men when women weren't around, except fallen women and whores and Catholics), no wearing of make up or lipstick or nylons, (mostly applicable of women but you never knew), no card playing (use of the Devil's image was found on the pictures, and besides, this was a complete pastime for fun, and therefore not consistent with the serious business of saving one's soul and all the others—lost on all the sinners and the invincibly ignorant Catholics and Mainline Protestants), no watching movies at the "show"; no homosexual activity (which was for the exclusive use of Satan, queers, faggots, boys or men "light in their loafers", opera lovers, most Hollywood male actors, university professors, Satan, Catholic and Episcopal priests-duh, dress like mother, etc., music directors, male organists, opera loving university professors with lisps, and anyone friendly with Dean Acheson, Gore Vidal, Adlai Stevenson, Truman Capote, Walter Philip Reuther, the French, Rex Reed and Liberace). This very last sin was the unpardonable sin. And there was to be no asking of serious questions challenging the rather shallow theological or historical or Biblical understanding of my parents as well as most Officers. They could never answer the key question: Where did the Bible come from?

Thus, most of the Salvation Army's preaching, exemplified by mother's articulated moral code, was about having the right feelings, verified in avoiding all the behaviors above. This was a mostly negative approach to being and living "saved". It is a spiritually, intellectually, and emotionally suffocating way of living, and continued expressions of the love of Jesus, came across to me as a wished for but ultimately doomed hope. (Why is this the case? St. Paul masterfully dissects the problems with searching for salvation through the Law in *Romans 7*.)

In the 1940s, my mother got a job working for Bell telephone. She was a marvel at this kind women's work, and an athlete as well. She could do anything administratively, and steadily rose in position and salary within the limitations set by this business for women. Then she encountered conflicts within the Company. The softball team she played on, sponsored by Ma Bell, was in a league which began scheduling games on Sunday afternoons. She made a point of refusing to go along with these changes, a matter of principle for her because Sunday was the Sabbath. And Holiness churches, like the Salvation Army, without any considered understanding of how the Bible was to be interpreted, lacking any catholic or historical perspective, believed the most juvenile and insipid ways of reading the entire Bible as "inerrant", as wholly "God's Word", setting both Old and New Testaments as equally inspired, despite Jesus' own teaching and acting revealing Himself as the very "Word of God", against whom the rest of the Bible and even all religions are to be understood. So if the Commandment of Moses, which he received directly from the Lord (YHVH) on Mount Sinai, stated that the Sabbath was given for rest, and not work, so that God would be honored, that included no playing softball. My mother refused on principle. But this was only the tip of the iceberg, because Bell Telephone next required work on Sundays. She therefore quit. The Sabbath was actually from Friday sundown until Saturday sundown.

How one could follow so many Laws as communicated in both *Exodus* and *Leviticus*, especially, but then Commands of our Lord and other New Testament moral demands, with this kind of hermeneutic, was then left to Salvation Army muckety mucks to determine casuistically, as *mutatis mutandis*, so do the Mormons. (Anyone note how convenient it is for the Prophet to suddenly come up with a new "revelation" whenever American *mores* change?) And one opens oneself up to the kind of question humorously stated in an open letter to Radio personality Dr. Laura Schlesinger, an orthodox Jew who dispenses all sorts of moral advice on her radio talk show. She said at one point "homosexuality is an abomination according to *Leviticus* 18:22, and cannot be condoned under any circumstances".

Dear Laura,

Thank you for doing so much to educate people regarding God's Law. I have learned a great deal from your show and I try to share that knowledge with as many people as I can. When someone tries to defend the homosexual lifestyle, for example, I simply remind him or her that Leviticus 18:22 clearly states it to be an abomination. End of debate. I do need some advice from you however, regarding some of the specific laws and how to follow them.

a. When I burn a bull on the altar as a sacrifice, I know it creates a pleasing odor for the Lord (Lev. 1:9). The problem is pleasing my neighbors. They claim the odor is not pleasing to them. Should I smite them?

b. I would like to sell my daughter into slavery, as sanctioned in Exodus 21:7. In this day and age what do you think would be a fair price for her?

c. I know that I am allowed no contact with a woman while she is in her period of menstrual uncleanliness (Lev. 15:19–24). The problem is, how can I tell? I have tried asking, but most women take offense.

d. Lev. 25:44 states that I may indeed possess slaves, both male and female, provided they are purchased from neighboring nations. A friend of mine claims that this applies to Mexicans, but not Canadians. Can you clarify? Why can't I own Canadians?

e. I have a neighbor who insists on working on Sunday (the Sabbath). In the Book of Exodus 35:2 it clearly states he should be put to death. Am I morally obligated to kill him myself?

f. A friend of mine feels that even though eating shellfish is an abomination (Lev. 11:10), it is a lesser abomination than homosexuality. I don't know. Can you settle this?

g. Lev. 21:20 states that I may not approach the altar of God if I have a defect in my eye. I have to admit that I wear reading glasses. Does my vision have to be 20/20, or is there some wiggle room here?

h. Most of my male friends get their hair trimmed, including their hair around their temples, even though this is expressly forbidden by Lev. 19:27. How should they die?

i. I know from Lev. 11:6–8 that touching the skin of a dead pig makes me unclean, but may I still play football if I wear gloves?

j. My uncle has a farm. He violates Lev. 19:19 by planting two different crops in the same field, as does his wife by wearing garments made of two different kinds of thread (cotton/polyester blend). He also tends to curse and blaspheme a lot. Is it really necessary that we all go to the trouble of getting the whole town together to stone them? (Lev. 24:10–16). Couldn't we just burn them to death at a private family affair like we do with people who sleep with their in-laws? (Lev. 20:14).

I know you have studied these things extensively, so I am confident you can help. Thank you again for reminding us that God's word is eternal and un-changing, and we should do what the Bible says.

Your devoted disciple and adoring fan.

Keith[4]

Once an individual or a group or voluntary association or a church-the Salvation Army never refers to itself as a church—has made this interpretive move, one is back with the Pharisees in attempting to apply all Scriptures equally to one's life. I never could understand why one would consider the Decalogue or Ten Commandments more authoritative over one's life, than say Jesus' commands to "Do this . . .", regarding the Eucharist, or "Go therefore . . . and Baptize", with regard to Baptism. Sunday is not, and was never intended by early Christians to be "the Sabbath". Sunday very early on was the day of Christian worship, because it was the day of Jesus' Resurrection. So the New Testament writings refer to this day as "the Lord's Day", which trumps the Sab-bath, as the day of worship. (See *Revelation* 1:10) Of course, once you jettison Baptism and Eucharist (at Catherine Booth's command, relegating what Jesus said and did to matters of interest but not to be obeyed, replaced with some emphasis on the "Jesus special feeling" or the "Holy Spirit experience") then anything goes. The entire New Testament's clear teaching about the Church is thrown out, then the Church year, then bishops as successors to the Apostles, then basic traditional doctrine, then the Nicene (or better Niceno-Constantinopolitan) Creed as the basic statement of Faith of the worldwide Church, then knowledge and understanding about how all these matters were decided historically. All this occurs in neo-Protestantism removing a church to an entirely new "holier than thou" place, against Christ's message, against the New Testament, against basic reason. St. Augustine said, "Those who have no memories have no minds".

Go ahead and commission your own essentially lay ministers, who set the "mes-sage "or very long spontaneous prayers or "special musical package performances", or lengthy altar calls as the heart of a worship service. I was teased at one point by my Uncle Bill, Commissioner William H. Roberts, about what the Episcopal Church was doing with regard to same sex matters. "Don't you read the Bible?" he needled me. " Can you show me where Scripture allows that?". "Yes, I will," I bluffed," if you

---

4. Ashcraft, "An Open Letter to Dr. Laura", Online

will please let me know what the Salvation Army's Scriptural authority is for calling ministers major, or general, or commissioner. Where can I find in the Bible Jesus' command to wear faux Victorian British Military outfits?" I don't see why these questions should be so unsettling for the Salvation Army or any Fundamentalist group or church which states it believes in the literal, inerrant Bible as the Word of God. (By the way that "credo" is not found anywhere in the Bible. It is made up in the 20th century by Fundamentalists, who derive their authority from John Nelson Darby and "eccentric" ideas of Dispensationalism which he fabricated entirely in the 1860s, as a Church of Ireland crank. Richard Hooker, in his late 16th century *Of the Laws of Ecclesiastical Polity*, warns about such foolery: "When they and their Bibles were alone together, what strange fantastical opinion soever at any time entered into their heads, their use was to think the Spirit taught it them."[5]

A key statement of the paradox of much contemporary American Christianity with its total amnesia about its own history is this: "There is that special moment when you think have more Spiritual insight than the first Christians and their Churches because you possess a Bible they gave to you".

---

5. Hooker, *Laws*, Preface, VIII.7, 88

III

AFTER MY MOTHER WAS commissioned an officer in 1948, she was posted to Howell, Michigan. There she oversaw her first Army Corps. She did well, a born preacher and teacher, cared for those under her charge, and was moved in 1950 to Hillsdale, Michigan. At Hillsdale, a young handsome Red Wing shoe salesman, whom she had met while searching for shoes for her daddy, then came to hear her lead an "open air" service and was transfixed! My mother was 26 and my dad 19. Both had grown up during the Depression in extremely difficult personal circumstances, without the normal mother/father parenting. Both were Holiness Christians, my dad having attended Wesleyan Methodist worship services with his slightly older brother, Jack, and his Aunt Rill and Uncle Gilbert. They were both physically attractive, self-reliant, independent minded. I imagine my mother looking for someone youthful after all the years of being her elderly father's caretaker, and following two failed engagements, being swept off her feet by this charming handsome Romeo, who loved laughing and singing. My dad on the other hand would look upon Eva Rebekah Roberts as a young-ish mother he was searching for, attractive, intelligent, stable, with firm convictions, and someone to give him the uncritical love he craved and had received from Aunt Rill. They were both strong willed individuals, who could tangle and argue at the drop of a hat. Their first date was to go to a Detroit Red Wings game. This was a great team in the early 1950s, and they shared a great affection for the Detroit Tigers. Sports was a huge part of my growing up. (If they shared their dreams with one another, I'll never know, because as I and my siblings came along and became more knowledgeable of our parents as adult human beings, with their own individual histories and identities, we received their love for us, but perhaps little intimacy, either with us or with one another.) My dad became aware of my mother's great determination early on in their dating. They saw each other twice, and then my dad was informed Eva was seeing someone else, because of a fight. Dad told how he found out where the guy's house was, and circled it for two hours one night. My mother was always active and never one to brood over problems.

They married in February, 1952, and in a wedding picture I saw mother's father, looking distinctly Victorian, soppy stern and old style hat as in Larkin's poem, "This Be The Verse". My mother had left the ordained ministry to marry my dad, which the Salvation Army insisted upon. One could be a single officer, male or female, but with marriage both spouses had to be officers. And mother became pregnant fairly quickly, and my older sister Dawn Anne was born 13 months later. I followed 12 months after that—so obviously they experienced sex,(and this was without the aphrodisiac common for those after the war, martinis or any alcohol). Next was my brother Billy, "William George", incorporating my maternal grandfather's Christian name, and Uncle Gilbert's middle name. (My mother said she refused to have a child named Gilbert. So there!) Dawn's birthdate was March 3, and I came along on March 24, 1954, nearly ten pounds. (My younger brother Billy's birthdate was also March 24. That led to hilarity when we were teens, imagining what "I love Lucy" show might have inspired them exactly two years apart.)

I have told folks for fifty years that I was born one month before the McCarthy/Army Hearings of April, 1954. I am not sure if this was watched by my family with the same avidity of those millions who tuned into this great ratings success for the new medium in our country. It simply wasn't too important to my parents, who were otherwise uncritical humdrum small town Midwestern Republicans, the kind of local boosters Sinclair Lewis described in *Babbit*. Both my parents were Eisenhower/Nixon supporters. They trusted J. Edgar Hoover and his red hunting FBI. They would have cheered the Republican rise to power in 1950 in the House of Representatives, and then also in the Senate in 1952, and they opposed the last Presidential administration of Harry Truman, with heavy emphasis in their pokes at him on his "swearing" and "drinking" in spite of his claiming loyalty as a Baptist. They read local newspapers, and the *Detroit Free Press*, for information about sports and then the country, without ever asking searching questions about any details or specifics. They both preferred Ford automobiles. So much in Jean Shepherd's short stories about growing up in late 1940s Hammond, Indiana, including the Salvation Army's bell ringing at Christmas time, and in the subsequent opening shot of the 1983 movie called "A Christmas Story", remind me of the 1950s in Michigan. The drama of the confrontation between Senator Joe McCarthy's anti-Communist crusade, led by this truly fascistic fear—mongering demagogue, ruining mostly low level government workers in order to feed McCarthy's insatiable need for power and publicity for four years, and the Senate's Democratic members on the Senate's Permanent Subcommittee on Investigations, has always been thrilling to me. McCarthy was an alcoholic and bruising bully who lied and cheated his way to reach the Senate in 1947, having defeated the incumbent Republican—with a well-known Progressive name in Wisconsin, Robert M. La Follette, Jr. McCarthy rose spectacularly to popular power and headlines in 1950 with his red-baiting *modus operandi*, namely speeches in which he claimed the existence at first of 205 communists in the Government known to the Truman Administration. His numbers varying widely after that, sometimes 51, sometimes 130, he rode the tidal wave of the great fear engendered in this nation from the Soviet Union's possession of Nuclear weapons, which had been achieved by them in part due to espionage by Soviet "moles" in the

Government, notably in the nuclear facilities at Los Alamos, New Mexico, and at Fort Monmouth, New Jersey. [1]

There really was a Klaus Fuchs, a Soviet agent working as a theoretical physicist at Los Alamos under Hans Bethe from 1944 until he was caught in 1949, who confessed to passing secrets to the USSR through his longtime Soviet case officer Harry Gold. (He was arrested on a little bridge in Santa Fe about three blocks from the Church of the Holy Faith.) He was convicted in 1950, and sentenced to fourteen years in prison. Later his testimony and that of Harry Gold helped convict another scientist at Los Alamos, David Greenglass, who then implicated his sister and brother-in-law, Ethel and Julius Rosenberg (with the Soviet Venona records of the KGB files, opened finally in 1995, and disclosing Julius was in fact a spy, but not Ethel) in 1951, with the subsequent executions of the Rosenbergs in 1953. Whittaker Chambers, a long time hero of mine, had courageously ended all ties with the Communist Party and the Soviet Union in 1938, along with a great many disillusioned intellectuals, such as the author of the influential 1940 *Darkness at Noon*, Arthur Koestler, due to revolting purges of Party members inside and outside the USSR by Stalin, and mass murders of tens of millions of innocent men, women, and children within the Soviet Union. The final straw for even the most diehard glassy-eyed communists came with the 1939 Non-Aggression Pact between Stalin and Hitler. Chambers described in 1938 to the FBI what it was like to be a member of a communist cell in the United States, and finally received a public hearing with his testimony in 1948 before the notorious House Un-American Activities Committee chaired by Martin Dies. Chambers accused Alger Hiss a high serving member of the Roosevelt and Truman Administrations, and in fact the man who had chaired the United Nations conference establishing that world body, of having been a Communist and fellow member of Chambers' own cell as late as the 1930s, and possibly a Communist even to the very moment of his testifying. Hiss categorically denied the charge, and the intelligentsia, information class, and politicos in the country chose sides, either the clearly dapper cultured well educated upper class liberal Democrat Hiss, or the working class, earnest short dumpy anti-communist Chambers, with noticeably discolored teeth. Of course, this came at a time when HUAC was led by resentful Republicans who hadn't tasted power in some time until 1946, and kept up a barrage of unsubstantiated charges against the Roosevelt and Truman Administrations which they believed had been coddling Communists all along. Richard Nixon made his name in the Chambers/Hiss controversy by alerting the press to the "Pumpkin Papers", 65 pages of re-typed Government papers from Hiss' own typewriter. Hiss was eventually convicted at a second Federal trial, following a mistrial which had ended in a hung jury, for perjury, i.e. lying under oath to a Congressional Committee. (Any possible criminal charges involving espionage were disallowed in fact due to the five year statute of limitations.) The passions this case engendered hadn't subsided when in 1978, Allen Weinstein published *Perjury*, which

1. See Reeves, *Life and Times*, 536–637

came to the conclusion Chambers had been telling the truth, and Hiss had been a liar.[2] This was confirmed in 1995, by the US final release of the Soviet Cables, the US Army's Signal Intelligence Service (later the National Intelligence Agency) had collected and decrypted from 1943 to 1980, the "Venona" documents. There were nearly three thousand decrypted. Alger Hiss, Julius Rosenberg and Klaus Fuchs were all named. However, this conclusion was disputed because of the discovery that one of the SIS cryptologists, Bill Weisband, was a secret NKVD agent himself, and had leaked the information of the cables existence naming a number of Soviet agents in the US in 1945. Was Soviet intelligence then attempting to deceive the US with these names? Finally, the NKVD and GRU secret files from the height of Stalin's height of power of gaining access and influence with dozens to more probably hundreds of Soviets agents in the United States, the 1930s—1940s, were made available for the first time in 1993. Two scholars representing the US and Russia were chosen to study the thousands of files detailing the Soviet activity in that time. Five years later, Allen Weinstein and Alexander Vassiliev published the fruit of their study in *The Haunted Wood*. Their book exhibited for all to see that Soviet espionage was rampant throughout the United States Government, and the secrets attained at Los Alamos alone, could very well have affected the Soviet aggressions beginning with the Korean Conflict, by emboldening Stalin with an atomic bomb which was detonated in 1949.[3] For myself, I had been a Chambers' fan from the time I read while in high school his autobiography *Witness,* which he published in 1951. To read that book is to move back into the fiercely fought world of the Cold War—indeed Chambers' strong belief was by leaving the Communists he was joining the losing side—and how this polarized America for decades, eventually ending with the implosion of the Soviet empire in 1989.

But I was digressing as a reminder of how the geopolitical power struggle after World War II, especially between two antithetical political, cultural and religious systems, played out in sometimes unbearable tensions affecting 1950s Americans in their everyday lives. And for a few months the country was riveted by the televised Army McCarthy hearings.

The issue was a simple one. McCarthy's closest aide on his Senate Permanent Subcommittee on Investigations was his chief counsel, Roy Cohn, who brought along his new special friend G. David Schine as an unpaid consultant. Both men were Jewish and born in 1927. Cohn was a small dark intense hard charging reckless prosecuting attorney always looking for a way to prove himself, who had been involved in prosecuting the Rosenbergs. Schine was a ditzy blond playboy, and wealthy heir to his family's hotel chain built over the years by his Latvian born father, Junius Schine. (G. David Schine would later marry Miss Sweden 1955, Hillevi Rombin, a hopeful actress, whose own career fizzled.) When in 1953, at Cohn's suggestion, McCarthy sent them on a fact finding mission to check out the libraries of United States Information Agencies

2. Weinstein, *Perjury,* 565
3. Weinstein, *The Haunted Wood*

for books by communists or "fellow travelers", these high energy "junketeering gum-shoes" were seen running all over major European cities, giggling and tittering, enjoying luxurious digs, and attempting to intimidate various government bureaucrats to cough up their pink and red books. Of McCarthy's rather meager anticommunist successes, this was not one. And shortly after returning in November, Shine was drafted as an Army private enraging his bereft partner in crime. Cohn insinuated that the Eisenhower Administration, through this chicanery, had reacted to the Cohn/Schine pressure, by deliberately drafting Shine, possibly even at the President's orders. Cohn thereupon began an ill-advised campaign to threaten various Army officials who were colluding to keep his friend from the immediate promotions Cohn demanded, given Shine's obvious "qualities" (unknown to anyone else, even Shine's own family). He then actively intervened to ensure the private was stationed at an Army base close to Cohn's residence. The Army brass were not amused. And they remained unmoved. So, Cohn worked doggedly through his fatuous boss, Joe McCarthy, to investigate the Army, which unlike numerous other entities, had not kowtowed to Cohn's previous pressure. And behold! This would take place by means of McCarthy's inquisitional Permanent Subcommittee on Operations. Now the President—against conventional wisdom a deeply thoughtful man who had made his way to the top of the most fiercely competitive of all professions, the modern military—believed it was the right time to stop this bully boy from embarrassing his own beloved U. S. Army. (McCarthy had also called Eisenhower's deeply respected friend, General George C. Marshall guilty of treason.) And after some months of increasing criticisms of McCarthy-most notably by Edward R. Murrow—and a number of journalists and news agencies-some of them the very ones who had helped create McCarthy in the first place—and a steadily growing chorus of liberal Democrats and then moderate Republicans on the Hill, Eisenhower finally determined it was the right time to act. (Anyone who considers that the President lacked toughness and resolve, is underestimating the rare qualities Eisenhower exhibited—of restraint, tact, deep intelligence, not showing his thoughts—needs to take a good hard look at this extremely admirable leader. He was not usually cowed or surprised.) So the President ordered—as was his habit—the Secretary of the Army, Robert T. Stevens, to make public the charge that McCarthy's Committee, and pointedly the chief counsel, Roy Cohn, were repeatedly attempting to intimidate the Army to get Cohn's new best friend within striking distance of his "friendship".

Vice President Richard Nixon, at 41, arranged with the leaders of the Senate, the newly elected California Senate majority leader, dull, slow, humorless, William Knowland, and one of the most wily, skillful, successful Senate leaders, Lyndon Johnson of Texas, to have McCarthy temporarily removed as chairman for the committee to hear the charges and determine how to resolve this political hot potato. At the time, the Senate Democrats held more seats than the GOP. But Independent Wayne Morse of Oregon had agreed to assist the Republicans in organizing the Senate, and Vice President Nixon provided the tie-breaking vote. The Committee was chaired by one of the stupidest Senators ever, Karl Mundt of South Dakota.(He was possibly even more clueless than dumb—as—a—post Roman Hruska of Nebraska, whose most famous statement came in support of Nixon's choice to be Associate Justice on the Supreme Court in 1970, G. Harold Carswell of Florida. Hruska acknowledged on the Senate floor that Carswell was "mediocre", and then went on to blurt out that seeing we have so many mediocre people in this country, shouldn't they be represented also? The Senate rose to the occasion and voted no.)

Edgar Murrow's "See It Now" television critique of McCarthy ran on March 9, 1954, and the televised hearings of the Army/McCarthy matter began on April 22. Mundt and the Republicans chose Tennessee litigator Ray Jenkins as their counsel, and among those on the Democratic side was 29-year-old Bobby Kennedy. The Democrats had a widely respected and courtly Southern WWI Army veteran as their ranking member, John L. McClellan. McClellan was renowned for his legal abilities, having become a member of the Arkansas State Bar at age 17, and for his outspoken racism. He was supported on his side by Stuart Symington (D. MO), and Henry Jackson (D. WA).

McCarthy's most implacable foe, however, was the special counsel for the Army, Joseph Welch, from the prestigious Boston law firm of Hale and Dorr. He was himself a moderate Republican, a native Iowan, born in 1890. His soft spoken manner, and gentle wit, came to magnify his very clever barbs aimed at the blustery, ruthless, acidic Roy Cohn, until finally McCarthy had had his fill, when he personally attacked a young junior attorney in Welch's law firm, Fred Fisher. (Fisher had for a couple years during Law School been a member of the National Lawyers Guild, an organization begun in 1937 as an alternative to the American Bar Association. They supported the New Deal, and were early on integrated unlike the ABA. HUAC and especially Chairman Martin Dies had worked with J. Edgar Hoover to name them a communist front organization. Attorney General Herbert Brownell refused to include them on the list of subversive organizations.) This rather surly outburst came in flagrant disregard of an agreement the senator had reached with Welch, that Fisher would not assist Welch, nor be named by McCarthy; and Welch would not question the Cohn/Shine relationship. In Emile D'Antonio's finely edited documentary, "Point of Order", from 1964, the fascinating confrontation is dramatically displayed. This had followed a moment of sparring when Welch had called into question a "cropped" photograph of Schine standing with Secretary of the Army Robert Stevens which seemed to show only the two figures present. Welch exhibited the original photograph with Shine's McGuire AFB wing commander Colonel Jack Bradley, and a fourth person's arm visible near Bradley, which belonged to another McCarthy aide, Fred Carr. During an exchange when Welch requested that McCarthy staff member James Juliana reveal the origins of the edited exhibit, Welch asked, "Did you think this came from a pixie?", which caused McCarthy to have the question re-read.

Senator McCarthy: Will counsel for my benefit tell us-I think he may be an expert on that-what a pixie is?

Mr. Welch: Yes. I should say, Mr. Senator, that a pixie is a close relative of a fairy. (Laughter).

Senator McCarthy: As I said, I think you may be an authority on what a pixie is.

The moment then came for the key exchange between Welch and McCarthy. On June 9, day 30 of the hearings, McCarthy turned on Welch who had been showing Cohn as an opportunist regarding his numbers of communists in the Government. When McCarthy blusteringly attacked Fred Fisher personally, Welch pounced:

Until this moment, Senator, I think I have never really gauged your cruelty, or your recklessness. Fred Fisher is a young man who went to Harvard Law School and came into my firm and is starting what looks to be a brilliant career with us. Little did I dream you could be so reckless and so cruel as to do an injury to that lad. It is true that he is still at Hale and Dorr. It is true that he will continue at Hale and Dorr, It is, I regret to say, equally true that I fear he shall always bear a scar needlessly inflicted by you. If it were in my power to forgive you for your reckless cruelty I would do so. I like to think I am a gentle man, but your forgiveness will have to come from someone other than me.

When McCarthy, obviously stung, tried again to go after Fisher, Welch interrupted him:

Senator, may we not drop this? We know he belonged to the Lawyers Guild. Let us not assassinate this lad further, Senator. You've done enough. Have you no sense of decency, sir? At long last, have you no sense of decency? (Great applause)[4]

I found this recording on a long playing record at Madison, Wisconsin in 1974, and it became something of a touchstone for me. McCarthy had been on a rampage destroying people's careers by simply insinuating guilt through his accusations. He had become far more harmful to the cause for which he claimed to be fighting, by his methods. "McCarthyism" is known to this day by recklessness and desire to do harm to anyone by smears, and counting on one's opponent not having any opportunity to respond. Actual laying out a case with one's cold hard facts, and providing a forum for a response-the very basis for justice in any free society, is airily swept aside by these bullies.

A postscript. Joseph Welch tried acting, and plays the judge in Otto Preminger's outstanding film, "Anatomy of a Murder", from 1959. It is set in the Upper Peninsula of Michigan. Joseph Welch's acting was an excellent debut. But he died in 1960, three years after McCarthy.

4. Reeves, *Life and Times,* 536–637

IV

MY YOUNGER SISTER, ROBIN Joyce, was born in 1958. By then my dad had gone to Officers' Training School, and my parents were both engaged in their first appointment in Alpena, Michigan. In the Salvation Army, officers generally receive notice of a move on June 1, and they are told two weeks later where they are expected to be in two more weeks. We lived in this small northeastern Michigan town from 1956–1961, the longest we lived anywhere growing up. (For the longest time as an Episcopal priest, I would get restless after three or four years, and wish to move.) What I remember was a happy childhood, with joyous Christmases, with my role being the peacemaker. My older sister, Dawn, was attractive, headstrong, high-strung, emotional, generous, an A student, the one who gave my parents-I should say my mother—the most trouble, and who looked after the other three of us. My younger brother Bill and I were very close, slept on bunk beds, talked endlessly at night, although he was far quieter than any of us, phlegmatic, and the sibling closest to me. In both looks and personality he was and remains most like my dad. My youngest sibling Robin was the child who could do no wrong. Everything she did had approval from both mother and dad, so that if there was ever a fight, she was exonerated. She was the spoiled brat of the family.

We all grew up close-knit, with the week always moving toward Sunday. Sunday meant going to church at my parents' Salvation Army. For years I remember my mother polishing our shoes on Saturday night, because, "God expects your best". We grabbed a ride to church either with mother or dad, both picking up several Salvationists on the way. These were for the most part extremely poor white folks whose entire sense of worth and stability was set by church. Years later when I watched Robert Duvall in the "Apostle", I recognized the people as the same sort among whom we worshiped, society's losers, those who in many towns grew up literally on the wrong side of the tracks. We left about nine every Sunday morning, picked up various folks like Jacob Geiss, Mrs. Trevithick, Gus Sjoblum, Anna May Knueckle, Frank Byron, Mrs. Duchane, Alma, and got to the "hall" about 9:45. Sunday School then met from ten to eleven, with the simplest of exercises, coloring the apostles blue-something I was never good at, or reading for a few minutes from the *King James Bible*-with very little sense of the grand sweep of the Biblical narrative. And every story had little to do with us; they were simply taught as God's Word with their own individual moralistic meanings. What I mean is if the story was about Daniel and the Lions, it all happened and was true, and we had to be true to God. (Nothing was taught about Daniel and his companions in Babylon, and their kosher food discipline, or the meaning of the Sabbath for Jews, or that these first few chapters in Daniel were written down as parables for the Jewish people suffering at the hands of their enemies.) Just take it as it lays for very simple minds. If the story was about the importance of marriage and family, then the most dysfunctional married folks you would ever come across: Abraham, Sarah, Hagar, Lot and his wife (pillar of salt by day, ball of fire at night), Isaac, Rebekah, Esau, and even Jacob-the one considered the key player—who would be named Israel—with his tricks and chicaneries and deceptions and shrewdness, all the lying and whoring and thieving, even the selling of prissy spoiled Joseph into slavery by his brothers, all this was taught approvingly, without humor and as moralistically as possible. If there were two contradictory stories of creation, and two different names for God, no matter, they're both true. If there ran side by side two different versions of the flood, with two separate numbers of animals, or two versions of patriarchs, all were told as God's Word. If some nutty number of 4004 BC was calculated (by Anglo-Irish Archbishop Ussher in 1650 using the Bible and other ancient sources) as the time for creation, well there it is. If Joshua made the sun stand still, then it happened. A whale swallowed Jonah? So? The Bible says it, I believe it, that settles it.

Sex was a taboo subject, although it figures in many of the stories about Patriarchs and Matriarchs, and of course, in *Song of Solomon*-with the breasts and so forth—even the "feet" euphemism found in the *Book of Ruth*, none of this was mentioned or hinted at. What was "taught" were moral lessons from the Old Testament using "flannel graphs", if anyone knows today what that impressive pedagogical tool was. All of this was dull, dull, dull, before finishing with an inane Sunday School chorus or two.

At 11:00 am came the "Holiness Meeting". This was the big show, with my sister Dawn playing the songs by ear with a lively unique honky tonk style. "All to Jesus, I surrender", "I Come to the Garden alone", or the dreadful blind composer Fanny Crosby's "I Love to Tell the Story", or "Jesus Keep me near the Cross", or "Love Lifted Me", were all made somewhat less unbearable by Dawn's playing. The worst songs were "Storm the Forts of Darkness, Bring them Down!", and "I'm Climbing up the golden stairs of glory", if you can believe it. Any of this stuff could also be accompanied by bandsmen (and women) playing cornets, trumpets, an alto horn, or tuba, and bass drum. There was not a single great Biblical theme that could not be eviscerated and enervated, and brought down to the level of this schmaltz. My dad even had hand puppets like "Lifford the Lion" and Jesus and the mean Pharisee to act out the Gospels' main themes. In both Alpena and Ann Arbor these were great public favorites. (Our attendances blossomed, and a newly purchased Baptist church was renovated for our worship use in Alpena. My parents also gave away special gifts like yo yos which would light up with a "Jesus Saves" message at the end of the drop.)

Finally, after endless talking in a "tone", the tone that proved your officer or Sunday School Director or Sergeant Major was "truly saved", my dad would give a 35–40 minute "message" about some piece of a *Psalm* maybe, or something obscure from *Second Chronicles*, or the meaning of Zacchaeus who was short but tall in God's eyes, with everything leading to Hell for all of us unless we got the right feeling in our hearts because then we would have allowed Jesus in; all this tyrannical fear and guilt and horror that God was going to bring down on us because of His love for us; so we've got to find Jesus in the next few minutes; the altar call winding down with Dawn playing "All to Jesus, I surrender", and then the service was over. This meant the jibber jabber my parents had with all these folks, before taking the forty-five-minute trip to get them all home.

For years after we got home and ate roast beef and potatoes and terrible tasting cooked carrots, we were confined to the house with no television. I couldn't understand this at all. I also never remember reading this encouraged by Jesus. At five in the afternoon, we got around to go to YPL, the young people's league, at six, and the Salvation meeting at 7:00 pm. I especially hated the Sunday evening service. There was never a set time to end. This was the big emotional service, with testimony time interspersed with choruses about our feeling Jesus in our hearts, warnings about going to Hell, long prayers for all of us to get our lives right with God, because Jesus died for us, and off to Hell he'll send us unless we get the right feelings, and yes a literal Hell complete with fire burning us up, with the maggots and their razor sharp teeth, and the awful company we'll keep but not notice because of the terrible pain, world without end , Amen. And then my dad would enjoin us to find Jesus, and if we didn't get saved and other family members did, we would never see them for all eternity. He would elucidate this to the quiet playing of "Just as I am" or "Throw out the Lifeline", or "Almost Persuaded", then more emotional guilt trips. It would go on and on and on. I prayed most Sunday evenings no one would go up to the altar, because if someone did, one of my parents or a soldier or the sergeant major would go and comfort that person with great emotion and weeping and wailing, which would encourage my dad to go on with a new burst of energy. "O God, I want to see Swamp Fox on Disney; don't let anyone go up", I would pray quietly. My brother Billy was the absolute worst at putting up with this religiosity. During any Sunday service, morning or evening, he would hit, pull hair, jab, bite, shove us all sitting together one way or another on his best days. At his worst, he pinched very hard anyone he could reach by crawling around the pew. One time in Ann Arbor, my dad got so pissed off by Billy's antics that in the midst of his "The Beauty Of Holiness, Part 2" message, he came down off the platform with such speed it scared everyone, scooped up Billy—who began shrieking, "No, daddy, no daddy", while yelling loudly at my mother, "Eva, lead them in 'Let the Beauty of Jesus be seen in me' ". It was very effective drama, and at least two soldiers quit on the spot. If the Sunday evening service went on too long—too many weeping penitents, too many testimonies, too many "Jesus weejus" prayers, and sad songs about Jesus suffering and waiting, or softly and tenderly and quietly calling—which may have been the problem, couldn't He speak up a little?—then Billy would go into action. When the congregation of 45 or so, again at Ann Arbor, were all on their knees weeping and wailing, my dad intoning, "with every head down and every eye closed, our Lord will respond to you in quiet for He can see into your hearts", the real fat ones (usually women) would lean way over onto the seat back in front of them in the prayer squat, and Billy would begin his submarine pew scooting. He would shoot himself from pew to pew and look up women's dresses. They didn't know this of course-they dutifully had their eyes closed, and many were hard of hearing. He would then report his "findings".

Our family life besides Church, was for the most part enjoyable. Our public school life in Alpena, then Ann Arbor, then Bay City, all in Michigan, were settings for learning by rote, and in addition to beginning to read-which was an absolute thrill to me—we all did well in arithmetic, spelling, geography, science, and music. We had music teachers who taught us the scales and singing to autoharps! "Listen to the music of the Indian names in Michigan", "All things will perish from under the sky, music alone will live . . . never to die". Once I had an important theological question about this fine piece of music—I mean how could everything perish when we were promised a happy beyond or a damned beyond eternally? What kind of eschatology were we dealing with when music is "alive" and "never will die"? I did what I always did under these circumstances, at home, with teachers, with Salvation Army officers, viz. raise my hand and ask why. In this case, "Why am I taught at church that God alone is eternal and now I'm hearing this about music?" In this case, Mrs. Vaughn my third grade teacher at Haisley Elementary School, used a word I'd never heard before in the following sentence: "This is a German folk song expressing their Metaphysics". Wow! What an incredibly wonderful answer! How do you argue with that?! There was something about that word that stayed with me, so I tried using it in my own sentences. "Dale, why are you in the bathroom so long?" "Because of my German Metaphysics!" This generally silenced anyone from asking for details.

My teachers at Haisley Elementary School in Ann Arbor were my favorites. I had lovely Mrs. Sorenson in second grade, Mrs. Vaughn in third, and Miss Whaley in fourth grade. Miss Whaley had giant flaps of skin under her arms which wibble wobbled constantly. I would watch them when she prayed at the beginning of class, just after we had removed our "wraps", and begun settling down. They did huge wobbles. Mrs. Vaughn was odd. She constantly pointed out the two star lovers in her class, Todd and Mary Jo . She would write their names on the board and circle them with a massive heart. (It seemed odd for me that an adult would have these obsessions.) For myself, I was in love with Dana . She was the nicest girl in second grade, so that was that. (Years later I thought the school scenes in Woody Allen's "Annie Hall" concerning a boy's latency period so obviously true.) Then in third grade I found out Mary Jo was the prettiest girl. I thought, "How can that be? Besides she's a brunette". And then and there I switched allegiance. I also think that's the day I got kissed by Mrs. Vaughn. Her much feared form of punishment for boys would be to bring the errant one to her locker in class, let him pick out a wild colored lipstick, carefully apply it to her lips, then kiss the boy on his forehead. The mark of the beast! I only got this once. Never was my best friend Gary Melvin so marked. He did tend to freak when an alarm bell would ring, and we went into "nuclear blast position" of cowering under our desks.

V

GARY MELVIN AND I were very good friends. We talked about books we were reading, since both of us read voraciously. (It was about this time that I took to reading by flashlight under the sheets.) His parents both taught at the University of Michigan. My parents could get along with just about anyone, and they met Gary's parents at Little League games, where Gary and I played for the same team. Before I entered third grade I had joined Little League in Ann Arbor when the boys could hit off tees. Both our parents found each other because they had the greatest time watching little boys of all shapes and sizes make wild-eyed swings and fall over. I was part of a family that was very athletic and loved baseball. Gary and his family were not. They were "intellectuals". ("An intellectual", according to Billy Connolly, "is someone who can listen to the William Tell Overture without thinking of the Lone Ranger". He also said that "Christianity, Islam, and Judaism all have the same God, but that he's telling them different things".) My parents were not. But they hit it off. For Gary, Little League was a team sport where his parents thought he could become more socially acclimated. For me it was the most fun thing to do ever. From the time I was three or four I had learned very easily how to bat, throw, catch, and pitch. Baseball was the magical sport all my heroes played in Detroit. The Detroit Tigers were the entity that seemed at times another religion that held us together. You lived and died with the Detroit Tigers. Going to Tiger Stadium was incomparably beautiful, with grass on the infield! (We would go to twi-night doubleheaders, arriving by 6, and leaving in the seventh inning of the second game. At no time did we ever see the end of a single game, or the second of a twi-night double header, for the simple reason that my dad was obsessed with "beating the crowd".) Bob Costas on Ken Burns' Baseball series comments that it was the most incredible sight to see Yankee Stadium as a kid for the first time. When he walked around the stadium that first day and then the field itself, he saw all the greats' plaques on the outfield wall and was sure that was the Yankees' burial ground. And watching pitchers and players on television in 1961 (when I first remember) I could even listen to the most mellifluous voices of George Kell (A longtime Tiger player and Hall of famer) and Ernie Harwell calling the game. In 1961, Detroit had three great hitters in Al Kaline—Right fielder, great arm and glove, batted .324, my personal favorite Rocky "The Rock" Colavito, left fielder who crossed himself before every bat, had a great stretch that many of us mimicked with taking his bat up over head to his back, and bringing it back, 45 home runs, and "Stormin' Norman" Cash, left handed first baseman, wad of chew in his cheek, hit left, batted League leading .361. Detroit also had one of the finest fielding center fielders in Billy Bruton whom they had acquired from Milwaukee in the National League, who had led the Nationals in stealing bases three times, and a solid infield. Their pitching staff was excellent. Their best pitcher that year was "Yankee Killer" Frank Lary who won over twenty games. They also had future Hall of Famer, Jim Bunning, who had pitched a no hitter in 1958 for the Tigers, and would deliver a perfect game later with the Phillies, had a sidewinder style of pitching that was a thing of beauty to behold. For those who only knew him from his rather undistinguished dim years as a senator from Kentucky should not be held liable for thinking Mark Twain was right: " It is better to keep your mouth closed and be thought a fool, than to open it and remove all doubt". Don Mossi was not stupid so much as he was frightening to look at. This excellent left handed pitcher was known as "Sphinx" to his face, and damned ugly behind his back. He had sad deep inset eyes, a huge nose, and wide flapper ears. Bill James wrote this about Mossi: "Don Mossi was the complete, five-tool ugly, he could run ugly, hit ugly, throw ugly, field ugly, ugly for power. He was ugly to all fields, behind the runner as well as anybody, and you talk about pressure . . . man, you never saw a player who was uglier in the clutch."[1]

The Tigers were the center of our lives in a year when they won 101 games, and still ended eight games behind the hated Yankees the year of the home run race between the M&M boys, Maris and Mantle.

Two of those Tigers that year I followed them very closely-and learned how to keep a scorecard—two key starters were black, Billy Bruton and Jake Wood. The American League was far behind the National League in bringing African American players onto their rosters, after the great Jackie Robinson broke the color barrier in 1947. It's true Larry Doby came up to the Indians shortly thereafter, and helped them win the World Series in 1948. (He was soon joined by Monte Irvin.) David Halberstam, who in 1972 published *The Best and the Brightest*, about the brainy worthies Kennedy surrounded himself with in running the U S when he became President in 1961, only to conclude that there were limitations to what technocrats and bureaucrats using empirical social science methodologies could accomplish when dealing with the unpredictability of human beings and human societies, wrote a terrific book on the 1964 Pennant races which saw the St. Louis Cardinals and the Yankees as league champions, and then face one another in the World Series. Halberstam's theme in his *October 1964* (published thirty years later) is that from 1964 on when the National League Cardinals triumphed, the National teams were in ascendancy due to their bringing up more Black players than the recalcitrant American League.

My point is about my parents, especially my mother, never exhibited any prejudice against Blacks, and it was only by happenstance that I found out Bruton and Wood were "colored" hearing this in my second grade classroom. After all my criticisms about their constricted views of being Christian, they gave to their family the

1. James, "The Man Who Invented", 245-6

gift of growing up without experiencing racism at home. The same was true of anti-Semitism. I found out much later that our doctor in Alpena, Michigan, Dr. Kessler was Jewish, a very compassionate family doctor, the best in town, whose only criterion that mattered to my parents was his expertise. Living in Ann Arbor, the Melvins and the Colemans hit it off from the first time they met. We were guests on numerous occasions at each other's houses including Christmas, and Hanukah dinners. My mother in particular would preach about the importance of God creating everyone, regardless of color or race or religion. And of course with my mother an ordained Salvation Army officer, we didn't hear about sexism, or one sex dominant over the other. If I had ever had to choose, I would have said females are stronger and dominant. (I, later on, never questioned women's ordination for the Episcopal Church or any other Church. I will discuss this further below.)

November 22, 1963. On that day, a Friday, I was heading downstairs at the Salvation Army's large kitchen and dining hall, smelling some of the worst cooking ever to hit my olfactory system. It was boiled cabbage! YUCK! The odor permeated everything in the Corps (church building), and you'd think you were swimming in an open sewer. It was about 2:15 in the afternoon, and I overheard a couple women crying. I inquired as to the reason. "The President has been shot! They don't expect him to live." What, I, thought. That young energetic handsome elegant man? Shot? What on earth! The television at the Coleman house never changed from CBS with Walter Cronkite et al., from that day until Monday the 25th, the day of the State funeral at the Capitol and St. Matthew's Roman Catholic Cathedral; and burial at Arlington National Cemetery. The details I remember were John John saluting the casket being carried on a horse drawn caisson, the huge crowds of quiet weeping people, old and young, black and white, from all backgrounds, dressed nicely, and the burial at Arlington National Cemetery with the eternal light. I found the whole chain of events fascinating , including the shooting of Lee Harvey Oswald by Jack Ruby, LBJ's becoming President, the sudden turn of personal happenstance affecting everyone, especially Kennedy's own family and friends. It wasn't too long after this event that more and more news began covering the conflict in Viet Nam.

I have never believed the assassination was a conspiracy. Americans somehow believe we are above the horrible matters affecting the world, but we are too idealistic and naïve. The Warren Commission appointed by President Johnson, seemed to be good honorable men. I may have thought that because of my parents' view. Not too much later when the paranoid style of questioning the Commission's solid report (which I have read a couple times), beginning in 1966 by the attorney Mark Lane in *Rush to Judgment*, and then the mushrooming of skepticism engulfing our nation in the decades to follow, becoming a huge cottage industry, I have challenged those supposedly seeking the "true answer" about the Warren Commission's work itself. I am aware that so much of this gullibility on the part of so many in the midst of great fear and anxiety in the country-exhibit #1 being the constant threat of nuclear warfare with the Soviet Union-came about due to the 1960s terrible public events: Kennedy's assassination, an entirely different seemingly untrustworthy successor as President, the beginning of race riots at numerous major cities (including Detroit in 1966–8), the tremendous upsurge in the War effort against Viet Nam, Robert F. Kennedy's and Martin Luther King's assassinations, the realization that we US citizens were being lied to by Johnson and then Nixon about the War, and not once but repeatedly-as we finally saw shaken out by the publishing of the Pentagon Papers, and on and on. The televising of all these events affected such a great number of our people that there was nowhere to hide. I remember my dad, and then a looney Baptist minister spelling my dad and mother's vacation to Britain, hollering at us about "the End Times". First Khrushchev was the antichrist, then the Beatles (right!) with their filthy music, then LBJ, then Mao, then Ho Chi Minh. Henry Kissinger was named this any number of times after Nixon was elected President, in my hearing.

Anyway, I have remained with my firm conviction the Warren Commission got it right. Have the doubters read the report? Do they know how reputable the members were? Since I came to meet Congressman Gerald Ford several times, Congressman Hale Boggs (Democratic House leader from Louisiana, and father of Cokie Roberts), and I sat for many hours with the flat out most honest and noble and wise Senator from Kentucky, John Sherman Cooper, I find I trust them. (Any who have known or knew about Senator Richard Russell would say the same thing.) And the evidence is overwhelming to anyone who comes at this subject objectively, that there is no doubt there was one shooter. (This tragedy is now narrated masterfully by Robert Caro in the fourth volume of his massive biography of Lyndon Johnson, *The Passage of Power*.[2])

2. Caro, *Passage of Power*, 308–318

VI

IN 1964, IN ANN Arbor I have some happy memories. My dad and mother had four weeks every year to take vacations, which in our circumstances were limited to trips with our travel trailer. Many times we would visit the Smokey Mountains National Park, or Hannibal, Missouri, or the Upper Peninsula of Michigan, Yellowstone, or on a couple occasions even Florida.

All of us got along, even in the Pixie Trailer we had for traveling. We swam and hiked, played catch, sang songs in the car, and attended the evening gatherings at National Parks. We saw Washington DC one summer, I believe in 1964, and I began to aspire to be a member of Congress. What better life could there be? We all heard President Johnson speak at the University of Michigan stadium, in May, when all the schools were closed for the event. I don't recall whether his "Great Society "address nor the fact that this was the first time a sitting President spoke on campus made much of an impact on me. I do remember seeing my family's personal political hero, Governor George Romney, at close view. His being a Mormon never came up at home, but his experience running American Motors, supporting Civil Rights issues and neutrally dealing with union matters, were what I remember from those years. He and the President looked distinctly uncomfortable together. The Big news from Washington DC that I knew about was the Civil Rights Legislation passed in June. I also came to realize that a larger percentage of Republicans than Democrats voted in favor, with e.g. both Republican senators from Delaware, from Vermont, and from Kansas supporting this great bill. Even the two Republicans from Kentucky, both noted for their Civil Rights leadership, John Sherman Cooper and Thrustan Morton were on record in favor. (In 1965, again with the Voting Rights Act, Republicans achieved a higher percentage in voting in favor. The Minority Leader in the Senate, Everett Dirksen of Illinois, led both fights. This man was the oratorical champion of Congress who with his stately annual speech on the Marigold left not one dry seat in that chamber.) The Presidential election of 1964 between Goldwater and Johnson saw my getting involved chiefly by attaching Goldwater stickers on every Johnson Street sign I could find. I don't know why I was strongly for Goldwater. Gov. Romney had joined Rockefeller forces in the walk out from the Republican Convention at the Cow Palace in San Francisco after Goldwater's nomination.

Billy and I did everything together. We were a formidable team playing baseball, or football, or basketball. We could both heave a baseball a long, long distance. Once we were having supper, and the phone rang. My mother talked quietly for a minute or two, and then asked, "Dale and Billy, did you throw rocks at the windows of those new houses being built? A couple kids are saying that a group of you threw them from behind a dirt pile, and only you two hit them. They're broken". "What, mother? We did? No, we couldn't throw that far. A couple of those guys must have gone closer after we left to break them", I lied. We were with friends that day, riding our banana seat bikes with the "ape hanger" handle bars. A whole new subdivision was being constructed with great little hills everywhere, perfect for playing army with rocks, or just racing up and over the landscape. It was boy heaven! Of all the boys, most older than Billy and me, we tired of this and from 175–200 feet away we lined up from one of the top of a pile, and heaved rocks at new bay windows in one of the unfinished houses. None of the other kids got close. They were off in their direction, or short. Both my brother and I could throw over the house, and finally throwing simultaneously, with perfect arcs, we hit one of the windows at the same time. What a kick shattering that window, and both of us doing it together! To me it was a sign from God that we would both play in the major leagues! I bragged that I bet Don Wert or Jerry Lumpe couldn't throw that straight that far! I was probably right. They were lowly "utility" players for the Tigers that year. Anyway, my mother said into the phone, "No. They didn't do that. Quit blaming my sons." She hung up the phone and in a huff said," They blame you two for a lot of stuff. I wonder why they do that. They just pick on Christian kids". (Perhaps she was making a prejudicial statement about all our Catholic friends.) And she looked at us while sitting back down at the table, smiling at her two angelic appearing boys! (Honest to goodness, when I finally made my first confession at age 22 before I was baptized, that lie was the first sin that came into my head. So, not stealing a pear from a neighbor's tree like St. Augustine (commented on by Justice Oliver Wendell Holmes—"Rum thing seeing a man making a mountain out of robbing a pear tree in his teens"); nor Dr. Johnson's standing for several hours in the rain at Uttoxeter in Eastern Staffordshire, as penance for his youthful disobedience of his father's request to open the bookstall there when he was a young teen. This was the kind of thing that I thought about late at night when I couldn't sleep. At age 6, my parents concerned about my insomnia, asked, "What do you think about at night?" I said, "I lie awake and think about the past".

One other memory I have about speeding around that construction area. Aunt Rill was taking care of us. That was terrific because of her home cooking and giving us ice cream before supper, or even for breakfast on some occasions. She was brighter than Aunt Muriel, who never seemed to be playing with a full deck. Aunt Muriel had a little head with stringy grey hair, and a funny eye that swiveled in strange directions behind her coke bottle glasses. "What! What! Which one of the little devils are you?", she would holler at any one of us, not inspiring any change in our minds about how dim her bulb shone. I can only imagine what difficulty she, or poor old Clara Wolf in Alpena, or Miss Brunke would have had with four young whirling dervishes swooping-in and out of the house. Aunt Rill brought with her medicines. Once around the time of the rock throwing incident, while Aunt Rill was drawn to her favorite "story" or soap opera, about whose characters she fretted sometimes to the point of actually praying to God to help them, I went in to the bathroom in the hall, and found some chocolates among her things in the cabinet. I popped three in my mouth and swallowed them even though they weren't quite as tasty as Hershey bars. "Oh, well", I remember thinking, "What do you expect from old people candy?"

It wasn't fifteen minutes while Billy and I were zooming around the construction site with three or four other friends, that I went over a hill into the air and landed with a loud explosion occurring in my "bottom" as my mother would say. For maybe two or three minutes after that I heard weird gurgling sounds resembling piglets squealing, and experienced two or three more blasts. The odor was something nasty, more foul or putrid than any odor you would smell around Aunt Muriel. I hopped on my bike which felt squishy, raced back to the house, while Billy accompanied me giggling. I reached the downstairs bathroom and locked the door. My blue jeans were filled. Aunt Rill yelled from outside the door, "Did you shit yourself? I saw the Ex-Lax wrappers". I looked down and noticed the wrappers which said "extra strength", and "stimulant laxative for extra hard stools". "Rut Roh" as Astro would say. (May I add once again that Aunt Rill only knew farm life?)

After three years in Ann Arbor, we were sent to Bay City, Michigan. Dawn began the sixth grade, I the fifth, Billy the third, and Robin first grade. I remember three events very clearly: in school, I began to have doubts about what I heard from my dad and assorted Salvation Army officers about evolution. I had begun to question how Charles Darwin was being portrayed as an agent of evil, when his writings concerned his careful research involving evolution, especially *On the Origin of Species by Means of Natural Selection*, published in 1859. Evolution never seemed false on its face to me, given the fact that after years and years of listening to and then questioning various Bible stories' historical veracity-particularly in the Old Testament—it was baffling to see why there weren't different ways of approaching life and reality. I didn't know why these matters had to be considered with such defensiveness. I was not allowed to ask important questions. I do remember making a statement on Sunday night in response to my dad's teaching that we avoid all evil and "paganism" in our world, among our neighbors, and especially at school. I stood up and asked about what specifically? My dad looked at me for a long time and answered, "Many of the customs around Christmas are totally sinful, including the Christmas tree. And all of Hallowe'en is nothing but demons and witches and celebrating Satan." "Really", I thought. Then why do we participate as a Christian family in these customs? I brought up the two matters I had been thinking about at night, because I remembered reading in an encyclopedia about how the English language incorporates much from our past what we had experienced hundreds of years before and took for granted. "Dad, if we get rid of Christmas and Hallowe'en, shouldn't we also give new names to the days of the week? Should we go along with a day for Thor? Or Woden? Or the day of Saturn? Or what about the names of the months of the year? This month is named for Mars, a Roman god. Or Juno or Julius Caesar, or Augustus. What do you think?" My dad did not like my obvious skepticism, and my need to ask these questions. He mumbled something about he would check that out.

It was also at Bay City that at eleven years of age, I came across the most astounding picture of a woman. At downtown's Mill End store, there were suggestive 3D photos of a San Francisco performer, which I found in a "view master". These photos were of a heavenly beauty, an adult woman, who "knocked my socks off", in the phrase my parents used. Only a few weeks before my anxious dad had brought out "special books" on sex, a male for me, a female book for my sister Dawn, with graphic but more scientific pictures of the male and female anatomies, with cut away drawings of the male and female reproductive organs. EWWWWW!!! It was horrible to sit on my bed listening to my dad stutter his way through what was obviously a painful subject for him, using words he couldn't quite pronounce. I even think he said "public" for "pubic". "And when a married couple who love each other carry out what God intended-because this is a good thing—and they love each other—he will insert his 'penis' into her 'virginia'" and so forth. He had the same uncomfortable tone saying much about "sex" from the pulpit, and how it was the way the devil enticed us in visions of women who cause us, against our Christian duty, blah blah blah. In the 1970s when the angry religious right became politicized with opposition to public school students being taught basic sexual information in Health classes, along with anti-homosexual and anti-abortion propaganda, led by the likes of Fundamentalists Jerry Falwell and Phyllis Schlafly , I remember hearing once again in the public square what I heard from my dad and other ministers, the same old fear and anxiety and the quivering bodily expressions that go with them—talking about these subjects with frowns, through clenched teeth, with the body language of Joe Cocker at his weirdest. The message was something like: Sex (uh) is dirty (uh). It must (uh) be taught carefully by true American *Bible* believing Chris-tian (emphasis on "Chris") parents (uh) or at *Bible* believing Churches (uh) where you can *Hear* this in the environment (uh) of a Christian community where God is *Lifted Up*! Our culture is spewing filth, and pornography from all media, and that is where the public school teachers get their information. Let's *Stop* this (uh) from ever hap-pening (uh) to our innocent girls and boys! (Great applause) This was all duplicitous, all false. In my sixth and seventh grade health classes, a nurse or a doctor talked as best as they could with a bunch of edgy nervous kids about sexual matters, in a mostly scientific or medical way. Who would want Jerry Falwell or Billy Graham or Pat Robertson teaching anything, let alone about sex? A photo of Phyllis Schlafly would have been enough for me to lose any sense of eroticism.

Of course one may find vacuous and foolish teaching on sex in all Churches. (My favorite word was *jejune*. This use of mine now strikes me as affected.) In the mid-1970s, I actually came across an elderly priest in the Anglo-Catholic Diocese of Milwaukee, who told me he provided thirty minutes of sexual instruction to the couples. "What do you talk about?" I inquired. "I never have to say too much", he replied. "I bring out the models I was given in 1936 when I was ordained, and show the couple the right position for intercourse, and let friction take over." "I see. They don't ask questions? Or become curious about other possibilities at all?" I deadpanned. "What? What else is there to say?" The Rev. Father demanded. "You show them what Adam and Eve did, and bang bang that's it!" Oh, my.

My sixth grade teacher was Mrs. Anderson. Until my parents met her in late October, they didn't know she was an African American. This was 1965. My mother later said to me that she knew her children had been properly brought up when she met my teacher. There was one exception. My behavior was awful that year at school. I had begun reading all sorts of books from the school libraries, and never was without one or two or three to enjoy and keep from getting bored. My worst fear for all my life has been boredom. Attending the Salvation Army with my dad's preaching and teaching was fatuous beyond endurance. And in the sixth grade, school was a close second. For church I learned to take a book I liked or wished to read, and kept quiet with my head down. At school we were consigned to paying attention. So I read in the classroom, holding up my desk top a crack with my book laid out inside. This would get me in trouble. And then I would answer questions with wisecracks. And some of these one liners were pretty good, with Mrs. Anderson—not possessing a sense of humor at all—getting frustrated. She would become increasingly upset. When she reached her limit, she would gesticulate and yell, and be my straight man, declaring the downfalls ahead for me and for a friend of mine, Bob Shearer. So, out in the hallway I'd be sent on an average of once a week, as would my friend. Thank God for Bob Shearer. He was enormously clever, and the comedy team of Coleman and Shearer entertained the troops passing outside of class. We did imitations of teachers and the assistant principal of school, including their walks. We would get laughs. This was hugely gratifying, to hear the laughter and joy which one could evoke with a sense of humor.

Another first occurred in Bay City.

For the first time I heard my mother on the telephone arguing with the Salvation Army's Divisional Commander. It was so strange to find out the muckety mucks of the Salvation Army operated like the Politburo in Moscow, or the Exalted Elders of the Mormon Church, with the same arguments, viz. officers were informed that Divisional Commanders and Territorial Commanders, who prayed every spring about who should stay or who should go, so to speak, simply then sent out orders. These orders were not to be questioned and there was no opportunity for appeal. If one did question a Commander, one would be told that they were under Satan's influence, and would therefore need repentance and learn obedience, which the Holy Spirit would provide. In this specific case, my mother believed the house in Bay City provided for our family was inadequately furnished, and that the previous officers had left it in disarray even filthy. Her D.C. ordered her to quit complaining, that the "corps" (church) in Bay City had little money, so that was that. My mother with her strong sense of fairness, and the knowledge that she and my dad had offered very fine leadership in their previous two "appointments", now continued her protest. Many of the divisional leaders in the Salvation Army were average men (mostly) without the education or necessary skills to know how to manage various officers, especially women, who could be as strong in their leadership positions as my mother. And for the most part, conflict resolution was a very simple matter in the hierarchy of the Salvation Army, the Divisional Commander issued an order. This is the authoritarian system established by William Booth himself (angels singing whenever his name is mentioned). When my mother did not back down (and she rarely did in any conflict in which she might find herself, including matters of defending the poor and powerless who sought assistance to deal with corrupt local politicians or unfair landlords or crooked local businessmen) but put her views on paper, and sent them to the D.C., Colonel Marlin Cohn, she was seen as a nuisance. After two years in Bay City we found ourselves in Bismarck, North Dakota. This was extremely disruptive and upsetting to my parents. Salvation Army officers learn to cultivate friendships among other officers, obviously an important part of surviving when one's family is moved very often due to the arbitrary decisions of the Holy Spirit, communicated by the Salvation Army Officer in charge. My folks were both Michiganders, and both had extended family that mattered to all of us. My mother's brother, my uncle Bill and his wife Aunt Ivy were officers in Eastern Michigan. Mother's older sister Lillian and her husband, Uncle Chuck, lived in Livonia. Dad's Aunt Rill (Uncle Gilbert died in 1965) lived in Hillsdale, and counted on my dad for assistance of all kinds. When our family had vacation time, a week or two would include attending a Divisional Camp, for music lessons, fellowship, recreation of all kinds, friendships, and the bonding that occurs with other Officers and their families. Now we were told, ordered actually, to be publicly shamed by being sent to North Dakota. Bye. I think this led to my dad's beginning disillusionment with the Salvation Army.

A favorite video on YouTube is the one of Bruno Ganz's portrayal of Hitler's last few days with his dearest and best in the bunker in Berlin, a scene taken from the film "Downfall". It has been subtitled with hilarious English "translations". No Nazi wishes to talk candidly with Hitler about their impending plight, that Soviet and American troops are closing the circle around central Berlin with fewer and fewer able German soldiers to defend the Fuehrer. Hitler's top generals finally ask him what to do, and the video shows his very high military leaders informing him they have made plans to send him to North Dakota. He explodes in rage: Not even the North Dakotans want to live there, he will be the darkest person in the whole state (even after all these months in the bunker), there is nothing to do, he will have to eat horrible Mexican food which he will defecate into the Red River, they use expressions like Uffda, he will freeze his nuts off, and so on. I sympathize with Hitler.

So we moved to Bismarck. Away from most friends and family, we lived in the Salvation Army's witness protection program, or so it seemed. I found seventh grade challenging and of course with Dawn, Billy, and Robin, had to make new friends all over again. Since we had each other as playmates, this wasn't too hard for Robin and me, the more extroverted of us. I remember dad not enjoying this move or the Salvation Army as he once had. He and mother had worked tirelessly, at the last three appointments. But my parents' concerns were far away from me, because we heard all sorts of pop and rock music as sirens calling us. Both my parents were uneasy about this. "Do you hear the words, Dale!" my dad would say. Really? "I'm going to cry 96 tears? Dad is that what you don't like?" I was becoming a bona-fide know-it-all jerk. I had to have something to latch onto in my favor because I was a fatty tubby. I see pictures of myself in sixth or seventh grades, and I have a Dumb and Dumber bowl haircut, short sleeves on dorky undersized shirts, tight "husky" pants, everything about me screaming stupid dork. And I was blind. So, I was a squinty eyed fatty in dork clothes. Why blind?

Uh, oh. I was at the age when boys discover "that". And outside of "that", I simply can't think of much that happened in North Dakota. (Dorothy Parker named her pet canary "Onan" because it kept spilling its seed. See *Genesis* 38:9.)

My dad said to me about this—more helpful advice—that if I did "that", I would go blind. I said, "Dad. I'm over here". A Catholic friend of mine said that a nun told him that if you touch yourself, the saints cry. Get this: not famine or dropping bombs on Japan. Fundamentalists of course would talk—in their herky—jerky spaz ways— about going blind from masturbation. My spiritually mature advice is this: if you start going blind, you're doing it wrong.

English men of letters may of course write at length about these matters, well into their dotage, because they're . . . well . . . *Englishmen*. In a longstanding feud Auberon Waugh (son of Evelyn) responded to a silly comment Cyril Connolly made in the midst of a review about the memoir *Conundrum*, which Jan Morris published concerning her major change in her life switching "teams". Connolly noted:

> It's bad luck on her that the reviewer chosen for this book should have a cas-
> tration complex, for there is nothing I dread more than injury to those parts
> whose activities are still in the private sector, and which I regard as the source
> of so much intellectual authority, lucidity, judgement and visual pleasure.

Waugh responded, "Poor Connolly!", and then he commented:

> Visual pleasure indeed. If this horrible old man can't keep eyes off himself at
> the age of 70, he might have been better advised to experiment a little earlier
> like everyone else. [1]

No comment.

1. Auberon Waugh, *Will This Do?*, 223

VII

WE WERE SENT IN 1968 to Ottumwa, Iowa. This was a much better appointment as Salvationists said, and in fact my Uncle Bill, Aunt Ivy and their family were now close by. Uncle Bill had pulled strings to arrange for us to come into his division, as he was on his way to the very heights of Salvation Army officialdom. My dad did not like this. He would not be beholden to anyone and certainly not to his brother-in-law, whom he considered pompous and a bore. As far as the rest of us were concerned, Ottumwa was a much more pleasant place to live, and to attend school. I celebrated our move by coming out, so to speak, and joining those Salvationist teenagers planning to become Officers, that is, the Salvation Army way of announcing one had the "Call". The group met several times in one's own Division-Iowa, and were called the "Future Officers Fellowship". It seemed I had known for as long as I could remember having a vocation to the ordained ministry, but I was unsure of this taking place in the Salvation Army.

The Public Schools of the Midwestern states in which we lived took seriously teaching, music, athletics, and learning how to socialize, the importance of home-work, and encouraged regular meetings between parents and teachers. Public School in the 1960s was very solid, focusing on a child's education, and seeing to it that the young people who graduated were prepared to face the world, knowing how to read and write, the basics of State and Federal Government, what citizenship meant, and provided for band and choral music, extra science study, class and school government, various athletics, and yearbook and journalism opportunities. The teachers were fully capable of disciplining students, and keep order in their classrooms to benefit the learning of those pupils. I am and will always be grateful that I was able with all this help from my community and State Board of Education to learn the basics and keep learning to the extent I was able. When I got to College, I was well prepared, including knowing how to write a sentence.

Schools and their personnel and other resources were not expected to take care of other basis needs of children such as nutrition (except at lunch time), parental responsibilities like teaching basic discipline, extensive psychological evaluation and treatment, all of the social needs now provided in public schools. The near breakdown of the family unit, especially among the poor and working classes, and the tremendous rise of cycles of poverty, crime, and substance abuse, which have now been America's stock in trade since the 1960s, and multiple questionable political attempts to alleviate the basic needs of children, even involve them in heavy handed social engineering (to arrive at bureaucratic solutions for integrating communities for example) have not kept the major cities from suffering under this weight of social need. Daniel Patrick Moynihan's study from the mid-60s warning about the collapse of the basic family unit in African American communities, and what this foretold for the future seems to me prophetic and accurate. (This was known as the "Moynihan Report" or *The Negro Family: The Case for National Action*, 1965.)

Eighth grade was more challenging for me, especially because of science. English literature, American history, math, social sciences all came easily. Part of the reason for me might have been how wooden science teachers were in their styles of presentation. I enjoyed chorus tremendously. Music has ever been since I can remember a way of pleasure and delight. This was true mostly at school. Church music was dreadful, and the elevator music or country music my dad listened to was unspeakably bad. I was repeatedly abused musically in my youth. To this day, I know and can hum on cue several different Leroy Anderson tunes: "Sleigh Ride" , "Syncopated Clock", "Bugler's Holiday", "China Doll", "Trumpeter's Lullaby", "Fiddle Faddle", even "Typewriter", and "Plink, Plank, Plonk". This is the kind of yucky stuff PBS brings out when they're begging, and they want to suck in the proles. Or what the Boston Pops play when they're slumming. It's awful. To my parents, this was cultured music, only topped by Lawrence Welk. Christmas music played for an entire month sung by Bing Crosby, Danny F. Kaye, Dean Martin, Johnny Mathis, the Chipmunks, "I saw Mommy Kissing Santa Claus", even the song which I think should cause the waterboarding of the composer: "All I Want for Christmas is my two front Teeth". In mixed chorus, a 13 year old boy who liked looking at girls could indulge in that, and sing music a step or two up from what I was forced to hear at home or church.

Another area for my more competitive and athletic streak was football. Mr. Gullian was a nice dumb guy whose idea for getting the players' attention was to holler out, "Men! Get your fingers out of your asses and listen up!" Great. I played all season as either a left guard on offense, or a right tackle on defense. I got through the season. It was not enjoyable. Once or twice when I moved to outside linebacker on defense, I actually enjoyed playing. I did notice something important: I could either sing in the choir or play football. With a new awareness in girls, I saw there were not any attractive ones in football. What was the point of football then?

I found I was reading any number of books, history, literature, but now I discovered what I thought would be my profession, politics. I had become obsessed by watching the Evening News, either Walter Cronkite or Huntly and Brinkley. Once in a blue moon, it was ABC. In late summer, I caught the ABC Convention coverage for both the Democrats and the Republicans. They offered for our viewing pleasure two fascinating, intelligent, articulate gentlemen and intellectuals to put forward their views on why the viewers should consider either the Republican or the Democrat. They were William F. Buckley and Gore Vidal. In the months leading up to the conventions,

I remember times of great anxiety at school affecting students and teachers. Rioting occurred in one large urban city after another, including Detroit, over the inequalities and injustice so many sensed in black and white racial matters, and especially among black citizens in the US, who felt and endured manifest racial prejudice. At the same time, well to do college kids on campuses across the country were marching to call attention to the Viet Nam War, which had become a volatile issue as we watched the scenes night after night on television. Many of us in Ottumwa had family members or friends of our families, and members of our churches who were drafted to fight in Vietnam (which reached over 500,000 in 1967). Events in America seemed to me, and many many others, to show that our nation was coming apart. If you looked at news stories on the domestic front, cities were burning, any number of people were crying, including children, and if you watched stories from Viet Nam, the scenes were just as tense and horrific. Governor George Romney was himself running for the presidency as a Republican, along with the other "R"s, Nelson Rockefeller and Ronald Reagan. The sleeper candidate looked to be to be former Vice President Richard Nixon. As for me and my house we were Romney people. My mother's view was straightforward, both Rockefeller and Reagan were divorced and therefore unqualified. The Bible said it, she believed it, that settles it! She did not see Romney as a non-Christian, because the Salvation Army was as eccentric in its views as the Mormons. The Salvation Army had no "Canon", no measure to say who was in or who was out, beyond the "outward and visible signs" of smoking, drinking, card playing, Hollywood loving, skirt chasing, homosexing, divorcing, gambling, et cetera, who were all out. On Sundays, the "Singing Colemans" even sang about this: "The ole ark's a moverin', a moverin', a moverin', and I'm going home". "See that sister, dressed so fine? She ain't got the Good Lord on her mind. See that brother, dressed so gay? The Devil's gonna come and carry him away." And so forth. This was a Negro Spiritual that a large number of white Fundamentalist male quartets and choirs would take and alter. In this case there were verses that covered all the obvious sinners whom you could point out on your own block. And Romney was none of those. Mormons and Salvationists don't drink or chew or kiss girls that do—unless they are looking for a really good time. (An actress and comedian-whose name I shan't mention—said, "When I'm good, I'm very very good; but when I'm bad I'm better"; and "When I get caught between two evils I try the one I've never tried before"; as well as, "Those who are easily shocked, should be shocked more often". Finally, "I'll try anything once, twice if I like it, three times to make sure". I will give you a hint. It's not Hedley Lamarr.)

Our churchly world changed in Ottumwa, Iowa, as I implied above. At some point Dawn, Robin and I sang with dad in a mixed quartet. Dawn accompanied on the piano and sang alto; Robin sang melody; dad sang high tenor; and I sang bass. We sang well with a fine harmony. (Whatever chances my mother had singing ended when she had her larynx scraped following the discovery of polyps attached to it due to talking too much while hoarse.) Billy of course was too incorrigible to sing, and not considered saved. And we sang, and sang. Every single worship service we sang at least twice. Mostly we sang such Holiness standards as "Mansion over the Hilltop", "On the Jericho Road", "Just a Little talk with Jesus", George Beverly Shea's awful, "I'd rather have Jesus", or Stuart Hamblen's "It is no secret what God can do". Gag me with a spoon. I reached a point of informing friends at school who had heard of the "Singing Coleman Family", that Shea had originally written his song during his 1936 Nazi period with the lyrics "I'd rather have Himmler, than Jodl or Krebs . . .", which had then been greeted with approval by Magda Goebbels. I firmly believe Hell will be forcing large groups of stinking humanity with their cigarette breath, into tiny rooms with the continual communal singing (while having pitch forks stuck into their nether parts to force lobotomized smiles) of all the hits of "Bev" Shea. I know this to be 100% true because this Good News was channeled to me by George Beverly Shea after his death at age 104. (Not a lot of peer pressure at that age. And he didn't look good for 104. The last candles on his birthday cake which he spent several minutes blowing out had reduced the cake to pudding by the end of his effort.)

With regard to the Presidential contest, my mother (and I) supported George Romney, while my dad, who had come unglued by the world, he thought, coming apart, was continually alarmed, and began doing what Fundamentalists do when they can't figure out what is happening in the country or world making them anxious and fearful (which is often): They go Apocalyptic. This is predominantly an American Christian phenomenon. The whole "Last Things" nonsense was the brainchild of a Church of Ireland (Anglican) kook, (mentioned above) who made up the Rapture, the last days, spooky *Revelation* stuff, even wildly misunderstanding what Jesus says in *St. Mark* 13 (which is so obviously about Jerusalem's last days in 70 AD, when the Temple was destroyed by the Romans of Vespasian and Titus). With John Nelson Darby's new bizarre way of using these Apocalyptic lenses, he read these texts as secrets which he could discern and weave into his crazy quilt of an interpretation. When he came to the Plymouth Brethren in the United States, he found a huge willing audience ignorant of Christian doctrine and theology, lapping up this toxic teaching. (The idea that everything is so wrong and frightening, and therefore the times are ripe for Jesus' return has been a continual theme in American history, from Columbus' eschatological notion that God wanted him to evangelize the inhabitants in the New World, right up to the Mormons, the Jehovah's Witnesses-who completely get "The Lord's Name" wrong, Seventh Day Adventists, who got the day wrong, to the reactions of so many Christians North and South during the Civil War. (Julia Ward Howe's "Mine eyes have seen the glory of the coming of the Lord", uses choice language to interpret these horrific four years in which as many as 700,000 men died. She sees the altar of the Lord on the battlefield, sacrificing men left and right, with his terrible swift sword. Lincoln also interpreted the war theologically, but very differently and more faithfully to the meaning of judgment in the Bible.) Darby published tracts and books on his theory of "Premillennial Dispensationalism" which led to *Scofield's Reference*

Bible, influencing Evangelist Dwight L. Moody and the Moody Bible Institute, as well as the Dallas Theological Seminary, and Hal Lindsey and Tim Lahaye and their more contemporary goofy writings. All of this "premillennial dispensationalism" is entirely false from any Historical Credal Christian belief. My favorite bad piece of "Christian" music remains the Gaithers' "The King is Coming!".

My dad had come across a bizarre religious book by Clarence Larkin, *Dispensational Truth* (1918) by this business man turned preacher. Larkin follows Scofield in taking Darby's views as mapping out all of the history of the world to show the seven dispensations as secretly laid out by God in the Bible. Larkin was directly ordered by God (as all these nutty folks were) to draw pictures of the dispensations, for those who were challenged by the words on the page of Darby's and Scofield's works. My dad— from one of his Salvation Army officer friends—discovered these pictures, to put before the congregation on large sheets pulled down like window shades or the maps in your public school classroom. Here's God, here's Adam, here's the Fall, Oh, here's the Second Coming (right around the corner) here's Satan, here's the Anti-Christ, here's the great pit, (I like abyss-sounds vaguely like a Catholic nun) and so forth. In my dad's teaching, Stalin, Hitler, the Pope, the Beatles, Henry Kissinger, Leonid Brezhnev, Ho Chi Minh, the present State of Israel, Vietnam, all had their key parts to play in these so obvious last times. Only true and special Christians were given this knowledge, unlike all nominal Christians and hypocritical Christians—Episcopalians, Lutherans, most Methodists, all followers of the Pope, and Liberace. This teaching earned a reputation for my dad, and soon, people were coming quietly and respectfully to the Sunday night worship service when my dad would unveil his latest revelation. The musical Colemans supported this in great measure by belting out all the latest Fundamentalist music available, but I refused to sing "Do Lord", "He Touched Me", and "When the Roll is called up yonder I'll be there".

At one of the Salvation Army's Iowa Divisional Councils, the Divisional Commander Birger Justvig, who spoke exactly like George Jessel, and therefore easy to imitate, announced to a stunned audience that an officers' family, The Singing Colemans, were going to perform "a musical package", like no one has ever heard before! Since my mother couldn't sing well, she was the MC. She narrated this splendid package; and then outdoing even ourselves, Colonel Justvig related in quiet George Jessel tones, that the Colemans regularly had evening devotions including reading from the *King James Bible*, and each in turn prayed. "So, we have set up a table here with five chairs, and they will each pray. This is so powerful and an answer to all the families in this country who are broken and lost. Captain Eva will narrate." So, the incredibly spiritually gifted Colemans walked over and sat at this makeshift supper table and the audience was transfixed with this scene of our special piety. My dad even worked in a reference to these being the last days, before my mother continued her narration about how if everyone listened (see if you can hear a pin drop) then they could hear every Coleman child (I was 14) pray for their Aunt Rill, now widowed.

In the real world, Eugene McCarthy came close to defeating the sitting President in March, and then Bobby Kennedy-who had assured Richard Goodwin and others he did not intend to enter the race—jumped in. Goodwin had worked hard to persuade McCarthy to enter the race, which he had done reluctantly. As soon as Kennedy went after McCarthy's spoils, Goodwin shoved everyone and everything over to sign up with Bobby. Gore Vidal issued a classic statement, "Goodwin is an Iago always in search of Othello". Years later, I mentioned this anecdote of Vidal's to a professor of mine in political science at the University of Wisconsin. Dr. Robert Booth Fowler, informed me that years before, he had dated Doris Kearns before she left him for Richard Goodwin.

At the end of March 1968, Johnson himself withdrew from the campaign. Then a few days after that, Martin Luther King was assassinated in Memphis. The Vice President, a noble old fashioned Democrat-Farmer-Labor member from Minnesota who as mayor of Minneapolis had roused the 1948 Democratic Convention with a stem-winder on Civil Rights, Hubert Horatio Humphrey, now ran as the mainstream Democrat. Humphrey had been instrumental in founding the modern Democratic party in Minnesota by his leadership to merge the Farmer-Labor and Democratic parties. He worked with Senator Paul Douglas of Illinois to found the Americans for Democratic Action, a liberal anti-communist movement, focused mainly on Civil Rights. At the 1948, Democratic Convention these two led the fight from the floor of Convention to make their minority plank the main plank of the Party on Civil Rights. He stated it was time that Civil Rights for all African Americans come out into the clear air in American politics, and not continue beholden to States Rightsers. When they won, several State party leaders from the South got Senator Strom Thurmond of South Carolina to lead the Dixiecrats, an out and out segregationist party. They hoped to defeat Truman that year, and drive the now Northern led Democratic Party back into "bed" with the Southern States Rightsers. Instead, Humphrey campaigned vigorously for Truman, and won a Senate seat himself. He was known for being a senate leader on issues of a "Test Ban" treaty, the Peace Corps, agricultural relief, and relief for the poor, in addition to Civil Rights. His sunny disposition and ability to speak at length about almost any subject extemporaneously with feeling, led to his being called the "Happy Warrior".(This had also been the nickname for Gov. Alfred E. Smith, the Democratic Party's nominee for President in 1928.)

Humphrey was in 1968 at the Democratic Convention in Chicago burdened with the necessity of defending the war he despised in Vietnam. So, a key chant from the antiwar and radical protesters was "Dump the Hump". (Jimmy Carter once referred to him as "Hubert Horatio Hornblower".) He said during the Convention, "No sane person likes the Vietnam War, and neither does President Johnson".

For the Republicans, my favorite (and my mother's) Governor Romney was stalled in his attempt at a run for their nomination, with some ill-chosen words on being brainwashed by the generals in Viet Nam. Gene McCarthy said brainwashing wasn't necessary; a clean rinse would do. Lyndon Johnson won the insult contest for that year in mocking tones by saying, "Watching George Romney run for Presidency was like watching a duck fuck a football". He dropped out before the first primary in New Hampshire, as Nelson Rockefeller entered the race.

So, back to the Conventions being broadcast on ABC with two wordsmiths, authors, intellectual heavyweights—who had both run for offices themselves—both unsuccessfully. William F. Buckley, a leading conservative intellectual, and Gore Vidal, a liberal who had published *Myra Breckinridge*, in February of 1968, a painfully boring stab at a satirical novel about feminism, transsexuality, male machismo, and sexual perversions. These men were considered two of the finest professional debaters in the country, both patricians, wealthy, and well educated, and they hated one another with a white heat. Their small talk included Buckley's comments on Vidal's "decent book" about the fourth century emperor who pretended to be a Christian until his reign began in 361 AD, known as *Julian*, whose sobriquet was Julian the Apostate, which had come out in 1964. Vidal said he liked Buckley's account of his failed run for Mayor of New York City in 1965, entitled *The Unmaking of a Mayor*. Then Buckley said something about Vidal's ambivalent sexuality, and Vidal asked why if Buckley was such a faithful Roman Catholic he only had one child. Then they were on the air, and to me it was watching something akin to lightning flashes. Their rapier attacks on each other had me off my seat and sitting right in front of the television. They were both very clever and droll, with moderator Howard K. Smith not knowing if he should call them to order or applaud. I had never seen anything like this, and this was fun! Both men were knowledgeable about a great many subjects, and called important facts to mind about the Roman Empire, the Viet Nam war, literature, World War II, religion, philosophy-contemporary and medieval and ancient, Lenin, the Soviet Union and its present designs to become an empire, Churchill's career and his "Iron Curtain" speech in 1946, the US's becoming an empire, quotations in Latin, the French, and of course Nixon and Humphrey. Wow! Whatever they had I wanted. To be more precise, whatever Buckley had I wanted. The next day I knew I wanted to get involved in politics and start by reading William F. Buckley. I went to Ottumwa's Public Library. I found his mayor book, a couple of his collections of newspaper columns, and a Ralph de Toledano biography of Richard Nixon, and Nixon's *Six Crises*. I loved the Buckley books, and found Nixon's account of the Hiss case thrilling, but not much else-such as the treacly story of the "Checkers Speech". From Buckley I got interested in Whittaker Chambers' *Witness*. This gave me a first person narrative of the Soviet Union's attempts at espionage in the United States, from Chambers' own life. The *caveat* by Chambers that by leaving the "religion" of Stalinism for the West, he was joining the losing side, startled me. Was this true? My dad informed me that in the Book of *Revelations* (sic), there was no mention that the great nation or the Beast would be destroyed as it shows in *Revelations* 13 (sic). So, I learned not to ask my dad anymore questions about the Bible if I were expecting a helpful answer. On Sunday evenings however, during the "window shade" teaching, I would ask publicly how *Revelation* could have been written in the first century AD, in Greek!, and have nothing to assist John's first century readers. How do we know the translation we are utilizing in English, is accurate? And why did a first century writing known as God's Word, and inerrant, come to be considered as intended for "true Christians" living in the United States in 1968? After a few weeks of insistent questioning, my dad glared at me and said, "Dale, your learning has made you mad." I immediately answered that that had been spoken in the *Acts of the Apostles* by a non-believer about St. Paul. So, I stopped attending church for a while, and turned my full attention to American politics.

I also began reading books, which showed Christianity was false on its face, because how could anyone believe the Virgin Birth, the miracles, the salvific death, the Resurrection, these nonsense doctrines were true? Several writings by Thomas Paine were bracing, especially his noting that Christianity was invented lock stock and barrel, and the Old Testament was worthless and shows us a cruel god, which worship then leads to cruel men, that there is at most one god, whom we can come to know through reason alone, a natural philosophy. This is deism. Immanuel Kant once said one would be embarrassed or confused if caught at prayer.

In eighth grade science, I gave a presentation on tornadoes during which I inserted a few *bon mots* ,which led to great laughter for the best of thirty minutes. I found I liked this gift. And, if I had made friends and family laugh on private occasions, why not in public? At the Central Music Institute of the Salvation Army's Central division, the annual camp at Camp Lake Wisconsin, two events occurred which stayed with me. I came to realize my cousin Betty Anne Roberts was kind and caring. She was a year older than I , and as with all her family, especially Uncle Bill, highly intelligent with a dry sense of humor. Wow! Plus, she let me articulate my skeptical views about the Christian faith. Who would do that in the powder keg tensions of my family? Later I went out to the Salvation Army Divisional Camp Laurie near Boone, Iowa, partly to see my sister Dawn who was working there that summer, and to get a chance for another visit with Betty Anne who was normal. Her friendship mattered to me.

The second thing was I decided to sing at the music performance finals at CMI. I chose a song which was one of the more interesting to me among the drab and dreary Salvation Army *repertoire*, "The Love of God". A German immigrant, Frederick Martin Lehman, had written it in the early twentieth century as I announced. Then I said that the third verse had been attributed to a Jewish man, who had scrawled this on the wall of his insane asylum. Well! That got a laugh! Dawn of course accompanied my singing this astounding piece of testimony! So I began, "The Love of God, is greater far, than tongue or pen can ever tell", at which point my voice broke, and I lapsed into silence, totally embarrassed at this incredibly shameful display of cowardice. Then the worst thing happened, I tried coming in on the chorus, a series of middle D notes. "O Love of God, how rich and pure . . ." except I only croaked out "O, Love" and again went silent. What a disaster! Grown men were weeping at this sad *denouement.*

Youngsters were laughing, led by my smart-ass brother. For several days after that, Salvationists, supposedly Christian, would sing the first four notes of the refrain, and then imitating my voice cracking, would serenade me. Great.

VIII

I WAS HELPED BY the major event that fall to get over my cousin's new friendship because her family had moved away. In October 1968, the Detroit Tigers played the St. Louis Cardinals in the World Series. From May 10, Detroit never looked back and won 103 games, behind Denny McLain's 31 wins—first time over 30 since Dizzy Dean did this with the Gas House Gang in St. Louis, and an earned run average of 1.97. He won the Cy Young ,and the American League's Most Valuable Player's awards that year.

The ex-convict Gates Brown pinch hit .370, both Norm Cash and Bill Freehan hit 25 homeruns, Willie Horton-hitting in the .400s as late as June—hit .287 with 36 home runs. Jim Northrup had 90 RBIs and five grand slams-including three in one week in June. Mickey Stanley won a gold glove playing regularly in center when future hall of famer Al Kaline was injured and center fielder Northrup was moved to right. Dick McAuliffe with his open batting stance similar to Mel Ott's, scored 95 runs and hit 16 home runs. Mickey Lolich won 17 games. And then there was another of my heroes, Earl Wilson, a pitcher acquired from Boston in 1966 following a vicious racist event which took place in Florida, when he and two white players entered a bar, to be greeted with "We don't serve niggers here". Wilson sought relief from his manager who told him to forget it and not to tell the media. (Wilson was the first African American on the Red Sox team in 1959, the last team of 16 to break through the color code.) Wilson was disgusted with this order to keep quiet, and he found himself traded to Detroit for Don Demeter and Julio Navarro. He proceeded to hit seven home runs as a power hitter, twice as a pinch hitter, in 1968. He was 13–12 with an earned run average of 2.85.

Detroit then played the great Cardinals team in the World Series. They were led by Bob Gibson, an overpowering fast ball pitcher, who was 22–7, with an era of 1.12, fleet of foot—sounds like Achilles in *The Iliad*—Lou Brock , sure fielding and hitting Curt Flood, and the essential team which had won the previous year's World Series. Down 3–1, Detroit came back with sterling pitching performances by Mickey Lolich (three complete game wins), and Denny McLain in game six. Two key moments occurred in the seventh game. In the sixth inning of the low scoring pitcher's duel between Bob Gibson and Mickey Lolich, Lolich picked off both Lou Brock and Curt

Flood. And then next inning, Jim Northrup hit a fly ball into center field, which Curt Flood initially misjudged. It sailed over Flood's head and allowed two runs to score on the triple. That was all Detroit needed, to win only their third Series of all time. (I am grateful to my friend Randall Balmer, Episcopal priest, fine scholar, and interpreter of American Evangelicalism for helping me with this.)

This was a fabulous year for Michiganders and Tigers' fans. I missed most of the World Series however. My parents had become somewhat anxious about our Junior High years, and Dawn who had been wild already with several James Dean-esque boyfriends much older than she, was hesitant about attending Ottumwa High School from rumors she had picked up from friends. Also, my mother in particular had grown concerned about my lack of interest going to church, and reading free thinking materials and verbalizing my religious doubts. They wanted us to attend a Christian start up private High School in Stanzel, Iowa, southwest of Des Moines, on the road between Greenfield and Winterset. So, off to Stanzel we went in September of 1968. There were twenty or so of us in four grades. The school was associated with the Christian and Missionary Alliance Church, with a church on the grounds. The staff were for the most part Fundamentalists, and I have never heard a group of teachers mention "petting" and "heavy petting" like this bunch. There was a young, sad, red-haired, spinster school marm type named Marcia N. , who was alarmed by anything to do with sexuality, especially what she might witness as she stared out her window each night like Alice Kravitz on the television program "Bewitched". Everything that Dawn and I said and did alarmed this nervous Nellie who would run and tell the headmaster of the school, a Rev. Cruttwell, a CMA minister, married, with three lively teens. I was a freshman with four others in my class; Dawn was part of a similarly small group in the sophomore class. The juniors had seven members, and there were three seniors. We had daily 45 minute prayers-where we were supposed to "unburden ourselves" of any and all sin. We had morning and evening worship at the CMA church, and three times a week was evening prayer time with our dorm "families". Just about everyone there was a "type". Gordon Seiler was the not very bright out of touch teacher, who couldn't communicate with teenagers if his life depended on it. He was married to a petite, whiney, church lady type who would interrupt class to alert Gordo to what he had promised. Cruttwell himself was a know—it—all martinet, constantly ordering everyone around, and watching out for any sign of moral "turpitude" as he said. We had the dreamy, tolerant liberal type, Ray Block, who disagreed with all the rigid en-forcement of the "Cruttwell Rule System". No dating was allowed without a chaperone. No handholding. No kissing. No watching "shows", i.e. movies. There were strict hours for watching television, 7:30—9 every night, in one's dorm parents' living room. Those who watched over the teenage males were Bill and Gloria Lewis, who were waiting the entire school year to find out if they would have a future as missionaries letting the Hottentots in on all of their vast fortune of knowledge. They had little. I think about ignorant stupid clergy what Johnny Carson once said about a starlet on his show hawking her autobiography: "I have a starlet rule. You should be forced to read one book first, before you write one". This couple somehow learned to read and write, I think. They were overweight, dumb, and inarticulate. And that's no way to go through life. Unless you are a CMA missionary.

At least twice a week, at evening prayer time, they asked each of us in turn if we had committed any sins in our beds, because of specific noises they heard. We were four to a room in bunks. I spoke up first, "The only noises we heard were coming from downstairs". How weird could these people be? This happened a number of times with these unnecessary intrusive inquisitions. These folks were fixated on anything sexual that was in their heads. The Lewis's got turned down in their being sent to Africa, and consequently stayed vigilant watching us for all nine months. I do not know how we could have endured all year without their unique brand of Christian moral teaching.

By the end of November, Dawn had gotten the heave ho for arguing with her Dorm mother, Marcia. It turns out that during one of the girls' evening sessions of endless prayer, Marcia got them to pray for Dawn, that she would begin acting like a Christian or some such stupidity. So, they circled her and began praying one by one for Dawn to come out from the snare of Satan. Dawn reached her limit and told them to fuck off. I am grateful to write these many years later that Dawn is safely in Satan's arms today, playing honky tonk in the Methodist Church. Honestly, this authoritarian "mind control" or "mind fucking" as Fr. Robert Cooper called it in Seminary, especially by so-called religious people, is something rarely noted in our tolerant society. In his autobiography, William Sloane Coffin said that the behavior he found most prevalent and neurotic among Fundamentalists was that of mind control. He wrote in his pastoral *Letters to a Young Doubter* that he was part of a Bible study group while a student at Union Theological Seminary in New York City in 1949. At one such gathering, he had vigorously disagreed with a particular point being made and found himself alone, and under attack for his dissent. They would "pray" for him. This elicited a marvelous comeback from Coffin: "And how does your prayer list differ from a shit list?" I will bet that got him on more lists.[1]

This news of Dawn's leaving was communicated to me during the same evening's boys' prayer meeting, during one of the Lewis' opening lengthy emotional harangues masquerading as prayer. This passive aggressive power play is another common ploy to make religious groups conform. I remember getting very upset and praying aloud for Dawn, for her wellbeing. Bill Lewis came over to me, put his hand on me, rubbed my back (ewwwww!), and prayed that Dawn would confess her sins and stay at this holy place. I felt violated, and left the group and sought out Dawn to offer her my support. Well, she had had enough of this sick place, she said. Mother and dad were coming that night. She was absolutely correct.

I have found how destructive and dehumanizing religions can be, especially those with little accountability, and situations including family groups, being based

1. Coffin, *Letters to a Young Doubter*, 38

on the projections of a founder's or leader's psychology. And, it strikes me that many of these projections are narcissistic, reflecting one person's solipsistic desires. Quite often thinking about several examples, like Stanzel, someone whose upbringing and interactions with their own family which was pathological may develop a particular systemic approach, which then becomes consciously or subconsciously engrained in a person's psyche causing certain attitudes and behaviors which can have serious deleterious repercussions, both for the individual and for those with whom that person interacts, especially if this does not come to the person's awareness. Ludwig Feuerbach pointed this out, particularly in his atheistic *The Essence of Christianity*,[2] in which as a philosopher he studied the psychology of individuals and groups in Christian Churches, to show how psychological preconceptions determine everything in theology, mores, cultic , and behavioral ways in which religious people operate, all a false consciousness. This can be observed easily in the study of some community of religion as Freud did specifically in his *Future of an Illusion*, 1927, Ernest Becker, *The Denial of Death*, 1973, and especially in family and congregational settings by rabbi and scholar Edwin Friedman in *Generation to Generation: Family Process in Church and Synagogue*, 1985. Of course, this was already noted in the Old Testament, with the prohibition of idols. Human Beings from as long as anyone can remember have been inveterate idol makers. And, we especially enjoy worshiping ourselves. We can make anything under the sun into our own god to worship. Moreover, we take on the characteristics of that god. Bishop Michael Marshall once said that we become what we worship, as is seen in the resemblances between dogs and their owners. Arguably, for many people, fear or anxiety guide what they think or what they do or how they behave. It is now a platitude that our families of origin deeply affect us, twenty, thirty, forty years or more later.

2. Feuerbach, *The Essence of Christianity*, 12

IX

PERHAPS THE ONLY REASON I didn't leave with Dawn was because of noticing girls, including and especially Joyce. Like many pastors' kids, she was among the wildest. She had a very wicked sense of humor, was very quick witted, and great to be around. And she was lively. One night she came over to see me in the boys' dorm while the others were on a hay ride, and I suavely played her my favorite music, Herb Alpert's "Marching through Madrid". Whoa! Who could resist that hot Latin beat! Well, Joyce for one. Maybe if I put on my other favorite LP by the Ventures that would do the trick! Nope. She suggested taking a walk, so it was sweater time. We ended romantically in a ditch, and kissed, my first kissing adventure. The next day I sought out Joyce for more of this excitement, and she said in a deadened tone these incredible words, which haunt me to this day with their finality: "Get away from me creep." For a fourteen year old seeking out female encouragement, that sent me back to what was my solace of choice, the Lettermen. This fine group had the major heartache song any one my age would want, "Hurt So Bad". Or perhaps "Cathy's Clown" by the pop group the Everly Brothers. Maybe even "Love is Blue". What choices. I went with the Lettermen.

Later, the pastoral Mr. Block clued me in on what had occurred. Joyce had become guilt ridden about this breach with her father's rules, and needed solitude. OK.

With a few guys in the school, I enjoyed starting on our purple and gold Stanzel Christian High School basketball team. I started because everyone started. We had one senior, two juniors and two freshmen. We played five or six physical games with other fundamentalist private schools, won one, and otherwise received a pounding every time. At one time three of us were down on the floor because of Fundamentalist knees to the groin. Premillennial Dispies may say that Jesus is returning any day now, but they'll try to thrash you in the meantime. Or as my dad said, "clean your clock". He had quite the gift for phrasemaking. I also sang several times in the Iowa All-State Music Festival that spring. I found the rehearsals and preparations for these competitions intense in this state. Who knew? Iowa was known as a farm state with corn cobs-while no longer used-supposedly—in outhouses-are still a hot commodity. And hogs were everywhere. In the rural atmosphere of Stanzel, I expected to see hogs and cattle run through the towns blocking traffic. What else was there to do? Well, sing for one thing. Or wrestle. (While I was all for physical contact with someone of the opposite sex, and proved it in a ditch, wrestling another guy wasn't for me. This was the time for a number of outstanding Hawkeye wrestlers who went to the Olympics, like Dan Gable.) And everybody sings coming from fundamentalist churches. In fact, one comedown for many a great soloist without much pressure to polish one's singing style and sound in your little country church in the wildwood, where you were the belle of the ball (mixed metaphors running amuck) was to sing in various high schools in music loving Iowa, or even at the University of Iowa, and find you are now eighth or ninth best as an alto, and nowhere close to being the diva. (I'm thinking mostly of men.)

State competitions were greatly anticipated everywhere in Iowa. At Stanzel, Gordo Seiler "directed" the music. He had one song he thought appropriate, namely, "I Walked Today Where Jesus Walked". This is filled with hopelessly inane, non-sensical, maudlin lyrics to thrill its targeted audience. Let me assure you of a Holy Spirit blessing with this poetry:

> I walked today where Jesus walked
> In days of long ago.
> I wandered down each path He knew,
> With reverent step and slow.
> Those little lanes, they have not changed,
> A sweet peace fills the air.
> I walked today where Jesus walked,
> And felt Him close to me.
> My pathway led through Bethlehem,
> A memory's ever sweet.
> The little hills of Galilee,
> That knew His childish feet.
> The Mount of Olives, hallowed scenes,
> That Jesus knew before,
> I saw the mighty Jordan row (sic),
> As in the days of yore.
> I knelt today where Jesus knelt,
> Where all alone He prayed.
> The Garden of Gethsemane,
> My heart felt unafraid.
> I picked my heavy burden up,
> And with Him at my side,
> I climbed the Hill of Calvary,
> I climbed the Hill of Calvary,
> I climbed the Hill of Calvary,
> Where on the Cross, He died!
> I walked today where Jesus walked,
> And felt him close to me.

*This is the version we sang. There are variations on this.[1]

1. Twohig and O'Hara, *I walked Today Where*

Well, you may need a moment to come out of your spiritual reverie. I know I did. This has become a favorite for me to sing with great emotion whenever I shower. Perhaps if you are educated and actually read books, you may recognize some obvious errors in this otherwise beautiful George Beverly Shea-esque piece of something. 1) It's awful. 2) You can't walk today where Jesus walked because of the buildup of nearly twenty feet of sediment, almost wherever you go, over the last two thousand years. 3) One cannot wander down the "little lanes" Jesus knew, because we don't know for certain where he walked (with a few exceptions), and there are dangerous people all around, and what "little lanes"? If you've been to Bethlehem or Nazareth or Jerusalem, even in the old city of the last, you wouldn't use this expression. 4) Galilee's hills are not "little". They are rugged, and the kind that easily sheltered guerrillas who wished to take down Roman soldiers and spread terror. Many of these "bandits" hid out in the Galilee area from years before Jesus to years after, until the tremendous military force of Rome wiped out resisters in fortresses in the north and the south of Palestine (so-called after 70 AD), totally razing Jerusalem and the Second Temple of Herod. Then they completed the job in 135 AD. 5) I haven't a clue what it means that the "mighty Jordan row". What? The old Negro spiritual is "Roll, Jordan, Roll". Not "row". It's not like "row, row, row your boat . . ." And 6), why did the Incarnate Son of God have "childish" feet? What is being implied? That the average height in his day for a grown man in Galilee would have been 4'8"? With size 3 ½ sandals? And he may have been shorter?

Nothing is said about the Resurrection, and that both the tomb and Calvary are now enclosed in the Church of the Holy Sepulchre, which tends to frighten the kinds of pietistic American Christians attracted to this sentimental pablum. They would go to the so-called Gordon's Tomb, which is first century, but in no way possible for it to be the historical site. However, it has a nice little garden with little birds singing, and American yokels are drawn in droves to this spot and "feel" Jesus' presence. Or whatever.

All of the students at Stanzel sang this, first in solos, then duets, then trios, then quartets, and finally all of us sang it as a choir. By the end of the afternoon, teachers and students were roaming the halls aimlessly, pathetically screaming, "Make them stop!" A couple of the configurations got "ones".

I was released from this hellhole in late May. Back at home in Ottumwa, I read more political and American historical books, and began reading Theodore White's books in his series "The Making of the President". His most recent one, on 1968, was a book I treasured for years. He began with Tet and the disaster facing Nixon who had been elected even though George Wallace had picked up 46 electoral votes while Nixon won with 301. (Wallace a third party contender, nearly scored the 52 electoral votes Goldwater had won in 1964.) Nixon himself had begun working on the "Southern Strategy" to turn FDR's southern bloc of states Republican, and he succeeded. Harry Dent was the point man for Nixon in carrying this out, later described by Kevin Phillips in *The Emerging Republican Majority* (1969), as he analyzed voter patterns in the

Presidential elections, by region. Dent worked on John Tower's campaigns in Texas and he was the first Republican elected to the Senate from Texas since reconstruction. Dent also worked to turn Senator Strom Thurmond of South Carolina to the GOP, and he made the connection for Nixon of Winton (Red) Blount of Montgomery, Alabama, whom Nixon named to his Cabinet in 1969 as Postmaster General (when this was still such a position). Nixon's general theme was what has been called "the politics of resentment", the notion that working class whites were under attack by the levers of the federal government, in the control by various "elites" in the country, and were in danger of losing their hard earned place in American White Protestant society. The key concerns were Civil Rights—what in the 1950s right up to political races in the South in the 60s, was called "nigger, nigger, nigger"—also the taunt used against black baseball players in the 1940s and 50s, beginning with Jackie Robinson, a Republican. But the specific racist language started changing according to Lee Atwater, in the 1960s to "coded language" of opposing forced busing, opposing the "Federal Government", opposing Voting Rights' Acts (which Tower and Thurmond did) , developing private "Christian" schools, and consistently supporting "States' rights". Nixon was very skilled at this. Reagan was a master. Reagan kicked off his 1980 campaign in Neshoba County, Mississippi, the location where three young civil rights workers had been murdered in 1964 by Klan members, including the Deputy County Sheriff. The killers were finally brought to justice after a key witness was paid for her testimony (changed at this point in the 1988 "Mississippi Burning" film). Reagan said not a word about this infamous case, but assured his predominantly white audience he was there to support States' Rights. Everybody knew what he meant. It shouldn't mystify anyone as to the reasons for race continuing to be such a polarizing issue central to American politics in 2018. The White Deep South today is solidly Republican.

During the summer of '69 I worked at the Salvation Army camp as a pot and pan boy. That was the significant time when on July 11, 1969 Neal Armstrong walked on the Moon. And Woodstock occurred in August.

X

IN THE FALL OF 1969, I began to enjoy High School at Ottumwa High School as a sophomore. The word itself alerts us to this stage in one's high school education. Writing in 1509 the clever Erasmus put forward his wicked satire about the clergy and religious, their pomposity and venality, entitled *Encomium Moriae* or *The Praise of Folly*, writing it as he did with the play on his host's (Thomas More's) name. The eighteenth century word sophomore was coined (from what I can tell) in part to get at a distinctive behavior of second year students, first at Harvard and Colleges, and then picked up also for second year students in High School. It refers to morons, idiots, the socially inept, inflated, bombastic in style, proud of themselves for no apparent reason. Sarah Cook's line of never arguing with an idiot because they will pull you down to their level and then beat you with their experience is instructive. I should know. I worked at growing out of my occasional habit to be a sophomoric show-off. I did this by finding a mentor, even father figure, who was wise (*sophos*—from the Greek used in philosophy for example, the love of wisdom), and could assist me to grow up, and learn basic manners. Lord Chesterfield wrote in the mid eighteenth century to his son about learning manners and courtesy and that the "most well-bred person in the room is the one who makes the fewest people uncomfortable".[1] Well, up to a point. Chesterfield also wrote that,". . . in my mind, there is nothing so illiberal, or so ill-bred, as audible laughter." [2] Of course he also famously wrote in the same work-or infamously if you are a prude or a Freudian, " . . . a gentleman who was so good a manager of his time that he would not even lose that small portion of it which the call of nature obliged him to pass in the necessary-house; but gradually went through all the Latin poets in those moments. [3] In a way, that man was Merlin Schneider, the choral director at the High School. I wished to become better mannered socially, while being tutored in classical, baroque, renaissance music, and he offered me the opportunity. I sang in the choir, as well as the Madrigal of the School. So I learned some of the classics of fine music which have stood the test of time (even though some composers go in and out of fashion), Tallis, Byrd, Weelkes, Purcell, Bach, Handel, Mozart, Beethoven, Mendelssohn, Poulenc, to name a few.

1. Chesterfield, *Letters*, xxxv

2. Chesterfield, *Letters*, xxxviii

3. Chesterfield, *Letters*, xxv

My try out included singing something having absolutely nothing to do with any of the highbrow stuff. I was to sight read, "You are my Special Angel" a Bobby Vinton song from 1963. What irony! It's a terrible song. However, I didn't suffer my solo break down, and several junior students and one senior came up to me to talk afterwards. All of the choir members were juniors and seniors, I was the only sophomore. By far the most interesting was a senior, P., who was trained as a soprano, and as an organist. She was open and cheerful. She also came with a plan to attend the University of Iowa, and then Oberlin. (My musical training involved Salvation Army bass drum, and attempting to learn the accordion in Fifth grade. This is what the Fates do to you when your middle name is Duane. Both instruments will be ubiquitous in Hell.)

She didn't seem to mind I was two years younger than she. And she drove her own Volkswagen! Wow! I began seeing her every day, following Madrigal rehearsal, and by December, we were an item.

I asked P. out, in fact to see "The Miracle Worker", a school play. I did this by staring at the telephone for at least two hours, then finally screwing up the courage to call, and she said yes! So the Thursday night of the play, I dressed up with a sports jacket and aftershave, and came down stairs to see my dad waiting for me. He had some advice for me before my seeing this young woman. "I'm only going to tell you what the best advice is for a Coleman: whatever happens, keep your pants zipped up". End of dad wisdom. I stared out in bewilderment for a minute or two and pondered what kind of message this might be. And then P. arrived and we were off for my first official date (not including J. in the ditch). It was splendid! We double dated with a senior couple, who seemed vaguely uneasy the whole evening, but we still all went to a hamburger joint, to pick up "made rite hamburgers", a highlight in Ottumwa. The play itself was about watching Helen Keller run around the stage and bump into things. (She was blind.) I remember fumbling at my various attempts at putting an arm around this young woman or stabbing at her hand with a terrified sweaty palm. After dropping off her friends, I asked about their nervousness. "Oh, you know; they didn't know what to expect from you." Oh, I thought. Later I would find out this was the first of many evasions to which P. was accustomed providing. Her friends were tight with P's longtime boyfriend, a large menacing surly looking football player. So, we went to see Helen Keller while she kept me in the dark.

I loved that year in the tenth grade. I enjoyed classes, especially American History and English Literature, and I sailed through Algebra II. From January on, the Madrigal Class prepared for the Iowa State competitions, with my singing either baritone or bass. We sang "And the Glory of the Lord" from Handel's *Messiah*, Michael Praetorius' "In dulci Jublio"-with its moving back and forth between Latin and German, Vittoria's "Eram quasi agnus innocens" from his "Tenebrae Responsories". I loved Vittoria's music. I had never heard anything like this before. Nor had I been aware of its existence. It was late 16th-17th century sacred music, and at the Public Library I found more of the same composer. "O Vos Omnes", "Sancta Maria", and especially the deeply intricate and haunting "O Magnum Mysterium". While listening to this music, I lost track of where I was, and what I was doing. Before I knew it I had been listening for a couple hours. When I then read the translations of the texts, they were from the Catholic liturgy. They involved devotional and corporate prayer at worship. Where would one find this?

My parents were clueless over what I was talking about, and my dad actually became somewhat defensive. When I talked to my girl friend about this, she said sacred music was sung and listened to at her Lutheran Church. Why didn't I come with her? I gladly went, and found I was deeply peeved with my parents for not informing me of liturgical prayer. My dad would answer, or try, and then leave the room when he realized we weren't able to communicate. On this subject as on many involving Christian theology, Church history, the Mass and the worship of the Western Church over two thousand years, my parents had no intellectual or spiritual resources to respond to my questions. I was beginning to view an entirely different world. My mother attempted to argue with me, and told me that true Christians did not use written prayers at all, but prayed from "the heart". I responded that she read prayers in her regular morning devotions, so did that not matter? And I inquired about what is said in the Bible about prayer. Didn't we use a written prayer taught by Jesus called "The Lord's Prayer"? She said "authentic prayer of the heart" was spontaneous. Was it? I questioned. I had been around enough Salvation Army folks in and out of worship to recognize there was "spontaneous" and there was "spontaneous". My mother had more variation in her prayers than my dad, but she used pet phrases. In fact everybody did. My mother often prayed that we be spared from "harm and alarm", and that her children and others present would let Jesus into their hearts. Her prayers always began with "Heavenly Father . . ." The less educated people, or more emotional people who prayed, especially on Sunday nights, almost to a one, began with "Heavenly Father, we just lift up . . ." (I hated that phrase with the phony "just" as though we had nothing really in mind for God to do.) What was missing in language they would make up with volume. When my mother said read prayers were insincere, and spontaneous prayers were from the heart, it meant certain "tones" would be used. That's how you could tell them apart. The "tones".

Then there were the Catholics. Why emulate them in prayer when they so obviously have departed from the Bible? They have the Antichrist, the Pope. They believe in salvation by works. They engage in idolatry by worshiping Mary. The Reformation saved us from all the hypocrisy and superstition they revel in. I alerted my mother to what I had observed at the Lutheran Church; they had the very parts of the Mass she identified with those loathsome Catholics. There had been an announcement about the Gustavus Adolphus choir coming from Minnesota to sing Bach's "B Minor Mass". How was that liturgy different from the Catholics?

So I argued. I felt distinctly impatient and unsatisfied. For years I had naturally asked questions (as most children do born with minds) and if my curiosity concerned anything to do with the Salvation Army, I was told to believe and not to question. This wall of separation caused me such frustration, that I wondered where I could go for satisfactory answers? *Selah*, as it says in the Psalms.

The Public Libraries in the cities in which we lived were always my favorite haunts after school. When I read presidential biographies or about other significant figures in history, say Lincoln-by far my favorite-or Harry Truman, I would note how important their books were to them. Truman haunted his local library. Later, in Merle Miller's book about conversations he had with Truman, entitled, *Plain Speaking* (1974), the President makes the point that when one is mostly self-taught, or an autodidact, one did not pronounce words and names properly because for long times he only had read them, not heard them at home. (So Plutarch was Ploo-tarsh.) I also found books on Mark Twain after seeing Hal Holbrook's performance on Twain on television. I read voraciously beginning usually with an Encyclopedia, and allow my eyes to roam in doing so to read other articles on other subjects, after finishing the original one. Dinosaurs, baseball, famous lawyers, presidents, the American Revolution, the American Civil War, the various books of the Bible and whence they came, Jesus, the Salvation Army, Bach, Mozart, the Mass, who on earth was Bishop James Pike? Without a good library at home, or even a few classics of non-fiction or books of literature, many of my selections were hit and miss. My dad didn't read much, and he was becoming increasingly restless during the time we were in Ottumwa. My mother read pious trash, either devotional books or Christian fiction, the kind with sixty exclamation points per page and picked up at pious trash Christian bookstores or grocery stores. My own view is that a book of fiction or non-fiction does not get a pass if it's "Christian". It's either well thought out and written as a decent book needs to be—based on the subject—or it isn't. The spate of faux Christian books on dying and returning to write trash on Heaven, is trash.

(Our time is not the only time for Christian trash fiction. I have discovered that a number of ancient Coptic writings found at Nag Hammadi-in Upper Egypt—in 1945, with twelve or so papyrus codices (books) dating from the very end of the 2nd Century AD to the 3rd and 4th centuries, including the Gospel of Mary Magdalene, and the Gospel of Thomas, are Gnostic—not concerning real historical lives, but fantasies—are actually a kind of ancient Christian fiction. Or trash.)

I believe my view holds for "science fiction". It's either good fiction, or it isn't.

I know because I read some trash authors, Irving Wallace, James Michener, Allen Drury, Leon Uris. Uris with *QB VII* did lead me to books by celebrity lawyers—F. Lee Bailey, Louis Nizer—a variation on trash.

P. gave me a John Updike novel to read. This was *Couples*, a 1968 book. I think she gave it to me for aspiring reasons, but I found it to be a hilarious skewering of the lives of a number of suburbanites in a fictitious upper middle class New England town. This was good writing and not trash, although it was called "a dirty book" by bluenosed Puritans. It actually concerned the moral decadence, even spiritual emptiness experienced by bored suburbanites, constantly, ever obsessively on the prowl for sexual experiences with numerous partners to fill the void. Updike was fascinatingly luminous at describing this, and in so doing held before the reader what Post World War Two life of seeking constant thrills was like in America. This was the America of sexual experimentation, pill popping and booze. And the need for more and more. It is about (in Wilfred Sheed's words), "the relation of individual to collective decadence".

I remember one night after finishing this particular Updike novel, and starting to do what is my predilection (over analyze almost everything), P. told me to shut up because she wished my full attention. I began listening to the kinds of music on the record player she liked, the Lettermen, and Ed Ames, the really daring stuff and her absolute favorite, Rod McKuen singing about the sea. "Do you know my friend, the sea? He watches everything you do . . ." And more wonders of this kind from this magical mystery poet. My heart was strangely warmed by kitsch.

So, in addition to studying, and reading (Theodore White's *The Making of the President, 1968*; Robert F. Kennedy's *To Seek a Newer World*; William F. Buckley's *God and Man at Yale*; Winston Churchill's *My Early Life*; even the new *The Greening of America* by Charles Reich), P. and I were an item. I liked her, and she said she liked me. I did have to ask her not to sing Beatles music in opera style. (It's hard to listen to "I want to hold your hand" like it's Verdi.) She then told me I had to listen to good rock, not just the Ventures. So, I listened and began enjoying the really hard stuff: Simon and Garfunkle, Stevie Wonder, "Suite: Judy Blue Eyes", CCR, Three Dog Night, Paul Revere and the Raiders, the Moody Blues, even my favorite: Dusty Springfield's "Son of a Preacher Man". I did say no to Joe Cocker.

I got my learner's permit to drive, and when school let out, I was hired to work in cornfields, which lasted all of one day. Then I was hired the next day at J. C. Penny's selling shoes. I began earning money which was a good thing because P. and I were seeing each other three or four nights a week. One night my older cousin Chuck came for a visit. Both my mother and Aunt Lillian were daughters of Rebekah Sampson, who were, as I noted above, of the Lumbee Tribe.

However, while strikingly similar physically, with prominent noses and cheek-bones, my mother was very fair complected , and Aunt Lillian was much darker. My cousin Chuck had the dark complexion of his mother. His father, Uncle Chuck, had been dark and handsome, my mother said, when he came back from WWII, but had lost much of his youthful looks and charm from having become a drunk. He drank himself to sleep every night having worked a six to three shift at the Detroit GM plant. P. arranged for her closest friend B. to join the three of us in partying around the county, and B. provided her auto, an old Plymouth. We had a blast, and imbibed from a jug of wine. At one point I took over driving-with my permit—and tested the acceleration of the car. It could go 70, even 80 miles an hour. It was really stupid. It was pure luck we weren't killed or injured. We got home about two in the morning. Mother and Aunt Lillian were fit to be tied. Where had we been, etc. It was crazy tag team by these women. When they got shrill (obviously not dissuaded by our laughter), they lit into Chuck. And the rest of us quietly removed ourselves from watching Chuck twist in the wind. Great!

Selling shoes at Penny's involved learning the stock, measuring feet, letting women (mostly women—men would come in, point at a pair and say sold) know how nice particular shoes look , and get caught in occasional uncomfortable games with vampish customers of all ages who wanted to be noticed by a 16 year old, and show off their tiny little feet.

At the end of the summer, P. was leaving to attend the University of Iowa, while I would be entering the eleventh grade. Something wasn't quite right about her. Her father had become a drunk and her parents had divorced when she was seven. For many years P. had been the stable force at home, with a nutty, anxious, prying, gin drinking, panicky, reclusive mother named Margaret, whom I called Loony Tunes mostly out of her hearing. The main power in the household was her grandmother, Baba. On a number of occasions we had visited Baba who was the companion of a loopy blue hair millionaire old crone named Mrs. Farney. When we visited, Baba would announce that since P. and I were music students of Mrs. Stoltz, Mrs. Farney wished me to sing her favorite songs! They always began and ended with "I Left My Heart in San Francisco", with my girlfriend accompanying on piano. If I didn't sing this to Mrs. Farney's liking-which meant Baba's, since she was the one to interrupt and tell me to try harder or sing slower-I would be at this exercise for quite a while. The wild-eyed trio of witches, Farney, Baba, and Loony Tunes, increasingly didn't mind as they enjoyed cocktail hour far more than real food. Baba would mix this vat of brandy old-fashioneds, and fill the glasses of the coven with assorted fruit. Watching the three of them all close in on the vat in the music room and then take turns stirring the concoction made me think of the witches in *Macbeth*: " Double, double toil and trouble; Fire burn and cauldron bubble". Honestly, this was insane! P's own psyche was damaged to the extent that she would get panicky if I tried to stay away from Baba's clutches, because Mrs. Farney paid for everything for Baba, as well as Looney Tunes and P. She couldn't imagine life without the old bag. She was also extremely needy emotionally. Growing up as she had with these generations of narcissistic women had not been pretty. And that meant seeing other and older guys, not just a sixteen-year-old novice. Occasionally she cancelled dates at the last minute out of illness. What? Baba would call me from time to time and inform me that she would not let P. see me for a while, that she would not be allowed to go steady. She will date older guys, other guys. Other guys who were not named Dale Duane.

Later I suspected that P. had put Baba up to this, because she had difficulty with closure with a couple of former boyfriends. Baba and P. seemed to have a strange symbiotic dynamic.

It was late June when the Salvation Army brass told us the Holy Spirit wanted us in Sault Ste. Marie, Michigan. We loaded up our truck and we moved to the Soo.

XI

EXCEPT FOR MY DAD, we all enjoyed Sault Ste. Marie, at least away from home. My parents' marriage was breaking down because my mother thoroughly loved the Salvation Army and her vocation as an officer, and my dad did not. Once again, my Uncle Bill had arranged for this move, to get us back to Michigan. This entire system of a few high ranking Salvation Army officers making these arbitrary decisions had come to cause feelings of such loathing and revulsion in my dad, that he and mother now found it difficult to communicate. And I imagine dad at age 39 was dealing with mid-life issues as he saw the rest of his life being determined by narrow minded ignorant despots, since many of the ones with whom he came in contact were mediocrities, or just plain stupid. And the Salvation Army bigwigs cloaked their will to power by resorting to "we prayed and the Holy Spirit revealed" anything they wanted themselves. My dad could be enjoyable company, and I saw this side of him whenever he was at Rotary or Kiwanis clubs, when he didn't have to worry about being judged—for his friendliness or educational level. Among any ecumenical ministerial associations, he was very self-conscious of his lack of a higher education. A future boss and friend of mine, Bishop William Wiedrich, whose time as rector of the Episcopal Church in Sault Ste. Marie coincided with my dad's, informed me a few years later that he and dad would stand way in the back of any such association they found themselves in, and mutually encourage each other in disliking having to be present. It was at this point I noticed dad carrying a chip on his shoulder about feeling trapped in the Salvation Army, and trapped with my mother. Neither would have considered seeing a therapist or a shrink. That would have caused them to feel shamed, I think, believing that they might have psychological issues. Their frame of reference would be: God takes care of all our problems because "Christ is the Answer". She blamed my dad, passive aggressively, for his lack of spiritual wellness. If he were right with God, everything would be perfect for their marriage and ministries. For my dad, he saw mother and her insidious relationships with the Salvation Army, particularly or focused especially on Uncle Bill, as the cause of their problems. They had a strained relationship, and avoided taking any responsibility individually for what was happening. Instead, they found the key button to push in the other's emotional make up. The sense of anger and unease emanating from their repressed emotions and issues hung over our family for the three years we lived at 247 Ridge Street, Sault Ste. Marie. About once a week, it would come to a head with loud arguments between mother and dad. On two occasions, my dad punched holes in the walls of the kitchen. My mother would cry, leave the house and drive off for awhile. On Sundays, we were all at church to sing for the one-hour radio program the Salvation Army had long established with a local station, and smile and make a show of how perfect our family was because "Christ is the answer".

Dawn, now a senior at Sault Area High School, handled this by denying it was happening. Bill, an eighth grader, was like my dad in not wanting to deal with unsettling emotions. He stayed away from home and discovered cigarettes and alcohol. Robin, entering the 6th grade, became the wild child, acting out in all sorts of ways and making sure everyone saw her doing so. Since I was the second child, and first son, I was the peacemaker, the reconciler. Both my parents sought me out to hear their sides to the weekly fights, and attempt to draw me to each one emotionally. I did not like this.

Fortunately, I discovered a number of opportunities to get out of the house and began enjoying a wide number of activities. I walked into J. C. Penney's, and was hired on the spot by a strange, dour, little, balding man named Eldon Chesnut. He was not talkative, and mostly one noticed him looking frustrated and angry. He would not speak for two or more hours, and then begin to breathe very noisily like Freddy Kreuger hiding in a closet with the microphone catching his heavy breathing. Then he would bark out his orders hurriedly, not ever inviting dialogue. He was a pillar of the Presbyterian Church in town. He hired me at 4:00 one afternoon in August, and I began working in the shoe department at 4:15. So, I had a steady job, with hours on Tuesday and Friday evenings, and all day Saturday.

By far what I enjoyed the most was the brand new Sault Area High School. It was designed it seemed to me like a huge Pentagon style building with a great many classrooms, language and scientific laboratories, audio visual rooms, study areas, a large lunchroom, auditoria and many places where one could find privacy. But the building didn't affect me as much as the wonderful, delightful, intelligent students my age, with our class numbering nearly 330. The great variety of so many charming people my age, who were for the most part easy to befriend was a source of enjoyment to me. I liked the faculty, an excellent English Literature teacher, Mrs. Ewing, Mr. Nelson in American Government, Mr. Kosinski in Algebra II and Geometry. There was a creepy guy who spent a lot of time staring at girls' blouses, named Mr. Beadle. There was a far out guy teaching English whose favorite color was pink: Mr. Fifer. And there was even a Nancy Sinatra look alike teacher in French, with long tresses, attention getting clothes and long white boots which " were made for walking". Her name was Mrs. Ludwig. Her classes were always full. Add to this mix the fact that the Roman Catholic High School had just closed, and the most charming girls from anywhere around now attended this High School. And they were all Catholic and even taking over the school. I was totally entranced and motivated to be on time every day. I thought that if the Pope were on the ball he would use such Catholic teenage girls to ensnare unsuspecting dumb Protestant guys as the basis for evangelism. No, wait.

That is the Catholic strategy. Among my male friends were Paul, Kim, Bernie, Rich, and three seniors: Bill, Duncan, and Bruce. All of us were high spirited, politically minded, intellectually curious, and enjoyed laughing. Among the guys with whom I was especially close, Paul, Bill, and Duncan, we were all suspicious of what President Eisenhower had called the military-industrial complex, those industries supported by the Pentagon, and numerous Congressmen and Senators in Washington, which produced armaments and various supplies for the military at a time of war; and we saw this "complex" lobbying in Washington D.C. to continue the Viet Nam War. We all saw the importance in a free country-meaning the United States—of having freedoms key to the health of our Constitutional Republic, namely freedoms to vote, speak, assemble, publish, worship as laid out in the First Amendment to the Constitution. We were all staunch supporters of Civil Rights, and approved of the 1960s movements for full equality for all citizens, especially for those needing support in overcoming oppression, blacks in the South, the poor throughout this supposedly wealthy country, for women everywhere—we were all feminists. We were critical of many aspects of our parents' generation: going along to get along; accepting religion uncritically; believing that the good life could be achieved in this selfish consumerist society through hard work, disregarding dignity or purpose, and purchasing goods continually promoted in advertising. One's life would only have value if it was viewed mostly in acquiring material goods, which propaganda from our American culture harangued the entire nation. And not only were we bombarded with these messages of materialism, but women's sexual images were used in selling products, bringing about very dehumanizing notions affecting women and men.

We were all to a person aware of perceived evils of the United States. (This kind of talk upset my parents.) It was part of our heritage that White Europeans had destroyed the native American cultures and peoples, enslaved hundreds of thousands of Africans in the name of producing wealth, calling this freedom, ended the Second World War by the use of fire bombing innumerable cities in Japan with the clear targeting of civilian areas in total disregard of any moral standards for a "Just War" as established for hundreds of years, and then dropping the two nuclear weapons on Hiroshima and Nagasaki, destroying 200,000 human beings within minutes, almost all civilians. (David Peace writes about the human experience of this horror affecting the entire civilian population of Tokyo, which is truly apocalyptic in his novel of 2007, *Tokyo Year Zero*.) This barbarism, this horrific destruction, was then rarely debated within the US, in terms of Christian or humanist understandings of a Just War. Ian Buruma has pointed out how the irony of the Nagasaki bombing by a supposedly Christian nation—which destroyed the entire Christian ghetto in that city—showed something seriously wrong with the United States.[1] If we were operating solely along the lines of might makes right, then we were not far from the amoral totalitarian societies which had destroyed so much of humanity in the "heroic materialism" (Kenneth Clark's

1. Buruma," The War Over The Bomb", *NYR*

phrase in his *Civilisation*) of the twentieth century. From the time of the genocidal "cleansings" of the oldest of all Christian nations, the Armenians, by the Turks; to the horrors and murderous rampages of Lenin and Stalin, and the Gulag; to Hitler's attempts to rid Europe of Jews, Eastern Europeans, Gypsies, homosexuals, physically and mentally crippled, and all deemed misfits; to Mao's establishing of his rule by terror; to the atomic bombings of Japan by the United States; to the extremist wiping out of all opposition of political opponents by Pol Pot; all these attempts to establish an ideal society according to an individual's sense of what was fair and just, or to that of an elite, with little concern for what it meant to be human made in the image and likeness of God, all ended in hopelessness and darkness, in the pit and in the grave. (This culture of death, as Pope John Paul II called western societies to account, shows abortion, capital punishment, military power, gun violence to be extremely problematic and exhibiting evil.)

From a seemingly continuous dialogue with these thoughtful and well informed young people, I had been able to judge liberal democracy and civil rights as necessary and superior to other forms of government. We all approached this rather naively as though we were always rational, and human beings were by nature rational. We could not account for all the horrific actions one person could take in harming another. We did not take into account "sin". We made special pleadings for each of the terrible spiritual forces involved in our own American history: the Southern planters needed more education to recognize the humanity of the African slaves; Truman had only come to the presidency completely unprepared for the atomic bomb decision and was told it was a matter of hundreds of thousands of Americans or the same number of Japanese who would die—and what could he know as a former high school educated haberdasher beholden to the Prendergast political machine in Kansas City? Stalin was the product of Russia and its backwardness; yes, Hitler was Austrian, but he wished to make the depressed economy of Germany get back on its feet, especially after it had been tremendously enfeebled and humbled following WW1, and weren't his Nazis all monsters? We had our rationalizations for everything awful or evil. They didn't involve a flaw very deep in humanity and even in ourselves as such.

In various ways, we believed our generation, all born in the 1950s, were going to make something positive of the world, and bring about the great liberal values necessary for our nation to thrive. Liberal civilization was what mattered, "the rule of laws, not men, of argument in place in force, of compromise in place of violence", as summarized recently by Canadian parliamentarian and philosopher, Michael Ignatieff. He continues with the value of the "liberal virtues-tolerance, compromise, reason . . ."[2] We were committed to these. And we were going to work to achieve peace (sung rather grandly by Cat Stevens in his "Peace Train") by getting college degrees, for many of us the first in our families, and exert ourselves politically.

---

2. Cited in Paul Wilson," The Road to Rejection", *NYR, 28*

Several of us, all guys, Paul, Bernie, Bill, Duncan, Kim, Rich, became acquainted with a husband and wife teaching team at High School, Art and Dana Vandewater, two eccentric characters, one who looked like Ichabod Crane, and one who resembled a shorter Miss Jane from the "Beverly Hillbillies". They were looked on suspiciously by the principal, Mr. Dubow and his vice principal, Mr. Waters. That made them credible in our eyes. They lived in a small attic apartment which seemed very anti-establishment and vaguely—to us—Left Bank. They talked to us about our concerns, the inauthenticity and consumerism of American life, and the strong possibility any of us would be drafted to go to Viet Nam. If we did, we would be upholding an American system which divided citizens in this country. We were earnest and loquacious in our discouragement about the war, that gung ho Americans had led us in with the generation which had won WWII, and what interesting knowledgeable journalists were saying now about this imperialistic war. David Halberstam's *The Making of a Quagmire*, of 1965 was our text; later, *Fire in the Lake*, by Frances Fitzgerald. Our music was stating the crisis in our country, "Ohio" by Crosby, Stills, Nash and Young, for example beginning with the lyric, "Tin soldiers and Nixon's coming" about the on-going conflicts in the nation, including the anti-War movements, the continued and growing racial divide (sung about by Neil Young in "Southern Man"), the polarization in Congress over the management of the War, the funding of it, the sending of more soldiers to die there-meaning ourselves in a couple years, and even the distrust we all had in various presidential administrations about our reasons for going in in the first place-now summed up with one word: *Nixon*; all these we talked about. Granted, much of this was bullshit from a bunch of high school kids in the Upper Peninsula, but we learned how to think with careful arguments, informed from books and articles we read, and all of us understood that we would soon be able to vote, and that the vote was crucial to our political power. And speaking up at meetings of different kinds was necessary for issues to be addressed. In our Constitution, we all of us knew better than Haldeman and Erlichman, when they appeared before Senator Ervin's Watergate Committee: The people, not the president, were sovereign.

The book which had most affected me at that time in the fall of 1970, was Garry Wills' just published book, *Nixon Agonistes: The Crisis of the Self Made Man*. Chapter after chapter, this former associate of William Buckley's, at *National Review*, and a one-time seminarian, and classicist, wrote brilliantly about the myths prevalent in America, especially of those of Nixon's generation. Richard Nixon had been born in 1913, son of poor hardworking Quaker parents, in a family struck by tragedy. He rose to attend a local college, Whittier, and through very hard work, and chicanery, and claims about his World War service, he took on Democratic incumbents, to be elected first to Congress in 1946, and then the Senate in 1950. He was a vicious anti-Communist, and as a member of HUAC, the House Un-American Activities Committee, he had come to the fore by exposing the lies of Alger Hiss and the truth of Whittaker Chambers. Wills' book was a revelation to me of a careful scintillating political, philosophical and sociological analysis of our country in the twentieth century. He spends a great deal of time establishing how Ralph Waldo Emerson's writings about self-achievement and success in the nineteenth century, affected the country's paradigm of what it meant to be an American male who lifted himself up from nothing to become something worthwhile, and how that myth still affected Richard Nixon and those who supported him.

Another book, by an evangelical Christian and Senator, Mark O. Hatfield of Oregon was presented to me at Church. It was entitled, *Conflict and Conscience*, and it affected me greatly. Hatfield, who became a longtime hero of mine, wrote largely about the apprehension he felt with too many Americans wrapping the Bible in the American flag. He himself had become an outspoken critic of the War in Viet Nam, and saw how the support of the War by the Nixon Administration, after Nixon had promised during the campaign to end the War-with a secret "plan"—had coarsened the political discourse in the country, and harmed greatly the civility in Congress among our political leaders. In the United States Senate, various coalitions of Republicans and Democrats were speaking out against the War, and Senators John Sherman Cooper (as noted above, a Republican from Kentucky) and Frank Church (Democrat from Idaho) bravely, honorably, put forward an Amendment to a military spending bill to end any appropriations for the extension of the War into Cambodia and Laos. It failed at first in the House after being passed in the Senate. It was re-tooled and passed in December of 1970. In between the times Cooper-Church came up for votes, two outspoken Christian men, Senators Mark Hatfield and George McGovern, prepared an Amendment to end all expenditures for the Viet Nam War. The vitriolic language attacking them personally, for their showing clear leadership in the country, politically and morally, especially from the President's men, caused many to see this political position a necessary one for our country.

Senator George McGovern eloquently spoke in an impassioned speech on the floor of the Senate about the reasons for putting this Amendment forward. It struck home to many (including me) about what was at stake at this point in Viet Nam:

> Every senator in this chamber is partly responsible for sending 50,000 young Americans to an early grave. This chamber reeks of blood. Every senator here is partly responsible for that human wreckage at Walter Reed and Bethesda Naval and all across our land-young men without legs, or arms, or genitals, or faces, or hopes.
>
> There are not very many of these blasted and broken boys who think this war is a glorious adventure. Do not talk to them about bugging out, or national honor, or courage. It does not take any courage at all for a congressman, or a senator, or a president to wrap himself in the flag and say we are staying in Vietnam, because it is not our blood that is being shed. But we are responsible for those young men and their lives and hopes. And if we do not end this

damnable war those young men will someday curse us for our pitiful willingness to let the Executive carry the burden that the Constitution places on us.

So before we vote, let us ponder the admonition of Edmund Burke, the great parliamentarian of an earlier day: "A conscientious man would be cautious how he dealt in blood." [3]

These were the prophetic words of this honorable man. John F. Kennedy in his *Profiles in Courage*, noted the tribute Governor Franklin D. Roosevelt paid to Republican Senator George Norris, who—among many unpopular causes-gave his support for Governor Al Smith in 1928, and in whose mold was McGovern, to whom I think these same words apply:

History asks, "Did the man have integrity?

Did the man have unselfishness?

Did the man have courage?

Did the man have consistency?[4]

As Roosevelt answered in the affirmative about Norris, so I answer about George McGovern.

While their legislative attempts failed, repeatedly, professors, students, activists, Civil Rights leaders, clergy, religious, professionals, women, journalists, politicians, and military leaders were coming to view the war as immoral, unnecessary, damaging to the United States standing in the world, and horrifying to the people, landscape, ecology, and cultures of South East Asia. And our own Presidents were doing all in their power, including using police, military, intelligence agencies, the IRS, the media to restrict the flow of accurate information, from the people of the United States to affect our having adequate knowledge of the war in order to vote in the responsible way the framers of the Constitution intended in 1787. We had, as Arthur Schlesinger said, an Imperial Presidency, and one acting with increasing dictatorial powers.

Among our group, I was the most astute and aware about the goings on in Washington, who the key players were, and what particular Senators were doing to draw down and phase out the Viet Nam effort. The Vandewaters themselves weren't so passionate as we were, and had another agenda. They were entirely cynical about anything to do with the US government, and after our reading a number of Bertolt Brecht plays with them from the Weimar Republic days, e.g. *Life of Galileo, Mother Courage and her children, The Caucasian Chalk Circle,* and my favorite, *The Threepenny Opera,* which were all new and exciting, they began introducing Ayn Rand! What?

I had been a close reader of William F. Buckley. His television show "Firing Line", and his magazine *National Review*, were mainstays in my life weekly since discovering him. I had read in his introduction to the book he edited about American Conservative

3. Mann, *A Grand Delusion*, 666–9

4. Kennedy, *Profiles in Courage*, 210

thought, *Did You Ever See A Dream Walking*, his quotation from Whittaker Chambers' review of Ayn Rand's 1957 novel *Atlas Shrugged*. Chambers had written:

> The book's dictatorial tone is its most striking feature. Out of a lifetime of reading, I can recall no other book in which a tone of overriding arrogance was so implacably sustained. Its shrillness is without reprieve. Its dogmatism is without appeal . . . resistance to the Message cannot be tolerated because disagreement can never be merely honest, prudent, or humanly fallible. Dissent from revelation so final can only be willingly wicked. There are ways dealing with such wickedness, and, in fact, right reason itself enjoins them. From almost any page of *Atlas Shrugged*, a voice can be heard, from painful necessity, commanding: "To a gas chamber-go!" The same inflexibly self-righteous stance results, too, in odd extravagances of inflection and gesture . . . At first we try to tell ourselves that these are just lapses, that this mind has, somehow, mislaid the discriminating knack that most of us pray will warn us in time of the difference between what is effective and firm, and what is wildly grotesque and excessive. Soon we suspect something worse. We suspect that this mind finds, precisely in extravagance, some exalting merit; feels a surging release of power and passion precisely in smashing up the house.[5]

So, our group began to break up. None of us was searching for a guru, or a weird extreme right wing cult. Ayn Rand's absolute opposition to God, and altruism, or to reality, in truth, and her trumped up "objectivism" was too weird. That was beneficial to me, because I had sacrificed my desire to have any other social life while being with the attic bunch. I was working two nights a week, doing my homework, reading extra about American poets who had caught my ear in class with Mrs. Ewing, reading everything I could find about how congress was battling the President on the war, and discovering a new author, Walter Kaufmann.

Kaufmann was a professor at Princeton, who had written *The Faith of a Heretic*, which I found challenging and interesting. I remember liking the title because even at this stage, I imagined that all Christianity was fundamentalist and desiccated and empty of thought as was the Salvation Army. One officer visited Sault Ste. Marie, Dwight Garrington, who had assured me God wanted us to use our minds and reason. But he was alone. And he had given me a copy of Evangelical (Anglican) John Stott's book, *Your Mind Matters*. It was to me especially dry, and not engaged in what the world was about, or literature, or philosophy, or even theology. It didn't answer any questions I had raised with Garrington, but at least he tried. Kaufmann was a convert to Judaism, (which he later discovered was the faith of all his grandparents) and an existentialist. He had emigrated to the US from Germany just as Hitler came to power. His heroes I found fascinating: Hegel, Goethe, Kierkegaard, Nietzsche, Martin Buber, Leo Baeck, Karl Jaspers, among others. In his book, he totally skewered much of

---

5. Quoted in Buckley, *Did You Ever See A Dream*, xxi

liberal Protestant thought, particularly of Rudolph Bultmann and Paul Tillich, as they had made a cowardly retreat from traditional Credal Christian theology, by following the psychological approach to religious experience as established by Friedrich Schleiermacher. This was a cop out as far as Kaufmann was concerned, and failed to answer questions of truth. This was new to me, and something I began exploring by reading quietly on my own, not part of an intense group debate format. Not many folks whom I knew could talk about any of this.

Now, when I was in class with a number of friends, I found they were all not only thoughtful but could hold up their sides of any argument they entered. I asked Cynthia to go out. She was a very devout Christian, tall , friendly eyes, extremely kind. She was also the first person I had met who hadn't ever been out of Chippewa County. I spent awhile in front of our phone one day, and then called to ask her out. Yes, of course, she said. We went to my idea of a fine restaurant in the Soo, which didn't cost an arm and a leg, on Ashmun Street, Elias' Big Boy! Whoo hoo! I picked up Cindy and she did much of the talking, including letting me know how much she liked being asked out by "the son of a preacher man"! This was beginning on an auspicious note. We ordered salads-a whole new experience to me, and she asked for French dressing! Wow! She had never been outside the county but knew how to sound cosmopolitan! As we got down to our grilled chicken sandwiches and fries, I talked politics, particularly the War. I was now seventeen and I would be facing the draft within a year. She heard my skeptical reasons for thinking of refusing to go, and got alarmed. "I can't imagine dating someone who doesn't support the Vietnam War", she said. At her church, the preacher had even stated that only communists and America's enemies opposed the War. What church I asked. She said the Foursquare Gospel Church. "That's kookier than the Salvation Army", I opined, charmingly. "Wasn't that started by Aimee Semple McPherson? ". Cindy wasn't sure. It was Pentecostal though and adhered to the Bible. "Where in the Bible does it say Jesus spoke in tongues?" I innocently inquired. For the next 45 minutes or so we traded jabs at each other. Or rather I jabbed and she sat mortified, and asked me to keep my voice down. The evening ended on an unsatisfactory note. I realized Cindy was a Fundamentalist, and a noticeably unquestioning one at that. Wait. That's redundant.

So, I got up the nerve to ask another Pat out. Patricia was sophisticated, clever, intelligent, and didn't believe in premillennial dispensationalism, which now was becoming a real plus. She was enjoyable to be with, and within a few minutes, I realized I was out of my depth. Listening to her critique the novel we were presently studying in English class, Harper Lee's engaging and moving *To Kill a Mockingbird*, helped me think through character development, plot, the entire ethos of southern Mississippi in the 1930s, the young girl's (Scout's) point of view maintained throughout this classic. I especially appreciated Atticus Finch and his noble, dignified way of going against the grain of the systemic racism of Macomb as he defended the young African American, Tom Robinson, described by the author. Largely I found this paralleling the South

African apartheid condition, so bizarre because both societies claimed a Christian heritage. This has become my favorite novel, with splendid quotations, such as:

> You never really understand a person until you consider things from his point of view . . . Until you climb inside of his skin and walk around in it.[6]

> I wanted you to see what real courage is, instead of getting the idea that courage is a man with a gun in his hand. It's when you know you're licked before you begin, but you begin anyway and see it through no matter what.[7]

> People generally see what they look for, and hear what they listen for.[8]

> Sometimes a Bible in the hand of one man is worse than a whiskey bottle in the hand of [another] . . . There are just some kind of men who–who're so busy worrying about the next world they've never learned to live in this one, and you can look down the street and see the results.[9]

With Pat however, I was about five out of six on her dance card, and the rest were older guys in their mid to late 20's or so, with their own cars. (I was driving my dad's.) She had the steady wit of a young Dorothy Parker. What I had going for myself was my increasing enjoyment of politics. Pat and her older sister, Theresa, were daddy's girls, and their father was an old fashioned, courtly, confident gentleman attorney. In addition, he was the Republican chairman of Chippewa County. After a few dates, I didn't know if I was driving out sixteen miles to see Pat or Bernard Doll. He had been to many GOP conventions, and was to some extent the boss of the Upper Peninsula Republicans. He spoke very quietly with authority. He not only knew of all the people about whom I enjoyed talking: the William F. Buckley set and the National Review folks, the White House of Richard Nixon, the Governor of Michigan William Milliken, key Senators, but he also was well versed on the ways of the world, on culture, history, religion, philosophy, and the law as a practicing *attorney*.

I was leaving for a trip to Washington D. C. shortly after making Doll's acquaintance, and he made several contacts for me a young 17 year old Yooper. I would meet the two Michigan Senators, Philip Hart, and Robert Griffin, spend time with the congressman from the 11th Congressional District which included the U.P., Philip Ruppe, an additional appointment with lively Congressman Don Riegle of Flint, see Senator Mark Hatfield, and get a White House tour for VIPs. I loved this. I then asked for one more favor. Could I get a subscription to the *Congressional Record*? Mr. Doll arranged for all of this.

I went to the Capitol gathering with students from all over the US. There had been a contest the VFW sponsored on "Liberty and Freedom". Every contestant had to

---

6. Lee, *To Kill a Mockingbird,* 36
7. Lee, *To Kill a Mockingbird,* 115
8. Lee, *To Kill a Mockingbird ,* 174
9. Lee, *To Kill a Mockingbird,* 46

submit a 4–5-minute tape on the subject. I spoke about how we live in a Country with a rich heritage of free speech as laid out in the First Amendment of the Constitution, and that it was intended from what Madison said to counter ideology. The sovereign people of this government must have the freedoms of speech, press, assembly, and religion. Rah Rah! I won this along with classmate Terry. So, we took the bus to Detroit and flew from there to Washington. What a blast! We stayed in a huge dorm, and were among 120 High School kids. We were to see the Senate in action, visit the House of Representatives, hear from members of the Administration, and from several Senators and Congressmen. One of the Senators was Edward M. Kennedy, who had had his vicissitudes in the not too recent past. When I found out he would be one of our speakers, I brought along a couple of copies of the *Congressional Record*, and a book by Jack Anderson, then a well-known muckraker, who had worked for years with Drew Pearson-Joseph McCarthy's nemesis, and discovered so much graft and corruption, and hidden secrets among Washington's elite, that for a while he was targeted by E. Howard Hunt and Gordon Liddy for possible injury. Drew Pearson and Jack Anderson co-authored *The Case against Congress*, (1968), which I purchased in paperback with added material from Anderson's new assistant, a heavyset Britt Hume, after Pearson had died. Jack Anderson had exposed such fraud in government—the attempts on Fidel Castro's life by the CIA, the hidden reports on Vietnam, Senator Thomas Dodd's corruptions, how J. Edgar Hoover worked hand in glove with the Mafia, ITT's paying huge sums to Nixon's campaign in 1972 to hold off certain Anti-Trust charges, and much later, even breaking the Iran-Contra scandal. I took a trusty tape recorder with me to catch Kennedy!

We met first with Congressmen, Peter Frelinghuysen, R. N. J., and William Stuckey, D. GA. Both had illustrious names. Between the two of them they didn't have a single thought. Oh. Well. Then we met with Justice Byron Whizzer White, a famous college athlete and friend of the Kennedys. White from Colorado had been an All-American halfback for the Buffaloes, and was drafted by Pittsburg in 1938, before playing two further seasons for Detroit's Lions in 1939–40. His excellent start as a running back ended when he first attempted to enlist with the Marines, but was not accepted due to color blindness. He then served honorably with the United States Navy Intelligence during the War. Returning from War he was a deferred Rhodes Scholar, and then pursued a law degree. He was chosen by President Kennedy in 1962 to replace Justice Charles Whitaker, and won easy approval. He was a moderate-conservative Catholic Democrat (very much like the President himself) who would be one of two dissenting votes in *Roe v. Wade*. He was thrilling to hear, and we all stood and gave him an ovation.

I then had a chance to visit with Senator Griffin, and Senator Hart. Griffin had led the fight to keep LBJ's crony, Abe Fortas, from becoming Chief Justice. He was then elected Minority Whip in the Senate, when Hugh Scott of Pennsylvania replaced Illinois' Everett Dirksen as Minority leader, and mentioned above. (A favorite quotation of Dirksen's was, "A billion here, a billion there, and pretty soon you're talking about real money".)

While I considered myself a Michigan Republican, I found Senator Hart's views regarding ending the war compelling, in part, because I had moved to that position already. He gave several succinct arguments for the President to be opposed in this effort. (I remembered this later on, as I was considering becoming an adult Christian, needing thoughtful intelligent reasons for doing so. I believe that the role of theology is found in St. Anselm's maxim, "Faith seeks understanding". [10]) While I had reached the point of definitely opposing the War, I found myself in large company in the Republican Party. This was a time of far greater diversity among Republicans than one finds today. A number of GOP senators had joined with Hatfield-McGovern and Cooper-Church legislation. Senators Clifford Case, N.J., Edward Brooke, Mass., George Aitken, Vermont, Margaret Chase Smith, Maine, Charles Percy, IL, Richard Schweiker, PA, Jacob Javits, NY, as well as Mark Hatfield, and John Sherman Cooper, all regularly opposed Administration requests for expansion of or funding for the War, from 1971 on.

Congressman Pete McCloskey, CA, who had served with the Marines in Korea, and had been awarded the Navy Cross, the silver star, and two Purple Hearts, challenged President Nixon in the 1972 primaries as an anti-war Republican. McCloskey had defeated Shirley Temple in his first race for Congress. He later co-authored the Endangered Species Act, and took Pat Robertson out of the Presidential race in the primaries in 1988. Robertson had lied about his service in the Marines in Korea, claiming to have served in combat. McCloskey knew this to be false, as they had been shipped to Korea as part of a replacement draft to bolster the First Marine Division. However, Robertson's father, Willis Robertson, a powerful senator representing Virginia, arranged to have his son and a few college friends dropped off at Japan. McCloskey made this lie public, and Robertson quit the Presidential race. Robertson later sued McCloskey for 35 million dollars, but settled just before the case would come to trial, as McCloskey had several marines who were eyewitnesses of Robertson's non-combat role. He then was forced to pay McCloskey's $400,000 attorney fees and court costs.

McCloskey received one delegate for his effort at the GOP Convention, putting him second in the balloting to Richard Nixon.

Our group had great fun with the major star of the Congressional speakers, Senator Edward Kennedy. After all of us students were seated, many older folks came in, and I realized Kennedy was packing the room with his shills. What on Earth? Theodore White's book and others on John F. Kennedy's run for the Presidency in 1960 frequently spelled out the advance tactics used to ensure the best "buzz" among voters and journalists. One was always to have a smaller room set for a campaign stop than what the local politicians and campaign advance aides believed the number of folks

10. St. Anselm, *Proslogium*, 53

expected for that particular event. Our room had seemed fine and roomy for our 120 or so, but then these groupies came in laughing and cheering the senator. After the set speech for young people to enter the election process and bring their (our) ideals with us for the betterment of the nation, questions were called for. A couple students asked straightforward questions—what did the senator hope to accomplish in the Senate? What were his views on the draft? Kennedy (only 39 or so at this time) said he opposed the move to have an all-volunteer army, and then used what I surmised was a practiced ploy of asking the group: "How many of you are for an all-volunteer army? " Lots of young hands went up, including mine. "Now", he added, "and how many of you will volunteer?" A few hands went up. "See, we're all for volunteering for the army, but not so many about actually joining up." Oh, my, what great applause he got from the plants. They would jump up and applaud enthusiastically. And perhaps to end the question time, an lively and loud woman leaped to her feet and said how much all of us were waiting for the senator to run for the Presidency. Yayyyy!!!! went the old folks as if by pre-arrangement; and the yells and cheers and foot stomping and clapping went on far too long. This was only a year or so after Chappaquiddick, and around the time when Kennedy's Democratic colleagues in the Senate were to determine if they wanted this "fat, rich kid" (in Jimmy Carter's elegant phrase of 1980) continuing in the second highest leadership position in the Senate. He had defeated Sen. Russell Long, scion of the Longs of Louisiana, in 1969, to become Senate Majority Whip, and assistant to the leader (Senator Mike Mansfield, Montana) in rounding up votes for crucial legislation, along with extra perks that came with the position. Kennedy's colleagues gave him thumbs down-primarily because of his relentless exhibiting of horrible judgment at Chappaquiddick—and turned instead to a former Klansman from West Virginia, Robert Byrd. So his being surrounded by loud applause for everything he said to intimidate High School youngsters was obviously what he needed. I then got his attention, and yelled out could I ask the Senator a final question? He called on me, and I used some material from the Drew Pearson-Jack Anderson book to ask about his paying State Taxes for several years running. Why had he shown a big fat zero for the last four years on the income line when he filed his Massachusetts Taxes? Uh oh. This didn't follow the script for such events centered on Kennedy. He handled it like a pro and swatted me down as the bug I was. "Have you checked my State and Federal Taxes for the last few years?" I wagged my head hoping nothing would rattle. "Well if you did, you'd find my charitable giving and numerous property losses left me without income." The claque applauded this vigorously, and I turned red and sat down. But I had stood up and broached the subject I wished to one of the country's national leaders, knowing it would be unpopular. My clearest memory of Kennedy later was when he was making his only run for his party's nomination against President Carter in 1980. He repeatedly responded to any questions about abortion by answering (almost a mantra), "My religion is private, and I do not impose it on others", a dastardly evasive way of responding about a public policy matter on morality. William Buckley's response was, "Kennedy's religion is so private he will not impose it on himself".

Later that afternoon, our group met with the new EPA (Environmental Protection Agency) director, William Ruckelshaus. The man was passionate and fascinating about his job, and linking it to clear air and pure water for America's future. Nixon had initiated the move to establish the EPA. I asked him about DDT which had been in the news for some time. Ruckelshaus had managed to wrest control of pesticides away from the Department of Agriculture, and made the banning of DDT his first order of business. He considered it a carcinogen and harmful to humanity, as well as animals. He jumped on this question, and took some care to say it was being carefully studied, but he was himself deeply concerned about its use.

Our final speaker was by far the most thrilling orator I think I have ever heard from the armed forces. General Daniel "Chappie" James spoke to us about what was at stake for the United States in fighting in Viet Nam. He gave perhaps as many as three separate stem-winding speeches in answer to our generally skeptical and doubtful views on Viet Nam. This man was the highest serving African American in the Air Force, and a genuine hero. He had trained the Tuskegee pilots in WWII, flown 101 combat missions in Korea, and led an Air Force division in Vietnam while flying mostly dangerous combat raids over Hanoi and the North, 78 in all. He was well known for having no truck at all for militant Civil Rights leaders, such as H. Rap Brown, and Stokely Carmichael, and removed his Black Panthers emblem from his helmet. He was highly decorated with the Distinguished Service Medal, Legion of Merit, and the Distinguished Flying Cross among many awards. He had recently been named Deputy Assistant Secretary of Defense for Public Affairs when he came to address my group. He had only two years before been involved in a wild west showdown with Colonel Muammar Gadhafi, while commanding Wheelus Air Force base at Tripoli, Libya, in 1969. Gadhafi's forces overrode the gates of the Base, and he and Chappie James confronted one another packing pistols. James spoke out challenging Gadhafi, and the latter fled the scene. A little after that incident, while the US was negotiating with Gadhafi on the future of the base, two Libyan officers and a soldier brandishing a submachine gun burst into James' home, threatening his life. James again asserted himself, unflinchingly, and the team left. General James in May, 1971, was not very threatened by a bunch of kids still in high school! His words and tone were rousing about the cause of America and freedom, against Soviet style totalitarianism being spread into North Vietnam, and threatening the South. He even spent some time with the growing military rationale for our losing in Vietnam that the civilian control of the war effort was at fault. He noted the rules fighter and bomber pilots had to follow to lessen the possibility of their hitting non-combatants.[11]

(To me, later on, this came to remind me of General Douglas MacArthur's and General Curtis LeMay's bitterness about what is for the United States' axiomatic and

11. Grier, "The Chappie James Way", 70—73

Constitutional: it is imperative to our freedoms that we have Civilian control of the Military.)

At the end of James' effective Patriotic speech, all of us to a person stood up and cheered, and yelled for maybe three minutes.

Later that afternoon, many of us dealt with embarrassment for doing so, but we had responded to a master orator, and one who appealed primarily to our emotions, not our reason, exactly as a highly gifted preacher can. To me this ability can easily become an abusive and manipulative one, but it has always been held in high regard in the US, because of our heavy reliance on salesmanship and demagoguery in selling whatever product. This is not a new awareness: Dale Carnegie laid out how to be effective at selling whatever product, by selling oneself, in his *How to Win Friends and Influence People*, published in 1936. His basic statement about selling was: "It isn't about what you have or who you are or where you are or what you are doing that makes you happy or unhappy. It is what you think about it". So, be positive! This complete amoralism I believe to be one of the chief downfalls to any nation under the sway of Capitalism, and through American styled churches and businesses, how we have been destroying so much of the rest of the world. Our entire economy is based on consumerism, and responding to effective advertising: making people feel the need for something they don't need.

After the 1968 elections, author Joe McGinniss wrote a scathing book about *The Selling of the President*, which showed how Roger Ailes and others were "packaging" Nixon to portray a likable man, a "new" Nixon. It was in part an alternative to Theodore White's much more stilted and stately way of describing the political process in his series of books. McGinniss' observations about what has toxified and dehumanized our political process, came to larger expression about our entire consumer culture in Neil Postman's *Amusing Ourselves to Death: Public Discourse in the Age of Show Business*, 1985. Suffice it to say here, that I find these deceptive approaches in public communications exactly what St. Paul combats as the danger of "rhetoric" in the Christian Church in *First Corinthians* 2 and to speaking truthfully as human beings.

A last memory of this High School trip: After the Great Kennedy Fiasco of mine, I was threatened by a couple of huge thugs who were part of the group from New Jersey, one African American, one White, let's say Mr. T and Andre the Giant. I don't remember their names, but after telling me what they would like to do to teach me a lesson, I stood my ground, and dared them to follow through, which they did, starting with wrapping a telephone cord around my neck and tightening it. I remember not feeling fear, and a moment later they laughed and told me it was all in play. I told them we played differently in Sault Ste. Marie. Almost on cue, their senator showed up at our place, the residence hall where we slept. He was known to me by news photographs I had seen of this Democrat, Harrison "Pete" Williams. He had been in labor union and environmental and OSHA issues. However, he was convicted for his role in accepting bribes in the FBI ABSCAM sting, and sent to federal prison in 1980.

He served a number of years, making him the first US Senator to serve time in prison in 80 years. His story was included in the 2013 "American Hustle", a terrific political film, with his character renamed and played by Anthony Zerbe.

XI

I came back from my trip, having enjoyed every minute of it. Almost as soon as I got back I found out from my friend Duncan McMillan that the local radio station, WSOO was hiring. So I applied and got the job. My set hours were 3–11 pm every Sunday, and then fill in on other days of the week. I gave reports of my Washington trip to local service clubs, which from what I could tell were comprised by shockingly juvenile fat guys still yearning for their high school days, and playing pranks. So, I fit right in. I had great fun providing a few anecdotes, and especially joking about Senator Kennedy. The line no one thought funny was: Senator Kennedy's thoughts on the failing of a volunteer army was to ask how many of us wanted this? And how many would sign up? I then said to the group how foolish it was to base one's views on this issue, in Kennedy's fashion. I noted, "For example, how many of you are in favor of abortion? And how many of you are going to have one?" No laughter. No nodding in wise agreement. Nothing. Frankly I thought there was some correlation to these two questions, but I got blank stares from this audience. Even a gesture from the Tail Twister, one of the more cultured members. At least that was a reaction.

Home life continued being difficult and filled with tension. My senior year came, and I signed up to try out for "Hello Dolly". It seemed everyone in the class was trying out. I got Cornelius, a role I enjoyed, and found the rehearsals at night a welcome escape from home. "Out there, there's a world outside of Yonkers, way out there beyond this hick town Barnaby, there's a slick town Barnaby!" It was joyful and laughter all the time for this production. I remember learning how to waltz with Irene who was a fine dancer, and this helped me get confidence for our upcoming senior prom.

Many of us also got acquainted with the charismatic young Catholic priest in town, at St. Joseph's in Sault Ste. Marie. Fr. Terry H. was personality plus, and there was enjoyment being around him. Both my older sister, Dawn, and I were entranced with his magical kingdom which moved with him. I remember once or twice going over to the rectory, where a continual party—it seemed—was occurring, and noticing almost the entire wrestling team there. Fr. Terry was our baccalaureate speaker, and someone who connected easily with most folks no matter what the occasion. I attended Catholic Mass for the first few times in my life, and encountered what was for me a very strange way of worshipping, along with the Consecration of the Eucharist central to the worship. I had never seen or experienced this before. Liturgical prayer was different, and yet something completely sensible. Just as the Lord's Prayer or Our Father was so obviously a corporate prayer (our) and liturgical (said the same every time) so was this form of the worship of what was referred to as the people of God. I urged Dawn and my mother to go with me to St. Joseph's on Christmas Eve. The Salvation Army did not have services on that day, having lost almost all connection with the traditions of worship in the Christian Liturgical year. I found I loved the worship, and didn't understand why my mother and Dawn seemed to be offended by Mass. After all, we were celebrating the "Christ Mass". At the dismissal, and following the closing hymn, the monsignor invited everyone to come into the parish hall for refreshments, and he held up a six pack of Blatz (yuck!). Blatz? My mother hissed and said we needed to leave, and I said Dawn and I were going back to wish Fr. Terry a Merry Christmas. I wanted to see the crèche scene, and the altar, and the sanctuary, including the aumbry (where the Reserved Eucharistic elements are kept) . I made jokes to Dawn about Jesus being hidden away in the aumbry, crying to be let out: "Let me out! Let me out!". I liked this form of worship and something I couldn't quite express at the time. Generally, I noticed a difference between Catholic worship and extreme Protestantism, in that to the former, the Mass said: This is who you are as God's people. To the latter, the worship said: Are you sure? It seemed to me I found the former far more consoling and comforting, far more in fact like the Spirit of Christ who repeatedly called us not to fear. The Evangelical and Fundamentalist forms of worship, and these were the newer and to a great extent American forms of worship, expressed a sense of anxiety, the opposite of what Jesus called us in faith to believe and love. It is very hard for anxious and fearful people to love. I appreciated as well a sense of "holiness" in the Church, that God is addressed there, in straightforward language, not relying on histrionics. Later I was to find this even more intensely in the Episcopal Church with a sense of God's mystery.

Several times my senior year, I found that I was sensing something a little weird about Fr. Terry. On two or three occasions as I was getting to know him and enjoy his friendliness and thoughtfulness about religious matters, he would ask me a strangely personal question or in some way intrude into my interior life. I liked being around people and friends at school, but I protected my interior life, my "soul" if you will, my consciousness, my inner thoughts, from most people, as I assume human beings do who become aware of their soul and treasure times in solitude. For myself, both my parents would speak to me as though they knew of my own psyche, or that this could be spelled out in brief exchanges of conversation. This rather ignorant assumption by one person, even a family member, about another is foolish. Human beings are made in the image and likeness of God according to Genesis 1. So there will always be mystery in each person's life. In fact, various students of psychology building on Freud's work, have insisted that beneath an outer manifestation of one's persona, what mask one wears, how one presents himself or herself to the outside world, what one presents is the tip of an iceberg which is mostly chthonic, unseen, beyond at times one's own cogitations. This mysterious inner self is not readily accessible to others, and for those who have developed, attended to their interiority, there may be a great depth to such a person's self. At least it seems so to me. (Of course there are innumerable ways when one may show by slips of the tongue, or an expression of one's thoughts, and what one chooses to say, or by one reacting defensively about a subject which may come up in conversation spontaneously, what is at work subconsciously in someone. This can also be discerned in how an individual establishes filters in one's apprehending and daily negotiating the world around us.) I found Fr. Terry becoming uncomfortably intrusive by making quiet suggestions to me. "I watch you at these parties, and while you go from person to person, and pass on some charming remark to make them happy, you never reveal much of yourself. Let's get together and explore what makes you tick." This kind of remark was expressed to a sixteen and then a seventeen-year-old young man, and I would become extremely uneasy by the tone of what he was suggesting. Why would I want Fr. Terry H. to know what made me tick? I shuddered at the idea of going "exploring "with him. So, I would find a comment clearly to show that this is what I wished to have in a girlfriend, not a Catholic priest. Once at the university in Madison, Terry called me to come and visit him over a weekend at a very small town in the Western U.P. He had been assigned to a Church on an Indian reservation. I decided to go, and asked my roommate to go as well. It was a fairly uneventful time, but driving back, Gerald—a Ukrainian Roman Catholic from Ladysmith, Wisconsin—brought up Fr. Terry making him feel a little out of sorts. "He's got problems", Gerald said, and I knew I wasn't crazy, picking up on the way Gerald said it. (In the mid-1980s Fr. Terry H. was arrested, convicted and did several years' time in prison in Michigan for pedophilia, for molesting several teenage boys; and the last time I checked he was out of the priesthood.)

However, the dumbest thing I ever did was to take three different classmates-on different nights—to watch "The Godfather". They all laughed and joked about how especially a jerk I was to do this since they were all friends with one another and compared notes. This film remains my favorite, with the story of the rise and expansion of a particular "wise guy" family killing and intimidating every one of their enemies on their way to great power as gangsters in America after the second World War—a parable of amoral American politics and business. The scene with Michael Corleone escaping the gang war he helped start by going abroad to the village with his surname in Sicily, and marrying Apollonia is one of the most romantic I know. I remember Pauline Kael writing about Marlon Brando and commending his performance as captivating.

With my senior year rapidly coming to a close, I was asked by a woman in the homecoming Queen's Court, Cynthia , from the Big Boy disaster, to escort her to the Prom. This included a parade, which with all the chiffon and damask and lace and whatever else goes into clothing on such an occasion, prepared me for dressing up as an Anglo-Catholic priest years later.

My great joy occurred in that spring of 1972 was my meeting with the Chippewa County Republicans, chaired by Bernard Doll, to select delegates to the Michigan State GOP Convention, who would then elect delegates representing Michigan at the National Convention in Miami, where Richard Nixon would be renominated as President. I then filled out the forms necessary to get elected from my particular precinct. I registered as uncommitted on the Republican ballot, and running unopposed, received 81 votes. At the state Convention, I ran around meeting various pooh-bahs of the Party, Governor William Milliken, Secretary George Romney (in Nixon's cabinet), Senator Robert Griffin, House Minority Leader—and soon to be President—Gerald Ford. I greeted my Congressman, Philip Ruppe who with his wife Loret had already been kind to me, and who had enabled me to attend dress up affairs. The Congressman had asked me a couple of times to read speeches for him in the Soo. (Loret was more famous than her husband, as a shrewd smart businesswoman, heiress to her grandfather's Miller Brewing empire, and an outstanding Peace Corps Director in the 1980s, before ending her career as Ambassador to Norway.) Bernard Doll came and found me just before a series of votes to elect at-large delegates and a couple alternate delegates to the GOP National Convention. He wanted me to meet William McLaughlin, state chairman of the Republican Party. Doll knew what to say, including securing Congressman Ruppe's full support for my becoming an alternate delegate. A moment later, McLaughlin announced Ruppe's nomination, and then added that in the election of 1972, McGovern's young people would be promoting McGovern as a champion of the young! (boos) Now we have this fine young man from Sault Ste. Marie who will champion President Richard M. Nixon's support from young people as well! (Great applause) What? I was still an uncommitted delegate. And the youth were enamored with Nixon? Within a few seconds, Senator Griffin had stood up and requested my election "unanimously as first alternate". Loud cheers and I was on my way to Miami Beach in the not too long future! (Actually, if anyone wants to see how the youth supported Nixon, there it is in the comedy/farce "Dick", (1999) which, in part, is a satire of Nixon's White House in 1973–4, and includes a hilarious re-imagining of the Watergate break in, and a parody of Woodward and Bernstein.) This all got written up in the fabulous *Sault Evening News*! Woo Hoo! Bernard Doll went around the room and did an effective fund raising for this poor kid right out of High School. And then I had enough funds to travel to Miami and back, and stay with the Michigan delegation in the Fontainebleu Hotel.

A couple months following, I had taken a bus to Detroit and flown with the Michigan folks. The only critical news I remember noticing before leaving, were stories in the Detroit papers about a break in at the Watergate complex, and the immediate denials by the White House, and CREEP, (actually Committee to Reelect the President). I got to Miami, and our delegation was greeted by Congressman Jerry Ford, his wife Betty, and his daughter Susan, at a Michigan reception in the La Fontaine room! I was something of a minor celebrity because of my youth. I had my first martini, shaken not stirred. The cocktails were everywhere as well as happy folks, many of whom I knew from pictures in the news. The hors d'oevres were a huge variety of seafood, Mexican food, carved meats, everything a small town boy from Sault Ste. Marie could imagine and more. Coming from a distinctly low working class background and area, I would have thought cheese whiz and little weenies. But these folks were dressy, and after a while a little inebriated. (Have you ever attended a GOP mixer?)

I had an ability from years' practice in Salvation Army circles (and a new school nearly every year) to wander around and meet folks. I remember coming across some of the younger party goers: Susan Ford, Dick Posthumus, and Spencer Abraham. Posthumus was 22, and would go on to serve in Michigan's State Senate, before serving a single term as Lieutenant Governor. Abraham, from Lebanese descent, and Eastern Orthodox, was 20. He had a brief illustrious career in government, becoming United States Senator in 1994 and serving one term, then, after defeat, becoming Secretary of Energy in George W. Bush's Cabinet. Susan Ford was the youngest of the four of us, whom we only saw occasionally in these next several days. She was way under age to drink martinis (age 15) even though I remember her wanting to. (No joke intended—Betty Ford Center) I was with all these bright lights, and more to follow on the next day, Sunday, the last free day before the Convention.

Everything for me was a whirlwind. The floor of the Convention Hall was a huge blur, too many folks, too many loud noises, celebrities everywhere I turned, some very strange people doing clownish activities, a lot of carnies barking out their causes and wares. Any number of speakers were addressing the news cameras, and no one on the floor paid any attention. The details of the "GOP Platform" went on for a while, and who cared? As alternate, I sat in that section until a delegate came over and "tagged" me, which was often. So, I was free to roam and met Senator John Sherman Cooper from Kentucky who everyday gave me a thimble or two of his hooch in a jug at his feet. I sat and asked him questions, including his experiences during the great Civil Rights debates of the mid-60s. He spoke about the courage of many from back in his home state, especially white and black Christian folk who marched. Day by day I enjoyed his company enormously. I got Frank Sinatra's autograph and let him know how much I enjoyed "Fly Me to the Moon", "The Way You Look Tonight", "Nancy" about his daughter—"Bootsie". And who sang "Something Stupid" with him.(It is.) I said to the Chairman of the Board that I played a Rod McKuen song he recorded, while I was announcing at WSOO every Sunday afternoon: "Love's Been Good to Me". Next to him was Rocky (Governor Nelson Rockefeller), and Charlton Heston, and Henry Kissinger. All gave me autographs. I turned around and there were the Romneys, Senator Robert Packwood from Oregon who looked for me and talked several times, Senator Marlon Cook from Kentucky, Senator James Buckley, and two Senators from Colorado, Gordon Allott, whom George Will assisted and accompanied, and Peter Dominick. By Wednesday, I began to think most of the delegates looked like Zombies, without much enthusiasm, going through motions. Quite often, I found myself thinking that these actually weren't happy people, but desperately trying to prove something by being at the Convention. Maybe my reading of several John Updike novels was affecting me. Do these folks have any center? There seemed a little more energy on Thursday night as we went through the "Four More Years" chant incessantly, when the entire crowd turned toward the CBS news booth and singled Walter Cronkite out as the target for their anger or spite.

In Garry Wills' *Nixon Agonistes*, which I had read but not wholly absorbed when I first read it, the author had with crystalline precision, described the "lack of center" for these very Americans. These were the ones whom H. L. Mencken had skewered with his descriptive word the "booboisie", the ones about whom he stated, "No one . . . has ever lost money by underestimating the intelligence of the great masses of the plain people", who engage in boosterism, in Sinclair Lewis' novels, *Main Street* and *Babbitt*. Wills describes what he observes about a huge crowd at a George Wallace rally in 1968, I think like the Nixon *devotees* of 1972:

> Their happiness is enough to break the heart. They vomit laughter. Trying to eject the vacuum inside them. They are not hungry or underprivileged or deprived in material ways. Each has, in some minor way, "made it". And it all means nothing . . . The desire for "law and order" is nothing so simple as a code word for racism; it is a cry, as things begin to break up, for stability, for stopping history in mid-dissolution. Hammer the structure back together; anchor it down; bring nails and bolts and clamps to keep it from collapsing. There is a slide in things-queasy seasickness in these laughing tortured faces, vomiting emptiness.[1]

Wills concludes in his reflection on the anger, even the "cruelty" in these Americans who do not have the ability to answer their own children's skeptical questioning about the purpose for following in the American way of life:

> These parents] had 'done everything for the children'—-except answer them. And that failure was enough to undo all that they do all that they had done. They are angry not so much at their children as at themselves for failing the children. And it is anger itself that eats into the mind. Their faith—in hard work, good manners, obedience to the law, success, self-reliance—was being challenged. And their *grounds* for faith have through the years evanesced. All their religions are empty-beginning with the religion of religion. After that, the religion of progress (civilization had bombed our cities senseless). The religion of success (*they* had succeeded, and had ashes in their mouths). The religion of prosperity (for America has had a spirituality of materialism with millionaire saints now losing their faith). Finally, the last great belief, education. America had said, like the man in Chesterton, "I do not know what good is, but I shall give it to my children." The parents may not be able to defend

---

1. Wills, *Nixon Agonistes*, 51–2

"the American way"; but that was only because they were not educated. The children would do it; teachers had been hired to show them how. Yet the children, taught to doubt, far from defending their parents' way of life, question it with new rigor, mercilessly. Under that questioning, these parents fall back on a mindless faith in George's [Wallace] "good old America." But the faith is a desperate one, grown defensive. These people have neither an examined certitude nor a soothing oblivion. They do not have the comforting simplicities of the rebel. They defend an establishment they do not really feel part of, without weapons or joy, getting little for their effort. Caught between complacency and protest, their anger is a sterile thing, ejaculations in the air.[2]

I returned from the Republican Convention, wondering if politics was the right choice for me. Would I want to spend my life pretending this was a worthy vocation?

It almost seemed I was getting an answer with the serendipitous release of a film that summer, "The Candidate", starring Robert Redford. Redford plays the charismatic son of a former California governor (Melvyn Douglass), who has turned his questioning of the meaningfulness of secular politics in such a degraded political culture described in Joe McGinness' *The Selling of the President*, into a life as a caring legal aid attorney in leftist causes. The attorney, Bill McKay, is idealistic and wants no part of the propagandistic life embodied by his father. However, a cynical political operative, Marvin Lucas, played by Peter Boyle, recruits McKay, with the promise that he will be free to speak his mind, because the plan is to lose. McKay reluctantly agrees. Ironically, McKay begins to pick up momentum in the polls, and begins under various pressures to reign in some of his outspoken views. After he is greeted by his father ironically with the compliment that now he's a real politician, McKay wins. The last scene is of McKay with his top aide in a rest room, and McKay plaintively, asks "Marvin, what do we do now?" For myself, I came back to Sault Ste. Marie, and after criticizing the local paper in a letter to the editor for not running the stories on Watergate, I voted for McGovern.

2. Wills, *Nixon Agonistes*, 53

XII

In the fall of 1972, I began my college career at Lake Superior State College, a quaint picturesque liberal arts school in Sault Ste. Marie. Many of my graduating friends also attended, using the local college as a springboard for their later university plans. I enjoyed socializing with a number of very smart, vibrant women, as well as a number of male friends, and I was used to seeing one or more of either sex for much of every day. We all had the delight of enjoying each other's company, and talking well into the night. We were young! And we were friends! About this time I found the poem *Heraclitus* by Victorian William Johnson Cory which spoke of being part of this circle:

> They told me, Heraclitus, they told me you were dead,
>
> They brought me bitter news to hear and bitter tears to shed.
>
> I wept as I remembered how often you and I
>
> Had tired the sun with talking and sent him down the sky.
>
> And now that thou art lying, my dear old Carian guest,
>
> A handful of grey ashes, long, long ago at rest,
>
> Still art thy pleasant voices, thy nightingales awake;
>
> For Death, he taketh them all away, but them he cannot take.[1]

Now, in my 60s, this strikes me as a rather too "precious", maudlin, faux tragic poem, but it captures some of our late teen sentimentality. Evelyn Waugh parodied this poem in his *The Loved One*:

> They told me, Francis Hinsley, they told me you were hung
>
> With red protruding eye-balls and black protruding tongue
>
> I wept as I remembered how often you and I
>
> Had laughed about Los Angeles and now 'tis here you'll lie;
>
> Here pickled in formaldehyde and painted like a whore,
>
> Shrimp—pink incorruptible, not lost or gone before.[2]

1. Cory, *Heraclitus*, 653
2. Evelyn Waugh, *The Loved One*, 85

I met Dr. John McCabe, theater director at the College, who knew a great deal about American and British stage acting and directing, and he invited me to try out for a fall and a spring play, *The Importance of Being Earnest*, Oscar Wilde's delightful comedy of manners, and *The Boy Friend,* a Sandy Wilson musical. I was picked for Jack Worthing in the former, and Lord Brockhurst in the latter. McCabe had received his earned college degrees from the University of Detroit, a Master's from Fordham, and a doctorate from the Shakespeare Institute at the University of Birmingham in England. McCabe had been good friends of many theater notables, and wrote biographies of Stan Laurel, Oliver Hardy, George M. Cohan, and James Cagney. In addition, he ghosted Cagney's autobiography. McCabe encouraged me to see a film just out about Winston Churchill's youth directed by his friend Richard Attenborough, based on Churchill's *My Early Life.*

This began my enjoyment of reading everything I could about the great parliamentarian. The film follows the old-fashioned style of epics, with several scenes depicting an anecdote or one encounter Churchill describes, meant to convey a much longer time frame or more complex incident. But I found the movie entrancing and romantic. I wanted to be a congressman! I wanted to orate!

Here was a man born in 1874 at the time of Disraeli and Gladstone, who in 1898 took part in the last great cavalry charge at Omdurman, and as Prime Minister in 1954 looked over the Hydrogen Bomb. What tremendous changes occurred in that 56 year period for the human race to adapt to these new weapons created by science, which now gave human beings the ability to destroy everyone on the planet several times over. And in fact the twentieth century was a time period in which so much of humanity was destroyed in the name of modernism and science and "man come of age". Churchill's cavalry charge would have been understandable to Homer. (I must add the British also used Lee's Enfield rifles, the Maxim gun, and cannonry. But I am thinking of the charge itself.)

My reading of Winston Churchill included his World War I memoirs said by contemporaries to be egotistical on his part: Winston has written a history of the world with himself at the center! And then his World War II memoirs. Also, I was captivated in the movie by Winston's father, Lord Randolph, played by the extraordinary actor Robert Shaw-who had previously portrayed Henry VIII in *A Man for All Seasons*, the 1966 filmed version of Robert Bolt's play with Paul Schofield as Sir Thomas More. I found everything I could to read about Lord Randolph, from Robert Rhodes James' biography, to Winston Churchill's own biography of his father, to books on the Fourth Party Lord Randolph created with a future Prime Minister, Arthur J. Balfour. A son of the Duke of Marlborough, Lord Randolph had experienced a meteoric rise in the Tory Party, from a very early age. He was something new in British politics, a fiery campaign speaker, and coined the phrase "Tory Democracy" to attract young voters. He and his lovely, charming American wife Jennie, dazzled English society as "celebrities", and he assisted the Conservative Party in gaining a majority in Parliament in

1885. In that campaign, he frequently and effectively attacked Gladstone, calling him the "Moloch of Midlothian", referring to Gladstone's constituency in Scotland. Lord Randolph's oratory was never more successful than in his devastating "Chips" speech, lampooning Gladstone's hobby of demolishing whole forests!

> For the purposes of recreation, he has selected the felling of trees; and we may usefully remark that his amusements, like his politics, are essentially destructive. Every afternoon the whole world is invited to assist at the crashing fall of some beech or elm or oak. The forest laments, in order that Mr. Gladstone may perspire . . .

Now Lord Randolph comments on Gladstone's recent meeting with working men at his house, Hawarden, on the Welsh border:

> It has always appeared to me somewhat incongruous and inappropriate that the great chief of the Radical party should reside in a castle. But to proceed. One would have thought that the deputation would have been received in the house, in the study, in the drawing-room, or even in the dining room. Not at all . . . Another scene had been arranged. The working men were guided through the ornamental grounds, into the wide-spreading park, strewn with the wreckage and the ruin of the Prime Minister's sport. All around them, we may suppose, lay the rotting trunks of once umbrageous trees: all around them tossed by the winds, were boughs and bark and withered shoots. They come suddenly on the Prime Minister and [his son] Herbert, in scanty attire and profuse perspiration, engaged in the destruction of a giant oak, just giving its last dying groan. They are permitted to gaze and to worship and adore and, having conducted themselves with exemplary propriety, are each of them presented with a few chips as a memorial of that memorable scene . . . To all leaned upon Mr. Gladstone, who trusted in him, and who hoped for something from him-chips, nothing but chips-hard, dry, unnourishing, indigestible chips![3]

A failed Liberal Prime Minister, Lord Rosebery, a close friend and critic of Lord Randolph, and a remarkably cultured and literate man when that was unremarkable, wrote a brief memoir to assist Winston Churchill in the latter's attempts at writing the life of his father. When this consequence of his efforts was rejected, he published *Lord Randolph Churchill* in 1906. He noted a partisan speech in which Gladstone and the Liberal Party were castigated by Lord Randolph: "The Prime Minister, his colleagues, and his party-these children of revolution, these robbers of churches, these plunderers of classes, these destroyers of property, these friends of the lawless, these foes of the loyal".[4] Lord Rosebery wrote admirably about his subject's personality thus:

---

3. James, *Lord Randolph Churchill*, 136–7
4. Rosebery, *Lord Randolph Churchill*, 102–3

He had at his disposal the charm of conversation, and this was as various as his moods. When he felt himself completely at ease, in congenial society, it was wholly delightful. He would then display his mastery of pleasant irony and banter; for with those playthings he was at his best. Nor would he hesitate to air his most intimate views of persons and characters; he did not shrink from admissions which were candid to the verge of cynicism; he reveled in paradox. A stranger or a prig happening upon him in such moods would be puzzled, and perhaps scandalized; for his lighter conversation was not to be taken literally. He would hate this and that, embrace the most preposterous propositions, and defend any extravagance that might happen to enter his head; if he were opposed, he would carry it much further.[5]

When Lord Salisbury became Prime Minister, he named Lord Randolph as Secretary of State for India, and then Chancellor of the Exchequer, and Leader of the House of Commons-since Salisbury was in the Lords. However, within a few months Lord Randolph attempted a power play over demanding rigid cuts in the budget for the British military , and upon a very public resignation, Salisbury accepted it. At age 37 he was out of the government, never to return. His health went into rapid decline and he died, possibly of syphilis at age 45, in 1895. His son lamented that he only had a very few times to spend time with him, no more than a handful. And while there is a multiplicity of reasons for one to be considered a genius, his or her motivations could be considered along with all the rest, and the mysterious elements not open to measure scientifically. For Winston Churchill one was his great desire to please the father he hardly knew and wished to claim respect. For this marvelous man who did more, I believe, than anyone to save the Western World and civilization during WWII, who only won a single parliamentary election as leader of his Conservative party (in 1951); about whom Iain MacLeod said, "Nothing detracts from the splendor of his life"; he rose and fell several times before achieving greatness. He died on the same day as his father, January 24, seventy years apart, and exactly twice his father's age.

I had my first political science classes with a recent legislative aide to Senator Vance Hartke, Democrat of Indiana, Professor Jo Beth Wolf. One day she predicted a major fall coming for the Nixon fund raising "gangsters", especially Maurice Stans, based on information she was receiving from Hartke. She added that this forthcoming scandal might sink Nixon and his administration.

My favorite professor was James W. T. Moody, who taught Western Civilization. Professor Moody was a kindly, sagacious Methodist, who looked the spitting image of Mr. French on the television show, (trimmed beard and mustache, black suit with waistcoat, white shirt and bowtie). He had a ready sense of humor, and especially enjoyed encouraging students in their individual endeavors. His teaching was very popular and always began with a reading from A. A. Milne's Winnie the Pooh stories. I saw him every day, and talked with him about the disconnect I had having been

5. Rosebery, *Lord Randolph Churchill*, 82–3

raised in a home which was "holiness" oriented-coming from the Wesleyan notion of producing one's emotions supposedly at the inspiration of the Holy Spirit, and in some way measurable, and therefore anti-intellectual or obscurantist. And the Salvation Army *prided* itself: a) on having the emotional pietism which was all important to their sense of being "saved", despite what Paul said in *Romans* and *I Corinthians* (about one's own spirit being unreliable, even dangerous); and, b) consequent ignorance of the results of any careful historical or Biblical or theological study. Moody was himself from a "holiness" background as a Free Methodist, but had broken loose of the chains of anti-intellectualism, particularly in the areas of Creationism/Evolution, and premillennial dispensationalism. He gave me a paper to read from another Christian and biologist, who made the case that a literal reading of Genesis was a new heresy in Christianity (with the rise of the Fundamentalists), and was a willful misreading of the key passages in the Creation narratives of *Genesis* 1:1-—2:4a, and 2:4b—25. These were in fact not written by Moses, but from much later in Israelite history, the first in *Genesis* 1, the Priestly narrative which was post-exilic (c. 400–350 BC), and the second one much earlier, using the name of God, *Yahweh*, or *Jahveh*. This narrative developed by oral recitation over centuries until being written down in the eighth century BC, and was associated with the South of Israel, Judah. (In reading about Homer, and the process of orality to written work, I came more to appreciate this. Bernard Knox spells this out in his pellucid introduction to Robert Fagles' translation of *The Iliad*.) In *Genesis* 1, the Creator is known as *Elohim*, a plural for God and his retinue. In *Genesis* 2:4bff, the God of the Israelites is named: *Yahweh*, with only the consonants used in this sacred name, also known as the Tetragrammaton (Greek for Four Letters). It would be nearly sixteen hundred years before the vowel pointings were added by the Masoretes, from the Hebrew word for Lord, *Adonai*, because the priests and scribes, and much later rabbis, followed the convention after the Exile of not using or pronouncing the very name of the Lord. (Around the 16th century, Christian scholars attempted to write the sacred name putting the consonants for the sacred name, with the vowel pointings for *Adonai*, and came up with "Jehovah", which Jewish scholars particularly have found to be a great joke. It is now enshrined in a Christian sect, Jehovah's Witnesses. It is funny. When a simpleton founds your religion, you get stuck with that stupidity. Consider the Mormons.) All of this was new to me. Secondly, the purpose of the Creation stories was "theological" not "scientific". That is, we are told "why" not "how". In addition, the key to understanding the early chapters of *Genesis* was the Covenant which God was making with humanity, which entails "relationship". So, to get hung up on a literal "scientific" reading of *Genesis*, and treat it as a step-by-step scientific treatise was to engage in misreading *Genesis* entirely. In the words of philosophy, this is a grand "category error", or logical fallacy. It is misunderstanding one form or category, for the appropriate one, mixing them up.

The author then described what Charles Darwin discovered in the early 19th century, regarding the evolution of species as they interact with their environments.

All of this had made sense to me when I was in Junior High. One adjusts theory to fact, not the other way round. The author then spelled out his remaining a firm Christian and scientist. And, I have met innumerable scientists who were and are Christians. That has never, it seems, been a problem for Anglican theologians who in 1860, one year after Darwin's publication of the *Origin of the Species,* engaged in compiling a series of essays, including several referring to science, entitled *Essays and Reviews,* 1860. The future Archbishop of Canterbury, Frederick Temple, preached a sermon included in book, which he called "The Present Relation of Science to Religion" which fully accepted God creating through evolutionary processes, as creation was on—going and not a single moment in time. None of these Christians establishes that what we have is only a mechanistic or naturalistic understanding of creation, apart from the One who creates. In fact, in these essays and later nineteenth century Anglican theology, evolution was accepted with the proviso that the human soul was not part of any natural process.[6]

In Professor Moody's class, we read : Garrett Mattingly's classic *The Armada,* and how luck determined the rise of Elizabeth I on the world stage, and the failure of the Spanish in their attempt to conquer England for the Catholic Church in 1587; Carl Becker's *The Heavenly City of the Eighteenth-Century Philosophers,* with his skillful demolishing of the pretenses of the "Age Of Reason", and exhibiting the age's own unexamined metaphysics, their own "religion" one could say, based on a scientific leap of faith, and nothing more than a prejudice; Barbara Tuchman's *The Proud Tower* (1966), concerning Europe at the *fin de siècle* and her ruling families, all to be swept away by the coming World War I ; and, *Stilwell and the American Experience of China 1911–1945,* (1971), about America's own growing imperialistic designs in the world.

Privately, Moody gave me volume after volume of Loren Eiseley. *The Immense Journey* was a deeply stirring book from this extremely sensitive naturalist, anthropologist, philosopher, and poet. I to this day refer to it, and quote from Eiseley's meditations about the Earth and its creatures, including man. I have read many of Eiseley's books, *The Night Country, The Firmament of Time, The Invisible Pyramid.* One passage grabbed me and stands out in how Eiseley's love of the natural world reveals something very deep and rich about life all around us. It is found in his "The Bird and the Machine", in *The Immense Journey.* Eiseley has been describing being commissioned by a European city to acquire certain birds and animals from the Colorado Rockies. Coming upon a desolate and deserted stone cabin, he immediately recognizes the kind of place wild birds would nest. He entered and placed a ladder next to a wall to reach a shelf which would very probably yield birds seeking shelter and safety from coyotes. He quietly ascends to the shelf and uses the flash of a spotlight to blind whatever birds are there. Then he notes he had no idea what he would be encountering. Eiseley writes:

6. See Ramsey, *The Anglican Spirit,* 54–5,70

I snapped on the flash and sure enough there was a great beating and feathers flying, but instead of my having them, they, or rather he, had me. He had my hand, that is, and for a small hawk not much bigger than my fist he was doing all right. I heard him give one short metallic cry when the light went on and my hand descended on the bird beside him; after that he was busy with his claws and his beak was sunk in my thumb. In the struggle I knocked the lamp over on the shelf, and his mate got her sight back and whisked neatly through the hole in the roof and off among the stars outside. It all happened in fifteen seconds and you might think I would have fallen down the ladder, but no, I had a professional assassin's reputation to keep up, and the bird, of course, made the mistake of thinking the hand was the enemy and not the eyes behind it. He chewed my thumb up pretty effectively and lacerated my hand with his claws, but in the end I got him, having two hands to work with.

He was a sparrow hawk and a fine young male in the prime of life. I was sorry not to catch the pair of them, but as I dripped blood and folded his wings carefully, holding him by the back so he couldn't strike again, I had to admit the two of them might have been more than I could have handled under the circumstances. The little fellow had saved his mate by diverting me, and that was that. He was born to it, and made no outcry now, resting in my hand hopelessly, but peering toward me in the shadows behind the lamp with a fierce, almost indifferent glance. He neither gave nor expected mercy and something out of the high air passed from him to me, stirring a faint embarrassment. I quit looking into that eye and managed to get my huge carcass with its fist full of prey back down the ladder. I put the bird in a box too small to allow him to injure himself by struggle and walked out to welcome the arriving trucks. It had been a long day, and a camp still to make in the darkness. In the morning the bird would be just another episode. He would go back . . . in the truck to a small cage in a city where he would spend the rest of his life. And a good thing, too. I sucked my aching hand and spat out some blood. An assassin has to get use to these things. I had a professional reputation to keep up.

In the morning, with the change that comes on suddenly in that high country, the mist that had hovered below us in the valley was gone. The sky was a deep blue, and one could see for miles over the high outcroppings of stone. I was up early and brought the box in which the little hawk was imprisoned out onto the grass where I was building a cage. A wind as cool as a mountain spring ran over the grass and stirred my hair. It was a fine day to be alive. I looked up and all around and at the hole in the cabin roof out of which the other little hawk had fled. There was no sign of her anywhere that I could see. 'Probably in the next county by now,' I thought cynically, but before beginning work I decided I'd have a look at my last night's capture. Secretively I looked all around the camp and up and down and opened the box. I got him right out in my hand with his wings folded properly, and I was careful not to startle him. He lay limp in my grasp and I could feel his heart pound under the feathers, but he only looked beyond me and up. I saw him look that last look away beyond me into a sky so full of light that I could not follow his gaze. The little breeze flowed over me again, and nearby a mountain aspen shook all its tiny leaves. I suppose I must have had an idea then of what I was going to do, but I never let it come into my consciousness. I just reached over and laid the hawk on the grass. He lay there a long minute without hope, unmoving, his eyes still fixed on that blue vault above him. It must have been that he was already so far away in heart that he never felt the release from my hand. He never even stood. He just lay with his breast against the grass.

In the next second after that long minute he was gone. Like a flicker of light, he had vanished with my eyes full on him, but without actually seeing even a premonitory wing beat. He was gone straight into that towering emptiness of light and crystal that my eyes could scarcely bear to penetrate. For another long moment there was silence. I could not see him. The light was too intense. Then from far up somewhere a cry came ringing down. I was young then and had seen little of the world, but when I heard that cry my heart turned over. It was not the cry of the hawk I had captured; for, by shifting my position against the sun, I was now seeing further up. Straight out of sun's eye, where she must have been soaring restlessly above us for untold hours, hurtled his mate. And from far up, ringing from peak to peak of the summits over us, came a cry of such unutterable and ecstatic joy that it sounds down across the years and tingles among the cups on my quiet breakfast table. I saw them both now. He was rising fast to meet her. They met in a great soaring gyre that turned into a whirling circle and a dance of wings. Once more, just once, their two voices joined in a harsh wild medley of question and response, struck and echoed against the pinnacles of the valley. Then they were gone forever somewhere into those upper regions beyond the eyes of men.[7]

This quotation hit me strongly about life, and about who we were as creatures of a God who created a world in which a naturalist could write such a beautiful description of wildlife. Many years later, in discussion with Fr. John Claypool, I mentioned Loren Eiseley, and this particular passage. I said I had received this gift from a Free Methodist Professor of mine at Lake Superior State College, and how this moved me toward a Sacramental understanding of the entire creation. He responded that he had experienced exactly the same awareness in reading this passage, and that he quoted it in one of his books. I imagine that this is what Jim Moody had in mind for me.

I had also begun reading philosophy, A. J. Ayer's *Language, Truth, and Logic* (1936) to be specific, with the programmatic urgency of a twenty-six-year-old, who wished to limit all meaningful questions to those which could be answered with "verification", that is, empirical evidence. With this tricky move, this sleight of hand, this con job even, Ayer, a logical positivist, believed he had ruled out all metaphysical, aesthetic, and theological questions, all the truly important questions of life. Reading

7. Eiseley, *The Immense Journey*, 188-192

Eiseley, I began to remember many days as a five, six, seven, eight-year-old, lying on my back staring into the sky, seeing the upturned bowl or firmament as the writer of *Genesis* 1 identified. Many philosophers, especially Kant, have regarded the sense of wonder in the world as the beginning of philosophy. I didn't want to forget that. Nor did I want to rule out the other primary questions one has, especially of one's meaning in the world. Why should Ayer, and the dogmatic atheists and scientists he represented, rule out all other forms of knowledge? Isn't Ayer's view a "metaphysical" one, that is, of a particular kind? And, Ayer's very "verification" axiom is itself beyond the rules he attempted to establish. One cannot "verify" it with Ayer's own verification principle. A great strength of Ayer's was his lucid polemical writing. It was thrilling to follow the arguments of this fine stylist. I got ahold of his *The Problem of Knowledge*, 1956, and would shortly acquire his *The Central Questions of Philosophy,* 1973, this last his Gifford Lectures for 1972. I argued with him.

It was in May that the Watergate hearings began. I watched by myself or in company the Senate Hearings, chaired by Senator Sam Ervin, Democrat of North Carolina, and flanked by Howard Baker, Republican of Tennessee. Their assisting senators on both sides were Lowell Weicker (R. Conn.),Edward Gurney,(R. Fla), Daniel Inouye (D. Hawaii), Joseph Montoya (D. NM). Ervin himself was great fun to watch, as he kept the hearings moving forward with the help of Counsel Sam Dash. (Baker and the Republicans had Fred Thompson of Tennessee, who would later become a senator, nominee for President, and then an actor in Hollywood movies.) I found everything about this high drama riveting. Professor Moody had the insightful observation that the establishment of the country had been warning for years about hippies and those in long hair, and here were these advertising executives with crewcuts subverting the Federal Government. A major theme of the hearings was: is the President equivalent to a monarch, and therefore sovereign? Or are the people?

I was reading *Eleanor and Franklin* by Joseph P. Lash at this time. (It had been published in 1971.) I found out that this fascinating man had kept a diary with a few lines every day, and I decide to imitate him. Now, more than forty years later I can read what this young naïve student recorded day by day for five years, until I entered Seminary. Beginning in winter of 1972–3, I began noting how often mother and dad were fighting. I became determined to move away as soon as I could, for my own sanity and quiet. In the meantime, I persuaded them to let me move downstairs where I set up book shelves for my growing library, and a place to listen to classical music. I kept most of what I was thinking to myself, because both my parents would overreact to anything I wished, finding it threatening. When I heard that several of my friends were applying for Michigan State, or Central Michigan, I did too. I was accepted at both in March of 1973. Then a bolt from the blue occurred when the Divisional Commander of the Salvation Army for the Western Michigan Division ordered us to move to Janesville, Wisconsin. We would move at the end of June. I broached my plans to my parents at a rare time when they were talking to one another. (They were both now talking freely about leaving the Salvation Army.) I wished to attend Michigan State, and several friends were heading there as well. My dad responded that it was time to get a full time job, and my mother cried and cried. Bill was adamant that he would stay in the Soo, as he had become a star baseball and football athlete at Sault Area High School. It would be his senior year. Dawn volunteered to stay and work to take care of Bill. Mother said to me on various occasions that she wouldn't know what to do if I didn't move with them to Janesville. Mother was used to using her emotional control on me. (You may decide if you wish to attend church, but let me tell you how sad and disappointed I'll be if you don't.) Now she said she didn't know if she loved dad, and I was her mainstay. So, Robin and I moved with our parents to Janesville.

XIII

THE FIRST FEW MONTHS in Janesville were miserable. Mother hated the house, and worked for a long time to get permission to buy a new Salvation Army "quarters". I had left behind my friends and friendship with Professor Moody, and I had no idea how to find a job. There was an extension of the University of Wisconsin in Janesville, and I slowly made preparations to apply and get financial aid. From the first I was challenged by the fact that I would have to pay out of state tuition, unless I could get a legislator in Madison to approve me for a grant. I met with several, but they were already committed to other students. So I found out what I needed to do to attend U-Rock (Rock County). The class list looked very inviting, with a number of the professors coming from Madison or other extensions. I signed up for a survey of English Literature with Lars Christiansen, Post War Europe and the Cold War with Robert Storch, an introduction to Philosophy with a Buddhist, and a Theater class with Felicia L. I also was chosen to sing in Ted Kinnamon's Madrigal Choir.

Without a job, I spent much time in the public library. I read Chaim Potok, Bertrand Russell, David Halberstam's *The Best and The Brightest*, Solzhenitsyn's *August 1914*, more books by Walter Kaufman especially his *Critique of Religion and Philosophy*, *Existentialism From Dostoevsky to Sartre*, and his books about Hegel, Goethe— *Faust*, Part One and selections of Part Two, and numerous translations of Nietzsche's major writings at the time available in *The Portable Nietzsche*, and *Basic Writings of Nietzsche*, and Kaufmann's superb biography of *Nietzsche: Philosopher, Psychologist, Antichrist*. Kaufmann for the most part ignored the dead end of much American and British philosophy at the time, of Linguistic Analysis, and Logical Positivism. Neither, he wrote, were creative ways of approaching the great problems of life, and both were evidence of the desiccation of philosophy. Philosophers of either school were simply combing the hair of a corpse. This calls to my mind Browning's sardonic poem "A Grammarian's Funeral", the scholar focused on death:

> "Wilt thou trust death or not?" He answered "Yes:
>
> Hence with Life's pale lure"...
>
> [he] throws himself on God, and unperplexed
>
> Seeking shall find him.

So, with the throttling hands of death at strife,

Ground he at grammar;

Still, thro' the rattle, parts of speech were rife:

While he could stammer

He settled *Hoti*'s business—let it be!—

Properly placed *Oun*—

Gave us the doctrine of the enclitic *De*,

Dead from the waist down.[1]

Rather, Kaufman read Nietzsche, Buber, Dostoevsky, as great literature, speaking to cultured people with imaginative approaches to life and death. He especially bowed before Soren Kierkegaard as the man who fearlessly questioned the many decisions modern humans make in bad consciousness, cowardice, self-deception.

It was at U-Rock (University of Wisconsin at Rock County) that I heard some outstanding Classical music. Ted Kinnamon was a joy to be around. He brought the Czech Chamber Philharmonic Orchestra to our small extension, and the brightness and joy of their first piece, Vivaldi's Concerto in A minor, blew me away. What gorgeous music! I was now listening with Kinnamon's help to a great many recordings, as well as a number of soloists and chamber groups which came to school that year. Kinnamon was a delightful teacher, who would discuss literature, film, and especially American politics. He was a main stay in county and State Democratic political organizations, who would argue at the drop of a hat. He recommended I see the movie "The Paper Chase "which I did and loved the acting, particularly of John Houseman as the distinguished Law professor who constantly pushed his students to achieve to the strains of Telemann's "Concerto for Three Trumpets and Tympani in D major" about which I talked with Kinnamon the next day. I have over the years been deeply affected by musical scores by those with fine taste in music, and to a certain extent collect baroque and classical music from movie scores. And fairly quickly I fell in love with Mozart, while watching "Elvira Madigan", Mozart's Piano Concerto 21, andante movement.

In addition to Kinnamon, in my English Literature Professor, Lars Christiansen I found a stimulating teacher. In visiting him many times before the class officially began, he taught me to read Chaucer's fourteenth century *Canterbury Tales*, using a German pronunciation, which begins so famously with:

Whan that April with his showres soote,

The drought of March hath perced to the roote,

And bathed every veine in swich licour,

---

1. Browning, "A Grammarian's Funeral", (lines 111–12, 123–132) 280

Of which vertu engendred is the flowr;

Whan Zephyrus eek with his sweete breeth

Inspired hath in every holt and heeth

The tendre croppes, and the younge sonne

Hath in the Ram his halfe cours yronne,

And smale fowles maken melodye

That sleepen al the night with open ye-

So priketh hem Nature in hir corages-

Thanne longen to goon on pilgrimages,

And palmeres for to seeken straunge strondes

To ferne halwes, couthe in sondry lands;

And specially from every shires ende

Of Engelond to Canterbury they wende,

The holy blisful martyr for to seeke

That hem hath holpen whan that they were seke.[2]

This man loved English Literature and it showed. (From this time on I caught the desire to follow the path of the pilgrims and pray at Canterbury Cathedral where St. Thomas of Canterbury was murdered at the order of Henry II.)

Christiansen was a bachelor, and a WWII veteran, I believe having served in the Pacific, who whenever a class bell sounded, would run to a wall he was near, flatten himself against the wall, and stare wildly as though seeing a ghost, perspiring heavily. Obviously the wartime demons would not leave him be. He informed me that reading literature was serious business, that one must take time over great poetry and prose, and not rush this for the sake of getting to something else. Investing oneself in reading, would cause works of art to remain with one for one's entire life. I valued his counsel. I have discovered myself that since most people in our culture read for distraction or entertainment, the work of serious reading and study can be misunderstood as no more than a pastime. Many years later, in A.N. Wilson's distinguished, and I believe best biography of C. S. Lewis, the author notes the basic misunderstanding of Mrs. Moore, mother of Lewis' friend Paddy Moore who had died in September, 1918, from wartime wounds, had about Lewis' reading:

> [Lewis's] first major prose work—*The Allegory of Love*—took about eight years to complete. This was the price he paid for having thrown in his lot with a person who with all her virtues . . . did not have the concept of a working day. She belonged to that great majority of intelligent human beings who

2. Chaucer, *Canterbury Tales*, 81

think of a book as something to beguile the hours of solitude of an evening. After years of living with Lewis she still knew but did not know that 'a man' could regard reading as the main business of the day and everything else as an interruption.[3]

And Professor Christiansen talked with me freely about my religious doubts. He was a Christian, and let me in on his reasons for this, especially on account of faith: "Faith seeking understanding" he said, quoting St. Anselm's motto, *fides quaerens intellectum.*[4] (In this Anselm was following St. Augustine.[5]) One discovers one has faith in God, and seeks to know more about that. In this sense, faith is a gift from the Holy Spirit, and consequently one wishes to know more. How can that be? This is where I believe so much American religion is desperately mistaken. The general model at play is that by means of salesmanship or persuasion even using a "tone", a preacher can "make" Christians out of sceptics or nominal Christians, or atheists, or whoever. St. Paul is clear in *First Corinthians* 2 that to those who are constantly exposed to a selling or "rhetorical" environment (as in the United States with its incessant barrage of intrusive vulgar advertising) the Gospel needs to be presented without rhetorical tricks. God is actively involved in all human life as in all of His creation. Nothing lives without God.

In my sophomore year at Rock County, I also performed in three plays, As Sir Joseph Surface, a wicked man fun to play due to his being a wastrel, in Sheridan's *School for Scandal*, which the director Dr. Felicia L. moved from the author's eighteenth century to the "Roaring Twenties"; *Offending the Audience*, a play by Peter Handke; and *Three Penny Opera*. I found a whole new group of friends in getting involved in drama, which was good for me, since I was losing the circle I had counted on from Sault Ste. Marie. I met three remarkable characters, Gerald Mahun, an engineer from Ladysmith, and a Ukrainian Roman Catholic, who possessed one of the weirdest senses of humor I've ever come across; J. Leon Miller, an actor and conversationalist who went in and out of various dramatic roles at the drop of a hat, so that he would be Blanche Dubois, then Al Pacino in the Godfather, then Paul Robeson, and Queen Elizabeth II, all in a matter of 30 seconds; and Steven Hemming, a delightful and happy young man , to an extent J. Leon's protégé. Since this was one of the dramatic arts, J. Leon and Steven were clear about their sexual identities as gay. Felicia over the year's time got in the habit of including me in her dramatic dinner parties, something my warring parents never understood. ("You go and have what kind of chicken? Cardin blue? At a dinner party? With homos? And you talk for hours? You need to see a psychiatrist", was my dad's charming way of reacting to my informing him of what I did. Frankly, my entire family needed to have a team of therapists for a week. Especially when my

---

3. Wilson, *C. S. Lewis*, 93

4. St. Anselm, *Proslogium*, 53

5. St. Augustine, *The Trinity*, XV, pro,2, 394

parents left the happy confines of the Salvation Army. Thank God I was ensconced in my new theatrical dysfunctional family.)

U-Rock was not lacking in friendly female company. Especially was this the case in the cast of *Three Penny Opera*. This Bertolt Brecht/Kurt Weill musical in which I played MacHeath was a marvelous escape from home life. The play revolved around the low life of MacHeath (Mack the Knife) a shrewd dashing gangster without the hypocrisies of bourgeois world views. The music was strangely atonal and memorable, as we *petit bourgeois ingénues* pretended to be 1920s Berlin cynics. We began with everyone on stage in street clothes, stripping to underwear and then dressing before our audience. (Felicia was not anything if not *avant garde*.) I found this whole year unsettling, and keeping me off balance. I simply didn't know what was, but everything seemed upended in my life. I didn't know what to make of Felicia's attentions. She was kind and sought out my friendship, inviting me to visit her several nights a week, in various groups of ten, or six, or two. (I was one of the two.) Felicia had a crush on a one of her male students every year. Two years before on Roger Ames, then Gary Brill, and now me. Gerald said she was working her way through the alphabet. She was European, French-or so I thought, tall, graceful, and despondent, even morose. She was married to Wayne L. who taught French this and that at Ripon College. Wayne was in the process of changing his name to Venn, and was somewhat ambivalent in his sexual identity. So Felicia compensated, as they say. When the Swedish actress Viveca Lindfors, trained for the stage in Uppsala to play Strindberg and Shakespeare, having just divorced her fourth husband at 52, came to Janesville at Felicia's invitation, I was her escort (Venn was there). She was theatrical, melodramatic, expansive, "Marlene Dietrichesque" with low throaty or smoky voice, in fact I thought imitating Dietrich. She was at our UW-Rock school to perform her one-woman play ingeniously named "I am a Woman!". I remember at the dinner table her moving closely to me, which was fun, but soon in her cups, imitating Dietrich exulting over asparagus, while the rest of us watched her performance, one hand on her cigarette holder, one hand on my knee, while she leaned far too close to me, into my space, like the Beloved Disciple leaning towards St. Peter in Da Vinci's "Last Supper". (For all readers of Dan Brown's trash book, DaVinci identifies each disciple in his notebooks.[6]) When I asked what she was doing, she said she was remembering actors she had known, Clint Eastwood, Charlton Heston, Errol Flynn, and Jeffrey Hunter, the last in "King of Kings". Had I heard of it? "Isn't that about Jesus?" I asked. "Yes!", she exclaimed. (She would go on to win an Emmy for an awful television sitcom.) Great, I thought. Two narcissistic European women needing too much of *je ne sais quoi*. Who wouldn't get weary with this kind of "Glitter and be Gay" life? (Felicia gave me Bernstein's *Candide*, with this song on it. It summed up for me what was soul numbing around this frivolous social life.) On my birthday, I informed Felicia I couldn't come over for brownies, because I was seeing someone. That night at home, the young lady and I were freaked out hearing

6. Da Vinci, *Notebooks,* 232

XIII

something metallic scraping one of my bedroom windows, and hearing howling. I ran outside and saw brownies had been smeared all over the glass. Felicia was determined I get some brownies. We had a talk.

XIV

In the second semester, the spring of 1974, the focus was once again nationally on Nixon's fall. It would be a few months until his resignation. A new favorite professor whom I found completely balanced in his political and moral judgments, was Dr. Cedric Tarr, the chairperson of Political Science. Not only was his approach to American political thought balanced and judicious, but on two occasions he helped shift my way of thinking. First, he said he was an Episcopalian, and that at a seminary nearby (Nashotah House) was a professor of outstanding qualities, Dr. Robert Marsh Cooper. Tarr had heard him speak at a forum on several moral issues facing the country, and could carefully distinguish among moral, political, and theological ways of approaching issues such as homosexuality, abortion, women's rights, open marriage, with just the apt quotation to illustrate his point. He quoted (said Tarr) Latin maxims, Homer's *Illiad*, Thucydides, St. Paul, Karl Barth, and Freud, deftly weaving this into his presentation and responses to questions. Tarr had never heard anyone like this. He also mentioned a sentence or two of a quotation from George Steiner's *Nostalgia for the Absolute* (1974) which Cooper used, which book I found and bought (beginning my love affair with Steiner). The sense of the quotation concerned the consequences of the loss of nerve in the Christian sensibility in the West. We are now left with various entirely secular even nihilistic mythologies: Freudianism, Marxism, the religio-cultural or structuralist project of Levi Strauss, and the blatant superstitions or pseudo sciences now at work in the United States, Canada and the West generally. Steiner observes in the chapter "Little Green Men":

> The cults of unreason, the organized hysterias, the obscurantism which have become so important a feature of Western sensibility and behavior during these past decades, are comical and often trivial to a degree; but they represent a failure of maturity, a self-demeaning, which are, in essence, tragic.
>
> [In] terms of money and of time spent, of the number of men and women involved to a greater or lesser degree, in terms of the literature produced and of institutional ramifications, ours is the psychological and the social climate most infected by superstition, by irrationalism, of any since the decline of the Middle Ages and perhaps, even since the time of crisis in the Hellenistic world.
>
> An entire edifice of pseudo-science has been erected on the foundation of certain unquestionably interesting anomalies in human perception and in the laws of statistics, which are not, of course, laws in any irrevocable,

transcendentally deterministic sense. Coincidences, many of them grossly unverifiable, are assigned uncanny weight. Kinks, or apparently anomalous clusters in what should be a purely random series of happenings-the right card turning up, a better-than-average divination of concealed symbols-these are cited in evidence of an occult, animist view of the universe. Unbeknown to himself, but in many ways wholly familiar to adepts of Rosicrucianism, of the Golden Lotus, of the Hidden Atlantis, modern man is enmeshed in a network of psychic forces. There are reversals or synchronisms of time in which past, present, and future overlap. The astral presences will be made manifest; the die will turn up all sixes; the number on your dog license is the cube thrice halved of the telephone number of the beloved. The builders of the pyramids knew, Nostradamus knew, Mme Blavatsky whispered the secret to Willie Yeats. Send for the free introductory booklet.[1]

For the first time I thought I would like to attend a seminary which would include such a faculty member on their masthead. A short time later, I looked for a passage in a Mark Twain book, which I thought, spoke about the human possibilities with self-help or human potential movements. Hal Holbrook in his latest performances of "Mark Twain Tonight", had included a darkly humorous passage about humanity. In a monologue taken from one of Twain's posthumously published *Letters From The Earth*, Holbrook quoted Twain thus:

Man is the reasoning animal. Such is the claim. I think it is open to dispute. Indeed, my experiments have proven to me that he is the unreasoning animal. Note his history . . . It seems plain to me that whatever he is he is not a reasoning animal. His record is the fantastic record of a maniac. I consider that the strongest count against his intelligence is the fact that with that record back of him he blandly sets himself up as the head animal of the lot: whereas by his own standards he is the bottom one.

In truth, man is incurably foolish. Simple things which the other animals easily learn, he is incapable of learning. Among my experiments was this. In an hour I taught a cat and a dog to be friends. I put them in a cage. In another hour I taught them to be friends with a rabbit. In the course of two days I was able to add a fox, a goose, a squirrel and some doves. Finally, a monkey. They lived together in peace; even affectionately.

Next in another cage I confined an Irish Catholic from Tipperary, and as soon as he seemed tame I added a Scotch Presbyterian from Aberdeen. Next a Turk from Constantinople; a Greek Christian from Crete; an Armenian; a Methodist from the wilds of Arkansas; a Buddhist from China; a Brahman from Benares. Finally, A Salvation Army Colonel from Wapping. Then I stayed away two whole days. When I came back to note results, the cage of Higher Animals was all right, but in the other, there was but a chaos of gory odds and

---

1. Steiner, *Nostalgia For The Absolute*, 38, 41–2

ends of turbans and fezzes and plaids and bones and flesh-not a specimen left alive. These Reasoning Animals had disagreed on a theological detail and carried the matter to a Higher Court.[2]

How could humanity save itself? Young people my age had the generally accepted view that we would succeed where our parents (the World War II generation) had failed. Much of our music was about "Give Peace a Chance". The Youngbloods sang, "Come on people now, smile on your brother, everybody get together try to love one another right now". After all our parents' generation had accomplished in taking down the twin evils of Nazism and Tojo's imperialism, we had ended those great powers and their spreading of darkness into Europe and Asia. And we had come to recognize the reality of evil. (Perhaps not so much in ourselves, with all our naiveté and forgetfulness of our own history.) Walter Lippmann had written about this in the 1930s:

> The modern skeptical world has been taught for some 200 years a conception of human nature in which the reality of evil, so well known to the ages of faith, has been discounted. Almost all of us grew up in an environment of such easy optimism that we can scarcely know what is meant, though our ancestors knew it well, by the satanic will. We shall have to recover this forgotten but essential truth-along with so many others that we lost when, thinking we were enlightened and advanced, we were merely shallow and blind.[3]

We were now locked in this Cold War with our former ally, without which the West could not possibly have won the War, putting all our trust in our rational advantages as Americans to invent greater technological gadgets and weapons to bring total peace to the world. The best and the brightest of the Kennedy Administration had all come together to bring the American hegemony over the world, and peace would be the result. Vietnam would be the test case. And then we had gotten bogged down in the quagmire of that war, in a small third world country, which was devastated by our bombing and missiles, and should have pleaded for peace terms, but which stayed potent enemies of ours. And then after Tet, when the American people began to notice they were being lied to about our winning the War (which George Romney had stated), which began tearing America apart, our political and military leaders had no idea what to do. Maybe we couldn't do whatever we wanted with all the new technological advances we kept bragging about. Maybe human beings could not be subjected to the scientific methods as things and objects were, and be shown to act predictably. Maybe there is far more mystery in life than the Modernists and Enlightened philosophes and scientists had so confidently proclaimed. Maybe there was something to what Christians referred to as "sin" as something very dark and unmanageable and unfathomable at the heart of each human being, and at work in the world itself. How else do you consider the most enlightened men gathering in Philadelphia in 1787 to

2. Twain, *Letters From The Earth*, 181-2
3. Quoted in Pelikan, *Jesus through the Centuries*, 76

establish a Federal Constitution, which would be based entirely on reason, and the learning of the best from Roman and Greek and British traditions, and then leave the "sleeping serpent of slavery" of an entire race embedded in the same Constitution, "coiled under the table", in John Jay Chapman's words? And the word "slaves" wasn't even used, but "other persons".

Maybe as Robert McNamara, the most brilliant of the cool reasonable Kennedy people—the master of using objective statistical patterns and results to arrive at the correct and necessary answers—finally admitted, reason and empiricism have their limits. And America was suffering from the responsibility we had inflicting this war on Southeast Asia. (Pogo's "we have met the enemy, and he is us".) I saw that. Many of my generation came to that conclusion. Many of those who returned from fighting the war were also suffering. What could be said about war? A 19th century humorist put it: "War is God's way of teaching Americans geography". (Not Ambrose Bierce. Attributed to attorney Edgar Wilson, who wrote by the pen name "Bill Nye", a name famous from a Brett Harte poem.)

My generation believed that by the right "emotion", or "feeling", or "love", we would be able to bring about peace. All we were saying, was give peace a chance! Couldn't we with great feeling, sincerity, "authenticity", bring about the Utopia we all longed for? And we could sing about it with the most authentic instrument of all, the guitar. It makes me blush to think how I could get caught up in this *Weltschmerz* this great "feeling" as we had received this from the Romantics. My friends would laugh when I would mention that the Beatles had sung, "All you need is love", and then promptly broke up. But Cat Stevens, Seals and Crofts, James Taylor, Peter, Paul and Mary, for God's sake couldn't all be wrong? Charlie Brown put this as clearly as anyone, "How can I be wrong, when I feel it so sincerely?"

In the spring of my sophomore year, 1974, Dr. Cedric Tarr alerted me that I had won a scholarship to an adult education week in Door County, called "The Clearing". This remote picturesque location, housed in log cabins, just outside of Ellison Bay, Wisconsin, was hosting two scholars, Dr. George Anastaplo from the University of Chicago, and Dr. Leo Alvarez from the University of Texas/Austin. They would teach adult seminars in a graduate school style from August 5–11. And about that same time, my fellow student and new friend Gerald Mahun asked me to room with him in the fall at The University of Wisconsin, Madison. In April, Gerald and I drove the 45 minute trip north to Madison and signed up for housing across the street from the Brat und Brau, at the Regent Street Apartments, not far from Camp Randall Stadium where the Badgers play football.

XV

MY SCHOOL WORK IMPROVED greatly in the spring of my sophomore year. In part I found that I had finally learned to write a sentence that was sensible. My teachers at this little out of the way extension in Janesville had become friends, and they were to a person enjoyable in conversation as well as in class. My ability to use words, and even to enjoy the sounds of words, had been with me from early on in my life as I was always around adults. Constructing an argument verbally was what I particularly desired from about age 8 or 9 or so, and the use of facts, or axioms, or quotations, along with a humorous or clever expression was a gift I had and wanted to develop. So, I was attracted to well-spoken and well written statements, arguments, novels, political or biographical works, as well as any thoughtful writing on culture, philosophy, religion, science, which might evince the historical development of an idea, or concept. For some time from tenth grade on I read serious literature and non-fiction. And I found how much I liked analyzing the work and weighing if what I found was worthwhile, and what wasn't, and even more what might affect me "existentially". I began to affect being an intellectual snob, a *poseur*, and found the company of students or adults who lacked interest, reasoning, verbal skill, and especially imagination, not worth my time. From high school and subsequently, I liked William F. Buckley, Winston Churchill, Garry Wills, Barbara Tuchman, Mark Twain, Harper Lee's *To Kill a Mockingbird*, George Orwell, Oscar Wilde, David Halberstam, Loren Eiseley. In my first two years of college, I discovered Graham Greene, Evelyn Waugh, George Steiner, Thomas Carlyle, Jane Austen, G. K. Chesterton, Samuel Johnson. Having gotten my first taste of poetry lovingly, carefully recited with understanding by Prof. Lars Christiansen, I began reading poets and dramatists who had caught my attention in classes: John Donne, Alexander Pope, Spenser, Shakespeare, Edward Albee, Harold Pinter, T. S. Eliot, Robert Frost, Edna St. Vincent Millay, W.H. Auden, Chaucer, Wordsworth, Keats, Shelly, Byron, Robert Browning, Tennyson. I remember being thrilled by coming across Bruce Catton's Civil War books, Wilfred Sheed's *People Will Always Be Kind*, *Catcher in the Rye*, John Updike's novels. I read many biographies first, and then works by an author. Gore Vidal's *Julian* caught my eye, and for the first time I got an insight into Fourth Century A.D. Rome, the crucial century for the Christian Church in becoming legal, and then the religion of the Roman Empire. Julian (the Apostate) was a hero to Vidal, for his iconoclastic rejection of his family's faith in Christ, and grand gesture in returning the Empire to its pagan past. Vidal's novel is filled with colorful characters, Licinius—the cultured, aristocratic pagan who taught Julian and his friends, the Cappadocian Fathers as they were later called, Gregory of Nyssa, Basil of Caesarea, and Gregory of Nazianzus. These last three Church fathers were instrumental through their writings, leadership and diplomacy, in getting much of the now Christian empire, to support the great Athanasius, and affirm the Nicene Creed with its Trinitarian Confession. Julian lasted about two and a half years as Emperor and died in 363. The Cappadocians were instrumental in getting the second great Council of the Church at Constantinople in 381 to add the clarifying language of the full deity of the Holy Spirit as God, as well as Father and Son.

With a very few exceptions, I found various forms of Christian belief expressed in these writers, here and there, a Catholic statement, a quotation from Scripture, an allusion to the cross, or a basis for the truth of God. Or a desire to find the truth. Very early on in my freshman year, I began wondering how it was that there was an I, a consciousness, an inner self, a soul, my interior life. Cardinal Newman had written that of two persons in all truth he had no doubt, God and himself. I thought that also. I was aware of my consciousness. That the I that I am, both acts externally on the world, and negotiates life day by day, so to speak, and is very mysterious internally, even to me, in my imaginative inner life, which no one is privy to knowing, except that that I share, and reveal consciously or unconsciously, by what I say and do, and don't say or do. The questions of Who am I? Why Am I here? Why is there anything at all? Why was I born in 1954 and lived as Dale, to Dale and Eva Coleman, Caucasian and Lumbee, with those forebears, to parents in Michigan, in the United States, born with a sister already, and two more siblings afterward, with an insatiable curiosity about the world, and about books? Why? Is there a God? If not, how was I and indeed all of life created? Why is there something rather than nothing? And why is so much American religion so inane and anti-intellectual, and having nothing to do with real life, in fact not mindful of what is said in the Bible about God? Why is so much American Christianity individualist, reliant on feelings and moralism, or nationalistic? Or destructive? Why doesn't my mind matter? Or my inner self?

XVI

I MET AN INTERESTING man at one of the plays in which I acted, in May 1974. His name was Tom Misurek, and he enjoyed conversation. He had been a Roman Catholic seminarian a few years before, and continued to have a keen interest in religious matters. He and his wife Chris invited me to dinner several times, and I took a bottle of Madeira or port or cream sherry, to talk. Tom had found a brief book on Jesus helpful, himself, C. H. Dodd's *The Founder of Christianity*. We slowly worked our way through the book, which taught me to weigh historical evidence carefully in looking at first century writings about Jesus, and what kind of a figure he was. The book laid out Jesus' mission, and claims of his miracles, as well as his teaching, his gathering around him twelve apostles, whom he formed as disciples, and the announcement of all of this as the Kingdom of God. The book was the first of the kind I had read, and I was fascinated. We moved on to a new book just published by Catholic theologian, Hans Kueng, entitled *On Being a Christian*. In a review, Fr. Andrew Greeley had promoted this book by the Tubingen professor, stating he hoped readers would have the mental discipline to read the entire work, and take time with the author's footnotes. The book was important to me in that the argument of Kueng is that Jesus not be presented simply as a great religious teacher, but as the one who had come sent by God as Savior of the world. Kueng's approach had been that of a "Christology" from below, that is, by seeing the human Jesus in his time and place, and in the context of his Jewish life. Then Kung looked at the witnesses to Jesus' Resurrection, with a painstaking examination of the four Gospel writers' varied pictures of Jesus. Kueng had already published a much hailed ecclesiology, or theology of the Church in the 1960s (dedicated to Archbishop Michael Ramsey), and here tied the Kingdom proclaimed by Jesus to the historical Church in all its strengths and weaknesses. Kung pursued a central theme of the church witnessing through its very being Jesus himself, crucified and resurrected. Jesus commanded those who heard him to respond in faith, defined as intellectual assent in the Roman Catholic Church's dogmas, receive baptism, and receive the Eucharist. This seemed to me much closer to the meaning of following Jesus in the New Testament than anything I had come across in Fundamentalism.

I also discovered C. S. Lewis. This Belfast born Oxford Professor of Elizabethan literature, had taken up the cause of an avocation of Christian apologist. His broadcasts to war-torn Britain in the 1940s on the meaning of the Christian faith were electrifying in their meaning of what Christians believe and live as called by Christ

Himself. He had been born in 1898, baptized by his maternal grandfather, a Church of Ireland priest, and brought up in the Victorian home of a Northern Irish solicitor as he describes so famously in his autobiography, *Surprised by Joy*. This is the Lewis book which affected me most of all his entire *oeuvre*. He describes in all candor his childhood and the event which changed him entirely, the death of his mother when he was ten. His descriptions of the "public school" he attended with its graphic terror to a young sensitive boy, the Wynyard School in Watford, Hertfordshire, in 1908, are deeply unsettling. And he was sent there shortly after his mother's death. The headmaster of this school, Robert Capron, identified as "Oldie" by Lewis, was shortly after committed to a psychiatric hospital. Following a series of private tutors and private schools, he won a scholarship to attend University College in Oxford in 1916. Shortly thereafter he was drafted in the Great War, witnessed the horrors of trench warfare as a second Lieutenant in the Somerset Light Infantry, and was wounded, while his closest friend, Paddy Moore, was killed. He had solemnly promised to take care of his friend's mother, Janie Moore, noted above, if anything tragic happened to his friend. (And, she was the one who visited him in the hospital-not his own distant father.) So, after demobilization, he returned to University College, won three Firsts (highest grades) in Greek and Latin literature, philosophy and ancient history, and English, from 1920 to 1923. He then became a tutor in philosophy at University College in 1924, after which he was elected as a Fellow and Tutor at Magdalene College, Oxford.

Lewis lived with Mrs. Moore from the time he returned to the University. What was their relationship? Janie was 26 years older than "Jack", very loving, to whom Lewis was attracted. I think the evidence clearly points to a mother/son relationship, which included sexual intimacy. (Has anyone heard of Oedipus?) Lewis' longtime friend of twenty-nine years, Owen Barfield, said the odds were fifty fifty. The brilliant biographer of Lewis, A. N. Wilson, whom I have quoted above, believes it probable. George Sayer noted in his fine biography of Lewis that he disbelieved this possibility. Subsequently, in 1997, he admitted he now believed Lewis and Moore had a sexual component in their relationship. In Wilson's delightful book, the prologue and epilogue concern how Lewis' flame is kept, by conservative Evangelical Wheaton College in Illinois, and by aesthetic bachelor Anglo-Catholic Fr. Walter Hooper, who converted to Roman Catholicism in 1988. Both have their very distinct myths about Lewis. To the former, Lewis is a clear American Evangelical, and therefore his love of beer and alcohol and pipe smoking are only grudgingly acknowledged by his devoted worshippers, the way Elvis fans cannot imagine their King died on his throne. To the latter, Lewis was an obvious Roman Catholic wannabee, and a perpetual virgin, even after his marriage to the divorcee' Joy Davidman. (If anyone doubts the psychological projections of a totem by even highly educated people, one could do worse than meditating on these hilarious versions of Lewis by his acolytes, low church and high church.)

Lewis narrates his early life, and even his atheism from age 15. From an early age, he had shared with his only sibling, Warren, a love for the Norse Gods. While reading Longfellow's *Saga of King Olaf* as a youngster, he had come upon the phrase:

> I heard a voice that cried, Balder the beautiful
>
> Is dead, is dead . . . [1]

This caused Lewis a sense of an ineffable *mysterium tremendum et fascinans*; or identified perhaps with Rudolph Otto's *Das Heilige*, (1923), to which Lewis would come to refer in *The Problem of Pain* as the Numinous.[2] This experience was associated with Lewis as one of awe, and *sui generis*. Experiences of this kind are found throughout not only Jewish and Christian Scriptures, but those of other major world religions as well. (Schleiermacher spoke of this experience as that of "the feeling of absolute dependence" and spoke about the "God Consciousness" in everyone accessed through this feeling, and leaving the incarnate historical Jesus—the *Sondernkind* or problem child in Barth's word-out in the cold.[3] Lewis does not follow Schleiermacher's error of speaking of the Truth of Christianity reduced to a "religion" in which feeling—not faith-and especially not a reasonable one, takes the uppermost place in response to a "God event". Moreover, this "feeling of absolute dependence in one's God Consciousness" is filtered through the variety of religio-historical-cultural constructs, of which Christianity is one.[4] More on this "Gnosis" below.)

However, these experiences of Lewis', for there were others, were never integrated into a coherent religious doctrine, and he speaks of being strongly influenced by the clever skepticism of rationalist Edward Gibbon's *Decline and Fall of the Roman Empire*. He further remarks that the atheistic argument against God's existence came firmly from some lines of Lucretius in his *De Rerum Naturam* (*On the Nature of Things*):

> *Nequaquam nobis divinitus esse paratam*
>
> *Naturam rerum; tanta stat praedita culpa*
>
> Had God designed the world, it would not be
>
> A world so frail and faulty as we see. [5]

---

1. Lewis, *Surprised by Joy*, 17

2. Lewis, *The Problem of Pain*, 5–6

3. Barth, *Epistle to the Romans*, 30

4. Schleiermacher, *The Christian Faith*, 13

5. Lewis, *Surprised by Joy*, 65

C. S. Lewis' telling of his conversion despite the philosophical climate of humanism, empiricism and logical positivism, of skepticism, affected me greatly. He too emphasized that there are more forms of knowledge than positivism, which intimidated so many of his and my own age. He found around the same time G. K. Chesterton's *The Everlasting Man, which* provided him with a Christian outline of history. And that after believing what he described being in a "show down" with God, he got on his knees and accepted that "God was God"; the only God revealed in his Son, Jesus Christ. [6]

Lewis' books, written between the 1930s and 1960s, include his broadcast talks during the War years. These three sets of lectures, published as *The Case for Christianity, Christian Behavior, and Beyond Personality,* struck me when I first looked them over as rather old-fashioned and stilted. I still think that. Still less did I find his fiction writings interesting. I have never "gotten" his children's Narnia series books, nor his science fiction Perelandra series. It was his autobiography, his *Oxford History of English Literature in the Sixteenth Century, Excluding Drama,* (with its ten very fine pages on Hooker), *Allegory of Love, Preface to Paradise Lost, The Discarded Image,* and *Studies in Words,* and finally the mythic novel *Till We Have Faces,* which he wrote with his American divorcee' lady friend who became his wife Joy Davidman, which affected me most. My introduction to Lewis took place with the first book of his I owned, *God in the Dock,* edited by Walter Hooper. In this collection of Lewis' various articles, talks, reviews, supplemented later by *Christian Reflections,* I was deeply impressed first by his introduction to Sr. Penelope's translation of St. Athanasius' great work *The Incarnation of the Word of God.* (The man wrote beautiful prose, obviously influenced by his tremendously deep knowledge and love of the Latin language and classics.) In this "On the Reading of Old Books", Lewis made two points that have stayed with me for over forty years. The first has to do with someone who loves literature must be very careful if they wish to remain agnostic or pagan, because the "something" of the Christian faith sneaks up on the unsuspecting reader in a seductive way:

> I myself was first led into reading the Christian classics, almost accidentally, as a result of my English studies. Some, such as Hooker, Herbert, Traherne, Taylor and Bunyan, I read because they are themselves great English writers; others, such as Boethius, St. Augustine, Thomas Aquinas and Dante, because they were 'influences'. George McDonald I had found for myself at age sixteen and never wavered in my allegiance, though I tried for a long time to ignore his Christianity. They are, you will note, a mixed bag, representative of many Churches, climates and ages. And that brings me to yet another reason for reading them. The divisions of Christendom are undeniable and are by some of these writers fiercely expressed. But if any man is tempted to think—as one might be tempted who read only contemporaries—that 'Christianity' is a word of so many meanings that it means nothing at all, he can learn beyond all doubt by stepping out of his own century, that this is not so. Measured

6. Lewis, *Surprised by Joy,* 228–9

against the ages 'mere Christianity' turns out to be no insipid interdenominational transparency, but something positive, self-consistent, and inexhaustible. I know it, indeed, to my cost. In the days when I still hated Christianity, I learned to recognize, like some all too familiar smell, that almost unvarying *something* which met me, now in Puritan Bunyan, now in Anglican Hooker, now in Thomist Dante. It was there (honeyed and floral) in Francois de Sales; it was there (grave and homely) in Spenser and Walton; it was there (grim but manful) in Pascal and Johnson; there again with a mild, frightening, Paradisial flavour, in Vaughan and Boehme and Traherne. In the urban society of the eighteenth century one was not safe-Law and Butler were two lions in the path. The supposed 'Paganism' of the Elizabethans could not keep it out; it lay in wait where a man might have supposed himself safest, in the very centre of *The Faerie Queene* and the *Arcadia*. It was, of course, varied; and yet-after all— so unmistakably the same; recognizable, not to be evaded, the odour which is death to us until we allow it to become life . . . [7]

Later on in the same essay, Lewis notes the delight he takes in reading Christian "doctrine" rather than Christian "devotional works":

Now the layman or amateur needs to be instructed as well as to be exhorted. In this age his need for knowledge is particularly pressing . . . For my own part, I tend to find the doctrinal books often more helpful in devotion than the devotional books, and I rather suspect that the same experience may await many others. I believe that many who find that 'nothing happens' when they sit down, or kneel down, to a book of devotion, would find that the heart sings unbidden while they are working their way through a tough bit of theology with a pipe in their teeth and a pencil in their hand.[8]

I also began watching Kenneth Clark's brilliant *Civilisation* on PBS television and picked up the book to follow along. I found the series enthralling as Clark began by describing the decline of the ancient Greek and Roman world with an imagined "you are there" at the end of the Roman Empire, as he shows us the great aqueduct the "Pont du Gard" and Nimes not far from the Mediterranean. This is the World popularized in America of the 1930s to 1960s as the "Dark Ages" by the middlebrow Will and Ariel Durant, and described magisterially in Gibbon's breathtakingly capacious *Decline and Fall of the Roman Empire*, mostly because of (I believe) staunch prejudices against Christianity. [9] Gibbon famously wrote: "The various modes of worship which prevailed in the Roman world, were all considered by the people as equally true; by the philosophers as equally false; and by the magistrates as equally useful".[10] I had accepted the characterizing of the Catholic Church from roughly 410 AD to 1066 AD

7. Lewis, *God in the Dock*, 203–4

8. Lewis, *God in the Dock*, 205

9. Famously said by John Henry Newman, *Idea of University*, 195–6

10. Gibbon, *Decline and Fall*, II,2

(the Durants' dating) first and foremost due to the general *Zeitgeist* among academicians and journalists and pundits, and many others in what has been termed "the communications class", almost all "middlebrow". (In using this term I think first of Dwight Macdonald's describing and then satirizing the "middlebrow" in his *Masscult and Midcult* in 1960. The Book of the Month Club, and news weeklies *Time*, *Newsweek*, and the *US News and World Report*, along with the Oprah Book Club all fit in this category. Paul Fussell's lively little books, *Class: A Guide Through the American Status System*, (1983), and *BAD: or, The Dumbing of America*, (1991) designate and skewer the vulgarizing mass consumerism of American culture.)

Religion according to the Durants in the "Dark Ages" was mostly "primitive", superstitious, anti-scientific, and irrational. To this was added Freudian notions of projections of irrational fears. Kenneth Clark spoke quite differently about what the great Princeton historian Peter Brown would term "late antiquity" dated between 200–1000 AD, replacing the entire "dark ages" motif. In evincing the sense of "heaviness" in the dying world of the Graeco-Roman world which had lasted five hundred years, and quoting T.S. Eliot's "These fragments have I shored against my ruin" from *The Wasteland*, Clark spoke of the fragility of civilization, how seemingly "complex and solid", but actually quite evanescent it is. Clark goes on to say what was at the heart of the failure of this "complex and solid" world which crumbled:

> What are its enemies? Well, first of all fear—fear of war, fear of invasion, fear of plague and famine, that make it simply not worthwhile constructing things, or planting trees or even planning next year's crops. And fear of the supernatural, which means that you daren't question anything or change anything. The late antique world was full of meaningless rituals, mystery religions, that destroyed self-confidence. And then exhaustion, the feeling of hopelessness which can overtake people even with a high degree of material prosperity. There is a poem by the modern Greek poet, Cavafy, in which he imagines the people of an antique town like Alexandria waiting every day for the barbarians to come and sack the city. Finally the barbarians move off somewhere else and the city is saved; but the people are disappointed—it would have been better than nothing. [11]

By the end of his first chapter, Clark presents his considered thoughts about how Christian monasticism and the Christian Church saved the civilization of the Western world, and then by 800 AD infused this world with the new energy of the Christian Gospel. One might note in passing that the great stylist in Greek from the first century AD on-using the *Koine* form of the language common everywhere by then—was St. Paul. (This was realized with the 1896 discoveries by Grenfell and Hunt of the vast papyri fragments at Oxyrhynchus, South of Cairo, of *Koine* Greek used in all sorts of situations, including both every day communications, and literary writings

11. Clark, *Civilisation*, 3–4

dating from the Hellenistic world created by Alexander the Great, d. 323 BC Trained classicists had looked down their noses at the common or vulgar Greek of the New Testament writings, before this find.) Likewise, St. Augustine's Latin is arguably the finest style from the second century AD and later. Clark noted that one of the great easily remembered dates occurs with the coronation of Charlemagne on Christmas Day 800 AD.

Civilisation was for me a great discovery in teaching about masterpieces of art: painting, sculpture, monuments, buildings. His own inspiration for looking at civilization from this point of view was John Ruskin's maxim: "Great nations write their autobiographies in three manuscripts, the book of deeds, the book of their words and the book of their art. Not one of these books can be understood unless we read the two others, but of the three the only trustworthy one is the last." [12] Clark's book ends with deep concern about the twentieth century's "Heroic Materialism" and the prospect of facing life with the creations of destructive weapons holding every living thing hostage to the immediate prospect of annihilation. And we may not only foresee with Clark barbarians on the horizon, but realize how completely they have gained control as the rulers of this age.

12. Clark, *Civilisation*, 1

XVI

I FINISHED MY SEMESTER and prepared to move to Madison in August, 1974. I spent the late spring and early summer reading, following the drama in Washington DC with impeachment hearings of the President and debate taking place by the House of Representatives' Judiciary Committee. The final act of Richard Nixon and his sheer arrogance becoming almost daily more and more in focus allowed the American people to witness what happens when a President loses touch with his stewardship of the office and routinely abuses the grave responsibility to which he is entrusted. I watched this spectacle and found that Democrat Barbara Jordan of Texas, and Republican Charles Wiggins of California were by far the more able and eloquent among the congressmen in directing their legal cases for and against impeachment. When in the early summer, 1974, Special Prosecutor Leon Jaworski subpoenaed the White House Tapes, and argued successfully before the Supreme Court to have them turned over, the tapes were released in late July ,and the tide was turned in discovering the "smoking gun" of Nixon's own words on June 23, 1972. On that day, the President was heard ordering his top officials to get the director and deputy director of the CIA to pressure the head of the FBI, L. Patrick Gray, to stop investigating the Watergate break-in due to issues of national security. This was a criminal conspiracy to obstruct justice. Nixon's defense in both the House-where he would be impeached, and the Senate-where his fate would be determined, fell apart. Barry Goldwater estimated only 15 senators left to die in Nixon's ditch. On August 8, 1974, the President of the United States resigned from office, gave a strange pathetic speech comparing Teddy Roosevelt's loss of his first wife with the loss of the presidency, and flew away in a helicopter.

By that time, I was attending a gorgeous week at the Clearing, Door County, Wisconsin. I was assimilated quickly by thirty fellow students, who outside myself and a friend from U-Rock, were all older Jewish men and women from northern suburbs of Chicago, some bearing Nazi concentration camp tattoos. I don't think I have ever felt more at home in any educational endeavor than with those who were attending that particular session, because I had so much respect and affection for Jewish people, their love of questing for truth in Western civilization, their history of Israel, and their great courage in coming out of the Holocaust with the desire to reestablish their culture and heritage: their life rising from the ashes, after nearly being erased. They more than any other people, I think, suffered the most during the various pogroms of the twentieth century. They went through the worst of the tribulations granted by vision to St. John the Divine in the New Testament writing called *The Apocalypse*. They had faced the total destructive rages of those monsters or beasts (as identified in Jewish and Christian Apocalyptic literature) Hitler and Stalin. And this gathering of folks loved and admired our teacher for the class, Dr. George Anastaplo, who would focus our attention on Lewis Carroll's 1865 book, *Alice's Adventures in Wonderland*. Anastaplo was from St. Louis, born in 1925, of Greek heritage. He was a fascinating, erudite scholar, deeply knowledgeable about *Torah*, the Bible, ancient Greek and Roman cultures, the history of Greece, the classics, and all things American, especially its history, law, government, religion, and politics. In 1974, he was professor of Political Science and Philosophy at Rosary College in Chicago, and Lecturer of Liberal Arts at the University of Chicago. He admired scholars Alexander Meiklejohn (1872–1964), a renowned philosopher, university administrator (Dean of Brown university from 1901–1913, President of Amherst from 1913–27), educational reformer (especially establishing the Experimental College in Madison, Wisconsin from 1927–1932), and finally establishing the School of Social Studies in San Francisco, an adult education program centered on the great books of Western Civilization, from 1932–1964, dying in Berkeley, California. His great passion was the duty for American citizens to become highly educated for democracy, and keep the founding fathers vision of free speech for at least this purpose. (Recently both Supreme Court justices Stephen Breyer and Ruth Bader Ginsburg have argued the connection between free speech and democracy.)

Anastaplo's other great mentor was Leo Strauss, who was Jewish, born in 1899 in Prussia, a political philosopher and classicist, who had been trained by Ernst Cassirer, the neo-Kantian, at the University of Hamburg, and then studied with phenomenologist Edmund Husserl and metaphysician Martin Heidegger at the Universities of Freiburg and Marburg. He had ties with a who's who of Jewish and European intellectuals during the 1920s and 30s, including the German Zionists Walter Benjamin and Hannah Arendt, Franz Rosenzweig and Gershom Scholem, as well as Hans-George Gadamer, Karl Loewith, Alexander Kojeve, and many others. He wrote *On Tyranny*, and there developed his thinking about political philosophy in appealing to Socrates, Plato, Aristotle and Cicero. He taught Plato's *Republic* utilizing Cicero's insight that this is not about a blueprint for a change in regime, but rather "the nature of political things—the nature of the city"; in other words, descriptive not prescriptive. He warned about modern liberalism and its intrinsic tendency toward relativism, and in turn leading to two kinds of nihilism: the harsh totalitarianisms of Fascist Germany and Stalinist Russia, or the gentler form of liberal democracy and its value-free aimlessness, and a hedonistic "permissive egalitarianism", which he believed on display in the United States. His concern was that political liberty not be considered the end of political thought, but the means for acquiring human excellence and virtue as goals, with the continual question how, and to what extent, can freedom and excellence coexist. He urged political scientists, especially at the University of Chicago where he taught from 1949–69, to learn philosophy, including epistemology, ontology, and metaphysics. He was ever suspicious of Heidegger's ontology, which he believed a *gnosis*, a fantasy, not about actual human beings in societies, the work of a Crypto-Fascist wishing to see total control over human society. [1]

Every day at the Clearing—this vision and development by Jens Jensen, this beautiful spot with its views and flora and fauna on display, we rose at 7am, got around, joined together for coffee, juice and oatmeal, then gathered for George Anastaplo's teaching about Lewis Carroll's Alice, always finding his thoughts stimulating, interesting, even playful. Lewis Carroll was the pseudonym for Charles Lutwidge Dodgson, the strange little man with a quirky sense of humor; a mathematics don at Oxford's Christ Church, a friend of several Tractarians, especially Bishop "Soapy Sam" Wilberforce (whom Thomas Huxley squelched in a renowned public showdown on Darwinian theory), Dr. E.B. Pusey, and Dr. Henry Liddon. Not quite thirty in 1861, he was encouraged to consider Holy Orders by this circle, and he was ordained a deacon in December that same year. (He later refused to take priestly orders.) The Dean of Christ Church was the highly respected classicist, Dr. Henry George Liddell, known to everyone as the co-editor with Dr. R. Scott of the famous Liddell-Scott *Greek—English Lexicon*, of which the first edition was in 1843. It was revised and expanded several times before Liddell's death, the last the eighth edition in 1897. This very well known and handsome scholarly cleric was considered one of the most crashing boors in all of England. He was austere, uncomplimentary, aloof, a man of few words around whom—a friend noted—one would have to choose their words carefully; described by his own "disciple-biographer . . . as 'unsympathetic in demeanor'". [2] Dr. Liddell had married the lovely Lorina, said to be a "prude", and they had a son Harry, and three girls, Lorina, Alice, and Edith. Charles Dodgson got to know the family, on friendly terms, through befriending Harry. Dodgson had a stammer around self-assured men like the Dean. His own father was an eminent Churchman, confident, scholarly, a fine teacher and preacher, a theologian, who was in the 1850s Canon of Ripon, and then Archdeacon of Richmond. His mother is seldom mentioned in his letters or diaries. According to Morton Cohen's fine 1995 biography of Dodgson/Carroll, Archdeacon Dodgson was forceful and highly intelligent, a father who was said on a rare occasion to exhibit charm and wit. Charles both revered and was discomfited by the Archdeacon. And he found that socially he was happiest with little girls aged 8–10. He began visiting the Deanery of Christ Church at times when the Dean was out, and paid special attention to the four little Liddells, with his main focus on the expressive Alice. At times Dodgson would also arrange for a punt to row up and down the River Cherwell just north of the Christ Church meadow. When after a number of visits to see the

1. Strauss, "A Giving of Accounts", 461
2. Cohen, *Lewis Carrol*, 511

children, and some afternoon boatings, always relying on the nanny, Miss Prickett to assist him with the subterfuge of coming and going while the parents were unaware, he began to spin his enormously entertaining tales about little Alice, who became his favorite, most famously during a picnic in July, 1862. And he also photographed the youngsters, with one picture of Alice aged 10, vamping for the camera, even with clothes suggestive of some erotic pose. (Later, he would take innumerable photographs of her and many other girls naked.) This is the background for this strange mathematics don and Deacon of the Church of England. At some point in 1863 the Liddells refused access to his seeing and photographing the children—possibly because he proposed marriage to ten-year-old Alice—so he found many other little girls to photograph, losing interest in them when they reached puberty. He experienced a disgust at seeing pubic hair on women. It is well established that the most famous writer of late Victorian literature, John Ruskin, had a similar neurosis as Dodgson with his marriage to young Effie ending at his inability to consummate the marriage due to the sight of her naked body.[3] Psychosexual maladaptive behaviors, especially the fear of sexual intimacy with adult women, appear to have been a pervasive problem among Victorian men. (The fine writer A. N. Wilson writes about this as well as much more about Dodgson in his outstanding *The Victorians*, and compares him with Ruskin.[4])

The most enjoyable part of every day at the Clearing occurred after dinner. Then a number of the adults would gather in a large circle in the "long room" which had a fireplace and comfortable seating, and the stories would begin, including about Gerald Ford becoming President, and his pardoning Nixon for any crimes having to do with Watergate and the cover up; ahead of his being charged with any crime. Since those who gathered were Jewish, except for Anastaplo and myself, a number of folks would tell a variety of jokes, which I'm sure were hilarious! Except the punchlines were in Yiddish. So I had to ask. Let's everyone stop our fun and explain this to the goy. I loved being included with these vibrant, intelligent, and very funny folks. They even told "gentile" jokes! "One Gentile mother says to another, 'What does your son do?' The other says, proudly, 'He's a truck driver!'. 'Great' says the first one." They would be rolling in the aisles at this. And on it would go accompanied by a variety of wines, non-kosher. They were mostly Reform or non-observant.

And then about 8:30 pm Dr. Anastaplo invited me to sit with him to discuss his latest book, *The Constitutionalist: Notes on the First Amendment*, published in 1971. This tome of over 800 pages concerns various aspects of the First Amendment; a brilliant argument with illustrative stories, statistics, legal briefs before the Supreme Court, quotations from Roman, Greek, English and American jurisprudence, the *Bible*, Shakespeare, literary works, baseball anecdotes, theology, Church History, comic strips, poetry, classical and British philosophy, and American government and history, in the text covering 285 pages, and 400 pages of endnotes. (One reviewer said

3. Hilton, *John Ruskin*, I, 117–120
4. Wilson, *The Victorians*, 324–9

to study these notes would bring one the equivalent of a bachelor's degree.) There are nearly 50 pages of appendices covering various aspects of the First Amendment. And an appendix of 90 pages more or less concerning the most central event of Anastaplo's life: His being refused admission to the State of Illinois bar to become a practicing attorney. (This appendix is a short book in itself.) This was the result from his writing about the American Revolutionary War, and a number of quotations coming from the founding fathers, concerning the conditions under which citizens of the United States could be justified in rebelling against the government. Anastaplo had graduated with an AB and JD degrees from the University of Chicago after serving in the US Army Air Corps as a bomber/navigator during WWII. In a heightened atmosphere of anti-Communist anxiety sweeping the country, Anastaplo was requested to respond to a command of the Committee determining his fitness and loyalty to the United States Government, in writing, concerning what he believed to be the principles underlying the Constitution. He wrote:

> One principle consists of the doctrine of the separation of powers; thus, among the Executive, Legislative, and Judiciary are distributed various func-tions and powers in a manner designed to provide for a balance of power, thereby intending to prevent totally unrestrained action by any one branch of government. Another basic principle (and the most important) is that such government is constituted so as to secure certain inalienable rights, those rights to Life, Liberty and the Pursuit of Happiness (and elements of these rights are explicitly set forth in such parts of the Constitution as the Bill of Rights). *And, of course, whenever the particular government in power becomes destructive of those ends, it is the right of the people to alter or to abolish it and thereupon to establish a new government.* This is how I view the Constitution. (Emphasis supplied.) [5]

In meeting with a two-man Subcommittee of the Committee on character and fitness, one of the members immediately engaged Anastaplo in his meaning, and Anastaplo responded by saying, this sentence came from the Declaration of Independence, and that he believed this meant if the government gets bad enough, the people have a "right of revolution". Now both members began asking Anastaplo if he belonged to any organization on the Attorney General's list, and subsequently had he at that time or at any time been a member of the Communist Party. Anastaplo responded very simply, what were their grounds for asking that? Did they have any evidence whatso-ever that he had been involved in such political activity? They asked him to answer the question. He refused to answer, and stated that given the foundational documents for the United States government, especially the Declaration of Independence and the First Amendment to the Constitution, he would not cede the right to have this particular question answered. The two men then asked him about any other political

5. Anastaplo, *The Constitutionalist*, 368

affiliations he might have, including radical Greek political or paramilitary organizations to which he might be connected. He refused to answer, as he subsequently did refuse to answer questions about belonging to the Ku Klux Klan, or to the Democratic or Republican parties. When asked he gave as his rationale for the people's "right to revolution", that it was a "basic feature of Western Constitutional law". In the words of Anastaplo's counsel before the United States' Supreme Court, his own law professor Malcolm P. Sharp's summary:

> [This right to revolution] has been insisted upon by the Roman Catholic Church, elaborated by John Locke, expressed in the Declaration of Independence, strongly stated by Daniel Webster and Abraham Lincoln, among others, and now put into practice by [President] Kennedy in aiding a rebellion against the Castro Government in Cuba. Apparently it is not a part of the basic dogma of the Communist Party, which is reported to believe in its own revolution and then no others.[6]

In this appendix to his book, Anastaplo included the report of the Subcommittee recommending against admitting, the agreement to this by the Committee on Character and Fitness concurring after two hearings, the Committee refusing to issue a certificate of satisfactory character and fitness, and the Illinois' State Supreme Court's unanimous refusal to overturn the Committee's ruling, and Anastaplo's petitioning the United States' Supreme Court for review of Illinois' action. When the US Supreme Court refused to review Illinois' action (Justices Black and Douglas dissenting), Anastaplo petitioned both for a rehearing, and to admit himself to their bar. This was denied, and his case was over. He had litigated his case for nearly five years. In the meantime, Anastaplo had returned to the University of Chicago for a doctoral degree, and had begun teaching. At this point he knew about State and Federal Courts from experience.

In 1957, the Supreme Court signaled a change in what character and fitness meant for an applicant to a state bar, in two cases, especially *Konigsberg v. State Bar of California*, that the refusal of answering whether one was a communist was not to be held as sole evidence of lack of character. So Anastaplo requested again to be admitted to the Illinois State Bar, and again he went through the hoops, and was turned down for "recalcitrance", that is without any evidence otherwise concerning Anastaplo's character, his refusal to answer the question about belonging to the Communist Party was not being compliant with authority! His request was once again turned down by the Illinois Supreme Court, only this time 4–3. So once again he requested a hearing before the US Supreme Court for a review of Illinois' action, and this time he was granted the opportunity. This was May, 1960. Two statements stand out from the opinions for the Illinois Supreme court; first, that Anastaplo was to answer questions only, and he had insisted on asking a couple; and second, that he had insisted

6. Anastaplo, *The Constitutionalist*, 336

on stating that the Court should be questioned for their reasons in wanting to know Anastaplo's political activities. In a superb summary of this by distinguished Professor Laurence Berns of St. John's College in Annapolis, the author noted the "pampered elders of the Tribe" were not used to being questioned.

So, oral arguments were scheduled to take place in in the Supreme Court in December, 1960. Between the time of agreeing to review this second action of Illinois' Supreme Court, and oral arguments, my friend was expelled from Russia while on a family camping tour of Europe, for alleged "subversion of public order" which he denied in his meeting with Soviet officials. Oral hearings took place on *In Re Anastaplo*, in US Supreme Court, and on April 24, 1961, the Court held 5–4 against reversing Illinois' action. Justice Harlan wrote the majority opinion, joined by Justices Whittaker, Frankfurter, Stewart, and Clark. Justice Hugo Black was eloquent in a lengthy ten-page dissent, stating in the ringing words, " We must not be afraid to be free", on Anastaplo's right not to answer questions about his church, political, or organizational memberships, unless evidence was presented showing that he would not have the character and fitness to be admitted to the Bar. And he said, "The very most that can be said against Anastaplo's position in this entire matter is that he took too much of the responsibility of preserving that freedom upon himself". Black's dissent was joined by Chief Justice Warren, and Justices Douglas, and Brennan. (Brennan later said about Black's dissent that it would make Anastaplo famous, and Black requested that it be read at his funeral.) Anastaplo was praised for his clear, scholarly, unhistrionic and lawyerly presentation. However, his legal career then ended. And he became an impressive, provocative scholar.[7]

Anastaplo gave me a copy of his book, which has remained a treasured gift. He made the argument lodged in it of the necessity for a free country to have freedom of expression. He told me of his childhood, being the son of Greek immigrants, and growing up in St. Louis and then in Southern Illinois, and serving our country during World War Two as an Army Air Corps bomber navigator. He was honorably discharged in 1947, and began studying to be a lawyer. We talked about his famous case, as he pointed out what was in his book. Night after night I was privileged to talk with the man who got his Ph. D from the University of Chicago in 1964 after his legal hopes were gone, to become a teacher, something he said was the most enjoyable life anyone could have.

The inscription on Allard Lowenstein's headstone at Arlington National Cemetery states what I think true of this dear gentleman and scholar and for one week my mentor, called the "Socrates of Chicago": "If a single man plant himself on his convictions and there abide, the huge world will come round to him".[8] (This is a variation on a famous Emerson quotation.)

7. Anastaplo, *The Constitutionalist*. 331–418
8. Christopher Buckley, *Washington Schlepped Here*, 122

XVII

IN THE LATE SUMMER, 1974, I moved to Madison with my roommate Gerald Mahun. We were on the seventh floor of the Regent Street apartments, with another guy, Dennis Niesing, a Vietnam War vet who sighed and moped around because he had left a sweetheart behind. Much of that academic year, he and his Vietnamese fiancée worked to get her student visa to come into the country. Dennis was delightful, pleasant, kind hearted, bright, handsome, and within two days Gerald and I couldn't stand him. He played Stravinsky so loudly I couldn't hear myself think. (Of course within a month, "Firebird Suite" and "Rite of Spring" were fantastic and some of the most interesting music I knew.)

Absolutely everything about Madison was thrilling: a wonderful *joie de vivre*! I think now of St. Augustine's saying about arriving in Carthage at age 17, "I came to Carthage surrounded by a bubbling cauldron of illicit loves . . ."[1] , which T. S Eliot picked up in his *The Wasteland*. Or I thought of Wordsworth's lines from the eleventh book of *The Prelude*:

> For mighty were the auxiliars which then stood
>
> Upon our side, we who were strong to love!
>
> Bliss was it in that dawn to be alive,
>
> But to be young was very heaven![2]

I signed up for classes for my Junior year in Nineteenth century German philosophy taught by Ivan Soll, a student of Walter Kaufman; "Literary Aspects of the English Bible I" with Dr. Standish Henning the chair of the English Department; Ancient and Medieval Political Thought in my Political Science School-taught by Dr. R. Booth Fowler; Latin; and Spenser's *Faerie Queene*, taught in the Socratic way by Dr. Anthony Weiner. And Professor David Fellman's class on Civil Liberties.

I was deeply impressed by the professors, and sought out Dr. Henning immediately because he was Senior Warden at Grace Episcopal Church and said so. Henning was acerbic, clever, quick witted, a marvelous teacher, normal height, always alert with what was being said, and Anglican through and through. We talked about *The Book*

---

1. St. Augustine, *Confessions*, III,1

2. Wordsworth, "The Prelude, Book Eleventh" 106–109

of Common Prayer, some history of the Church of England, my love for polyphony, and my sense of calling to the priesthood. "Good luck", he said ambiguously. (Later I would come to know that his father was a prominent Rector, having served in a number of Episcopal Churches, especially in Memphis, and in Dallas. Stan himself had sought holy orders and had been turned down in the Diocese of Milwaukee.) He had a certain passive aggressive approach to any Episcopal clergyman, which Freud would have understood.

The other Professor who deeply influenced me was Dr. Fowler. I was relying on grants, loans, and a work/study program to get through college. This gentleman took me on, and provided a study carrel several floors up in the Wisconsin Historical Society building, in the middle of campus. Every day I checked in with him to receive his list of books he needed from the University Library, as he worked on his next book to be published, about the public intellectual in the United States after the Second World War. He was pursuing his general thesis about Liberalism having become deeply skeptical even pessimistic during the Cold War. In fact, liberals had even dragged the nation into the Vietnam War, and the Kennedy and Johnson administrations had suppressed freedoms of expression in various ways. I enjoyed assisting him, and as with other mentors, I learned a great deal out of the classroom, as I did inside. Booth Fowler was short and slight with sandy brown hair, almost dressed as a student, and very inspiring, highly intelligent, well read, a former Episcopalian who had become a Quaker, with his wife Emily. His classroom presentations were dramatic, fiery, and he easily held large classes of students spellbound. On a given afternoon, he was walking with his wife down impressive Bascom hill, and stopped to ask me to join them, which I did. What are you reading? (This was not rhetorical, he constantly asked me this, including how I was making progress in my finding a church, and my journey from the non-Sacramental life of the Salvation Army. Fowler loved finding out about his students, and if a question was answered, he would pursue it. He took genuine interest in students.) I said, Garry Wills' *Bare Ruined Choirs* concerning this former Jesuit seminarian's observations and analysis about the Roman Catholic Church in the 1960s. I quoted a reviewer who had written about Wills' book as "brilliant". He then made the distinction—there is "brilliant illuminating", and "brilliant dazzling", and then gave reasons for thinking the latter in this particular book's case. Both Fowlers were delighted by this, and they had me join them for a supper on campus.

The fall became a challenging time for me with the classes, keeping up with reading required, getting the gofer work taken care of for Professor Fowler, and discovering a new theologian to read. At the foot of Bascom Hill is the most important antiquarian bookstore I have found outside of New York City and Galway. Paul's Used Books stocked all kinds of books, most of very fine distinction and quality. Among other virtues, they had the best biographies for political or literary or psychological or classical figures. If I wanted David Herbert Donald on Lincoln (not yet his one volume biography), or Gibbon's volumes, or Boswell's Johnson, or Herodotus, or Plutarch, or

Chesterton on Dickens, or Karl Barth, that is where I went. Auden, Eliot, Joyce, and Richard Ellmann's *James Joyce*, or A. J. Ayer or Wittgenstein, or Tacitus or Suetonius, or Peter Brown's biography of St. Augustine, or still a favorite find: Albert Schweitzer's *The Quest of the Historical Jesus (Von Reimarus zu Wrede* 1906). I found Freud, a great deal of Nietzsche, Lord Rosebery's *Pitt*. I found *Honest to God*, the notorious religious book by Bishop J. A. T. Robinson of the Church of England, introducing the readers to Bultmann, Bonhoeffer, and Paul Tillich.

And I discovered Paul Tillich himself. I bought one of his books of published sermons, *The New Being*, and devoured it. I picked up *Theology of Culture, Ultimate Concern: Tillich in Dialogue, The Courage To Be, Dynamics of Faith*. I got Kegley & Bretall's interpretative essays about Tillich, by a variety of Philosophers and Theologians, and read about this theologian who had been trained in Germany before World War I, married to Margarethe "Grethi" Wever in 1914, then had experienced terrible disillusionment as a chaplain in the horrifying trenches. Tillich spoke about the great hope and belief in the human spirit affecting theology, that had swept over Germany and Europe before the War, such that there was vast confidence in science all problems and tragedies for humanity would be resolved. There would be no war, nor hunger, nor poverty nor crime with the coming utopia. Human reason and the human spirit especially in science would become manifest as the dynamic force given by God to achieve all knowledge, and overcome all obstacles. Hadn't Beethoven prophesied this in his Ninth Symphony? In the fourth movement is the Recitative, the great choral sound of *Freude!* Joy! All people shall become brothers and join in the religion of unity and harmony! The text of this possibly greatest of all symphonies in the Western canon, is based on a text by Friedrich Schiller, to which Beethoven appended an introductory stanza addressing all as friends:

O Freunde, nicht diese Toene!

Sondern lasst uns angenehmeren anstimmen,

und freuden vollere.

Freude!

Freude!

Freude schoener Goetterfunken

Tochter aus Elysium,

Wir betreten feuertrunken,

Himmlische, dein Heiligtum!

Deine Zauber binden wieder

Was die Mode streng geteilt;

Alle Menschen werder Brueder,

Wo dein sanfter Fluegel weilt.

O Friends, not these sounds!

Let us instead strike up more pleasing,

And joyful sounds.

Joy!

Joy!

Joy, beautiful spark of divinity,

Daughter from Elysium,

We enter, burning with fervor,

Heavenly being, your sanctuary!

Your magic brings together

What fashion has sternly divided.

All men shall become brothers,

Wherever your gentle wings hover.[3]

Here was the Sacred statement of what the future would be like, without any particular religion or religions fighting and killing human beings in the name of God (much as in the message of John Lennon's "Imagine"). Other great influences affecting the German populations elsewhere in 1900: Darwin's evolutionary insights, Freud's psychological ideas and methods for curing emotional and mental problems, Marx's new religion of social and political answers to the age-old inequalities economically and viewing all religion as ideologies for the few to hold power over the masses, about which he proclaimed a new Utopia which would put the means of production in the hands of the workers, and bring about fairness and justice everywhere. The preponderant sentiment of the general cultural environment, the *Zeitgeist* in Europe in 1900, when Tillich was 14, was of such heady optimism, that the Christian faith was reduced to a kind of private hobby one might choose, perhaps equivalent to mahjong, and in tremendous need of updating so that it might accord with the advances in the scientific age, the enlightened era. In his *History of Christian Thought*, edited from his lectures, and published posthumously by Carl Braaten, Tillich noted that the most influential professor in 1900 was Adolph von Harnack, the great historian of Christian Dogma, whose work affected all of intellectual society in Germany, not just the Church or Academy. Harnack's rather confident rational historical work, limiting Jesus to what for Harnack was in accord with his own heuristic core of the Christian Gospel, producing a cheerful universal religion, expressed in "the Fatherhood of God, the Brotherhood of Man". Outside of showing God's love, now open to all by God's grace, Jesus leaves the

---

3. Beethoven Foundation-Schiller's *An die Freude*

stage. In .January of 1900, Harnack's new popular book of this religion, *Das Wesen des Christentums*, (*The Essence of Christianity*) was observed by Harnack as told to Tillich stacked everywhere in the Leipzig Central Train Station, a sign to him of the prevalent form of Christianity ensnared to this easy going culture. The Roman Catholic writer, Fr. George Tyrell famously wrote: "The Christ that Adolph von Harnack sees, looking back through nineteen centuries of Catholic darkness, is only the reflection of a liberal Protestant face, seen at the bottom of a deep well". [4]

Tillich, was the son of a Lutheran pastor, born in Starzeddel, Prussia, in 1886. His father was an official in the United Church of Prussia, the amalgamated Church of Calvinists and Lutherans mandated by King Friedrich Wilhelm III in 1817, the three hundredth anniversary of the Reformation's beginning. Without a great deal of theological or doctrinal insight, the monarch was highly influenced by a personal matter-he wanted to receive Holy Communion with his wife the Queen, who was a Lutheran. With the assistance of a proposal Friedrich Schleiermacher wrote in 1808, based on little theology but pietistic platitudes, and the necessity of this State mandated and administered Church to help unify the nation, the bureaucratic structures of both the Evangelical and Reformed Churches were brought together. (There were several schisms, especially the significant one of Lutheran emigrants who fled this State run Church, to settle in Pennsylvania, and then finally in Missouri—the Missouri Synod Lutherans.) The theological educational center for the new Prussian Church was established in Berlin, involving the larger scale university reforms implemented by Alexander von Humboldt. Tillich studied and trained to be a pastor within this Prussian United Church, influenced first by Schelling-and spelling this out with his first work to achieve his Ph. D. in 1910; and then more deeply with Hegel's and Schleiermacher's ideas becoming especially instrumental in his own formative theological understanding. (Hegel and Schleiermacher were recruited to teach at the new University of Berlin.)

Tillich achieved his theological and philosophical degrees to begin his pastorate, which was short-lived due to his enlistment in the German Army as a chaplain in the Great War of 1914. He returned from a war lost by the Germans, and found his world turned upside down, especially with the forced abdication of the Kaiser, unemployment, hunger even starvation the prospect for hundreds of thousands in Germany, a severe breakdown in law and order, and the wait for the victorious Allies to determine Germany's fate. It was just at this time that the Influenza pandemic affected a great many including the now hated Kaiser Wilhelm (who fled to the Netherlands, and lived until his death in 1941). And when he discovered Grethi, his wife of five years, pregnant by another man, he divorced her, and tried settling down to university life as a Privatdozent of Theology for five years at the University of Berlin, 1919–1924. He had met Hannah Werner-Gottschow who was pregnant and married. They married, a second time for both, in 1924. In Hannah Tillich's first volume of memoirs, *From*

---

4. Tyrell, *Christianity at the Crossroads*, 49.

Time to Time, she describes the impact on her and of many others in class of Tillich's personality, and his charisma as a University lecturer. She also talks about his inviting her to his house, and hearing loud yelling and screaming all over the house coming from various women students who all seemed to have some claim on Tillich, one even pregnant by him [5]. In this atmosphere of utter chaos, she determined to bring some order into his world. In a Harvard Lecture in 1998, the Tillichs' son Rene spoke openly about his parents' marriage, how unstrung his mother could be as the abused child of her own father, and her great hardship coming to America, as the Tillichs did, following Hitler's rise in 1933.[6] (Rene suggested his mother had been exaggerating many of the claims made in her two memoirs.[7]) Tillich had by then made a name for himself along with Barth and Bultmann calling for a repristination of the Reformation message of the magisterial reformers. All these gentlemen were with Emil Brunner and others considered the rising Neo-Orthodox vanguard, Barth of course foremost with his Commentary on *The Epistle to the Romans*, published in 1919. Karl Adam, a Roman Catholic professor of theology at the University of Tuebingen, was quoted as saying the book fell like a "bombshell on the theologians' playground".[8] In this book, Barth wrote prophetically that any understanding of God's Word must come from God alone, especially in His Word about Christ. There was nothing that human "religion" could do to reach to God, in the easygoing way of liberal Protestantism before the Great War. God alone must speak the Word of Jesus Christ from (as Luther said) *extra nos*, outside of human experience, and human philosophy. Otherwise this human religion has been judged by God as idolatry, and in the twentieth century as psychology. Barth himself noted he was agreeing with Immanuel Kant in this regard. In his widely considered profound and seminal work, *Protestant Theology in the Nineteenth Century*, which was preceded by a lengthy introduction to the thought and culture of the eighteenth century, Barth quoted Kant's *Religion within the Limits of Reason Alone*, on "feeling" and its obvious inadequacies:

> The wish to feel the direct influence of the Godhead as such is a self-contradictory piece of presumption.
>
> Feeling is something entirely personal, and no one can assume its presence in others, which means that it cannot be taken as a touchstone for the truth of revelation. It does not teach us anything at all, consisting as it does merely in the effect of pain or pleasure upon one particular person, and cannot form the basis for any knowledge at all.[9]

---

5. H. Tillich, *From Time to Time*, 94

6. R. Tillich, "My Father Paul Tillich", 14

7. R. Tillich, "My Father", 14

8. McConnadine, "Teachings of Karl Barth", 385–6. I owe this reference to Stanley Hauerwas.

9. Barth, *Protestant Theology in the Nineteenth Century*, 315

Tillich would remain ambivalent about Barth, and move in the way he had first been inspired by German Idealism and Romanticism, the approach to understanding God through Mind, especially as Friedrich Wilhelm Joseph Schelling put this forward in his early philosophy, with a focus on beauty especially as discovered in nature. Tillich noted frequently that Schelling had helped him overcome Kantian pessimism of ever finding a way to reach the truth about God through reason alone, and that by pure luck he had come upon Kant's *Critique of Pure Reason*, and the entire works of Schelling in a book store when he was young. Tillich's own philosophical theology was eclectic synthesizing German Romanticism, Schelling, Hegel, and Schleiermacher, Heidegger, as well as twentieth century existentialism.[10] He spoke of God in the way of Medieval Theologians, stating that all language about God is metaphorical, with the exception of *esse ipsum*, "Being Itself". This reference to God, in God's totality of Being, considered metaphysically, was Tillich's way of overcoming the great abyss between Creator and Creation, including humanity. This occurred in the "Christ event", or the symbol of the "New Being" revealed in Christ. Tillich's language could be annoyingly psychological, and he emphasized Gestalt or depth therapy for overcoming our "split personality", as human beings in the grip of anxiety and "dread". (In his *History of Christian Thought*, my favorite of Tillich's books, he urged theological students to study Kierkegaard's *The Concept of Dread*, and *The Sickness unto Death*.[11] The editor of this book of transcribed lectures was Carl Braaten, who was grateful for Tillich's teaching him the tradition of the Church. When I met Braaten years later, he said "not the Faith, but the *Tradition* I learned from him".) The human condition is fraught with "dread", and only overcome in the New Being of the Christ. It was with his method of "correlation" with which he presented his theology, since philosophy raises the question of meaning in the world, and theology answers these questions. His term for the presentation of his thought, and of religion, was one's "ultimate concern". And note Tillich then asserts not Christian theology, but a "psychologism" as Rowan Williams suggests, something which is part of the psychological make up of all humanity.[12] For myself, I read Tillich enthusiastically for a number of years, until I came to the realization his "ultimate concern" doesn't preach. It is not the Word of God. There is no well thought out understanding of "sin" which separates human beings from God, and human beings from each other. And without any clear presentation of sin, there really is no need for a Savior. So the Christology of Tillich is rather shadowy, and unrealizable in his theology. He sees no necessity for a modern quest for the historical Jesus, because it's the symbol that counts, and because of the "ugly great ditch" Lessing said between historical knowledge and theological truth, echoed in Tillich's favorite New Testament Professor Martin Kaehler's book in 1892, *The So-called Historical Jesus, and the Historic Biblical Christ*. (In this case it may be instructive to note the German title:

10. Tillich, *A History of Christian Thought*, 438
11. Tillich, *History of Christian Thought*, 462
12. Williams, *Anglican Identities*, 105

Der sogennante historische Jesus und der geshichtliche, biblische Christus.) Tillich took pains to distinguish these two words for history/historic. *Geschicte* was considered the word to be used for the results of carefully investigated events in history resulting in reliable scientific answers. Kaehler was skeptical about finding much historically accurate in the Gospel record about the real living Jesus. On the other hand, belief in the Biblically presented Christ, who takes away the sins of the world, available to each individual who hears and feels this, was religiously historic, or *Historie*. I heard this taught at Seminary that to say Jesus died on a cross, was fairly reliable history. To say that Jesus died on the cross for me, was historic, and not in the same category of historical truth. Archbishop Michael Ramsey once said that this entire distinction was unhelpful, for something is true or it isn't; and he referred to this as "Bullgeschichte". The old saw about this was Tillich gets a telephone call from Jerusalem with the news that the real bones of Jesus have been found. Tillich responds, "Then he really lived?" [13] (A rigorous young theologian in 1964-German, 1968-English, got this completely right, Wolfhart Pannenberg's *Jesus-God and Man*. I found this later. I found this thrilling.)

Much of this was unsatisfying to me as I grew older and experienced more of life, prayed, led worship, studied the Bible, engaged in pastoral care with actual human beings, and read theology. I came to realize that Tillich—who in his later life moved from being a Lutheran, to becoming part of the United Church of Christ, (closer to his Evangelical and Reformed Church life), was a dedicated follower of the theologian of "feeling". Through "feeling" Schleiermacher taught were we able to overcome the problem of the limitations of reason to arrive at truth about God. Schleiermacher famously stated in his big book, *On the Christian Faith*, or *Die Christliche Glaube*, that religion was "the feeling of absolute dependence" on God, an experience known to all humanity, but mediated in accord with the varieties of religio-cultural expressions, in various historical and cultural contexts. (Schleiermacher's definition was "*das Gefuehl der schlechthinnigen Abhaengigkeit.*"[14]) This ambiguous statement meant that in the world of human religion-as is said in *Alice's Adventures in Wonderland*—"everybody has won, and all must have prizes". No longer is there one truth which comes to us in the Word of God, especially in the Incarnation of the Son of God, God's own revealed Word to save humanity from their sins. Tillich said that when this "feeling" became the basic message of Churches in the nineteenth century, preaching and hymns became all expressions of great emotion, and men stopped attending. [15] Well, for a long while, I was pleased to come to know Tillich's theology, because it asked so little of me, and gave me (and others) the impression of having learning and sounding like knowing theology in an educated way when speaking about the Christian faith. And one never had to speak about sin! Tillich's word for sin came from psychology, estrangement.

13. Neill, "Jesus and Myth", 58–9

14. Schleiermacher, *The Christian Faith*, 13

15. Tillich, *History of Christian Thought*, 393–4

He offered as a remedy found in the "symbol" of the New Creation, Christ, who is not personal or historical, the overcoming of this "contrary to our essential nature", insights from depth psychology.[16]

During the Middle Ages, the great archbishop of Canterbury, St. Anselm warned in his *Cur Deus Homo*, about recognizing tremendous destructive power in the human experience of sin. He wrote:

'*Nondum considerasti quanti ponderis peccatum sit*'

('You have not yet considered the weight of sin')[17]

New Testament scholar, N. T. Wright, commented about this in his dictum that Anselm was reacting to Abelard's belief that all that "the sinner needed was the loving example of the cross".[18] Abelard's view is parallel I think to Tillich's anthropology in his theology.

Or consider the ironic comment by H. R. Niebuhr about the easy going Christianity in the earlier part of the Twentieth century:

A God without wrath brought men without sin into a kingdom without judgment through the ministrations of a Christ without a Cross.[19]

In the article by Rene Tillich, mentioned above, he claims he once confronted his father about how a minister could engage in so many trysts outside of marriage; to which his father responded he never preached about adultery.[20]

I tried out for the University Chorus directed by Professor of Music, Sam Jones, who was also Director of Music at Grace Episcopal Church. It was extensive in that I had to sight read a couple pieces of music, hear chords played on the piano and say which note was the lowest or highest, or one in between, sing some musical piece I brought, and sing a few bars from the upcoming concert *repertoire*. The rehearsals for the singing of Carl Orff's "Carmina Burana" a cantata with large orchestra, and children's chorus, would begin the next day. I took to this choral work immediately. Orff encountered the texts of a great many poems originally satiric about monks of the 11th 12th and early 13th centuries letting off steam, through singing about the coming of spring, and the joys of lusting, drinking, gambling, and carousing. The Medieval use of Lady Fortune becomes the theme of Orff's work composed in 1935–6. On the same day I walked over to Luther Memorial Church, of the Lutheran Church in America, on University Avenue, with a highly regarded Pastor J. Stephen Bremer, whom Pastor Richard Neuhaus had praised in his fine memoir about pastoring in New York City, *Freedom For Ministry*. (I attended Luther Memorial one Sunday, and

16. Tillich, *Systematic Theology III*, 224–7

17. St. Anselm, *Cur Deus Homo*, 1, xxi

18. Wright, *Paul and His Recent Interpreters*, 153

19. H. R. Niebuhr, *The Kingdom of God in America*, 193

20. R. Tillich, "Paul Tillich, My Father",14

found its music and liturgy too Germanic feeling for my taste. That afternoon Pastor Bremer stopped over to welcome me. I was deeply impressed.) On that very afternoon were try outs conducted by Roger Petrich, for the Heinrich Schuetz Kantorei, named after the great Lutheran composer born 100 years before Johann Bach, and considered the most outstanding Lutheran composer second to Bach. I was accepted and began rehearsals the following Sunday for the most complicated and dissonant sounding music I had ever sung. We began singing the "St. John Passion", unlike anything I had ever heard, and strangely beautiful. Up to that point I was deeply in love with 16th century English polyphony, especially compositions of Tallis and Byrd. Those sacred musical choral works led me into "bliss" or joy in the way C. S. Lewis pointed out in his *Surprised by Joy*. St. John Chrysostom's rendering of how at the Eucharistic Prayer we are lifted into the very presence of God in Heaven, into the midst of the Holy Trinity, with angels and archangels, with the Mother of God, and all the saints, and all the hosts of heaven, was how I came to realize what my experience listening and praying with that opening chorus in which Bach named *Herr, Herr, Herr*, or Lord three times, and then repeated it three times in the mutations of the title of God, the *herrscher* and *herrlich* words. The three is representative of the Holy Trinity and Bach calls attention to this in this stupendous work of art. The Passion narrative was the great dramatic one from the *Gospel of St. John*, always sung on Good Friday. It was to be meditative, for worshippers to be drawn into the very means by which God saved the world by His Son our Lord's suffering and death. An Evangelist-tenor presents the *Gospel from St. John*, and the chorus and various soloists provide meditations to assist the prayers of those gathered. Following the sung "It is finished!", or better in the German-which thankfully we sang-" *Es ist vollbracht!*", the final chorus is emotionally powerful in stating "*Ruht vohl*", "Rest Well". For me this was powerful as anything I had experienced in the cumulative signs showing God's presence in His creation, and His sacrificial love for me (as Wesley said) even me.

In the fall and winter I was seeing a young woman, who was daughter to the sergeant major and wife at the local Salvation Army Corps in Madison. The officers were the Tregalleses from Cornwall, my maternal grandfather's home country. Her family offered to me an open dinner on Sundays after the worship at the Salvation Army. She was very much a dairy maid from Wisconsin, and wished to persuade me to become a Salvation Officer with her. We went our separate ways. My interests by now were seeing films by Lina Wertmueller, and concerts of Stravinsky, or Mozart, or Vivaldi, or lectures on philosophy or science or political science. And I had a great desire to hear Prof. Joseph Sittler from the University of Chicago, a systematic theologian whose books I had been reading, and someone who had known Paul Tillich well. I had come across his *The Care of the Earth and other University Sermons*, *The Ecology of Faith*, *The Structure of Christian Ethics*, *The Anguish of Preaching*. Sittler had written on ecology already in the 1950s, far ahead of many other academics in this area of general concern reaching the public (with Senator Gaylord Nelson of Wisconsin leading the way in the Senate, by getting the environment on the radar as a political concern of the first level, and working to have Earth Day designated for April 22, 1970). I listened to this brilliant theologian, who easily quoted philosophers, ancient and modern, as well as theologians from Eastern Orthodoxy and Western Catholicism, and poets, including Americans. In his *Essays on Nature and Grace*, he introduced me to St. Gregory Palamas.[21] He began by referring to a large sign he saw in the present Luther Memorial Church's nursery, which stated, "We shall not all sleep, but we shall all be changed". He spoke about the genius of St. Paul, and his theology of God's reaching out to all of the world through Israel's Messiah, Jesus of Nazareth, so that the covenant originally proclaimed by the Lord to Abraham, would now be fulfilled by all who became committed to His name in Baptism, the New Covenant itself. And everyone was equal in the sight of God, including males and females, slave and free, Jews and Gentiles. Sittler quoted Robert Frost, and Theodore Roethke, American poets. Sittler quoted Roethke's poem, "The Waking", which has become one of my favorites, based as he saw it on *St. Luke's Gospel*, 17:11–14, about Jesus' healing of the ten lepers, who are made clean "while they were on their way":

> I wake to sleep, and take my waking slow,
>
> I feel my fate in what I cannot fear,
>
> I learn by walking where I have to go.
>
> This shaking keeps me steady, I should know.
>
> What falls away is always, and is near.
>
> I wake to sleep, and take my waking slow.
>
> I learn by going where I have to go.[22]

Sittler's lecture was fascinating in his articulation about the coherence of the Christian faith, and in his very choice and use of words. He was a wordsmith. It was ironic then to hear him say about the great exclamation of St. Paul's in *Second Corinthians* 5:17 (So, if anyone is in Christ, New Creation! See everything old has passed away; see, everything has become new!), "When grace erupts, grammar cracks!". There was no verb in that exclamation. But, of course, this was a great insight.

Afterwards, I spoke with Dr. Sittler and asked him about his late colleague, Paul Tillich. I was fervent about learning this theology which spoke to me. He said he would give me a warning. Paulus' language was not the language of the Church. You simply could not change the great words of the Church: faith, agape, belief, sin, grace, forgiveness, all words the Church has handed down to us. So, if one wished to become an ordained minister of the Church, learn and practice the Church's grammar. (Later,

---

21. Sittler, *Essays on Nature and Grace*, 54–55
22. Roethke, "The Waking," 114.

I would come across the same *caveat* from Karl Barth, who spoke of the necessity of learning the language of Canaan.)

The Frost poem, "Revelation", has haunted me, both in my search for truth and love about God, and in my needing intimacy, which would enable me to love with all my heart, and receive the same. I continued to date various women, and then found relationships unsustaining. For myself, I was paradoxically suspect of anyone, including a woman, to get too close to me, because, at least in one respect, (apart from all unconscious motives not present to my mind) I couldn't entrust myself, and my heart, to anyone. I had learned this growing up with the suffocating love of my mother, and her suffocating Salvation Army. Heart speaks to heart; *Cor ad cor loquitur*. This was Cardinal Newman's motto. Pascal wrote "The heart has its reasons, of which reason knows nothing".

At age twenty, I became aware of my own form of study. Without a particularly solid education in public schools, and for the most part educating myself, I sympathized with Robert Frost's saying that organized education "was never my taste". And he famously said, "Once we have learned to read, the rest can be trusted to add itself unto us". In fact, I would read something, or hear something, a chance comment by William F. Buckley, or Dr. Stan Henning, or Prof. Sittler, and I would off and hunt and search to satisfy my desire for becoming fully acquainted with the biography or subject. The idea of the "hunt" for knowledge or Truth is deeply embedded in Plato's dialogues, particularly the *Laches*.[23] (I came to know later, that this may be a path taking us to the One who is the Way, Truth, and Life. This One alone promises us the full knowledge or wisdom given in unique relationship with God through His Son, the Word Himself. Our Lord says significantly: "Ask, and it will be given you; search, and you shall find; knock, and the door will be opened for you. For everyone who asks receives, everyone who searches finds, and everyone who knocks, the door will be opened."[24] I came to trust this promise.) This has been my way of becoming educated. At this time, I set as a regimen getting up and reading what serious book I had with my coffee. This first two hours were essential to my day. Afternoons were for school work, and evenings and before turning my light off, enjoyable reading. I came across a description of our greatest president's habit of learning from his contemporary, Carl Schurz. Schurz writes of Lincoln:

> His equipment as a statesman did not embrace a comprehensive knowledge of public affairs. What he had studied he had indeed made his own, with the eager craving and that zealous tenacity characteristic of superior minds learning under difficulties. But his narrow opportunities and the unsteady life he had led during his younger years had not permitted the accumulation of large stores in his mind . . . But when his moral nature was aroused, his brain developed an untiring activity until it had mastered all the knowledge within

23. Plato, *Laches*, 194b
24. *St. Luke* 11: 9–10

reach. As soon as the repeal of the Missouri Compromise had thrust the slavery question into politics as the paramount issue, Lincoln plunged into an arduous study of all its legal, historical and moral aspects, and then his mind became a complete arsenal of argument.[25]

I am not comparing myself to this giant of a man and President. I am comparing my habit of mind to his, as described so nimbly by Schurz.

25. Schurz, "Abraham Lincoln", 26–27

XIX

I SO ENJOYED BEING in Madison. Walking over to Memorial Union for lunch in the *Rathskeller*, a German Beer Hall lookalike, or upstairs in the same building to read or study in a large music room with comfortable seating, quiet and a record player, where day by day I heard Bach's "Easter Oratorio", or Handel's "Water Music", or Smetana, or Grieg, or a chamber work by Mozart, perhaps his Piano Concerto no. 23 with its hauntingly beautiful Adagio movement, or Andres Segovia's classical guitar playing the "Asturias" of Isaac Albeniz. If Mahler came on I'd take a hike. I remember reading *One Hundred Years of Solitude*, Michael Oakeshott, Hegel, Proust, or Ved Mehta, Garry Wills biography of Chesterton, *Candide*, John Fowles' *The Magus* and *The French Lieutenant's Woman* , listening to music. Tillich had a gift for interesting titles for his books, such as two mentioned above, *The Dynamics of Faith*, *The Courage to Be*, or others, *My Search for Absolutes*, *On the Boundary*, *Biblical Religion and the Search for Ultimate Reality*. In this last book, Tillich parted ways from the early lay Roman Church Father-and later Schismatic-Tertullian of North Africa who had asked what had Jerusalem to do with Athens? Tertullian was truculent in his denunciation of this possibility. Tillich-possibly seeing Barth's crinkled laughing visage while writing about the dour lawyerly Tertullian—was adamant in affirming philosophy's complementary role with theology in the search for truth. (OK, I know I'm going too far in this foolishness, but I can see Karl getting passionate in his claims of knowing the Word of God only in Jesus, and judge Tillich's libertinism, and Paulus pointing out that he may have had innumerable affairs, but then slyly inquire about Barth's longstanding codependent relationship with Lollo! This was Barth's nickname for his longtime muse, amanuensis, collaborator, confidante, travel companion, Charlotte von Kirschbaum, who wrote about her life with the Barths, and the alienation she observed between Karl and Nelly Barth. Barth referred to his wife Nelly as Frau Barth. Ms. Von Kirschbaum lived with the Barths from 1929–1966. All three and the Barths' son Marcus are buried together on the edge of Basel, Switzerland in Hoernli Cemetery.)

In the winter of 1975, I was invited by a kind hearted student in my English Class on the Bible to attend Evensong on the upcoming Friday night at Grace Episcopal Church. (We had talked after the Bible class about my searching for a church in which to worship.) I met Mary Beth at this magnificent Church on the Capitol plaza. The small group of worshipers met in the choir, and I balanced *1928 Book of Common Prayer*, and the *1940 Hymnal* of the Episcopal Church, in singing most of the traditional Evensong service. The folks present were all weird, and I fit right in. There was an English couple in their thirties, a couple students in wild hair , my Professor of Literary Aspects of the English Bible—Dr. Stan Henning, a music Professor of Piano—Carroll Chilton, a couple of very old women stooped, and one of them with a red coat on which made her look very much like a trollish wizened hag woman weirdly similar to Roman Polanski. Both women cackled through much of the service. The plainsong *Magnificat* and *Nunc Dimittis* were two of the most beautiful prayers I had ever heard sung. In fact, much of the service was sung, and the words made me somewhat emotional, especially when this Collect was sung:

> Lighten our darkness, we beseech thee, O Lord; and by thy great mercy defend us from all perils and dangers of this night; for the love of thy only Son, our Savior, Jesus Christ. Amen.

I broke down after this prayer, which upset me greatly. I knew this was against custom in this Church. But the prayers were so beautifully written, and economically stated, and yet said all that needed to be said. The general confession for example was this:

> Dearly beloved brethren, the Scripture moveth us, in sundry places, to acknowledge and confess our manifold sins and wickedness; and that we should not dissemble or cloak them before the face of Almighty God our Heavenly Father; but confess them with an humble, lowly, penitent, and obedient heart; to the end that we may obtain forgiveness of the same, by his infinite goodness and mercy. And although we ought, at all times, humbly to acknowledge our sins before God; yet ought we chiefly so to do, when we assemble and meet together, to render thanks for the great benefits we have received at his hands, to set forth his worthy praise, to hear His most holy Word, and to ask those things which are most requisite and necessary, as well for the body and for the soul. Wherefore I pray and beseech you, as many as are here present, to accompany me with a pure heart, and humble voice, unto the throne of heavenly grace, saying-

To be said by the whole congregation, after the minister, all kneeling.

Almighty and most merciful Father; we have erred and strayed thy ways like lost sheep. We have followed too much the devices and desires of our own hearts. We have offended against thy holy laws. We have left undone those things which we ought to have done. And we have done those things which we ought not to have done; And there is no health in us. But thou, O Lord, have mercy upon us miserable offenders. Spare thou those, O God, who confess their faults. Restore thou those who are penitent; According to thy promises declared unto mankind In Christ Jesus our Lord. And grant, O most merciful Father, for his sake; That we may hereafter live a godly, righteous, and sober life, To the glory of thy holy Name. Amen.

To be made by the priest alone, standing; The people still kneeling.

The Almighty and merciful Lord grant you Absolution and remission of all
your sins, true repentance, amendment of life, and the grace and consolation
of his Holy Spirit. Amen.

It was achingly true and even more beautiful because it was true. Why on Earth had
my maternal grandfather broken away from this language and sought emotional
comfort from clergy making stuff up? This Church knew how to pray. And no one
worried from what I could tell, about having the right tone, or emotion to prove one's
authenticity or sincerity. The words of this liturgy spoke truly. And the emotion one
could feel was constrained in the beauty such as I had never heard before. This Church
knew how to pray. This was a church at prayer. This was my home! Afterwards, I accompanied Mary Beth and the folks with their priest, Dr. Edward Lanphier, a scientist,
an oceanographer as a matter of fact, to a lovely tasty dinner. Aha! I thought. I don't
have to sit through one of those insufferable Salvation Army services to get a good
home cooked dinner!

I asked several questions, while eating, about the liturgy of the Episcopal Church.
I was not baptized I said. Oh! The table company looked at me quizzically. I began
explaining to them what practices the Salvation Army had regarding becoming a
Christian, and finally realized we would be there all night. "They have no Sacraments.
Things are different there." And I hoped we would talk about other matters.

What brought me there? "I was invited by Mary Beth from my Bible Class with
Dr. Henning", I responded. Mary Beth commented on the class's title, "The Literary
Aspects of the English Bible", and spoke of Henning's teaching of its derivation, from
Hebrew and Greek to Latin and the various translations in English up to the 1611
King James' Version. The group was a literate one, and moved into a discussion of
the *Septuagint*, the translation, or at times, paraphrase, of the Hebrew Scriptures into
Greek by cultured Jews in Alexandria around 300 BC. (Actually, this is something of
a misnomer. Long stretches of *Ezra* and *Daniel* are in Aramaic, the language of the
Babylonians for diplomatic correspondence and military communication, and then
widely the common language under the Persians. Both the Hebrew and the Aramaic
sections show a style and usage associated with late versions of both, i.e. the 2nd century BC.) It was only in Henning's class, which thrilled me half to death, that I began
hearing about the historical, literary, and cultural backgrounds of the Bible. I had never heard before that seventy per cent or more of the Old Testament used in the New
was derived from the Septuagint. I had only imagined that the reason for numerous
errors of wording and even meaning in the use of the Old Testament in the New were
due to poor translations, or forgetful memories. Particularly did I think this about St.
Paul's quotations from the Old Testament. Now, I was discovering that the Bible, *ta
biblia* in Greek, the books, or the library, *tas graphas* to Paul-the writings—of the Old
Testament was the *Septuagint* itself. Outside of *the Law, the Torah, the Pentateuch, the*

works of Moses, as the first five books of the *Old Testament* were called, there was no standard Canon at all for Jews in Jesus' day. Or rather, that the various parties in Jesus' time, were all vying with one another about the particular writings considered true Scripture. The Sadducees, the establishment running the Temple in Jerusalem, only believed that Torah was authoritative. The Pharisees added the Prophets, but disputed among themselves about the Writings, including which exact ones were of the Lord's blessing. And then these groups argued with their own counterparts in the Diaspora, those Jews who had been forcibly exiled, or who had fled dangerous times from the Holy Land, the Land, the *ha'aretz*. For after the great political seismic changes which had occurred with Alexander the Great's conquering so much of the Eastern geography around the Mediterranean, including the Holy Land, and imposing his Hellenistic language and culture on all those peoples, Jews living in his conquered lands had spoken Greek for nearly three hundred years before Jesus. The Jewish elders who had translated the Hebrew books into Greek, accomplished this shortly after Alexander's death in 323 BC. The many books of the *Apocrypha*, originally sacred books of the Greek speaking Jews, between 300 BC and Jesus' day, are actually quoted and understood as sacred by writers of the *New Testament*. They were read as inspired by God (or Canon) by the Church, East and West, Catholic and Orthodox, from the earliest times of the Church. And the Christian claims for their new Canon, caused the Jewish religious leaders in Palestine (called this hated name by the conquering Romans after 70 AD), to come up with their own Canon. (This is generally understood to be the decision made by the rabbis—successors to the Pharisees—meeting at Jamnia, or Jabneh, about 90 AD.) Those who spoke the sacred language of Hebrew-mostly in Palestine-by and large considered only the books written in Hebrew up for inclusion. And those who spoke Greek—and were taught the legend of Moses farming out the Jewish writings to seventy elders (hence the name Septuagint) believed the Jewish books written in Greek and hallowed by use and custom, considered those Canon as well. To the historic Catholic and Orthodox Churches, and those looking to the entire 2000-year history of the Church, they have continued to this day including the *Apocrypha*, or *Deutero-Canonical* books, as part of the Canon of Scripture. (Episcopalians, many of whom are suffering from Doctrinal and Biblical amnesia, don't know what to think, and have little more than "bumper sticker" sayings to go in one of several directions on this.)

In any case, between Dr. Henning's class, and talking with folks at Grace Church, I learned far more in an a few hours or so, than I had known in twenty years before that, about the Bible.

Dr. Henning's class was thrilling. From the first day, following a caveat about testifying to all his failings and heresies concerning the Bible's interpretation, he would provide the now generally and widely accepted views of Biblical scholarship, in laying out the historical shape of the 66 writings in the Bible, and then include the *Apocrypha*, or as the great majority of Christians around the world say, the *Deutero-Canonical* writings, which are read in his own Episcopal Church. His next statement surprised me: The Apocryphal books had been included in the King James' Version of the Bible, until being suppressed by Evangelical Anglican Missionary Societies in the late nineteenth century. He encouraged all of us to get ahold of the latest *Revised Standard Version* Edition, preferably the study version which was annotated. His class concerned providing basic information about the English Bible which was the foundation for so much of historical English literature, e. g. Shakespeare, Spenser, Milton, Blake, right up to the present century with T. S. Eliot, W.H. Auden, John Betjeman, even Stevie Smith. (Henning identified himself as an Elizabethan scholar.) Next, we began with an historical summary of the Israelites, and their claims for having been created and formed by God *Yahweh*. Wow! This was my chief focus for so many questions I had about the historical background of the Jewish people, and moving from the old covenant to the new covenant of Jesus, what was legendary and what was true. (Oh, my God, I thought. Bring it on!)

"How many of you have heard of Julius Wellhausen?" (Well, I had heard of the name so I raised my hand, the only one to do so.) "What do you know. And what is your name?" "I'm Dale Coleman. I know that Wellhausen put forward the documentary hypothesis of the First Five Books of Moses, and that's about all I know." I got through that relatively unscathed. "Well, what does that tell you, about the direct authorship of Moses? Is it true?", came Dr. Henning's immediate challenge. I struggled with an answer to this scary guy. "What is truth?" I asked nicely. There was laughter, that I had counted on. Henning, of course was not amused. "What's your name again?" "Dale, Dr. Henning. May I call you that?", I improvised. "No, we prefer Professor at this University. Call me Professor Henning." "OK!" I said as cheerfully as I could manage. "Well, Dale, and what a lovely name that is, I mean did Moses sit down with his number #2 leaded pencil and begin writing down on paper all that we now have as the First Five Books of Moses. Do you know what they are? And I don't mean the leaded pencil literally." This was said so acerbically that I wanted but chose not to challenge him on his worry about this.

Professor Henning laid out the Graf-Wellhausen Documentary view that there are four separate "strands" of narratives running throughout the Pentateuch, which is why there are so many "doublets "or duplicate narratives running side by side, most noticeably in *Genesis*, with differences and even contradictions glaringly obvious. Wellhausen proposed two ancient sources, what he called the "Jahwist" and the "Elohist", identifying the former the oldest from c 950 BC, beginning with the second Creation story in Genesis 2:4b ff; and the latter from approximately 850 BC beginning with the story of Abraham's migration to Canaan.

Two other narratives were also identified: the "Priestly" source from after the Exile, beginning with the first creation account in Genesis 1–2:4a; and the Deuteronomist account from around the time of the rediscovery of the Law by King Josiah who reigned from c. 640–609 BC. Josiah instigated major reforms in Judah, repristinating the Jewish religion which had become syncretic even eclectic mixing with the worship of Baal. Both the Priestly and the Elohist accounts refrain from using the tetragrammaton, the four consonants of the proper name of God, until the name is revealed to Moses at the burning bush theophany, and use the Hebrew word for God, *Elohim*. However, from the beginning of the Jahwist narrative, *Elohim* is named by YHWH, or *Yahweh*. So we have the first creation account by the Priestly writer, establishing from *Genesis* 1 a highly formal Hymnic way of God's going about creating the cosmos, *ex nihilo*. (This is a foundational Hymn of Praise to God. Not science.) Seven days are set forth for the Creation, with the seventh day the day of God's taking possession of all creation as His house or temple, and resting. This is the *Shabbat* or Sabbath day. *Genesis* 1 answers the first question of philosophy, why is there anything at all? The answer is: Because God spoke his Word, and everything was created. For myself, I have loved this revelation! And the scientific method, a method not a metaphysic, although it hangs on a Jewish-Christian metaphysics, cannot answer this mysterious question of its own. (Richard Dawkins, Stephen Hawking, Bill Nye, all do not get this. With their ignorance of basic philosophy 101, they fail to understand the fundamental ground for thinking, and coming to Truth. To me, this was always very simple: the reason human beings can communicate and reason about the world around us is because our minds cohere with one another, and there is coherence between our minds and the world around us. Our minds and the entire Cosmos have been created by the *Logos*, the principle of reason, in a rational way. If not, a human being could not make black scratches on paper and find understanding in this. He or she would simply see black scratches on paper. And there would not be any communication with another human being unless our minds were created reasonably, and by a First Cause.)

The second creation account in Genesis 2:4b ff, is anthropomorphic, having Yahweh (using the capital letters of LORD in English translations) walk in the Garden of Eden, calling out for Adam and Eve as though He was another human being. This creation narrative has *adam* created out of *adamah*, the dust of the Earth, into whom the LORD God breathes the breath of life. When *Yahweh* finds Adam lonely, and in need of an equal complement to himself, the animal parade starts in front of a perched Adam looking at each in turn like a beauty pageant or a suspects' line up, to pick his favorite. While Adam names them—showing he is superior to them—none is found to be his equal partner. The Lord then tries plan B, and takes a rib to ensure an equal and complement to one another. When Adam awakes and sees this enticing creature, this radiant lovely woman, he claps his hands in joy and exclaims God has finally gotten this one right—and none too soon as the sheep were nervous. This first male and first female run around the garden and fall to the ground and discover their parts fit! Their human sexual difference is central to the story.

In both these accounts, the created order highlights the importance of God desiring creation out of sheer joy, out of love; showing human beings as the height of creation, either created last in the Priestly writing of chapter one, or first in the

XIX

Yahwistic second chapter story. In chapter one, the very blessing of God is given to all the species of animal life-including humans-to reproduce and continue. In addition, humanity is made in the likeness and image of God, and may commune with God. In chapter 3 of *Genesis* is the story that humans can and do abuse everything God gives us, as Eve is seduced by the serpent to disobey God, out of distrusting the One who loves them, and then Adam is likewise seduced by Eve to disobey, because he's a dumb guy, and they both want equality with God. The ancient forensic scene which follows shows everybody blaming someone or something else, and not taking responsibility for one's actions. There is no hint as to why there is sin and evil in the world. There is simply this parable. Either one gets this Jewish story, or one doesn't.

Professor Henning provided the general overview of Salvation History, with creation, the fall, God's establishing the Covenant with Abraham which would affect as many people as the stars in the heavens; the slavery of the *Habiru*, a nomadic northeastern Mesopotamian people on the outskirts of societies, which developed into the ancient Hebrews, rescued out of slavery in Egypt, and then formed by God out of love, and necessity as a witness to His covenant, by the leadership of Moses, and his revealing God's Torah or Law to the people of Israel; the Lord's very presence leading the people by means of the Cloud by day, the Pillar of fire by night; the manna and water provided by God to sustain the people; the disobedience of the people and judgment on them for this; the coming to the Promised Land; the rule of the Judges, including a woman and a left hander; the Monarchy with Saul anointed by the prophet Samuel; the rebellion of David and his kingship; the civil wars; the kingship of Solomon, and building of the Temple; and splitting up of the kingdom into the Northern tribes—in land called Israel, and Southern tribes—called Judah; the sending of the northern and southern prophets to remind the Jewish people of their Covenant with God; the destruction of the Northern Kingdom by the Assyrians in 722 BC, the destruction of the Southern Kingdom and Temple by the Babylonians in 587 BC; The Babylonian captivity; The return from exile by the Persians and rebuilding of the Temple—539 BC; Persians rule until 325 BC with Alexander the Great's conquering and imposing Hellenistic culture and political life on Eastern Mediterranean world, and Persia, and as far as India; After Alexander's Death, the rise of the *Diadochoi* or Successor Generals of Alexander in Greece, with Antigonus in the North, Seleucus in the Middle, and Ptolemy in South including Egypt; *Septuagint* published 300 BC; Jewish writings in Greek; Hellenistic rule lasts to 164BC brought down by the growing power of Rome as imperialistic conquerors; Judas Maccabaeus and family rebel against Antiochus IV in 164 BC and with the Temple restored and rededicated (celebrated by *Chanukah*—not pronounced "Chaka Khan") during times of Apocalyptic literature—*Daniel* added to the Writings; rise of Sadducees and Pharisees in Judea; Essenes live in caves in the Dead Sea; Fighting among Jewish groups over rule and control of the Temple, and invitation to Pompey the Great to invade and control Galilee in North, Judea in South 63 BC; Romans rule at time of Jesus c. 4 AD—c.30 AD. Herod the Great was a client

King. Augustus ratified Herod's will, in 4 BC giving half of the kingdom to Tetrarch Antipas, especially Galilee, one quarter to Tetrarch Philip, much of the Transjordan, and one quarter to Ethnarch Archelaus, in Judea. When the last couldn't keep Judea well governed, Archelaus was removed for a series of Governors, Quirinius, Governor in Syria, in 6 AD, to which territory Augustus added Judea, and required a census.

For the most part, I learned this sketchy summary of political rulers and Kingdoms over Israel, from Prof. Standish Henning.

It was at this time I concluded that I would seek holy orders in the Episcopal Church. Now, how on earth does one go about that?

In the spring of 1975, I took classes in the Greek and Roman classics, reading the Greek tragedians and dramatists: Euripides, Sophocles, and Aeschylus; and then Romans Ovid and Vergil. My professor was Herbert Howe, a complete classicist and character, and Episcopalian, who attended the low church of St. Andrew's, not far from Camp Randall where the Badgers played football. I continued with Prof. Andrew Weiner, and studied Shakespeare's Comedies. I took Professor Henning's Literary Aspects of the New Testament. I had cultivated a group of five guys including Paul Burke and Ray Dague, who enjoyed beer and would stay out arguing until 2 am or so. It interests me that all of us were considering the meaning of Jesus, and His Church, but we had such different ideas about whether the Church was a gift from God through God's Holy Spirit as promised by Christ, and asserted in the *Acts of the Apostles*, or a voluntary society as Hobbes would have said, or a front for the dehumanizing power trips of certain kinds of men, as Marx deemed it. For myself, I would argue that this issue is one of truth, and then what I meant by truth. There were at that point so many different kinds and shapes and sizes of Christian Churches, or unhistorical churches, or made up churches, or sects, or televangelist para church ministries, all bellowing their own causes like salesmen, that one needed care and study to determine what Churches would be in continuity with the Church of Jesus' Apostles. Paul was a dedicated Trotskyite, who thought Jesus had some good points. Ray Dague was I thought a monarchist. My roommate Gerald was funny, dedicated to funny. As a Ukrainian Catholic, he argued out of practical necessity, and the "church was there when you needed it. Of course weird old Fr. Arkady was there too, and you had to stay agile and out of his grasp. Usually he would catch the slower boys". At times we would get to the "signs of the true Church". The first was that Jesus is proclaimed Lord and Savior in continuity with the Apostles, since he gave authority to them and (by inference) their successors. He had promised His Church would extend in time and space. Second, that God inspired the 66 and maybe more (I like Ray was moving in a more Catholic direction) writings found in the Bible in which the Word of God was found. Third, the Nicene Creed was essential as a complete summary of the Christian doctrine, and the lens through which we could discern the Gospel in the Bible. Fourth, that Baptism was the clear sacrament for entering the Church or Body of Christ, and the Eucharist the means of keeping us in that Body. For me, it became more and more clear that I would decide on the Episcopal Church in which to get Baptized, and become a member.

This was occurring for me in the spring and summer of 1975, during which time my own family life was in some turmoil. After years of quarrelling, and hearing loud angry voices and doors slamming whenever I visited home, my parents left the Salvation Army's active Officer Corps. They were both exhausted from the fighting, which had seemed never-ending. My dad was taunted by mother to find a job which could cover their essentials, and they found a house to rent and began hunting for second hand furnishings in Janesville, Wisconsin. My brother Bill wanted a way out after his graduation from High School, as well as the upheaval affecting the family, and he enlisted with a couple friends in the Marine Corps. Dawn (my older sister) moved in with my parents and Robin. My dad found work selling kitchen countertops, and my mother went to work at J. C. Penney's. I arranged to work for the Salvation Army's territorial camp at Camp Lake Wisconsin, for the summer, which kept me away from home life, and provided a space to work through what I was contemplating, as well as some spending money.

XX

CAMP LAKE WAS LOCATED not far from the Illinois border between Lake Geneva and Kenosha. The Camp in which I was employed was an outreach to children mostly from inner city areas of Chicago and its environs. For nine intense weeks, the other counselors and I (African American and White) stayed in bunk houses with the youngsters 11–16. We had probably 12 on either side of the shared counselors' room, and a counselors' bathroom. We led youth worship, activities, sports and swimming, as well as Bible Study. I found the pastoring exhausting, but immensely valuable for coming to know how Black and White teens coped and behaved, and how a common basis of shared Christian faith and emphasis could hold us all together, even though this was a temporary situation week by week. Many of the boys saw me and other young men as father figures, and they seemed starved for attention and affection, and extremely vulnerable. I could see how clergy and other church ministers could be dangerous to such young people. There was never a hint of any kind of abuse that I was aware of the entire time I was there. I had two claims to fame, I taught the children every week to play soccer. I had taken part in soccer when I was in elementary school in Ann Arbor, and this provided an opportunity for everyone to play and run helter skelter. Some of the kids even actually kicked the ball! Second, quite often I was asked to preach a sermon on Sundays if an officer couldn't be found to lead chapel services on Sundays.

This made sense to me. And obviously it did to any number of folks I knew in the Salvation Army, other churches, and classmates, who expected me to be a minister. Since the age of eight or nine, I had strongly felt a calling from God to build up His church. To tell the truth, there was not a time when I didn't know this. This was central to my own identity, and I prayed or was aware constantly of God's presence in my life. Later when I studied *Romans* 8, I noted St. Paul's teaching on awareness of the Holy Spirit. I further was aware of Jesus's presence in my life, and my decision to follow Him as my Lord and Savior. I hungered for times to pray, study the Bible, and express my faith in Christ, in a more effective fashion than how I heard the faith talked about and preached in the Salvation Army, and other like churches. It was so inane and boring! With no sacraments! My question then was, where was God leading me? In which church would God call me to serve? And wouldn't it be more fun to become involved in law and politics? That would remain a major temptation to me in the years ahead, to turn away from what I knew I was supposed to be.

So I found a Biblical passage, generally from the Gospels, and proclaimed as well I could God's love shown us in Jesus. And I became pretty good at this. I was also invited to preach a few times for the adult chapel. The sermon I found was much liked was about various kinds of sin, moral, intellectual, sexual sin, utilizing Job, St. Paul, and David. The easiest one to explain was David, because you got to work in Bathsheba, and talk about sex. Anything I said about Bathsheba or sex got everyone's attention, to the point where you could hear a pin drop, as my mother used to say. The congregation was about one third white, and two thirds black, and the black folks would actively encourage you with a "thas right", "umm hummm", "Amen!", "preach it!". I liked that and attempted to preach with a rhythm. I enjoyed using humor, jokes, clever lines. By the end of the camp in early August, I was ready to find an Episcopal priest and talk about becoming a member, and get on the road to ordination.

I attended Saturday evening Mass at Trinity Episcopal Church, in downtown Janesville. The service used was the "zebra" book, one of the experimental Books of Common Prayer in the process of rolling out a contemporary new Book. About 10–15 of us met in the chapel of the Church, where a lamp was lit signifying the reserved elements of Christ's Body and Blood in an aumbry, placed in a recess in the wall behind the altar. This was "low Mass", meaning no processional, no music even, usually one acolyte serving the celebrant, who announced his presence with the ringing of a bell on the wall in the back of the pews. The entire service took 25 minutes, including Holy Communion. The celebrant was Fr. Eric Heers, whom I assumed to be the local priest, but who instead was covering for the rector's vacation. The two times I attended, and received Communion with the others, I thought Fr. Eric looked as though he would rather be anywhere but there. He never smiled, talked in a monotone, forgot his place several times, got pissed at the acolyte, loudly ordered a couple folks not to "intinct" or dip their wafer in the chalice and "swish", and wore beautiful robes, which he told me were called vestments. He wore black shoes, a black cassock, a white alb and amice, a cincture or rope, a stole, and a chasuble. His posture was generally hunched over the Altar Book with his two hands held in front of him like a hold-up was occurring, or like showing off how large the fish was he had caught.

I caught up with the gentleman once the second time I was there through sheer quickness, because he never talked to anyone during the Peace, or afterwards. He didn't hang around. When I did catch up with him, he seemed a little grumpy about this, even surly. He had to find his check he said. I labored to introduce myself, which got an ironic, "That's nice" from him. I then inquired about becoming a member, and he said he was not the rector, but Fr. Wayne Smith, who would be back the following Saturday. End of discussion.

On Friday, August 1, 1975, I knocked on the Rector's door at Trinity Episcopal Church, and was greeted by Fr. Wayne Lamar Smith, a short pudgy guy with glasses, a black short sleeved clergy shirt with tab collar, who moved about with quick steps, pushy, smart, lively, voluble, who spoke rapidly with the quickest wit, and as I came to realize, a depth of knowledge in a great many matters that amazed me. And he smoked. He asked me why I was there. I responded that I wanted to become a member of the Episcopal Church, go to theological school-I hoped the University of Chicago Divinity School, and get ordained. "Oh", he said. "You already know it all!". And then he burst into laughter. And he invited me to come in, have a glass of sherry, and have a conversation. "Tell me about yourself", he said. I gave him a summary of my life up to that time, including my Salvation Army background, and my renewed interest in the Christian faith. "Oh", he exclaimed, "the Salvation Army! They play trombones in place of getting baptized!" (Great laughter.) "And do you have a favorite theologian?" " Yes, I adore Paul Tillich!" "Ohhhhhh, hahahaha!!!! Well don't tell that to our Bishop!!!!! I know about Tillich . . . didn't he screw everything on two legs, maybe four?" Just then the phone rang, and his secretary came in bringing letters for him to sign. There were parishioners and service people coming through almost constantly.

I looked around his office. There were books everywhere all around a fairly good sized room, some on shelves, some stacked, various binders and files around, stacks of newsletters and journals and magazines all around. At one point He asked me to step out while he took a pastoral call, about a parishioner drying out in alcoholic rehab outside of Nashotah House. So I cased that joint, and saw books everywhere in shelves in the waiting area outside his office. I saw Old Testament and archaeological books, such as the famous Wright, Bright, and Albright (G. E. Wright, John Bright, W. F. Albright). He had Camus and Sartre, Pascal, Kierkegaard, Nietzsche, St. Thomas Aquinas, St. Augustine, the two volume White and Dykman on the Constitution and Canons of the Episcopal Church, Bishop James Pike, T. S. Eliot, W. H. Auden, John Donne's poems and sermons, John Updike, C. S. Lewis, Emily Dickinson, W. H. Prescott's 1843 history of the conquest of Mexico, Francis Parkman, Karl Barth, Reinhold Niebuhr, histories of the Evangelical United Church of Prussia, of the Evangelical and Reformed Church in the United States, and the Episcopal Church, Luther's Table Talk, Calvin's Institutes, a shelf full of Civil War books of various kinds, including Carl Sandberg, and Bruce Catton. And I saw my friends Paul Tillich and Friedrich Schleiermacher represented. These were all his second-class books, which had not found room in his office.

He called me in and I commented on the library he had. "Oh, this is nothing. I have another large library at home." We then began sparring about religion, revelation, the Sacraments, theology. I argued that the purity of the heart was all that was needed for salvation. "Then you only trust your subjectivity?" he quizzed. "If I pray", I said. "So you don't really care about what Christ says in the New Testament? You don't think Baptism is necessary?" I assured him I had been "dedicated" as a child in the Salvation Army. "Well, let's see, the Risen Lord called upon his apostles to go into all the world, and make disciples by baptizing them, and teaching them. And he will be with them always. That's in *Matthew* 28:19–20. I don't see where it says "dedication". What does that mean anyway? Why come up with substitutes for what our Lord Himself says?" I replied that from my reading of the Bible, Jesus played fast and loose with the Law. He hardly worshipped as a Jew. "The Sabbath was made for man, not man for the Sabbath." Fr. Smith came right back: "Check out *Luke* 4 where it states it was Jesus' custom to worship on the Sabbath". "Do you have a Bible?", I asked. I've got about twenty, take your pick. I picked up a King James' Version. After a few seconds, I said OK, but what about Baptism? "How many verses do you need?" came his response. "Jesus was baptized, and we may assume his disciples were also because they baptized folks. Paul says clearly only twenty years after the Resurrection that baptism is necessary. Check out *Romans* 6. Do you want to obey Christ or don't you?" I didn't say much, and he added, "It is central to the Episcopal Church and to almost all Christians around the world, to have the Lord's commanded Sacraments of Baptism and Eucharist, or Holy Communion. Nothing is unmediated in our life in Christ". "What does that mean?", I asked. "It means that all of the world is God's creation, and that everything that God does to love us comes through His creation. The Sacramental principle is a simple one: The Physical is the medium of the Spiritual. You do not have one without the other. When God sent His Son into the world to save humanity, He did not send an idea, or a feeling, or something we can conjure up if we concentrate hard enough. It's not a philosophy or a religion, or a moral rule. It's not a service club like Kiwanis. God came among us as a human being, and through being human He saved us. We say in the Episcopal Church, 'a Sacrament is an outward and visible sign of an inward and spiritual grace'. Can you think of loving a person and not saying it? Or showing it? Or doing something? Even if you're thinking about the person, or feeling fondly, little neurons are firing away. There is nothing that you can do as a human being, which is not both spiritual and physical. Martin Luther said when he doubted his faith in God, he would hit his forehead and say, 'I've been baptized'. It really and truly happened. And he says baptized, not dedicated. Baptism is the instrument and sign of God making us His children, by water, and naming the Trinity. God *acts* through His Sacraments!"

All of this came at me with lickety split rapid fire. Here was a bright articulate priest of the Episcopal Church taking me on, and not letting me get away with bullshit. He was a staunch believer in Jesus. And he believed in the Church as the people of God, the Body of Christ. After nearly three hours of arguing (which I loved), Fr. Smith said to me to stop reading Tillich. He gave me Archbishop Michael Ramsey's classic from 1936, *The Gospel and the Catholic Church*. He told me to read that, and Bonnell Spencer's *Ye Are the Body*, from 1962, and for my sins, Eric L. Mascall's *Theology and the Future*. Finally, Fr. Smith told me to read the *First Epistle of John*, and note the sacramental importance of the Apostle's knowing Jesus as human, in chapter 1. His parting shot was, "It's time to become a Catholic, not a Protestant. Protestants want to sit around and debate the Kingdom of God. Catholics want to enter the Kingdom."

I left from meeting this priest very happily. Years later, when I had been ordained a priest, and had become acquainted with my colleagues in the Diocese of Milwaukee, it amazed me that the only priest who could have taken me seriously enough to sit and argue for three hours was the one I met that afternoon, when I simply knocked on his door. Over the next few weeks, I got to know Fr. Smith better, and discussed his assignments.

I had become a senior at the University of Wisconsin, with the intention to graduate in the spring of 1976. I took the second part of Dr. Henning's "Literary Aspects of the New Testament", which I found thrilling. He began with *Acts of the Apostles*, in order to show some chronological order for the preaching and witness of the Apostles, using C. H. Dodd's *The Apostolic Preaching and Its Developments*, (1936), and then providing some possible dates for the other writings. I had never heard the New Testament presented in this way before. I picked up Dodd's book at Paul's Bookstore, and I enjoyed it-including the handy dandy chart inside. Dodd's view expressed in this little book was that there was a bedrock *kerygma*, the Greek word for the preaching of the Apostles; and *didache* from the Greek word for teaching-which he believed could be disentangled one from the other, the former considered assured by historical judgment and primary, and the second, following from the first, and also of historical value. With regard to this attempted distinction of Dodd's, many misunderstood Dodd's intention, and considered it too simplistic, as though Dodd was simply declaring, himself, what was his Gospel within the Gospel, his own creed so to speak, his own interpretation of Scripture. He actually wrote taking exception to the "form critical" school about which Bultmann particularly was notable, staking his claim that their extreme skepticism of anything of historical value in the Gospels and other New Testament writings, was faulty and excessive. Not many New Testament critics were impressed with Dodd's thesis, at the time of the book's publication. New Testament scholars, especially in Germany, were too affected by the general *milieu* of looking askance on anyone who made some sort of claim for a bedrock historical Jesus. For myself I had found by reading the Gospels that Jesus' teaching was itself hard to separate into an entirely different form from his preaching, or from his presence manifesting the Kingdom of God. I had read a passage of George MacDonald's, from my C. S. Lewis enthusiasm, which concluded with, "Those who would do the will of God, must know the doctrine", *St. John* 7:17, noted above which seemed plain to me or would otherwise leave us misunderstanding what Scripture is as place of the Word of God. In *Romans*, when St. Paul has laid out all of the foundational doctrine of chapters 1–11, he begins chapter 12, concerning essential teaching about how then human beings should treat one another in the Body of Christ, "Therefore". He doesn't say, "Now about unimportant housekeeping matters". John Paul II impressed me deeply by saying so faithfully as a follower of Jesus, "For Christians the *supreme model of community is the Holy Trinity*, the mystery of Three Divine Persons in a perfect communion of love. Every word and deed of Jesus Christ, the Incarnate Son of God, was a revelation of the inner life which he shares with the Father and the Holy Spirit." [1] This runs in accord with the Eastern Church Fathers and more recently, St. Gregory Palamas' summation of the Trinity's "Divine Energies", available in God's existence. [2]

Professor Henning proceeded with explicating the meaning of the Gospels, beginning with *St. Mark's Gospel*. He called our attention to the statement of Eusebius of Caesarea from his *History of the Church*, written early in the fourth century, concerning this Gospel:

> Concerning Mark who wrote the Gospel, he (Papias, bishop in Hierapolis, d.155, friend of St. Polycarp of Smyrna, and St. John the Elder) expounds with these words: "And the Presbyter (St. John) also said this: Mark being the interpreter of Peter, wrote accurately all that he remembered, but not however in order, of the things which were spoken or done by our Lord, for he neither heard our Lord, nor followed him, but later as I said, he followed Peter, who provided instruction according to the need, but not as to make an orderly account of the Lord's discourses, so that Mark did not err in anything about writing some matters as he remembered them, for he was attentive to one thing, not to leave out anything that he heard, or to make any false statements in them". So then these things were recounted by Papias concerning Mark. [3]

The general historical dates of this writing are: Books I-VII, c. 303, VIII-X, c. 323. Papias is referred to as a hearer of St. John, and a companion of Polycarp, in Irenaeus, c. 180. [4]

Without knowing a great deal at this point about the prejudices against finding much or any historical knowledge discerned in the New Testament, as well as the Old Testament for that matter, and how the Quest to know nearly anything at all about the historical Jesus was muted with the impact of Albert Schweitzer's book, I was at this stage generally open to hearing the results of various literary historical criticisms. This was before I came across Schweitzer's devastating judgment on the inane and lackluster, dry and uninspired lives of Jesus produced in the 19th century—especially epitomized with that of David Friedrich Strauss-is accurate, I believe, even in the last few years with the same kind of writing about the historical Jesus by our own day's insipid rationalists. Schweitzer wrote:

1. John Paul II, "Pontifical Council for Promoting Christian Unity", 7, Italics in the original.
2. Palamas, *The Triads*, 93–111
3. Eusebius, *The Ecclesiastical History*, III, 39
4. Irenaeus, *Against the Heresies*, 5.30

The Jesus of Nazareth who came forward publicly as the Messiah, who preached the ethic of the Kingdom of God, who founded the Kingdom of Heaven upon earth and died to give His work its final consecration, never had any existence. He is a figure designed by rationalism, endowed with life by liberalism, and clothed by modern theology in an historical garb. [5]

I found that the *prima facie* evidence for Jesus' historical life and impact that he made on his contemporaries, highly credible. While the prevailing winds of culture in the West, affected by Marx, Freud, and Nietzsche, had brought about a distinct lack of confidence among clergy for preaching the Gospel at all, Dr. Henning showed the likelihood of Jesus' life, teaching, and miracles, by the inner evidence in the New Testament, as well as the exterior evidence. Flavius Josephus, the Jewish historian writing in the 90s in Greek for the Flavian emperors (Vespasian, Titus, Domitian), and even acquiring his surname from the family, had mentioned Jesus and others involved in the Jesus movement of the First century.[6] Tacitus, in the last book of his *Annals*, written about 117 AD, mentions the historical Jesus, called by him "Christus" or "Chrestus", as well as his death, and the large presence of Christians in Rome (c. 64) Nero had used as scapegoats upon whom to lay the charge of arson, leading to the devastation of the great fire which burned in Rome for over a week. Tacitus' report included Nero's use of various Christians, regardless of age or sex, to light his gardens at night, after dousing them with pitch.[7] There is also the famous official letter of Pliny the Younger, Roman Governor in Pontus and Bithynia from 111–113 AD, to the Emperor Trajan, asking for advice about how to treat Christians who are being anonymously accused by neighbors for crimes against the State.[8] These are all literary evidence of the Christian faith being spread quickly through the Empire.

Of course, there is the interior evidence of Christian writings, including the various Gospels, history (Acts of the Apostles), and various Epistles—13 attributed to St. Paul alone, making up almost 50% of the later canonized New Testament. Other writings are dated to the end of the First Century, or shortly thereafter, which were not finally accepted as Canon, such as *I Clement*, the *Shepherd of Hermas*, an Apocalyptic vision, and the *Didache*. The identifying of the Canonical writings of the New Testament, as clearly faithful witnesses to the Gospel of the Messiah, Jesus, the Savior of the World, as Christians believed in continuity with the Covenant promises by the Lord God to Abraham, took centuries, with the process lasting from the first century until the early fifth century. It was not until St. Athanasius' Festal Letter in 367 AD, and the round of Church Councils starting in Northern Africa by St. Augustine of Hippo, and leading to the Pope's agreement in 410 AD, that the Church Catholic and Orthodox, West and East found the Twenty-Seven Writings as Canonical and inspired

---

5. Schweitzer, *The Quest for the Historical Jesus*, 396

6. Josephus, *Antiquities of the Jews*, 18.3.3 (A few additions have been made by later Christians.)

7. Tacitus, *Annals*, 15.44

8. Pliny the Younger, *Complete Letters*, 10.96.97

for Church use by the Holy Spirit. As many people are aware, the greatest challenge to this agreement was *The Revelation of St. John the Divine*, or the *Apocalypse*. This apocalyptic writing was so misunderstood particularly by the Western Church, and generally believed to be a writing to cause division, that this in particular caused the delay. The Eastern Church fathers and church communities believed these visions were brilliantly written descriptions of the liturgy in Heaven itself, with Christians from around the world worshipping the Holy Trinity, in the company of the Mother of God, angels and archangels, and the saints who had died previously than the time of St. John's writing of the visions, c. 95 AD. And the caution of the Western Churches was obviously justified by the horrific ways *Revelation* has been interpreted in the following 1900 years by fervent Millenarians, or chiliasts. This was the belief that Christ would reign on Earth for a thousand years literally. This view was combatted by the Nicene Council Bishops who declared in the Ecumenical Creed: " . . . whose Kingdom shall have no end".

Once this historical fact is grasped by anyone, then one must consider how the Canon was agreed to in day to day real life. There were those who agreed and those who disagreed, but it was by the Holy Spirit acting in and through the Early Churches, that the Canon of 27 writings was accepted. One must have knowledge of the ancient Church to understand the meaning of this. And for those who are Christian, one moves to a doctrine of Pneumatology (doctrine of the Holy Spirit), and even Ecclesiology (doctrine of the Church). This is a logical progression. If a heuristic is set up as "Bible only", one has made what in philosophy is called a category error. There is no Bible without the interaction between God and the Church, the Body of Christ. There are always human intermediaries. The Canon is the gift of the Holy Spirit, received by the ancient Church in historical fashion.

The dating that I recall Dr. Henning put forward for the New Testament writings was:

St. Paul's undisputed Epistles—49—63

St. Paul's Pastoral Epistles—75–85

The Gospel of St. Mark—68

The Gospel of St. Matthew 85

The Gospel of St. Luke 85

The Acts of the Apostles 85

The Epistle of St. James 85

The Epistle to the Hebrews 85

The Gospel of St. John 90

The Johannine Epistles 90

The First Epistle of St. Peter 90

However, in the process of the writings being circulated to various Churches from East to West, by 150 AD there already look to be 22 writings, which by use, and certainly in Rome, were considered, inspired by God and had some authority as God's Word. These were the four Gospels, *Acts*, the Pauline Epistles, and *I Peter, James, I and II John*. So, the basis of the Canon to be finalized in the late Fourth and early Fifth centuries was present from about the mid Second century on.

I got into the habit of walking with Professor Henning after class, and hearing about the Episcopal Church, and his take on what was happening in 1975. Grace Episcopal Church had asked their rector to leave about nine months after they had feted him in a big celebration. Such is life, was Henning's summary for this. On the occasion of hearing his dating proposals for New Testament writings, he urged me to look for Black's Series of New Testament Commentaries, by very fine scholars. He liked Dennis Nineham's *Mark*, George Caird's commentaries on *Luke* and *Revelation*, and several of Paul's letters commented on by C. K. Barrett. These books were being published in the United States by Harper and Row. He recommended I get ahold of John Knox's *Chapters in a Life of Paul*, 1950, which provided an excellent study on dating Paul's writings. (Many years later I still find Henning's promoting of these books very sound, possibly with the exception of Nineham.) We also talked about my upcoming baptism, scheduled for the last Sunday after Pentecost, which took place generally in late November.

By far my favorite teacher for entertainment, was my Spanish T. A., Ms. Elena da Costa. She was the most caring, energetic instructor, who in the midst of our 1975 fall semester was awarded her Ph. D. in Spanish language and literature. I don't know how she found out but she startled me one day in Spanish lab, ostensibly to work on my rather limited speaking ability "*en espanol*", though wasting my time listening to Charo, a popular Spanish actress and personality, who was singing, "*Eres Tu*". Elena invited me to her apartment to drink sangrias. She was a pleasant hostess who insisted on our speaking only Spanish. She actually wanted me to hear her favorite music recording of Joaquin Rodrigo's "Concierto de Aranjuez", played by Classical guitarist John Williams, this beautiful lyrical lush piece. It had just been released in 1974. Now, forty years later, it is this music I still reach for first thing in the morning while I have my coffee. I have several CDs with Julian Bream, John Williams, David Russell, Angel or Pepe Romero, Paco de Lucia, guitarists. The melody carried first by the oboe and then guitar, particularly in the much-loved Adagio movement, is simply haunting, evoking the music this blind composer remembered hearing in his home town as a child. For myself, I got through my foreign language requirements for my Bachelor's Degree, with three semesters of Spanish, a single semester of Latin, and a year of German.

XX

In the fall, Gerald Mahun and I had moved out of the Regent Apartments, and we had discovered a nice upstairs flat over a hair salon on 1400 South Park. Our neighbor who became a friend of mine was Patti C., a philosophy student from Chicago. We shared Professor Ivan Soll's class on nineteenth century German philosophy, and we regularly got together at her place to discuss Hegel, Marx, Schopenhauer, and Nietzsche, depending on who was the focus for a particular time. With the reading of a great deal of Paul Tillich, I found I could navigate this class with steady work and long hours. However, I noticed on a few occasions of working to understand Hegel's idealism, in English translation, Patti and I would labor at length by reading particular passages out loud, until we had come to believe through discussion and arguing, to some beginning understanding of what it was he was stating. And then we would exult about this until we realized we hadn't subjected it to criticism. Did we think this way? Did Hegel's presentation fit epistemologically? Was there coherence between what he said and what we believed to be true in the world around us?

Our landlord was an elderly gentleman, who could not make himself speak clearly, so he was accompanied for every visit by his daughter and son-in-law. They both addressed him as "the Colonel". Gerald and I were in the habit of meeting this strange threesome at Bee's Tavern across the street from us, our home away from apartment, where we played pool on most nights. (Bee himself was an enormously fat old guy, whose corduroy pants and folds of flappy fat slapped around and made weird sounds whenever he walked. He spoke in a growly harsh way, always with a half chewed cigar in his thick lipped mouth. Gerald and I called him the Big Bee.) The Colonel could never say anything understandable, except at the end of his verbose statements, when he would add a loud "You Know?", and wait for me to respond. I would stare at him with fixed attention trying somehow to discern what the hell he had just said, and when that failed I would hazard a guess as to whether I was expected to say yes or no. Invariably I would get it wrong. Then the poor man's head would turn down and then towards me while loudly expostulating, with an ear-splitting "WHAT!", and remonstrate with me, with sounds and pops and burps, saliva flying, eyes blinking rapidly, body shaking, that I had gotten him wrong, and then once again finish with, "You know?" And the whole charade would repeat itself.

After a number of discussions with Fr. Smith, and attending Church regularly at Trinity, Janesville, I asked if I could be baptized. I had reached the point of wanting to be brought into the Church, the Body of Christ, as this excellent priest taught, so at age 21, I determined to go ahead. He scheduled this for the last Sunday after Pentecost, November 23, 1975. In approaching the date, however, I got cold feet, and wondered if I truly believed in the Incarnation, and especially in the Bodily Resurrection of Jesus. The second century *Apostles' Creed* was confessed in the Baptismal service of the *Book of Common Prayer*, the simple brief individual witness to God the Holy Trinity, and to the Revelation to the world of Jesus Christ. I had begun reading a newly revised biography of *Nietzsche* by Walter Kaufmann, originally published in 1950, but now revised for the fourth time. I looked up several references about Christ, and decided I had too many doubts to go ahead with the service. I called Fr. Smith and explained my change of heart, to which he responded with a curt, "Fine". Click.

The rest of November went uneventfully, except that I was coming across any number of signs of Christ all around. I had discovered Michael Harrington's writing, a Roman Catholic with a staunch social conscience, who styled himself a socialist. Later in life he would claim to have lost his faith in the Church, but he had been in his early life a protégé of Dorothy Day's. He debated William F. Buckley on Firing Line, and connected Christian concern for the poor as not private charity, but identified with justice as spelled out in the Bible. He was born In St. Louis in 1928, and had been educated by Jesuits, before becoming chairman of the Socialist Party in America, succeeding Norman Thomas. In 1962 he published *The Other America: Poverty in the United States*, in which he argued there was an invisible number of poor and working poor in our affluent nation, as many as 25% of our population, which could only be addressed by a "war" on poverty. Dwight MacDonald reviewed the book in the *New Yorker*, and it came to Walter Heller's attention, and then to President John F. Kennedy. The War on Poverty announced by President Johnson was directly attributed to Harrington's sense of urgency of overcoming this scourge of poverty. The social programs already in place of Social Security and Food Stamps were expanded, and others such as Medicare and Medicaid, and new opportunities for housing, and Head Start were all a part of Federal programs of Johnson's war on Poverty. At one point in a later book of the 1960's, Harrington wrote:

> One important aspect of utopia is to understand its limits . . . some socialist writer—it may have been Trotsky—said that the function of socialism is to raise men from the level of fate to that of a tragedy . . . that is to say, utopia is not going to solve everything by any means. As a matter of fact, I have thought for a long time about Marx's prediction that in a society where men are no longer murdered or starved by nature, but where nature is under man's control, there would be no need of God because God is essentially man's projections of his own fears and hopes—a curious image. In contrast to that, I wonder whether at precisely the moment all economic problems disappear, that there could not be a great *growth* in religion rather than a decline. It is a possibility, because we would have a society in which men would die not from . . . idiocies about the economy. They would die from death. And at that point the historical shell around the fact of death would be broken. For the first time society would face up to death itself. [9]

And, while on Christmas break, I picked up Plato's *Republic*, long passages of which I had read in Dr. Booth Fowler's Political Philosophy class. Now I was startled to come

9. Harrington, *Cacotopias and Utopias*, 21–2

across what Socrates talks about with Glaucon concerning a Republic for citizens who are seemingly just, but hide their injustice. At that point, Glaucon imagines what would happen to a truly righteous man if he were to appear—this from c.380 BC:

> . . . a simple and noble man, who, in the phrase of Aeschylus, does not wish to seem but to be good. Then we must deprive him of the seeming. For if he is going to be thought just he will have honors and gifts because of that esteem. We cannot be sure in that case whether he is just for justice's sake or for the gifts and the honors. So we must strip him bare of everything but justice make his state the opposite of his imagined counterpart. Though doing no wrong he must have the repute of the greatest injustice, so that he may be put to the test as regards justice through not softening because of ill repute and consequences thereof . . . We must tell it, then, and even if my language is somewhat rude and brutal . . . *that such being his disposition the just man will have to endure the lash, the rack, chains, the branding iron in his eyes, and finally after every extremity of suffering, he will be impaled or crucified . . . 10* (italics added)

Later, I went to church at Grace Madison, and heard their new rector, Fr. Robert Hargrove, recently called from Fort Worth, Texas. My experience previously at Sunday worship at Grace was enjoying the liturgy and the music. Now I was hearing a former Southern Baptist minister who could preach marvelously from the Gospel for the day, and in a different way from Fr. Wayne Smith who preached on Catholic themes which I appreciated more, but who was affirming and complemented Smith's approach. I had in a little more than a few months come across two of the finest preachers I had ever heard. And these were not academics who had the time to craft their sermons, or visiting firemen coming with a favorite sermon from the "barrel" as one said, but parish priests with cures of souls, in those particular parish communities. I also observed that Grace Church was beginning to grow in attendance. This emphasis on preaching without a lot of rhetorical tricks, in fact centering the sermon on the Gospel as one who believed this oneself, caused a stir in the moribund Grace congregation. Since I had attended Grace Church during a search, and then when the new rector arrived, I noticed Hargrove's preaching was attracting *men* first of all, then younger folks, then many others. Both Hargrove and Smith preached about faith in Jesus as the world's gracious Lord and Savior, and not in order to rehearse their doubts; and they both read Scripture in a critical way: this was the Word of God through human witness, attested or dependent on what the first generation of Apostles themselves witnessed and experienced. The opening four verses of *St. John's First Epistle* says as much:

> We declare to you what was from the beginning, what we have heard, what we have seen with our own eyes, what we have looked at and touched with our hands, concerning the word of life-this life was revealed, and we have seen it

---

10. Plato, *Republic*, II, 361b-e

and testify to it, and declare to you the eternal life that was with the Father and was revealed to us-

We declare to you what we have seen and heard that you also may have fellowship (Greek is *koinonia*-full Communion in and with God) with us; and truly our fellowship is with the Father and with his Son Jesus Christ. We are writing these things so that our joy may be complete. [11]

It was courageous for both these Episcopal priests to say: I believe this, and this is from God, and therefore beyond what mere "salesmen" or "ad men" or politicians can do. In the mid-70s, there were many foolish ideas by clergy to attempt varieties of presentation as a substitute for a sermon: clown acts, dialogues between clergy (unrehearsed), dialogues with the congregation, having children preach, or teenagers taking a whack at it, or readings at length from secular literature, more as an effect, to humor or entertain the congregations. At times, dancers would appear and dance around the Sanctuary, around the altar, and into the Nave. African drummers, or Native American drummers, or an altar guild member on the bongos, would appear and do something, at first no one knew what. I found most of this bizarre and a sign of insecurity on a priest's or bishop's part of what it was to be the chief proclaimer of the Gospel. They were losing confidence in their own vocations, in their churches' purpose, indeed, in their faith in Christ. Meanwhile I, and I imagine many like me, were coming to the Episcopal Church seeking a reasonable and serious awareness of God Almighty in the traditional Anglican liturgy of the worship in the Catholic Church, and the Sacramental awareness of our lives in this world God had brought into being to love us and the Cosmos. What is the purpose of the Church for countless folks who have had their lives sucked out of them by a world that then just slithers off?

Fr. Smith's preaching also set forward a new way for me to see God and ourselves. He utilized a great variety of stories from the Bible, from literature, from church fathers, from American history or world history, from science to present the overwhelming mystery of life all around us. This was not an inane or shallow presentation of humanity as sinners needing God. He spoke of the creation of God as Good, made by a loving God out of sheer joy, who wished to share its goodness with human beings. We were made in God's likeness and image. He quoted Gerard Manly Hopkins: "The world is charged with the grandeur of God. It will flame out, like shining from shook foil . . ." And Elizabeth Barrett Browning: "Earth's crammed with heaven, and every common bush afire with God; but only he who sees takes off his shoes, the rest sit round it and pluck blackberries." He depicted this beautiful world of creation (not the mere nature of the Enlightenment) filled with God's presence. He spoke from Scripture itself about the creation in the first few chapters of Genesis, and showed the differences of the two creation myths, but more, their similarities, and why they

11. *The First Epistle of St. John*: 1—4

were revelatory. God had created through His Word, and so the creation, the Cosmos was brought into being, alive, living, and in accord with general principles of reason, so that our minds (also created by God) could apprehend outside of ourselves, and even communicate. God had created us to be in Communion with Himself, to be in relationship with Him, and through Him to be in relationship with other human beings, all humanity in fact. The Created order was to show God's majesty, and these signs of God's presence were adumbrated in art and science, by literature, philosophy, in music, even in the ways we attempted to order human society. But we knew God chiefly in worship, which involved all of ourselves, our postures of prayer, our senses-music, flowers, incense, books, our receiving the Eucharistic body and blood of Christ himself. The Holy Eucharist was the reason for Christians' worshipping on Sundays, in that we gather together on the day of our Lord's Resurrection to receive what Jesus gives us to nourish us as He promised to His disciples. While the Episcopal Church had neglected this great gift of God's for some time, it was being restored not only in this Church, but in the entire Anglican Communion—of which the Episcopal Church was the local manifestation. Gradually the Churches of the Anglican Communion found throughout the world were restoring this central act of worship on Sundays, by the means of the liturgical renewal movement which swept through the Anglican Communion and the Episcopal Church in the 1940s and afterward. We were made God's people in Christ through our participation in Baptism, the action of the Holy Spirit, in continuity with the Covenant God made with Abraham, as stated in *Genesis* 15, and now renewed in Christ's Baptism. And we lived as the Body of Christ through the Word and the Eucharist, the continual action of Christ's sacrifice on the Cross, thereby redeeming humanity, and making Himself accessible to us in Holy Communion.

I attended church on Sundays and heard the great themes of God comforting His people, and promising to come to us, because of His love for us. "Comfort ye, comfort ye my people saith your God! Speak ye comfortably to Jerusalem, and cry unto her that her warfare is accomplished." "He shall feed his flock like a shepherd, and he shall gather the lambs with his arm, and carry them in his bosom, and gently lead those that are with young." "O, that thou wouldst rend the heavens and come down!" "And the glory of the Lord shall be revealed, and all flesh shall see it together, for the mouth of the Lord hath spoken it". I confess that I heard the themes from the "Messiah" of Handel, which impressed me tremendously. This was not the sentimental mush of "I come to the Garden alone",(with the word I thought was God's name when I was a kid, Andy; "Andy walks with me, Andy talks with me . . .") but the announcement of God coming to His people in the future with compassion. And that included me. "The people that walked in darkness have seen a great light, and they that dwell in the land of the shadow of death, upon them hath the light shined." All these prophecies of what God will do, I began to see in global terms, affecting all of human history, not pietistic or escapist or—the bane of American Christianity—individualistic religion.

On Christmas Eve, I went to the 11:00 pm solemn high Eucharist, and went up to receive Communion. Fr. Smith grabbed my hand to show he was glad I was back. After the service, I told him I was now ready to be baptized. He invited me to come to the Smith house (not the rectory-the Smiths owned their house), and we could talk. So off I went to the Smiths' reception, where twenty or so church members were in attendance, including the Smiths' three daughters. The celebration had been glorious, and the sermon was a knock out about the meaning of God's coming into His world in the baby Jesus. What other religion has such a story with its god as vulnerable as coming as a baby, entrusted to humanity? Smith preached this with energy and good humor, theological acumen, and pastoral awareness of his congregation. I stayed and got to know several folks easily when Fr. Smith introduced me as getting baptized on Sunday, January 4, 1976. Which I did.

XXI

FR. SMITH SAID THIS was a decision for a lifetime, and I had the rest of my life to come to terms with what it meant. He was in the habit of quoting T. S. Eliot's line from "Little Gidding" in his *Four Quartets*:

> We shall not cease from exploration
>
> And the end of all our exploring
>
> Will be to arrive where we started
>
> And know the place for the first time.[1]

Besides, I was asking God and the church community to support me, the local part of the entire Church of God, which was Catholic and around the world, and having Apostolicity, meaning it traces its heritage to the witness of the Apostles themselves. Fr. Smith informed me I would make my first confession on Saturday, the day before the Baptism. What? This was new. I met my priest in the chapel at Trinity Episcopal Church, Janesville, and as was my custom, argued awhile. After ten minutes or so, I began the Sacramental service of reconciliation. "Bless me, Father, for I have sinned. This is my first confession." I named about twenty-five sins that came to mind, having prepared for a couple hours, and I received the absolution promised by our Lord who had given this power over to His Apostles in *St. John's Gospel*, chapter 20. I realized it was good for me to say these things aloud, because it was so easy to pretend they were not really weighing on me or bad for my soul and my relationship to God if I never said them to another person. And the Sacramental principle of a mediated action of God's through human beings, namely priests, has come to seem wise to me. The think method for believing had not worked for me in the Salvation Army. I needed to hear a human voice say, "Our Lord Jesus Christ, who has left power to His Church to absolve all sinners who truly repent and believe in Him, of his great mercy forgive you of all your offenses; and by his authority committed to me, I absolve you from all your sins: In the Name of the Father, and of the Son, and of the Holy Spirit. Amen." (I found I believed this, and making my private Confession at least once a year has become part of my personal spiritual discipline.) The next day, I was presented for baptism by two

---

1. Eliot, "Little Gidding", 145

lovely older folks, George and Rose Melan, two Lebanese immigrants, who gave me a donkey carved from olive wood from Israel. I was presented and stood between two infants—not between two thieves—something Mr. Day couldn't imagine doing in Clarence Day's *Life With Father*. My parents were also present, having decided to come and witness the sacrament.

I returned to Madison to begin my last semester to graduation. I was finally giving a serious reading to Archbishop Michael Ramsey's classic on *The Gospel and Catholic Church,* which has been easily the most influential theological book in my life.

In it, this marvelous young man (only 32 when it was published in 1936) laid out the identity of the Christian Church, which was formed by Jesus Himself during His ministry involving the twelve apostles, and then fully brought to life by the power of the Holy Spirit at Pentecost. The Gospel is the saving proclamation of the Incarnation of Jesus, His work, His mission, His Death and Resurrection, and His Authority as Messiah or King of all creation especially humanity. Christ preached and made whole all who through Him were reconciled with God. The Catholic Church is the extension of Christ Himself, as St. Paul states explicitly-especially in *First Corinthians*, through His Body, the Church. And Ramsey never identifies the Church in a triumphalist manner, but always as Christ dying and rising. The Church is known in continuity with the Apostles having themselves received the Spirit of Christ from God the Father. The essential marks of the Church were the same: Apostolic order, found in the Episcopate; The Word of God as attested in the Old and New Testaments; The Nicene Creed as the Catholic statement of faith; and the two essential Sacraments ordained and commanded by Christ Himself, Baptism and the Holy Eucharist.

Not too long after this, Fr. Smith took me to see Bishop Gaskell, for the necessity of the bishop's imprimatur, so to speak. The process of ordination in a particular Diocese is finally the bishop's own. We drove to the Diocesan Offices next door to All Saints' Cathedral in Milwaukee, on East Juneau Avenue, and I followed the two clergymen to lunch at some swanky place with "highballs" (!), which I seem to remember as gimlets. Fr. Smith warned me that the Bishop would flash his Episcopal ring, and at such moments when it would appear in an obvious way near my face, I was to kiss it. I remember it coming close to me once, and I got a lip on it, but two or three more times it came around and I missed, once nearly landing on the floor. I had hardly said anything at lunch, with Smith giving my credentials, including my having read The Book (Ramsey's Classic), which the Bishop heartily approved and said I was to read it annually. I found that for once in my life I was completely intimidated by the Episcopal presence! Frankly, I was shocked after my less than debonair behavior that the Bishop gave approval for me to meet with the Parish Vestry, and get on with the discernment process.

In mid-March at a Spanish Class party, with a tub of sangrias in the middle of our Spanish teacher's living room, nearly thirty of us had a blast with everyone contributing various fruits and red wines. It was only two months or so until graduation, and I remember feeling happy and expansive. The entire party was one of hilarity. I struck up a conversation with a friendly young woman, with long "dish water" blonde hair. She was pleasant, with an easy courtesy. She spoke articulately in a low voice always seeming to be holding back her true feelings and thoughts. (As I did.) Her name was S. She and I began bantering about politics, especially the national Presidential race heating up. She was a labor Democrat, liking the Pro-Israel, hawkish Cold war liberal senator from Washington State, Henry Jackson. I liked him as well, although my favorite was Congressman Morris Udall from Arizona, who unlike Jackson had a deserved reputation as a wit.(Udall, on being asked at an exhaustingly late day during the 1976 Democratic Convention, "Hasn't everything been said?" He responded, "Everything has been said, but not everyone has said it.") I began imitating Jackson, who at times could sound mentally challenged, and portrayed him as having great difficulty remembering his nickname as "Scoop", calling himself Scope, and stating he was proud to be the whore of Boeing! With sangria flowing, and everyone relaxed and laughing, I proposed a geekish game to the entire party, name any state and I could come up with their two senators. (I was a real weirdo. And of course, I named all one hundred.) After much hilarity, I was asked by someone what my career plans were. Was I going into politics? I responded "Yes. I am going to be an Episcopal priest". This brought peals of laughter, especially from my new woman friend. And then she realized I was serious, which caused her some disquiet. She asked if we could find a quiet place to talk. I must have allayed her fears, because we made plans to see each other again.

Once weekly I would drive to Janesville to visit with Fr. Wayne Smith. I began to find out about him. He had grown up in poverty in Lancaster, Pennsylvania, reared by his grandmother. She was a great cook (shades of my Aunt Rill), and he described what she could bake or make with a few simple foods. He had acquired a love of reading and verbal skills, and he had competed throughout Junior and Senior High Schools as a wrestler. A Grappler! He had become a state champion in High School, in the early 1950s. He had grown up a fierce champion of the underdog, with passionate support for farmers, coal miners, working men and women, and unions, any who were poor, and African Americans. He hated with burning zeal well to do people who identified themselves as Christian, and opposed Civil Rights for Blacks. He possessed a great depth of historical knowledge about slave owners who brought over to America hundreds of thousands of Africans, claiming that this was only an economic matter, and ought not to be messed up in morality and religion. He had been a member, and then a Pastor of the Evangelical and Reformed Church, which for a longtime had emphasized the importance of education for their clergy, and the mission for the Church of seeking social justice. Since the large Protestant Church had originated in the forced amalgamation in Prussia (see above), it really had no solid theological foundation. It had Schleiermacher, who equivocated on just about everything, even the truth of the faith in the Incarnate Son, who died for the sins of all humanity, and was raised on the third day. If your church cannot summon the moral courage to confess this, then you talk about everything else, especially your partisan political causes you name as God's special agenda, revealed to you through your special emotional authenticity. May I suggest this is wearing? It is nothing less than the proclamation of the Law right out of *Romans 7*. But I believed with Fr. Smith, that the Gospel does involve us in issues of naming and protesting against injustice, when human beings are being treated as means and not ends. I find Martin Luther King's *Letter from Birmingham Jail*, addressed to his clergy colleagues in 1963, deeply moving and right.

Wayne Lamar Smith reached an aha moment, and saw that the creation and incarnation, the passion and crucifixion, the Resurrection, appearances, Ascension, Pentecost, the Church itself, the Church order as found in the New Testament and the first five hundred years of the Church, the Dominical sacraments, the Ecumenical Creed, the Scriptures (including the Jewish Writings in Greek), all led him to the Church of England's American expression, the Episcopal Church, warts and all. And he loved America, and the continual political and social progressions towards this country's promise of equality for all. He fought for labor unions and working men and women, for children, for immigrants, for Civil Rights, for Equal Rights for women, and at the end of his life, for equality for same sex partners. He not only studied and kept up with the historical, economic, political, social, theological, religious, and psychological literature, concerning society at large, he lived it. (Once at St. Matthias's Episcopal Church, in Shreveport, Louisiana,1993, which I served as Rector, where he came to preach and teach, he was asked at the Forum had he ever been to the deep South before. "Yes! Once!", he exclaimed. He had traveled as part of a seminarian group from Lancaster, Pennsylvania, in response to the call from CORE and the SNCC for clergy and divinity students to come to Mississippi for Freedom Summer 1964, to register as many African Americans to vote as possible. He had stayed overnight at the Robert E. Lee Hotel in Jackson. He went down for breakfast, and a surly, bristling angry waitress plopped down a breakfast plate. "What is this white stuff?", he inquired. "Those are grits you goddamn Yankee son of a bitch!", was the response. His audience roared with approval.)

He did the same for women's equality, and was the lone vote at the General Convention of the Episcopal Church in 1976 and 1979 from the Diocese of Milwaukee, for the ordination of women to the episcopate and priesthood. He was this fireball of extremely highly intelligent, deeply knowledgeable—even erudite, energy force to be reckoned with, wherever he went, no matter who he was with, always preaching, lecturing, fighting, backing down to no one, no how, not ever. He loved to talk! He loved all kinds of people, women, children, men, even clergymen and women. He hated pretension and could knock anyone off their high horse so quickly, they didn't know what hit them. And he had a great sense of humor, which was constantly present as a central part of his personality. He was a wordsmith well deployed both verbally and through the written word. His wit was very quick, and apt, with a series of perfectly grammatical sentences and paragraphs, or pithy with a word or three. Loyalties mattered to him. As did telling the truth any time anywhere, and especially when it was uncomfortable. One of the first times I saw him in action, Bishop William Wantland was roaring at the clergy of the Diocese of Milwaukee, in the somewhat rigid Anglo-Catholic days of the late 1970s, about his burning opposition to the ordination of women. He had those men-all men—on the edge of their seats, and leaning forward red-faced in anticipation, to hear this attorney lay out his case. When he had offered the usual arguments against, he came with one that deeply impressed many present. He stated that the Catholic tradition was clear from Jesus and the apostles that one must have—as he said not to put too fine a point on it-a penis to celebrate mass at the altar. Fr. Wayne immediately responded loudly, "Bishop, I've been a priest for fifteen years at the altar and I have never brought mine out yet. Have you?" Bishop Gaskell detested Smith, because of the latter's outspokenness, and strength of character. One summer meeting, several clergymen began complaining of not being able to get anyone in the Diocesan Office in the summer. "Well, they all leave at noon, because that was the policy of my predecessor. I don't know what to do about it." Fr. Smith bounced to his feet and said, "We believe in Apostolic Succession Bishop. Tell them to stay!". The same bishop was loudly stating there were many bishops who at Port St. Lucie, Florida, a "gentlemen's agreement" had been reached in 1979, to disallow any coercion of bishops who opposed women's ordination to do so. "I would hold out until this Church comes to its senses and returns to ordination for men only, as we believe in the catholic tradition. And it will happen!" Fr. Smith yelled out, "In twenty years, bishop, I predict the only hold outs will be like the lone Japanese soldier found on an island in the Pacific, who hadn't heard in 1960 that Japan had lost the war." (This prediction was amazingly accurate; in fact, Roger J. White was elected the very next bishop of Milwaukee in 1983 with the promise to ordain women. By 1995, only six or seven of the Episcopal Church's 106 Dioceses were still hold outs, and more than half the Churches in the Anglican Communion had followed suit in approving women's ordination.)

Fr. Smith was married to a registered nurse Dona, with three daughters in their family. They were all involved in church life, and happy together. They now included me, and then S. when she came with me to Janesville. The Smith family life was loud, interactive, everyone knowing a strong sense of belonging. Wayne and Dona did have a habit, however, of angrily yelling at each other, sometimes from rooms two or three apart. (It reminded me of how a television personality on PBS, Leo Buscaglia described his own noisy family life. He said he would put on the refrigerator a large sign, which read, "Opera Rehearsal Taking Place".) Yelling at each other was an integral part of their own dynamic, how they communicated disagreement, or Wayne's feeling cramped married to someone who didn't have the same intelligence or quickly registering mind. And church was so much intertwined into their lives that it was brought up and talked about constantly. At any time, if I mentioned something I was reading, say about politics-from a Republican point of view—which was quickly challenged, or the Civil War, or the Influenza epidemic of 1918, or Hitler, or Nietzsche, or about ancient philosophy-say the differences between Plato and Aristotle, or T. S. Elliot's poetry, it would launch Wayne and me into a fervent discussion or debate, which anyone was welcome to join according to their wits. It was also at this time that Fr. Smith set about to gather support to have the Trinity Church renovated so that the architecture of the Nave and Sanctuary would reflect the liturgical insights he had gained studying with Nashotah House's outstanding Liturgics Professor, Fr. Louis Weil. This wonderful scholarly cleric had been teaching influentially for years about the anatomy of Catholic worship, that the most accurate and faithful form of worship could be pictured in the New Testament, and especially in *Revelation*. The Church at prayer or better, the entire *Laos* or people of God who are gathered to worship in the Holy Eucharist Sunday by Sunday is depicted best by the general design found from the time of Constantine, when Christian churches and worship were de-criminalized, and then later approved, when Christianity became the official religion of the Roman Empire. Those floor plans could be seen in archaeological digs, and in Basilicas mostly in the East. This model was one generally opened up, and experienced in a semi-circle, with parishioners of all ages standing and praying with the celebrant who is facing them from behind an altar. This showed that the much later Medieval style of cruciform shape in the church with the people far back in the long narrow nave passively watching and listening as observers to what the priest did at the high altar with his back to the congregation, even obscured by a Rood Screen, reflected a theology difficult to justify from the New Testament. It suggested the priest as the hired gun, and the sacred person alone, as the one who by his own ordination becomes the magical wizard. (I heard this theology of priesthood summarized very recently by an old style Anglo-Catholic in the Episcopal Diocese of Springfield thus: The priest (male only) stands in the gaps between the world and God. For myself, this is patently false, and contradicted by *I Timothy* 2:5: "There is one God and one Mediator between God and man, the man Christ Jesus." This is not even the Roman Catholic understanding of priesthood since Vatican II. Instead , Sacramental Theology insists on all who are baptized are brought into the very life of God, by the action of the Holy Spirit grafting us into the Body of Christ. And then liturgically this is manifested in the priest (from the Greek *presbyteros*, not *hiereus*) in accord with his or her order, assisting the Bishop in the Diocese, by celebrating the Eucharist and Preaching the Gospel-generally overseeing the Parish worship on the Day of Resurrection. Others in accord with their orders do the same: The Deacon, or icon of servanthood, proclaims the Gospel, leads the Prayers, and takes part serving at the Holy Table, as head waiter. And the laity, from the holy people or *laos*, engaging in the liturgy from the Greek word *leitourgos* or works of the people, reading the lessons, ushering, serving at the altar, singing among the musicians. Of course when the Bishop arrives, the priest-as stand in for the Bishop, he/she oversees this local expression of the Diocesan people, by virtue of his/her ordination to the

Episcopate, who in their person, is the one representing both the apostolicity and the catholicity of the Church itself.

At the same time, Smith had founded the *Cursillo* Movement in the Diocese for two sets of *Cursillo* weekends thrice annually held at various parish churches. This was a renewal ministry for the laity of the Diocese seeking this short course in the Christian Faith. It was lay led, with various *rollos* or talks laced with inspirational witness stories by the team of folks involved. In every Diocese utilizing *Cursillo*, the Bishop had to attend first, then a rector or vicar of a particular church, and then men and women had separate weekends. The weekend began on Thursday evenings and last until Sunday late afternoons. Fr. Smith was the key adult teacher in the Diocese, and his teaching educated a great many Episcopalians in the Diocese, many of whom had received very limited adult teaching, particularly during Confirmation instruction. This man was always coming or going. And he took me under his wing. I found a caring, highly intelligent pastor who would begin debating just about everything at the drop of a hat. He epitomized St. Paul to me, who mentored various assistants according to his Epistles, and who loved arguing. In the *Acts of the Apostles*, the author relates how Paul would enter a Synagogue and begin arguing, which is noted especially after the "we" sections of the writing from Chapter 16 on.

So, at this point, I had met the Episcopal priest who from that moment on would become a mentor and close friend. In my diary, I wrote how my life was beginning to take shape and have meaning after my baptism.

XXII

MEANWHILE MY PARENTS HAD come to the decision to request being re-admitted into the Salvation Army as officers. My uncle Bill helped arrange for this, and they were sent to Lawrence, Kansas, and Robin moved with them. This was most fortuitous, because it was around this time (1976) that my dad began to find symptoms of a possible cancer in his testes. Dad was just about 45 at this point, and coming as he did from the rural background, he had always been suspicious of doctors and hospitals. Generally, his rule of thumb was not to see a doctor for as long as possible, and never enter a hospital as a patient due to unforeseen circumstances which will result in your losing most of your important parts and then dying. His sense was "one thing leads to another" and then death. (Hitler served in WWI, and the Germans were treated horribly by the Allies, and one thing led to another, and six million Jews were murdered.) In the meantime, dad and mother had the Salvation Army's health insurance, and could cover most of any medical costs, including a health crisis. And they enjoyed the Corps in Lawrence. When I visited them in April, I saw they had a very nice house and yard, which was roomy. The town itself was pleasant, with an enjoyable used book store called "Hood's", the kind of place I found I needed. There is nothing I enjoy more for relaxation than to roam through a book store, and check out titles and sit and read. I found Karl Rahner's first five volumes of his *Theological Investigations*, which have been important to me ever since, and especially in his brilliance with a simple statement about the Holy Trinity.

Please indulge me this extended note: For hundreds of years Western Catholic theologians since St. Augustine's time, followed this profound philosopher and Church Father in an unstated desire to "protect" the mystery of the Holy Trinity in a way unlike the East. (St. Augustine was deeply hampered in his theological and Scriptural work, by not knowing Greek. [1] St. Augustine, and especially St. Thomas Aquinas, were "essentialists" about knowledge of God's very life. They hesitated beyond thinking about God from the "outside" so to speak. The Eastern Orthodox had the seminal writing of the Cappadocian Fathers of the Fourth Century, who with far less hesitation could say not only that the Holy Trinity reveals in "economic" action of salvation towards humanity, which is revelatory, but we also see within these actions themselves the "inner life of the Three Persons", because of Jesus, the Eternal

---

1. St. Augustine, *Confessions*, I.xiii 20, Ixiv 23

Word, becoming Incarnate, and interacting with humanity. This was developed in the Fourteenth Century by the great St. Gregory of Palamas, in his references about the "Divine Energies" of God, in his book *The Triads*. Rahner stated in words I find thrilling: "The Trinity of the economy of salvation *is* the immanent Trinity . . ."[2] (I must note that I didn't begin to understand the deep significance of this until reading Lutheran Robert Jenson's marvelous *The Triune Identity* a couple years after seminary.)

In addition, I came across Jacob Burkhardt's *The Civilisation of the Renaissance in Italy*, a 1921 fourth edition, which would be one of five to ten books I would take with me if I were exiled to an island. Moreover, I got ahold of Paul Tillich's *Systematic Theology*, Volume One, which I found disappointing. I started to find that *A History of Christian Thought* and his three collections of sermons, *The Shaking of The Foundations*, *The New Being*, and *The Eternal Now*, were my favorite books of his. I also found my way to the religion department of the University of Kansas, and two professors welcomed me to visit and audit their classes: one was James Woelfel, a former Episcopal priest, now teaching on Existentialism, Bonhoeffer, Kierkegaard, and Camus; the other was Richard Jeske, a Lutheran Pastor and Professor of the New Testament. Woelfel struck me as very weary and burned out, and now here he was teaching existentialism, what I imagined one does when the parish ministry sucks all the life out of you. Jeske on the other hand was a rock star, young, handsome, dashing with flowing Lohengrin locks. (Moody Blues' fans might know if I said he resembled John Lodge.) He had graduated with his Divinity degree from Concordia, in St. Louis, and then received his Th. D. degree from the University of Heidelberg. "Of course, come and join us, and take part in any of our discussions!" He was enthusiastic, welcoming, and personable. "We will begin studying the historical life of Jesus, using John Reumann's book, *Jesus in the Church's Gospels*, and then delve into the world of Paul, with Guenther Bornkamm's recent book. Please pick those up!". I did. I also decided to take an introductory class in classical Greek, to learn the basics, and prepare for the *Koine* Greek of the New Testament at Seminary.

For the summer, I had arranged to work at the Diocese of Milwaukee's summer camp, called Camp Webb. I had also found a position with the Diocese of Fond du Lac's summer camp, but with the opportunity to work at both, Fr. Smith urged that I take the Diocese's camp offer—I would become acquainted with a number of parish priests and others from the Diocese.

I graduated from the University of Wisconsin in May, 1976. I disappointed my mother by not going through the graduation exercises. My roommate Gerald left for home in Ladysmith, Wisconsin. Patti C. also moved out. The job at Camp Webb would begin in some three weeks, and I got a call from a Christian Bookstore in Lawrence, Kansas that a job I had applied for would be held for me, beginning in September, following my move back with my parents, as I would await word on my hopes to be accepted into the process of moving toward ordination in the Episcopal Diocese

---

2. Rahner, *Theological Investigations* IV, 87

of Milwaukee. And I would begin to seek admission to Nashotah House Episcopal Seminary for the fall (Michaelmas) term, 1977.

XXIII

WHILE AT TIMES THE pressing number of matters weighing on me seemed burdensome, everything also seemed to be falling into place. Fr. Smith arranged for me to visit in Nashotah House, and we drove to this beautiful spot in wooded land set apart for the Mission (as it was originally called in 1842), with views of the picturesque twin Nashotah Lakes. The sight of the buildings blew me away. This appeared to be a small Oxford University College, with Gothic style architecture. We parked and I immediately recognized Archbishop Michael Ramsey slowly walking from the fairly new refectory towards the Library and Chapel. My God! I leapt from the car, to meet this archbishop.

Arthur Michael Ramsey was born in 1904, just three years into the reign of Edward VII. He was born one of five children, an older brother, Frank, a younger brother and two younger sisters. His father, Arthur Stanley Ramsey, was a Cambridge Mathematics don, later President of Magdalene College in Cambridge, and a Congregationalist. His mother, Mary Agnes Wilson, was an Anglican, socialist and suffragette. He was educated at Repton, in Derbyshire, a public school (meaning a private boarding school) in the Midlands, dating to the 1550s. When Ramsey matriculated there, the headmaster was the Rev. Geoffrey Fisher,who had just followed the Rev. William Temple, later both Ramsey's predecessors as Archbishops of Canterbury. The future writer Roald Dahl was a classmate of Ramsey's. Ramsey followed in his father's footsteps and continued to Magdalene College, Cambridge. When I eventually visited Magdalene College, I prayed in the Chapel, with small plaques showing both Arthur's and Michael's prayer stalls. Ramsey's older brother, Frank, only a year his senior, was the singularly brilliant member of the family. He was educated at Winchester College, as the highly regarded public school is called, and therefore a "Wykehamist", referring to the founder of Winchester, Bishop William of Wykeham in the 14th century. Frank then continued his studies at Trinity College, Cambridge, where he came under the tutelage of John Maynard Keynes, the foremost economist of the day. Frank was a militant atheist. Ramsey spoke on the day I met him of the continued "rankling" arguments they carried on, which upset Michael to no end due to Frank's machine gun approach with analytic philosophy, and reductionist psychoanalytic attacks he had absorbed from Freud and his followers. Michael couldn't keep up with him. Frank as a fairly new student at Trinity, and with Keynes' help, came to know Bertrand Russell,

G. E. Moore, and especially Ludwig Wittgenstein. At age 18 he greatly assisted in the translation of Wittgenstein's *Tractatus Logico-Philosophicus*, first published in German in 1921; the English one—the Ogden/Ramsey translation, introduced by Russell, in 1922. This was a key text for many different philosophers from various philosophical schools, as they all tried to work out exactly what Wittgenstein in his notoriously gnomic style, actually meant. This work greatly strengthened the confidence of the logical positivists, Morris Schlick, Rudolph Carnap, and Friedrich Waismann of the Vienna Circle. The positivists, of course, were working to undermine any *a priori* metaphysical and theological possibility, for which they had nothing but contempt, and leading to their insistence, indeed ideological use, of the empirical methodology for any *a posteriori* scientific knowledge to do this. So, the key to any future philosophy was a method which could not be established by their very method. This is in part what Frank Ramsey thought-that any metaphysical talk was incoherent, and meaningless; and any possibility of truth was not to be found in dogmatic religion, for which read Christian Faith. With science, and the empirical method deftly employed to state which truthful statements were possible, how was it that anyone could believe in these childish pipe dreams? All of these folks had for whatever reason, an animus against the Christian beliefs of their countrymen.

Why? This was just after the horrendous carnage of WWI, the Great War, into which many Christian nations had plunged, with their military units all dutifully prayed over by their churches (so much "holy water" Marx had caustically pronounced about such matters) calling on God's help to support their causes, of slaughtering other Christians. This war is now viewed as signaling the end of the 19th century, of the age of the monarchy, nobility, the military, and Christian Established Churches, ruling the people in their respective countries. This entire edifice wobbled and then came tumbling down. If one lived in Britain, one noticed the rapid changes taking place in Ireland, the Easter Rising having occurred in 1916, and one of many signs of large fissures in the social fabric which had held sway for at least one hundred years. (Not least, as a huge sign of change, than a Prime Minister, who was a Welsh Dissenter and Liberal, and who had opposed the Imperialistic engagement of the British government in the Boer War only twenty years before, David Lloyd George. This lower-middle class Welshman, and attorney, something of a demagogue, a charmer, a "bounder"-in the quaint condescending words of the English upper class—a ladies' man, held the reins of Government, and steered Great Britain successfully through the War years of 1916–1918, to Allied victory, and then continued in power until 1922. His term in office presaged many great socio-economic changes in Britain: among others, the weakening of the Liberal Party to the point where it never again gained office by its own majority. In many respects, this brilliant politician, orator, and statesman, was the equal of the Second World War's Leader, Winston Churchill. I believe this to be the judgment of no less an authority than John Grigg, sometime Lord Altrincham, whose four volumes of scintillating and erudite scholarship, and masterful writing are on display in his unfinished biography of Lloyd George. The final volume, *Lloyd George: War Leader*, encompassing his first two years of the premiership, was published in 2002, posthumously. Grigg's father had been private secretary for Lloyd George from 1921–2. The fine historian, Margaret MacMillan, great-granddaughter of Lloyd George, wrote the "afterword" to the book brought to publication by the author's wife and son. (I have been drawn to reading much about this great man ever since viewing Anthony Hopkins' portrayal in the 1973 BBC television show on Lloyd George, in a series called "The Edwardians". It must be said that Lloyd George was not without his many peccadillos; chief among these being his womanizing. While Prime Minister, British Music Halls and pubs regularly were the scenes for the singing of "Lloyd George knew my father/My mother-wink wink-knew Lloyd George"; repeated over and over to the tune of "Onward Christian Soldiers".) It may interest some Anglicans that Grigg as Lord Altrincham (before he renounced his title in 1963) wrote articles urging the reform of the monarchy, and favoring the ordination of women to the Episcopate and Priesthood in 1957, saying about the latter, "those who say women are unfit to be priests belong in spirit to the vanishing world of tribalism and taboo". This is a man after my own heart . . . His view on Confirmation was equally bracing: " . . . a kind of spiritual sheep dip—a brief interlude of priggishness and religiosity in a lifetime of indifference".[1]

Perhaps the Post War malaise has to a certain extent been explored within the general ethos of the Bloomsbury set, which while overlapping with the Cambridge Apostles, had quite a definite sensibility, flaunting their disgust for any bourgeois loyalties, or moral codes associated with the Victorian era. A number of these people—including many who were later recruited to engage in spying for Soviet Communism-the same Bloomsbury/Cambridge Apostles—also flagrantly displayed forms of sexual and moral experimental behavior and "poses", incurring the disapproval of their elders and countrymen. This collection of varied intellectuals and artists looked first for their ideological justification to G. E. Moore's *Principia Ethica*, as Paul Levy describes in his biography of philosopher *Moore: G. E. Moore and the Cambridge Apostles*.[2] One historian has noted about Moore's book, " . . . the essence of what Bloomsbury drew from Moore is contained in his statement that 'one's prime objects in life were love, the creation and enjoyment of aesthetic experience and the pursuit of knowledge'". [3] And they were influenced by the writings of their own number such as those of Goldsworthy Lowes Dickinson, Aldous Huxley, Roger Fry, Clive and Vanessa Bell, Duncan Grant, E. M. Forster, Lytton Strachey, Leonard and Virginia Woolf, Vita Sackville-West, and most notably, of course, Frank Ramsey's own tutor John Maynard Keynes. Pleasure and personal relationships seem to have been in the forefront of this

1. *The Telegraph* Obituary, "John Grigg", 2 January 2002

2. Levy, *Moore*, 140

3. Blythe, *The Penguin Companion to Literature* 1, 54

group, with various folks flitting in and out of sharing of love, and even sexual relations in other configurations, with different partners.

Frank Ramsey, along with Russell, Keynes, Ogden, empiricists/positivists, and many others (at this point including C. S. Lewis), were totally aghast that anyone outside of the proles actually believed these laughable myths contained in the Christian Faith or even any metaphysics at all. Frank Ramsey was among the most electrifying and aggressive in his outpouring of brief almost journalistic articles expressing these views. And of all these philosophes, he at his very young age of 18, had succumbed to Ludwig Wittgenstein's charm, and then, following a disastrous love affair with a married woman in 1923, had made his way to Vienna for the new healing promises of psychoanalytic therapy as designed by Dr. Sigmund Freud. A second concern would converge with the confronting of his depression, meeting with Wittgenstein in Puchberg, some 80 kilometers or 50 miles from Vienna in Austria. Wittgenstein had been living the life of a monk, or recluse, for some time, and trying to quell his demons by teaching elementary school in this rural area. He had believed that with his *Tractatus*, the last word on philosophy had been written, and his project was finished.[4] He was notoriously touchy, and didn't like responding to questions or criticisms concerning his work. However, Frank Ramsey slowly cultivated his friendship and gained his trust. Ramsey knew how to break through to this little man-scion of a great aristocratic—if also rather psychologically unhinged—family. At the time of Ramsey's becoming re-acquainted with Wittgenstein and the latter's kin, three of the latter's siblings had recently committed suicide, and another played as a concert pianist with one hand.[5]

Wittgenstein's former tutor at Cambridge, John Maynard Keynes, provided a steady flow of letters to Ramsey, to assist in cajoling Wittgenstein back to Cambridge, and gaining a BA as well as a Ph. D, for Wittgenstein's already published work. Ramsey's diplomacy worked. Ramsey in addition to translating Wittgenstein's *Tractatus*, now became the latter's muse and intellectual sparring partner. This lasted for a while until Ramsey finally was worn down by his friend's finickiness. In 1925 they became so quarrelsome that Ramsey left and returned to Cambridge.[6]

Ramsey then proceeded to provide a much more adequate philosophical basis for mathematics than Russell had provided in his *Principia Mathematica*, about which in a letter earlier to Wittgenstein, Ramsey had been quite scathing in his denunciations.[7] In November of that year, the fruit of Ramsey's intense work became known in a paper he presented in London on "The Foundations of Mathematics." This was heralded as a superb achievement by this 22 year old, and along with several incisive, provocative articles on philosophy, economics, and the theoretical foundations of mathematics, would be posthumously published by Keynes as The *Foundations of Mathematics,* in

4. Monk, *Wittgenstein*, 155,160
5. Monk, *Wittgenstein*, 205–7,215–24
6. Monk, *Wittgenstein*, 231
7. Monk, *Wittgenstein*, 219

1931, considered to this day as one of the classic texts on the subject.[8] Ramsey later married Lettice, a much loved woman with "a robust sense of humor and earthy honesty" who when Wittgenstein finally came back to Cambridge in 1929—resuming his close friendship with Frank—became Wittgenstein's confidante. [9]Wittgenstein's own love life had been centered on one Marguerite Respinger, a Swiss woman he had met in Cambridge, and who traveled to Austria to be with Wittgenstein. That relationship was doomed in part by Wittgenstein's insistence that their future marriage be Platonic and childless. She would remain the only woman Wittgenstein romantically loved.[10] This idyllic friendship with the Ramseys was ended soon after when Frank suddenly died in January, 1930, following a serious spell of jaundice, and an unsuccessful emergency surgery. Wittgenstein had remained a few feet away from his friend's hospital bed in a death watch. Ramsey was just 26 when he died.[11]

At the time of my first meeting with Archbishop Ramsey at Nashotah House, I had read what A. J. Ayer and Bertrand Russell had said about Frank Ramsey's genius, but little else until a day before. While researching for more information, I came across John Maynard Keynes' *Essays in Biography*, 1933, and his portrait of Ramsey, so trenchant and insightful, painting him in swift strokes, as indeed was his artistry about all the men described in his outstanding book. Keynes' writing about Winston Churchill's *The World Crisis*, the latter's memoir about WWI, is judicious and pungent.[12] Same with his essays on Lloyd-George, and the Allied leaders in Paris for the plans for peace after WWI, Keynes himself being a chief participant and close observer of the proceedings. He resigned as Lloyd-George's economic advisor, and published a lively and exacting indictment of the War leaders' decisions in his justly famous *The Economic Consequences of the Peace*, 1919. No one who reads it will forget how President Wilson comes in for a severe rebuke, and for his inept attempts to deal with Germany justly.[13] It may be difficult for Americans who are not historians to imagine the place and influence Keynes held even while a fellow at Trinity Cambridge, where he taught philosophy, mathematics, and economics; then as the key foreign expert in the Treasury of Lloyd-George's Wartime and Conservative Coalition Governments, and after that for Bonar Law's subsequent Conservative rule. A favorite writer A. N. Wilson, whom I have lauded above, has produced three delightful provocative and arch books on Britain from the accession of the young Queen in 1837, right up to the present in *Our Times: The Age of Elizabeth II*. (Published 2003–2008). They are exhilarating reading, with wonderful detail, and a delightful wit with which he pillories

---

8. Monk, *Wittgenstein*, 244–7

9. Monk, *Wittgenstein*, 258

10. Monk, *Wittgenstein*, 258

11. Monk, *Wittgenstein*, 288–9

12. Keynes, *Essays in Biography*, 53–67

13. Keynes, *Essays in Biography*, 18–31

nearly all the insufferable boors among the great and the famous (such as Archbishop of Canterbury, Cosmo Gordon Lang). He notes about Keynes:

> Immensely tall, mustachioed, lofty in all senses, Cambridgey, John Maynard Keynes (1883–1946) is a name which still divides all who speak or think about twentieth-century British history . . . As economic advisor to Lloyd George's government, he had attended the Peace Conference and left in order to publish the damning indictment entitled *The Economic Consequences of the Peace.* His view was that the politicians had concentrated so myopically on political solutions that they failed to see that the only way to build a lasting peace in Europe was by getting the economy right. The old days of laissez-faire were over, and some form of controlled economy was to be necessary to weather the vicissitudes ahead. The French would always see his book as a piece of troublemaking, if not a cause of the Second World War itself. By making the thinking classes in England believe that German war reparations were both unjust and economically unviable, he had weakened the case for resistance to German rearmament . . . Keynes' book alerted the world to the fact that inter-Ally war debts and German reparations were a recipe not merely for economic but for political disaster. We can now see these factors to be the 'giant step in the descent' to totalitarianism and world war.[14]

I quote from Wilson's book about Keynes, in order to establish some sense of the stature of this philosopher, mathematician, economist, and diplomat, as well as statesman. It was Keynes who welcomed Frank Ramsey back and to Cambridge, and who wrote about the influence of Ramsey's brilliance and tremendous promise. His three pieces on Frank Ramsey consider this genius as a man, as a philosopher, and then as an elegant and especially lucid writer, even about formal logic, in a series of aphorisms-exactly the way Wittgenstein—or Nietzsche come to think of it-wrote. Keynes' brief articles were quite extraordinary, and note:

> The loss of Ramsey is . . . to his friends, for whom the personal qualities joined most harmoniously with his intellectual powers, one which it will take them long to forget. His bulky Johnsonian frame, his spontaneous gurgling laugh, the simplicity of his feelings and reactions, half-alarming sometimes, and occasionally almost cruel in their directness and literalness, his honesty of mind and heart, his modesty, and the amazing, easy efficiency of the intellectual machine which ground away behind his temples and broad, smiling face, have been taken from us at the height of their excellence and before their harvest of work and life could be gathered in. [15]

The nature of Frank Ramsey's writing may be observed in a few short paragraphs Keynes quotes providing a sense of the meaning of philosophy:

14. Wilson, *After the Victorians*, 286–7

15. Keynes, *Essays in Biography*, 295–6

Philosophy must be of some use and we must take it seriously; it must clear our thoughts and so our actions. Or else it is a disposition we have to check, and an inquiry to see that this is so; *i.e.* the chief proposition is that philosophy is nonsense. And again we must take seriously that it is nonsense, and not pretend, as Wittgenstein does, that it is important nonsense. [16]

I used to worry myself about the nature of philosophy through excessive scholasticism. I could not see how we could understand a word and not be able to recognize whether a proposed definition of it was or was not correct. I did not realise the vagueness of the whole idea of understanding, the reference it involves to a multitude of performances any of which may fail and require to be restored. Logic issues in tautologies, mathematics in identities, philosophy in definitions; all trivial, but all part of the vital work of clarifying and organising our thought.[17]

The chief danger to our philosophy, apart from laziness and wooliness, is scholasticism, the essence of which is treating what is vague as if it were precise and trying to fit it into an exact logical category. A typical piece of scholasticism is Wittgenstein's view that all our everyday propositions are completely in order and that it is impossible to think illogically. (This last is like saying that it is impossible to break the rules of bridge, because if you break them you are not playing bridge but, as Mrs. C says, not-bridge.)[18]

And then the last few pages of the aphorisms Keynes provided, includes this revealing candid confession of this remarkable logician:

My picture of the world is drawn in perspective and not like a model to scale. The foreground is occupied by human beings and the stars are all as small as threepenny bits . . . I apply my perspective not merely to space but also to time. In time the world will cool and everything will die; but that is a long time off still and in its present value at compound discount is almost nothing. Nor is the present less valuable because the future will be blank. Humanity, which fills the foreground of my picture, I find interesting and the whole admirable. I find, just now at least, the world a pleasant and exciting place. You may find it depressing; I am sorry for you, and you despise me. But I have reason and you have none; you would only have a reason for despising me if your feeling corresponded to the fact in a way mine didn't. But neither can correspond to the fact. The fact is not in itself good or bad; it is just that it thrills me but depresses you. On the other hand, I pity you with reason, because it is pleasanter to be thrilled than to be depressed, and not merely pleasanter but better for all one's activities.[19]

16. Keynes, *Essays in Biography*, 303
17. Keynes, *Essays in Biography*, 304–5
18. Keynes, *Essays in Biography*, 306–7
19. Keynes, *Essays in Biography*, 311

I find this to be a commixture of both sophistication in expression, but his cogitation based naively on nothing but feeling. Feelings come and go. He uses the word "corresponded" which would set up a red flag for anyone who has had some training in classical philosophy, and is aware of the necessity for epistemology, that is, how is this warranted or certain? How can he justify his statement? And what he says is not based on anything reasonable, but on his feeling. Frank Ramsey for all his brilliance, was an atheist who had a robust belief in Freudian Psychology, and the Psychoanalysis offered by Freud and his followers. (At one point Freud candidly offered what the goal was of his psychoanalysis: "To move the patient from hysterical misery to common ordinary unhappiness". *Studies in Hysteria*, 1893. Well, Freud never promised a rose garden.) Indeed, there is no warrant at all for this to be considered a "science", but in the words of George Steiner, a "meta-religion" or a mythology. Sir Karl Popper called Freudianism a "pseudoscience", because it had no organic or physical grounding at all, it could not be "subject to falsification through crucial experiment". Nor could it be verified, as the logical positivists all insisted upon, empirically, as they pontificated from their lofty height of what propositions were meaningful and what were meaningless.[20] (Now also see Frederick Crews' demolishing of any scientific foundation for Freud's psychologizing in *Freud: the Future of an Illusion*, 2017.)

This is the especially formidable brother of Michael Ramsey, whose own interests lay elsewhere, especially while attending Magdalene College, Cambridge, in political life. He had been elected President of the Cambridge Union, a debating society of long and sterling heritage, and he traveled with other debaters on a lengthy trip to the United States, taking on various college teams from all over America, in 1925. It was after this when he had experienced what he would later say was his call by God to the priesthood in the Church of England. A public speaker, Lord Hugh Cecil, a Liberal Party leader-representing Ramsey's own inclinations—stated somewhat off the cuff, that it was the Church which changed people, much more so than politics. Shortly thereafter he began bicycling twelve miles or so past Saffron Walden to Fr. Conrad Noel's church in Thaxted on weekends, where he deeply appreciated the Anglo-Catholic worship and thoughtful Christian socialist sermons of the priest. For those who have visited, this little charming village with a part 14th century Cathedral-like Church and 15th century Guild Hall, in the gentle rolling hills of Essex, would bring peace to anyone. And he needed this for the tragedy that struck in 1927, when his beloved mother was killed in an automobile accident, causing him to descend into near madness, and follow his brother to seek out a lengthy period of psychoanalysis. Then his brother died at age 26 in 1930. By that time, he was attending Cuddesdon, an Anglo-Catholic seminary for the Church of England, founded in the 1850s by high churchman Bishop Samuel Wilberforce, and located in a tiny village just outside Oxford.

I had heard some of the stories about Ramsey's eccentricities. It was commonplace for him to yes, yes, yes, if he had nothing else to say, or to whistle, lapse into silence or

---

20. Steiner, *Nostalgia for the Absolute*, 12

repeat something said to him to which he would offer no other response. At a picnic with another bishop and their wives, Ramsey was not listening to the joke being told, and was asked if he didn't thing that was funny? "Yes, yes, yes, very funny, very funny, very funny", which killed the mood, to which he was oblivious. As Bishop of Durham, nominated by Winston Churchill, in 1951, whom I heard Ramsey imitate, he stepped out of an antiquarian book shop, and right into a bus waiting there. Without any idea of where he was or that it was for the local asylum, he next heard an officious conductor counting out the people heading back from their day trip. "One, two, three, who are you?" Ramsey laughed as he said he was the Lord Bishop of Durham. Without missing a beat, the conductor pointed at him and said "four" and went on. It was some hours before he was found. A little later he was mandated as Bishop of Durham to stand at the new Queen's right during Elizabeth's Coronation at Westminster Abbey.

My first conversation with Archbishop Ramsey began badly. I was anxious, not knowing what to expect. I asked about his thoughts concerning his well know statement that we could trust God, because God is Christlike and in Him is no un-Christlikeness at all. Had he read about the "dark side of God"? I quoted something by Jacob Boehme. "That's nonsense, and has nothing to do with the Holy Trinity", he said. And he made an allusion to Trinitarian metaphysics, ending with "distinction without a difference". I replied, "Like Englishman and homosexual?" Watching him scowl, I referred to the Liberal Party leader in Britain, Jeremy Thorpe, in the news at that time, having just resigned his position due to a scandal involving his having paid for "rough sex" with a male prostitute. The archbishop glared at me and informed me Thorpe's son was his godson. Oops! He followed this with, "And where are you getting this awful stuff about the dark side of God?" "Paul Tillich has made reference to Jacob Boehme about this", I answered. "Oh, and do you read Tillich?" "I've read nearly everything by him over the past two years!", I said. "And don't you think that's enough!", Ramsey retorted. "Well, I'm also reading a couple of little known provincial British theologians. One is John Macquarrie; the other I can't now remember, ah . . . he wrote *The Gospel and the Catholic Church.*" At this Ramsey smiled at me-par rum pa pum pum—and asked about other books of his I had come across. I listed several: *Introducing the Christian Faith, The Resurrection of Christ*, and one I had just finished, *God, Christ, and the World.* "And what do you think?", Ramsey asked. "You're having more influence on me than Tillich!", I noted. "And are you coming here for Seminary?", he inquired. "I very much hope to." "It's my favorite seminary", was Ramsey's comment. I then asked him about literature he read or liked. He indicated he read mostly history, theology, biography, and particularly political lives. "Not Samuel Johnson? Your brother was compared to Samuel Johnson", I offered. "Ah, you've been reading Keynes", he responded. "Yes, he and I bickered constantly about what was meaningful language. I'm still answering his attacks. We will talk more."

What Samuel Johnson said about meeting Edmund Burke summarizes my thought that day and every time I talked with Ramsey: "You could not stand five minutes with that man beneath a shed while it rained, but you must be convinced you had been standing with the greatest man you had ever seen."[21]

Wow! That was the one-hundredth Archbishop of Canterbury! Fr. Smith was stuck hearing about the entire conversation several times over when he drove us back to Janesville. Everything about Nashotah I liked; the smell and feel of the old books in the library, the Chapel of St. Mary the Virgin with its medieval look, I thought, of sanctuary, choir, and "court of the Gentiles" or nave—the smallest area in the chapel; with the large choir within the Rood Screen in which all Faculty and students sat. (It was a monastic style worship space.) The carved wood statues of our Lady and various saints on the *reredos* or altar screen behind the altar. There were two side "oratories" or chapels with altars and *prie-dieux* or prayer desks, one where the sacrament was reserved. In the nave, a *terra cotta* sculpture of the Blessed Virgin was to be found. Throughout the chapel, one's olfactory sense was overcome by the smell of incense, which pervaded the entire building. To me, I was in a holy place, where the Eucharist and daily offices, as well as private devotions and prayers had occurred for nearly 135 years. Fr. Smith asked if I knew T. S. Eliot's "Little Gidding" poem from his *Four Quartets*? He said that nearly all Anglo-Catholic clergy, and in particular Nashotah House seminarians and faculty applied a portion of that to prayer at Nashotah. It was a few lines from the first stanza:

> You are not here to verify,
>
> Instruct yourself, or inform curiosity
>
> Or carry report. You are here to kneel
>
> Where prayer has been valid. And prayer is more
>
> Than an order of words, the conscious occupation
>
> Of the praying mind, or the sound of the voice praying . . .[22]

This is where I wished to be formed as a priest in the Anglican tradition.

21. Piozzi, *Anecdotes*, 172
22. Eliot, "Little Gidding", 139

XXIV

S. AND I TRAVELLED to St. Louis to meet mother and Dawn, stayed overnight and continued on to Lawrence, Kansas. On the way, mother informed us that dad was ill which the physicians hoped to identify, and thank God they were back on the Salvation Army's medical insurance. After a few days, Fr. Smith called to say I needed to get confirmed. The Bishop would be at Trinity Church in a few days. Come and do this, he said, and this will show I was serious. (After that, I would begin my job for Camp Webb.)

We took the train to Chicago the next day, and then took the bus to Janesville. We arranged to stay with my sister Dawn, who had recently become engaged to an older, taciturn (to our eyes, at least) deputy sheriff of Rock County, Jim. They lived in a lovely, quiet wooded area a couple miles outside of Janesville, with a Milton address. I did miss the rehearsal for the next day's Confirmation, but I was sure it was mostly a matter of showing up on time at Trinity's 10:00 am Eucharist the next day, Sunday. (Woody Allen is credited with saying, "80% of life is just showing up".)

I remember distinctly kneeling before the bishop, and his praying while laying hands on my head. Then, out of nowhere, he slapped me! What the Hell! And it wasn't a slight tap, but a rather hard noise-producing slap. My head sprang up to stare at this purple loon! I wanted to knee him in the groin, a noise-producing one. S. had accompanied me to church, and we joined the gathering afterwards at a church picnic with Bishop Gaskell at Camp Rotamer. With the exception of one annoying woman, we had a pleasant afternoon. This turned out to be fortunate; for the next evening was my first interview by the Trinity Vestry. In order for my postulancy to ordination to go forward, I needed this group's approval. (In the Episcopal Church, the Vestry are elected lay leaders of the Church, which meets generally monthly with the Rector, the Vestry elected priest or presbyter, approved by the Bishop, who then chairs the meetings. By National Canon, the Rector, or priestly and spiritual leader of a Parish church, who, once elected by the Vestry, cannot be forced out or expelled by the Vestry or Bishop, without due cause and due process. The Vestry is elected by the Congregation at an annual meeting, and is the body to manage all fiduciary and legal responsibilities; not the congregation. Ideally, the rector and vestry work together cooperatively. (I must add the money and property are held in trust by the Vestry for the Diocese.)

The journey for one who believes he or she has a calling to the priesthood of diaconate, is a strenuous one in the Episcopal Church, necessarily so. A priest who is a rector is held in trust by a parish church, and has access to almost any parishioner at any time, as well as to money, little kids, big girls and boys, altar wine, and any number of temptations. And the motivations for anyone to seek the priesthood are as murky as the human condition. Since Freud, we have become aware that each of us is only presenting a persona to ourselves and others, not entirely rational, like the tip of an iceberg, and that much of what is going on inside us is like the rest of the iceberg submerged. So many aspirants to Christian ordained ministry are mostly only slightly aware of what is affecting one emotionally, and possibly have not become aware of how warped one may be from one's own childhood experiences. Many clergy I have known, myself included, have been working on "fixing" our own childhood experiences, and can be innocently engaged in this without even knowing it. And we may be unleashed to an unsuspecting congregation, and create great mayhem. (This doesn't begin to touch on congregational "systems" which can be at work destructively within churches for four or five or more generations. Lots more about this below!) An aspirant to priesthood must meet with various representative church bodies, and come to meet with a parish priest, a vestry, a diocesan bishop, a Commission on Ministry, a Standing Committee, and if they all give approval, he or she will be fully tested for medical, psychological and psychiatric health. This is all-important because it is the Church as the Body of Christ, which calls one, and the Church, which will discern whom to ordain. That is all part of one "track" an aspirant goes through. The other is to apply to attend an Episcopal Seminary, with references, academic transcripts, all of which is at the Bishop's direction. He or she will determine which Seminary to which one will be allowed to apply. My ignorance was showing when I thought I could seek ordination formation at the University of Chicago. As I said above, Bishop Gaskell gave me the opportunity to attend Nashotah House, and no other.

So back to the Vestry Meeting. I met with eight adults, two of whom I had met casually during the Sundays I attended Trinity before and after my baptism. They were formal and somewhat intimidating, but eased into the interview with me by Fr. Smith, who told about his getting to know me, and why he supported me. He then suggested I tell my faith story, which I did, with several questions about the mysterious Salvation Army. Almost to a person they had no idea this organization was a church, or something. Then with fanfare, the senior warden, cleared his throat to alert all he would now ask the severe questions. He was distinguished looking, wearing what seemed to me a well-tailored three-piece suit, dark grey, with a maroon tie, obviously a successful man of about 60, a well-trimmed beard and mustache, and he answered to the name of Mr. John Overton. Several of the people present were working class (Janesville being a working class city of 45,000, with a Parker Pen factory, and a large General Motors plant). One could observe a pecking order of the folks present, and among the Vestry members, a couple of the men had ties, several did not, and the obvious leader was John Overton. It was also noticeable that the members—including the Senior Warden—held Fr. Wayne Smith in high regard. John was my biggest hurdle. He put me off with his first question: "Now, Dale, you are I'm sure aware of the social problems affecting the Episcopal Church. Are you or are you not a homosexual?" I responded evenly, "I do like opera". "Yes, well, answer my question." I considered that my hero George Anastaplo refused to answer a question about any communist affiliation, due to his belief that he would not dignify such a request unless there were evidential grounds for doing so; therefore, I would not dignify this question. So I said, "Unless you have any evidence about this, I will not answer that question". Just then Fr. Smith intervened. "If you had seen Coleman with a woman friend yesterday at Camp Rotamer, you'd know about him already!" Laughter in the room eased the tension, and there were no more inquiries. I went to find S. who had accompanied me and told her about the exchange with this guy. After about 20 minutes, Fr. Smith appeared and congratulated me. I had received the Vestry's approval.

The next few summer months were a blur. I was a counselor for many weeks at Camp Webb, while S. worked in Baraboo. I worked fairly easily with the youngsters, and was responsible for assisting with the daily Eucharist at 7:30 am, using the Zebra book with its proposed contemporary language-which would be accepted in 1979 by the General Convention of the Episcopal Church—for our outdoor service. The Camp Director was Fr. Bryce Hunt, a rather dim conservative Anglo-Catholic, who with his wife Carol, made their life most of the year at the small Episcopal mission church in Wisconsin Dells. Fr. Hunt was pleasant, but he had a temper which would blow a couple times a week at the staff or the campers. The Camp staff were mostly good, solid college aged young people, including David Adams, the assistant director, who was far more mature, and better at personnel matters than Fr. Hunt.

Camp Webb was for me the perfect job for that summer. It was very quiet, alongside a lovely lake, with various clergy and families coming every week as well as Episcopal campers. We had maybe fifty five each week. Fr. Bryce Hunt assigned me the job of leading a simple prayer service daily, and providing a devotional talk, something that I enjoyed. I could reach the young people with humor and stories about my life, or what we see at Camp around us showing God's presence. I found myself counseling a number of the teens, boys and girls. Various concerns brought to me included sex, alcohol, drugs, birth control, jealousies, uncommunicative parents, bullying, promiscuous behavior, even a couple of these kids considering abortion. Among the clergy, I met the Stillings, Fr. Tom Ackerman, Fr. Hugh MacGowan, and the finest young couple—Fr. Russ Jacobus and his wife Jerri, who were lively and enjoyable to be around, and who have remained good friends since. I could talk with all these folks, all of whom were concerned about the coming Tsunami-it seemed to them—of the secularism which would corrode the Episcopal Church, especially in Anglo-Catholic black-shirted Milwaukee. Any of these clergy could barely talk about women's ordination without getting deeply unsettled. There had been "irregular" ordinations of women to the priesthood a couple years back, and they noted the unease of the House of Bishops in making a decision, including Presiding Bishop John Maury Allin's wobbly way of handling this matter. (Allin, an excellent priest and bishop from Arkansas, was elected Bishop of Mississippi at age forty in 1961. While being known as a progressive in Mississippi for supporting Martin Luther King, Jr., and the Civil Rights movement, he was outspoken in his opposition to women's ordination, after being elected Presiding Bishop in 1973. He requested to resign when the General Convention in 1976, in the late summer, after I was at Camp Webb, gave approval to bishops and dioceses wishing to ordain women. My mentor and hero, Fr. Wayne Smith, of course, was for this, and outspoken in his support for the equality of women and men in the Church, as I was.)

The priest who talked with me the most, and in some depth, was Fr. Gene Stillings. A kindly, older, gentle man, he spoke with me about his faith in the Holy Trinity, the Incarnation, the truth of the Resurrection, and the grounds for believing in the Virgin Birth, which he insisted on referring to as the Virginal Conception. (I have just checked on him by google, and I see he died in December 2015, at age 96.) He told me about his hometown, Baraboo, Wisconsin, because he was born there in 1920. He was at that time serving in the Diocese of Eau Claire. He gave me several books, including Jacques Ellul's *The Presence of the Kingdom*, 1948, from a well thought out socialist and legal position of the meaning of Christians engaged in governing. (While Ellul was a member of the Reformed Church in France, he was very close in thought to the Christian socialists I was beginning to read, the Anglicans F. D. Maurice, Bishops Westcott and Lightfoot, Henry Scott Holland and Bishop Charles Gore, Conrad Noel, Archbishop William Temple, all of whom had been re-introduced by Archbishop Michael Ramsey into the Anglican theological world by his several finely written monographs on the centrality of the Incarnation, a notable Anglican theme since the seventeenth century. Ramsey's seminal *The Gospel and the Catholic Church*, had brought F. D. Maurice into view for many Catholics in the Anglican world. He had followed this with *F. D. Maurice and the Conflicts of Modern Theology*, 1951. In 1960 came his *From Gore to Temple*, which included his thoughts regarding both of those theological giants' implications of social justice and political policy stemming from the coming of Christ into the world. When one reads the works today of Archbishop Rowan Williams, John Milbank, and many others, one may see the fruit of what Ramsey and some others accomplished by keeping the world and every woman, man and child in the forefront of God's salvific plan to save humanity.)

Fr. Tom Ackerman was possibly the most intelligent of the priests with whom I talked. His habit of mind was a Thomistic way of thinking theologically, which at times caused me to ask historical or phenomenological or even existential questions. This gentleman was the first to explain carefully to me the two forms of knowledge that St. Thomas delineates in his work. I had picked up an Everyman edition of Medieval Philosophy, with lengthy passages from various philosophers, and sure enough at nearly the beginning of his *Summa Contra Gentiles*, Book I: God, one reads:

> There is a twofold mode of truth in what we profess about God. Some truths about God exceed all the ability of the human reason. Such is the truth that God is Triune. But there are some truths which the natural reason also is able to reach. Such are that God exists, the He is one, and the like. In fact, such truths about God have been proved demonstratively by the philosophers, guided by light of the natural reason.[1]

Here is St. Thomas stating there is what we today call the scientific method for thinking about what is to be perceived through the senses or empirical reasoning, and then there is Revelation of Truth that God has now given through Christ. The five arguments for the existence of God are offered very straightforwardly and economically here in the *SCG*. I found this helpful, and Fr. Ackerman was the first to say to me that Thomas' five arguments were not to stand on their own, but instead were intended as providing a reasonable basis for the Faith, which precedes these arguments, and as revealed by God. I enjoyed talking with him very much. (In Anglican moral ethics, these are distinguished by "saving knowledge", and "general knowledge").

The strangest priest and spouse I met were the Urquharts. Fr. Sligger Urquhart was this tall very handsome man, who dressed well, and spoke as if he was from Oxbridge, almost an English accent. It took a while at first for me to discern just how amazingly empty-headed he was. He could barely get through the Mass in the morning, and provided me with much advice about seminary, about which he himself knew very little about Nashotah House. He could not bring himself to communicate with any of the children, and treated them dismissively. It made no sense to me that this guy had been ordained. (It finally hit me that Father was drunk every morning, a true dipsomaniac of the first order. Fr. Smith let me know that you could sniff scotch on Sligger at any time of the day, but Sligger always had to have a single malt. When I asked about how a priest could be so thicky thick, Smith's response came to me as a maxim, which I remember to this day. "Too many vestries and bishops believe something magical will happen when a jerk is ordained to make him an outstanding priest. It won't. That's called magic. *If you ordain a moron, you get an ordained moron.*")

For me however, a problem arose not with the Reverend Father, but with Mrs. Urquhart. Her Christian name was Gruoch. She, like her husband, was tall and handsome . Every day when I was one of the counselors assigned to assist the swimming staff watch the children at the lake, I would bring a book or two and watch and read. I had brought with me Tillich's *History of Christianity*, which had become my sacred text; Eric Mascall's very fine *The Secularization of Christianity*—which carefully applied an astringent criticism to Tillich, Bultmann, American Paul Van Buren, and many others for being false to historic Christianity—(with the clever doggerel, "Hark the Herald Angels sing, Bultmann is the latest thing; or they would if he had not demythologized the lot . . ."); the British Indian writer Ved Mehta's book on the changing

---

1. St. Thomas Aquinas, *Summa Contra Gentiles*, I,3,2

moods of Christian theology in Britain and Europe, *The New Theologian*, which began with the storm in Britain over the Bishop of Woolwich, John Robinson's *Honest to God*, included some very trenchant comments on Archbishop Michael Ramsey, and closed with the author's encomium to Dietrich Bonhoeffer, all very well capturing the mood of the *New Yorker* in the mid-60s in which this remarkable and blind author first published these articles. And, I brought *Winnie the Pooh*. It seems, the lovely Mrs. Urquhart was hoping for some attention from someone who was not falling down drunk, to which I was oblivious or uninterested. In my diary of July 16, 1976, I noted that the campers left, and I was summoned to Fr. Hunt's office, to hear several criticisms from this Gruoch. My diary notes, "Finally last day at camp. It passed quickly, (the day not the week), but I was upset after hearing that the Chaplain's wife (Gruoch) had said some harsh things to say about my lack of attention to the children". Fr. Hunt said he had to bring this to me, but they were both problematic. Especially Gruoch. I had misjudged Fr. Hunt.

My greatest enjoyment every week working with the campers and counselors happened on Friday nights. That was when the big bonfire was lit, and everyone sat on logs around it. I was the one who early on started all the fun songs and told the last of about four or five stories attempting to scare everyone. Mine was always about Old Lady Calabash who . . ." for many years from the 1930s had been chained up in the top attic room of an old house, in Wautoma, when that was the fate of the dangerously insane. The room itself was filthy with matted hair and rodents, and food would be pushed through the door. Moreover, if anyone got close to the door, they could hear grunts and growls, and strange sounds emanating from something inside the room. What was clearly heard all over town was this unearthly cackling when at 2 or 3 am, Old Lady Calabash would let loose like this: (and I would launch into very loud high-pitched witchy laughter). And then one night as a family member took food to her, the discovery was made that Old Lady Calabash had gotten free, by breaking the links of chain, and was somewhere in town looking for human blood! And very late that night, a couple kids were out walking without their parents' permission, and they heard this sound, (repeat loud cackling) on one of the low branches of a tree just before without seeing her, she attacked and took both of them, and they were never seen again. (Here a dramatic pause and then almost *sotto voce*) but some say she's still around this area, and if you listen very quietly you may hear this cackling, and movement in the trees. So quietly go back to your cabins, in twos and threes, and stay close together, and you will probably be safe." And oh, man would those campers get spooked but it would be a quiet night!

S. drove up to get me when Camp closed in Mid-August. We set a date for our wedding for the following summer, and figured out what we would do until then. That fall saw S. back at Madison, and she and her best friend Linda from Baraboo, found an apartment on N. Carroll Street, only a few blocks from the University and the Lake. My sister Dawn gave me a ride back to Kansas, where I planned to live until our wedding and then go to Seminary as a newly married couple. With my parents now living in Lawrence, Kansas, and Robin with them, having just graduated from a high school in Janesville, Wisconsin, I looked forward to this time before my formation as a priest. I audited the four classes I had arranged to sit in on, began my job at a Christian Book Store, and became reacquainted with my youngest sister, Robin. So, Dawn was now married and working with the County Sherriff's department in Milton, my brother Bill had enlisted in the United States Marine Corps, which made us all very proud, and Robin and I were with my unhappy parents in Lawrence.

I got to know the Rector of Trinity Episcopal Church in Lawrence, a kind man named Fr. Bob Matthews. I joined the choir, a fine parish volunteer group, and was given by Fr. Matthews charge over the youth group. I rather enjoyed this, which was helpful because of Fr. Matthews' advice that as a curate right out of Seminary, I would be responsible for the youth of the Church. My book store job was easy; I stocked shelves, clerked, placed books out, even did some ordering. At first my employers, a lovely Evangelical couple, gave me freedom to order whatever books I saw fit. However, their tastes ran to the Fundamentalist/Last Things/self-help ilk, with, for example, books by Pat Boone, Hal Lindsay, Marabel Morgan and her ideas to getting sexual desire going in "Christian" homes by the wife meeting her husband at the door in nothing but saran wrap. I think it was titled *The Total Woman*. There is not much I can say about Fundamentalist ideas about a happy home, or a happy family, without noting the woman was always responsible for seeing to the peace at home, with her role as mother, house cleaner, child-rearer, slave to her husband-at his beck and call as her dominant partner—and cook. Anything that I heard or read about the "Christian" family made me nauseated. There ran through a great deal of this sort of literature at the time, a sense of fear of sex, normally blamed on the woman. (From what I observed, among many couples, was the gaining of the sense that women generally were interested and enjoyed sex-with exceptions of course; and that many men by their thirties and forties were uninterested or disgusted or fearful of this desire, because they would have to engage a real live woman, who was not airbrushed. Later when I counseled men and women, I found this insight generally accurate.)

The books I ordered were in accord with my more educated interests. I got a hold of books by and about Friedrich Schleiermacher, Bishop John A. T. Robinson-especially *The Human Face of God*, Paul Tillich's single volume *Systematic Theology*, and his sermons, and his *Biblical Religion and the Search for Ultimate Reality*. I look at these choices now, for such a store catering to a demographic without hardly any person with a college degree, and laugh at my naïveté. I did discover Wilhelm and Marion Paucks' *Paul Tillich: His life and Thought*, which rapidly became the standard biography of this interesting theologian and philosopher. I discovered a fine anthropological approach to studying Christology in Fr. Gregory Baum's *Man Becoming*, which I believed in the school of thought which included Teihard de Chardin, Bishop John Robinson and Hans Kueng. When I noticed the introductory Church History course at Nashotah House, taught by Fr. William Peterson, recommended Dr. Jaroslav Pelikan's *The Emergence of the Catholic Tradition*, I picked that up and immediately discovered a great historical mind, so that with the exception of his enormous body of work on Luther, I bought anything I could find by him. For fiction I found John Fowles' *The Ebony Tower*, by this favorite author.

Two matters were of great interest to me that late summer and early fall. One was that the Episcopal priest and chaplain at the University's Episcopal Chapel in Lawrence, preached at Trinity on the approval given at General Convention for women's ordination. The church gathering erupted in applause, myself included. I assumed it was long past time for the Episcopal Church to agree with this. It seemed to me-and after knowing a woman minister all my life—right thinking folks would support this proposal. My own simple argument, which I had come to utilize with more conservative Christians and Fundamentalists, was this:

1. God created man (humanity) in his own image. Male and Female he created them. And God Blessed them and said: Be fruitful and multiply. In Creation, male and female are equal. (*Genesis* 1:26–28.)

2. By virtue of the Fall, the woman's punishment is to be dominated by the man. This is not what God intended in Creation, but by virtue of sin. (*Genesis* 3: 16)

3. Jesus came into the world to restore all of creation including humanity to the right way and relationship with God, especially with the complete equality of men and women, as first intended by God in creation.

4. Jesus showed this in his equal ways of treating men and women, talking to women publicly (cf. *St John's Gospel* 4: 1–43, especially v. 27. The Samaritan woman then proclaims the Gospel, and brings the entire villagers to meet Jesus. She is a preacher and evangelist.) Or treating women as disciples (Note *St. Luke* 13:38–42 in which Mary sits at Jesus' feet as until then only male disciples would have.) Jesus saw to it that his male and female disciples and indeed the restored people of Israel, would be a people of full equality, clearly exhibited in Baptism. (Located in numerous texts in the Gospels, and *Galatians* 3:23–26).

5. Paul attends to what this means in his churches as for example in *First Corinthians* 11:2ff in which Paul states forthrightly that women are leading worship and offering public pastoral preaching in worship. They are to keep their heads covered because loose hair diverts the attention of the men. It is important to remember that male/female equality in worship in the assembly was new, including and especially for former Jews. Women publically covered their hair and part of their faces when married. Women with loose hair in the streets of Corinth were advertising their availability to men.

6. With the freer forms of Eucharistic worship in a house, the liturgy allowed for women and men to step forward after the reading of the Gospel, one by one, and either add to what one's predecessor had said, speak another Word, or even disagree with what a previous preacher had said. (Prophesying was speaking the Word of the Lord, i.e. preaching in public Christian worship.)

7. With the freedom now that women—including married women—were exercising as their right as Baptized Christians, in the Eucharistic assembly, they sometimes abused this honor, and spoke against their husbands, possibly including denunciations of the men's peccadillos, or even major sins! This would cause a breakdown of order which Paul found disturbing, and bring shame to the household order practiced by Jews, and noted by Paul. (May I refer those wishing to follow up on this, to consult James D. G. Dunn, and now to see the magisterial Commentary on *First Epistle to the Corinthians* (2000) by Anthony Thiselton, in the relevant sections.) Otherwise, it is so obvious there would be a massive contradiction between what Paul states in *First Corinthians* 11:2, and *First Corinthians* 14:33–40. It has been observed by many that the successors to Paul failed to continue Paul's own practice, as referenced in the next generation's Pastoral Epistles of *First & Second Timothy and Titus*.

8. The argument that Jesus was male and therefore all ordained must be male simply fails. What is maintained in Scripture and brought to the point of revealed doctrine, in the Fourth Century's Ecumenical Niceno-Constantinopolitan (Nicene) Creed, is the soteriological one of Jesus becoming *anthropos* (human), rather than *aner* (male), in order to save all humanity, men and women. Further the soteriological point must be made: St. Athanasius stated "What God did not assume, He did not save (heal-same word). This is in his great book of c. 318 *The Incarnation of the Word of God*.[2] St. Gregory Nazianzus followed St. Athanasius in his polemic against Apollinarius by using this thought again: "But that which He has not assumed, He has not saved".[3] It is therefore in philosophy and theology, a category error, to recognize the central relevance of the Incarnation, and then regress from that to establish a male dominance implication with Holy Orders available only to males.

9. This view of falling back to the human tradition of male dominance/female subordination, is not from Jesus Himself, nor from St. Paul. The nonsensical view was the point, perhaps in the late first century or early second century in various churches, of moving toward a male only clergy, at least as far as bishops/presbyters were concerned. This regression from equality of male/female to a male only ordained leadership in the Churches was hardened by

2. St. Athanasius, *The Incarnation of the Word of God*, VII
3. St. Gregory Nazianzus, *First Letter to Cledonius, Presbyter*, 440

tradition, and by the resorting in the Greek Churches to the Platonic notions of differences between men and women anthropologically, as found in what has been referenced as the most influential of Plato's books in the Greek Churches, namely the *Timaeus*. Among the Neo-Platonist Church fathers and mothers-St. Macrina figured highly—the *Timaeus* held such a place of honor, that the Greek of Plato and the *LXX* became entangled and confused. After many centuries of joint use, Plato's reductionist notion of women as placed in creation with the animals rather than with men; and men alone viewed as capable of thought and reasoning, who by cowardice could be reduced to the status of women, was not helpful in assisting the Church to recognize the truth of *Genesis* 1:26–28, and put a damper on any sexist prejudices.[4] I have found studying the *Timaeus* instructive in this regard, as well as Jaroslav Pelikan's Thomas Spencer Jerome Lectures, published in 1997, with the title *What Has Athens To Do With Jerusalem?: Timaeus and Genesis in Counterpoint*. This erudite scholar, who writes gracefully and insightfully, with dazzling, even bracing observations on the Greek Fathers' considerations of Creation, and the climax of God bringing forth humanity, answers this with an entire scholarly apparatus on this historical question. It helped me think through why if one has the Creation hymn in *Genesis* 1 in mind, with the creation of male and female both together understood as comprising humanity created in the image and likeness of God, confirmed authoritatively by our Lord Himself in the tenth chapter of the *Gospel of St. Mark*, the Eastern and Western Churches could reach such intransigence to this day, in opposition to women's equality shown particularly in ordination, the most visible way of recognizing the Church's leadership.[5] For myself, I came into a Church determined to establish the ordained ministry open (to God's call) to both women and men. Forty years after the Episcopal Church approved this extension of ministry to women, it has by John Henry Newman's own criterion of *sensus fidelium* or the sense of the faithful, shown to be a right development in the Church. In Diocese after Diocese in the Episcopal Church, and then in other national Churches making up the Anglican Communion, women's ordination was accepted. This is a clear sign of the approval by the Holy Spirit of this change in polity. I cannot myself imagine being a member of a Church which opposes the equality of ordained ministry for men and women.

The second matter which affected me was my dad's illness. Mother alerted all four of us to what she believed was a growing health concern, without knowing exactly what was the problem. One day, at Lawrence, Kansas, dad came into the family bathroom while I was shaving, and said to me he was troubled about something physical.

---

4. Plato, *Timaeus*, 91 D, 90 E

5. Pelikan, *What Has Athens To Do With Jerusalem*, 108

"What's wrong?" He replied, "There's something strange in one of my testicles"; a strange remark of some vulnerability on his part. Dad rarely talked to me about anything beyond exchanging greetings, so this was disquieting to me. I asked him if he had made an appointment to see a doctor. He said no, and he wouldn't. He would wait it out. I urged him to see someone soon, meaning a medical doctor, and added how this kind of cancer was simple to treat. How long had he noticed something odd? For a few months he said. Then he changed the subject, and asked if I wanted my own car. Of course, I replied. He would sell me a 1965 Ford Galaxy for $300, one that a guy at Rotary Club had given him to use as he saw fit. In fact, I could go take it out for a drive. So, I had a car. He drove me to the Salvation Army Corps building, where I found the white Ford, and just before I drove my new Ford, I reminded him how important it was to see a doctor. It was yet some months after this that he would finally see a doctor. By then the cancer had metastasized into his lymph system. His days were numbered, and he was only 44 when he gave me this information. I did pass on word to Robin, who was staying at the house in Lawrence. Bill was away in the Marine Corps who after basic training had been deployed to Hawaii with a friend of his, Ron Atkins. I teased him about defending the shores of Waikiki from the dangerous hordes of sunbathing women. Dawn was now married and living with her husband Jim. Mother was carrying the burden of overseeing the Salvation Army's work in Lawrence, which she loved.

By December, I was finding it difficult to stay with my parents, and I called my fiancé, who had provided a helpful sounding board for the strain I was experiencing living with my parents at age 22, with their constant tensions. She suggested I move to Madison, and get a job. The day after Christmas, I did just that.

In a couple days, I began looking for a job, and found my options limited due to my expected matriculation at Nashotah House, in August 1977. I applied for jobs everywhere, and in a couple days was called back for a new restaurant position of waiter/host at Mr. Steak. This was a good job for me, as I got to know what was expected of me waiting on tables, taking care of customers-some of them very aggressive and rude-cleaning up, learning how to follow explicit orders from two generally nice guys, but otherwise rather dimwitted. From time to time, my friend and former roommate Gerald Mahun would come in and write all kinds of nonsense on the bills he received causing me all kinds of personal difficulty. Since this was a new Mr. Steak, the Company out of Denver, I think, demanded that anything written on one's check, be faxed to headquarters for immediate perusal and knowledge of the managerial oversight of the one restaurant. So, Mr. Anderson, manager, and Mr. Plymaster, assistant manager, were nervous as hell about ANY comments written down. Gerald had great fun with this: he wrote on one that the waiter would not take his order because he was constantly talking about Hegel and Nietzsche. On another time—during a contest by the wait staff to sell the most desserts and win dinner for two—he wrote that his waiter was begging him to buy some chocolate mousse pie so that the waiter could actually take his fiancée out to eat. Otherwise, it was not affordable. Well, the first one had caused a telephone call from the muckety mucks to Anderson, asking him about his training procedures for waiters. The next day I was dressed down by the manager and told to straighten up. Nothing I said was accepted as this being a joke. The second time caused a minor crisis. I had worked most of the late morning and afternoon shift, and got a call about seven pm alerting me that I would be fired, and if I knew what was in my best interest, I would get there immediately. Both Anderson and Plymaster were almost in shock when I arrived. They told me this ticket had come back from headquarters demanding I explain, before my getting the heave ho. Then I might get a neutral reference. I read what Gerald had written and burst into laughter. This was my former roommate again! He was pulling their legs! They both grumbled for a while, and said they would try and explain this. This was a first opportunity dealing with the dull, foolishness of bureaucrats.

What else happened which I found of interest, was after ascending the ladder of responsibility as a Mr. Steak waiter, with all the responsibilities accrued, I tried out to be a softball umpire and got the job. This meant two or three or four evenings of calling balls and strikes, and judging runners who were safe or out. I worked two or three slow pitch games for men, which I found fairly easy. On a Thursday in that first week as an umpire, after 6 hours at the restaurant, I found myself at a softball field on Mineral Point, handling my first women's game, which was fast pitch. I was very admiring of how fast a good woman pitcher could hurl the ball to home plate only 40 feet away, and a closer distance obviously than baseball, or men's softball for that matter. I arrived about 5:55 pm, a few minutes before game time, and finding I was expected to stand behind the catcher, even though there was no mask. OK, I thought, I can move with alacrity (a new word I learned from Gibbon). The first two pitches came in with lightning speed, and were both right over the center of the plate, and easy to call. The third pitch came a little high, and the batter hardly ticked it sending it at 75 mph into my upper lip. *Wham*! I felt like I had been knocked over by a truck. The women players immediately came to my aid; the men were mostly snickering, with a guffaw or two coming from the stands. My lip split and out gushed blood all over my clothes. What to do? There were no other umpires anywhere around, so I got up, and said as well as I could, "lethh play ball!". Oh, my, was my courage applauded! Except I announced to both managers I would call pitches from behind the pitcher. The rest of the game was uneventful, with the men spectators somewhat muted in their criticisms of me. (Afterwards, I was informed the concessions were affected by my gruesome injury.) I received my pay of $25, and drove to Mr. Steak, causing several fellow employees and customers to gag at what they saw. Suddenly the demand for steaks rare and medium rare were curtailed. I got to Mr. Anderson, and showed him my colorful damage, and added I obviously couldn't wait on tables the next day. "Nothing doing", he said. "We're counting on you, and you alone. You will show up for work or get fired." What kindness. The next day, after I had seen a doctor, who told me that mouth injuries were among the quickest to heal, I appeared for work. My upper lip was now curled up, somewhat like the Elephant man's, and split wide open, so everyone could gaze at all the various shades of red, with the darkest occurring in the middle of the wound. I was there for my shift beginning at 11:00 am, and worked into the afternoon by myself, then continued on throughout the evening, due to a couple guys quitting. Throughout my time, when I showed at tables, customers would gasp, with a number of comedians joking they would order chicken or fish rather than having any beef whatsoever. At least two older women screamed when I they looked at me with my order tablet waiting. If you can imagine Brian Wilson of the Beach Boys, communicating right after his nervous breakdown, you would know how I sounded. "Wthouldth thyouth liiike thome thaled?"

These were pleasant days. My fiancée studied and attended classes, and I worked two jobs and went over to see her with my pockets stuffed with bills and coins. I would get off from work, about 6 or 7 in the early evening, in my imbecilic Mr. Steak uniform, change out of it and empty my pockets of money, count it then decide with her roommate Linda what we do for supper. We would get Greek or Italian food, from restaurants on State Street, and eat there or back at their apartment. Then we would go for ice cream. At least once a week we would head over to Myles' Teddywedgers, which sold Cornish pasties. In February, 1977, I had my scheduled meeting with the Diocesan Commission on Ministry. This group of five priests and four laypersons, with only one woman among them, was advisory to the Bishop, concerning a postulant's sense of vocation either to the diaconate, as a calling, or to the priesthood. Normally, one's parish priest accompanied the person being put forward to holy orders, and Fr. Wayne Smith dutifully met me in Oconomowoc to brief me on being tactful—coaching I needed. We talked about the Episcopal Church, the issues of women's ordination, and homosexual concerns the Committee might ask me to address, and then he got to the gravamen he thought might be a major problem for me. "If they ask you about your sexual history, what will you tell them?" "I'll tell them the truth, anything they want to know." "That is the most stupid thing you have ever said, among all the other stupid stuff you've ever had a need to verbalize", and much more in this vein. Our discussions were generally passionate, but this was several decibels louder than usual. "You simply say you are attracted to women. That's it. Don't scare the horses!" I looked at him, driving his Volkswagen, and burst out laughing, which continued for some time.

The meeting itself was *pro forma*, with the request that I relate my spiritual journey, and my sense of calling. I was asked about my view of women's ordination, to which I responded that my mother had been an ordained a Salvation Army Officer since 1948, and was going strong. The group immediately got into a discussion of what they liked about the Salvation Army, and ended with the Dean of the Cathedral's comments to me about the importance of learning that priests "participate in the head of Christ, not just the Body". I attempted to meet Dean Stub's fervor, and said, "Imagine that!". And then I was released, to wait for their recommendation. In a couple of minutes, Fr. Smith came out of the conference room, and was all smiles. "You're in Coleman!", was his announcement. "Now let's schedule your appointments with the shrinks!"

When I got back to Madison, S. and I began talking about visiting Nashotah, and planning for a June 4 wedding. Several clergy had various opinions about marriage and seminary, but Fr. Smith said it would be best if both of us experienced this intense priestly formation time together. This coincided with what we both wanted. In a couple weeks, we would meet with Fr. Arthur Kephart at Trinity Church in Baraboo, and see about a wedding there in June. We scheduled a visit to Nashotah House, and especially we were anxious about housing—only single students could live on campus. And we made arrangements through the Diocesan Office for me to satisfy the Canonical requirement of being physically and psychologically fit to begin training to become a priest in the Episcopal Church.

Fr. Kephart was a smart, kind, conscientious Anglo-Catholic, whom I had met when I went before the Commission on Ministry. (He and two others, Fr. Robert Bates of Portage, and Fr. Tom Ackerman, Fr. Smith's successor at St. Peter's, West Allis, were all bachelors.) He gave approval for our wedding at Trinity, Baraboo, a quaint English Parish style church. In addition, he allowed Fr. Wayne Smith to officiate at the service, preach, and celebrate the Eucharist. All of these permissions had to be granted, because as Rector, he had complete charge of any use of the church for worship. (This is very clear canonically.) Fr. Kephart let us know that his friend Fr. Robert Bates was a highly trained organist, who would assist us with the music, and there would be no Wedding March by Mendelssohn, nor the "awful piece by Wagner!", pronounced Fr. Kephart, because of their *pagan* associations. We agreed. Fr. Robert Bates then joined us after an hour in listening to music, which, we had asked, he might recommend. We all agreed on the "Prince of Denmark's March",(known erroneously for a longtime in the US as the "Trumpet Voluntary by Purcell") by the very young English Baroque composer Jeremiah Clarke, and still young when he blew his brains out in St. Paul's Cathedral churchyard with a gun over unrequited love for a highborn lady in 1707. So we got death rather than pagan. My own requests were for two pieces from Handel's "Messiah", the alto aria "He Shall Feed His Flock", followed by the Soprano solo, "Come Unto Him", sung by my two sisters, Dawn and Robin, during Communion.

A day or two later we visited Nashotah House. This was my fiancée's first visit, and she broke down crying. To me, the House was astoundingly beautiful and English. She saw a medieval Catholic Monastery, with little regard for women. We noticed a couple seminarians walking purposefully toward the library, both wearing black cassocks, and we followed them and looked in on the library, before heading to the chapel where we prayed, and then to the Dean's Office. We met Fr. Louis Weil, professor of Liturgics, a tall slender balding gentleman with an old world courtesy, who greeted us in a well-modulated enjoyable voice, and asked several questions about our coming there in the fall. Then we met a rising senior student, Gary Fertig, and a rising middler, Rex Perry, both of whom were talkative and charming, and acted as though they owned the place. (There was something that felt slightly English Public School to me, and these were 6th formers.) What could we do about housing? Fertig informed us that there was limited housing for married students in the "flats", which had filled over a month ago. (When we later drove around these small apartments, all attached to one another, it appeared to be tenement housing.) He had heard of several students finding housing in Watertown, in Federal housing apartments. Perhaps if we hurried we might secure housing there. We decided to give that a try.

Before heading back to Madison, by way of Watertown, we stepped into the Dean's secretary's office, and inquired about meeting the Dean. She introduced herself as Sue Adams, a rising senior's friendly tall pleasant wife, who seemed on best terms with Rex Perry—who had insisted on accompanying us. "Let me see if he's busy", Mrs. Adams said. She entered the holy of holies, and a moment later, Dean John Samuel Ruef stepped out to greet us. Dean Ruef was a quite tall, balding, imposing man, a demonic version of Colonel Klink, with a voice that was weirdly similar to Truman Capote's, (with the mien and precise phrasing of Dr. Goebbels). When he spoke to us, he looked as though he was suppressing his disdain, and imitating someone who was affable. "Coleman, you're from this Diocese?", the dean asked, as Capote with a sneering look. "I am, Dean Ruef, and I hope to begin in the fall, if I'm accepted here", I replied hopefully. "Well, we were just going over applications for Michaelmas term, and you will have everything you need, except the psychiatrist and psychologist alerting us you're not as *nuts* as your Bishop. He should be locked up, haha." (The tittering at the end of his sentence had a Peter Lorre half suppressed breathy sound to it.) At this I felt a sense of foreboding. Would I be stuck in the middle between these two loons? My myth of the high standard of mental health of the clergy in the Episcopal Church began to wobble. I responded to the question with a quick, "I see them next week. Nice to meet you Dean Ruef", and left it at that. The Dean had not acknowledged S. standing next me. I grabbed her arm and let her know I wanted to get the hell out. Now! This was "Rocky Horror Picture Show"! Yikes! We darted out of the office, and then sprinted to our car, where S's look of horror and the situation itself caused me to break into gales of laughter. We lost no time, then, checking out the married housing and driving highway 16 to Watertown, to search for the federal housing. We found the apartment complex on the outskirts of the town, found an odd woman who managed the place, filled out the government form, and got assurances we could move there in August.

In the next few weeks, S. finished her classes and graduated, as with me, the first in her family with a bachelor's degree. Two days later we were married at Trinity, Baraboo. It was a strange collection of characters. Of the 100 or so guests, the rural German *volk* sat on the Bride's side, all looking uncomfortable, white shirts, narrow black ties, and suits, and dresses. My friends and family sat on the groom's side, with navy blue Salvation Army uniforms, also shifting uneasily at the liturgy. Both my parents were there from Kansas, my dad beginning to show the ravages of cancer. There were a few friends from Madison, but mostly the witnesses were our immediate and extended families. Dawn and Robin were there to sing ten minutes or so from the Messiah, which would occur during Holy Communion. That music and the Jeremiah Clarke and Purcell, I figured, would frighten the proles. There were also five Episcopal priests and two wives present. My friend from Janesville, Tom Misurek and his wife were there, and Tom began to snap away photos, capturing the general sense of *angst*, which almost everyone was displaying, all these family members unsure of themselves in this rarefied air of traditional Anglican liturgy. (The wedding photographer followed the rules, and took pictures as the wedding party entered the church, and then refrained during the entire liturgy. His photographs all looked staged, with the subjects looking like waxen or anemic, effigies hardly human. It was the wedding of the living dead.) I remember my brother unable to get leave from the USMC and be best man; Aunt Murial repeating—every time I saw her—a phrase she remembered from her own wedding: "It was raining . . .", stated with a grimness as though it was from *The Epistle of St. Jude*; Fr. Smith energetically trying to rouse this lifeless congregation by using the Scripture passage of St. Paul's, "It is better to marry than to burn!", which when he then explicated it further to refer to God's gift of "sexual intercourse", caused audible gasps on both sides of the aisle, only made more horrifying by his stating that the Sacrament of Marriage is fully effected by the consummation in the wedding bed! The reaction to this (over my nervous laughter) was as though Martin Luther himself had appeared, mooned the congregation, and emitted the most explosive breaking of wind since, well, come to think of it, Martin Luther. (His polemical writings are filled with scatological humor.) When it came time for receiving Communion, despite the invitation to any who were baptized to come forward, seven Episcopalians, and my best man Gerald Mahun, and the Misureks, were all that availed themselves of this sign of Christ's presence and love. So Dawn and Robin sang on and on, urging all to "Come unto Him", and getting nary a convert, from these Wisconsin Synod Lutherans and Salvationists.

The reception was held at Country Kitchen, a large supper club, just outside of town. As we entered we saw a swath of black in front of us as all the Episcopal priests had stationed themselves at the bar, and were taking the edge off. We also observed uniformed Salvationists, and teeth gritting farmers push past these shameless clergy indulging in turpitude, specifically, dipsomania. At one point I heard my mother say to me—while she pointed at the bar—there are all your future colleagues. I responded, "Isn't it great? They know how to have a good time". My mother had her flinty stare wanting to witness to the heathen. I requested that my mother not sell the *War Cry* to these drunks.

The next few weeks were a whirl of activity getting furniture, mostly from Dawn who had stored our parents' furniture when they went to Lawrence, Kansas and the fully furnished Salvation Army "quarters". We considered ours as "early Salvation

Army furniture". And I drove over to the massive INSTITUTIONAL looking HOSPITAL in Milwaukee, for me to be thoroughly examined by the medical team assembled for this purpose, as I indicated at the beginning of this first part of this book. I did not flood the psychologist with all this material of my early life, but I did let him know about my growing up in the Salvation Army, what my journey had been in getting to the point of pursuing Holy Orders in the Episcopal Church, and in response to his somber and specific request, an account of my sexual history. This is who I was.

Early the next week, Fr. Smith called and said that the Standing Committee (of which he was a member in the Diocese of Milwaukee) had received the results of my examinations. I had passed with flying colors. In fact, he reported my IQ was high, and my sexual identity and behavior considered "normal". In fact, the Bishop and the Committee considered my prospects to be the best—based on these results—and the most promising of all the men they had considered going back fifteen or so years. (I took all this *cum grano salis*, which was wise considering the seminarians and priests I came to know over the next few years as fruits and nuts. I admit I was on the continuum.) I was entering a strange small, hot house of Anglo-Catholic clergy, and seminarians, and alumni, and Nashotah could feel inbred. Or severely brain damaged.

Part Two

ANGELUS

V. The Angel of the Lord declared unto Mary,

R. And she conceived of the Holy Spirit.

Hail Mary, full of Grace, the Lord is with thee; Blessed art thou among women, and blessed is the fruit of thy womb, Jesus. Holy Mary, Mother of God, pray for us sinners, now and at the hour of our death. AMEN.

V. Behold the handmaid of the Lord.

R. Be it done unto me according to thy Word.

Hail Mary . . .

V. And the Word was made flesh

R. And dwelt among us.

Hail Mary . . .

Let us Pray: Pour forth, we beseech Thee, O Lord, Thy grace into our hearts, that we to whom the Incarnation of Christ Thy Son was made known by the message of an angel, may by His Passion and Cross be brought to the Glory of His Resurrection. Through the same Christ our Lord. AMEN.

(SAID THREE TIMES DAILY AT NASHOTAH HOUSE WITH THE THREE TIMES STRIKING OF BELLS.)

XXV

WE SETTLED IN TO our new life together at Watertown, and I was having the time of my life at Nashotah. I picked up my class schedule, and having asked lots of questions of various priests whose friendships I had cultivated, but particularly from Fr. Wayne Smith with his quick-wittedness and encyclopedic mind, I imagined the Systematic Theologian, Fr. James Griffiss, would be my favorite professor. He lolled around campus with a pipe in his mouth, trailing a dachshund. He was a single man, living with his mother, about six feet, ruddy complexion in a pockmarked face, prominent nose; who wore round turtle shell glasses, and balding. He was droopy. Everything he said was slow and in a drawl. At a welcome gathering for the new students, 33 of us in a combined student body of 100, (and at least 30 from the Diocese of Colorado alone), Fr. Griffiss was the man I wanted to meet. I introduced myself, and asked him about his theological influences, always a safe bet with intellectuals. "Well . . . the Angelic Doctor . . . of course . . .", he began. I had read enough to know this was St. Thomas Aquinas. "And . . . then . . . Hooker . . . who follows him . . . of . . . course; . . . and contemporary thinkers would be Karl . . . uh . . . Rahner. Have you read him?" "Yes", I eagerly responded, like a lap dog. "Yes, I've read through his first five *Theological Investigations*!". This elicited, "Oh . . . good . . . .that's really, ummmm . . . .good". "And I know you like Tillich, don't you?", I noted with childish glee. "Hmmm, yes . . . a lot. Have you ummmm . . . read Tillich?" "I love Tillich!", which I said with one of my loudest outdoor voices, because we were "outdoors". My enthusiasm woke the man up, for a moment. "Oh, OK. And what in particular?", he asked. "I've read his sermons, *The Courage To Be*, some of his *Systematic Theology*. My favorite is his *A History of Christian Thought*, which Carl Braaten edited", I offered. "We'll be reading Macquarrie for our basic text." He was referring to Macquarrie's *Principles of Christian Theology*, which I found mired in Heidegger, not surprising because of Macquarrie's translating Heidegger's big book, *Being and Time*. "I had a difficult time with that. I have read his *God-Talk*, *Existentialist Theology* and *The Scope of Demythologizing*. I've just finished *Studies in Christian Existentialism*", which I had. I had had nothing but time on my hands as a waiter at Mr. Steak, and I had been busy. Then Griffiss said something that electrified me. "You know he's here . . . uh, Macquarrie . . ." "Here? Now? Today?", I blurted out. "Yes, leave me alone and go plague him", which he said with a snarky smile. Griffiss ambled off to find his best friend, another bachelor, Fr. Louis Weil.

At that point I looked around, because from the time talking with Griffiss, I had been in a kind of trance. The House was now serving sherry at this reception, and we were outdoors in the close, the open area of the monastery-like Nashotah House, surrounded on three sides by the library, the St. Mary the Virgin Chapel, and the cloisters, the covered walkway running in an L shape from the Chapel to the classrooms, and including various "houses" or apartments in B House and C House, and the administrative and academic offices. The setting seemed brightly colored, with lush grass, clear blue sky, large trees, animal and birdlife evident everywhere. It was a stunningly beautiful place. Near where I was standing was the impressive wooden bell tower, which housed "Michael", rung three separate times of threes to lead the community in the *Angelus*, prayers which included the *Ave Maria*. When Michael was tolled by a seminarian (who had to "cock" the bell), everything stopped while silent prayers were attended to. I was in the midst of maybe 150 people. Yes! I would go hunting for Prof. John Macquarrie, whom I had heard was short and mostly bald with tufts of hair sticking out from his temples, like a hobbit. I was hunting a Heideggerian hobbit. Humanity begins "there" said this philosopher, thrown there, into existence. (This was *Dasein* in German.) It was with existential intensity I began searching for the homunculus. After what seemed like ages, I spotted him looking out from the steps of the library. "A ha! Professor Macquarrie!" I yelled, catching his attention. He saw me running towards him, and he scampered into the bowels of the library. I kept thinking what on earth, and picked up my speed. I entered the library and saw two pasty white hermaphroditic dead people walking. I yelled, "Did you see a lit-tle man run through here just now? Come on, people, I don't have all day". "Did he look like a dwarf with hair coming out of his ears?", one of them replied in a high eerie voice. "YES!", I exclaimed. "He went down there!", the more womanly seeming of the two responded, pointing down the stairs. (It would turn out they were both men. Sort of.) "Good!". And I bounded down the stairs three at a time. In the men's room-which along with the women's room, would become my haunts on Fridays—I saw the feet of someone standing in the toilet enclosure on the toilet. "Dr. Macquarrie? John Macquarrie?", I said, urgently. "Stop it. Please stop", came the strange gasping reply, sounding defeated. "I'm not Dr. Macquarrie. I'm Gus. Gus Cholas. I'm a veterinarian." "Oh, sorry!", I yelled, and ran back, bounding back up the stairs, past the walking dead, and emerged into the sunshine, and the quad. Turning to my right, towards the chapel, I saw Macquarrie. He was talking, and smiling, and nodding, holding a glass of sherry, with a group of seminarians around him. He was a little giddy, and speaking loudly at a high pitch, which I learned many Scottish and Irish men tended to do after several glasses of hock. Or sack. (I was working on my English slang.) He was in mid-sentence, "Yes, yes, that was the case for both cant and heegle", he was saying, and it took me awhile to realize he was speaking of Kant and Hegel. "I will address that in my public lectures", which as I listened, learned that he would give three or four lectures on Christology, the Doctrine of Christ. I wanted to hear these, because I wanted to hear this eminent

Anglican theologian (fairly recently converted from Presbyterianism), and because, like Tillich, I found Macquarrie's Christology one of the more glaring weaknesses of his work. I found an opportunity to meet him, when he asked if anyone had read a book by him, and I blurted out, "Five!". "Oh, yes! That's good!", Macquarrie gushed. "And have you read Heidegger?", he added. "I'm sorry; I haven't", I replied. He then asked my name and I told him very briefly, why I was at Nashotah. He said he loved the place, and would be returning nearly every year he could.

After that, I relaxed, and began meeting and chatting with students. I met several who were entering juniors, the big macho guys trying to intimidate others, like Irishman and USMC veteran, Patrick Ward, Ralph Evans, and Don Muller. There were guys who were "spikey" Anglo-Catholics, like Phil Weatherford, Greg Smith, Jeffery Hamblin, Harry Parsells. Then there were the somewhat aggressive Evangelicals, Frank Lyons, Rob Lord, Thad Butcher, Wayne Bulloch, Bob Wagenseil, Ken Costello. And the scholars, Al Kimel, Fr. Ian, George Kimball—an attorney, David Yancey, and John Cannell. There were the old guys, Bill Radant, Gus "I'm not Macquarrie" Cholas; a professor from Southern Illinois in Carbondale, Wyatt Stephens, Henry Stickler, and Arnold Hoffman. Hope Koski was the only woman in our class. Nashotah was not a very welcoming Episcopal Seminary for women, so the women who came and graduated were toughened by the experience. I rooted for them, supported them and offered friendship. Carole McGowan in her middler year was someone I met and talked with frequently. I would note that my class had a more conservative-actually at times fundamentalist—or traditionalist, or even regressive feel about it. This was combined in classes with defensive or boorish questioning of several professors, particularly Father Joseph Ignatius Hunt, who taught us the Old Testament. I chalked up some of this to many having sensed a calling to Holy Orders after attending a Cursillo weekend, an emotionalist renewal movement associated with the more charismatic and evangelical Episcopal Churches, or those catholic parishes and dioceses emphasizing experience in worship and spiritual life, what is known as pietism. Many from Bishop William Frey's Colorado were at Nashotah for this reason-over thirty of them. From what several said, such as Jerry Anderson, a very nice guy and one of my fellow juniors, Bishop Frey believed that anyone who sensed a calling to the priesthood, and could articulate that calling, would be approved for postulancy, and sent to seminary. This never made sense to me or any number of bishops and priests, whom I heard weigh in on this, for this left out the Church's crucial role of discernment for any aspirants, and because once out of seminary, if the person had satisfied all the academic and medical qualifications, he or she could not be ordained unless they had a cure, a clear call to a parish or mission church, for which a bishop had to plan. (A bishop could appoint a vicar to a mission church, but he did not have authority outside of suggestion for a curate or rector in a parish.) Already in the late 1970s, curates' and vicars' positions were beginning to decline. At my home parish of Trinity, Janesville, Wisconsin, Fr. Smith related how only a few years before, Trinity had afforded a rector and two curates. Now in 1977, Fr.

Smith could call a deacon, the Rev. Mary Ann Peters, at a much-decreased rate than that of a full priest. I believed then, and still do now, that flooding the Church at large with extra ordained clergypersons, would cause a certain amount of chaos and hard feelings, even bitterness and resentment, and was a bad idea. How long would such a person wait around to find a call to a church? For most bishops and other keen observers of the American church scene, hardly anyone foresaw the immense tsunami of losses that was coming out of great disgust or apathy in the mainline churches, which flourished for a while from about 1950 to 1975. That was the generation of clergy, mostly white males, who had found people flocking to their doors, without much evangelism or even work on the clergy's or the leading laity's part. In the fifties, the general message had been live and let live, with cues taken from society at large, such as the psychological field of Carl Rogers and his humanistic focus of client centered psychotherapy. His *On Being a Person: A Therapist's View of Psychotherapy*, 1961 was influential. It had at its core the secular individualistic view of "health", a nebulous medical metaphor, not thought in Christian terms, or at least not in any more than a vague and indirect manner. The therapist or counselor paid intense listening attention to the client, even allowing the patient to determine the path of recovery, through his or her very statements. Usually this occurred by utilizing something the client had said, and then repeating it back in question form. Clergy from this era aped the secular models, having lost a great sense, I thought, of being a pastor or priest for the Church, even confidence in the Church's mission, and generally aspired to becoming a counselor, or therapist, or psychotherapist, "the listening professional". Theologians in vogue for the mainline church clergy (Episcopal, fairly newly merged United Church of Christ—and the United Methodist, American Baptist, and Presbyterian) were: Paul Tillich, Reinhold Niebuhr, and Rudolph Bultmann, all of whom were strongly supportive of H. Richard Niebuhr's sociological paradigm: "Christ transforming Culture", from a 1951 book *Christ and Culture*. This may now strike many committed Trinitarian Christians as colossal wishful thinking, but it could possibly be summed up in President Eisenhower's statement: "Our form of government makes no sense unless it is found in a deeply felt religious belief, and I don't care what it is". It was during his administration that the words "Under God" were added to the Pledge of Allegiance. Eisenhower was the first President elected in the United States who was not baptized at the time of election. (He then hurriedly asked that it take place in the Oval Office with a Presbyterian minister to fulfill all righteousness.) It was the time of the heady days of ecumenism, and the building of the headquarters of the National Conference of Churches, with the *zeitgeist* involving the minimizing of theological and religious differences in order to form a huge united Pan Protestant Christian Church. This was a social religion, on a grand scale. Consultation on Churches Uniting, or COCU came into existence when Episcopal Bishop James Pike invited Presbyterian Clerk Eugene Carson Blake to preach at Grace Cathedral in 1960, who called for this union. Today, there is a much scaled down version of Church in Christ Uniting, and the work of the National Conference of Churches seems to have lost all its headwind. If one visits the Headquarters today, they will see a largely run down set of buildings, and the lot they sit on going to seed. With many palpable signs of goodwill and intercommunion among these and other Churches, this progress is now generally considered as the height of all the hopes and dreams of the 1950s and 60s.

The sixties saw many clergymen of the Episcopal Church become activists in various kinds of political activity, to be visible on the streets politically engaged in fighting various forms of inequality and injustice and war, transforming men and women through "liberation". (Liberation Theology took its cue for establishing "base communities"-rather than the *ecclesia* or church, and fighting politically for liberation, from Karl Marx.) Liberate the unhealthy in their "sex lives" (as though "sex" had a life of its own), learn to become "in touch" with their emotions, work to achieve civil rights on the streets. Drop various traditional ways of worship, learn to "groove" with guitar services, without the oppressive signs of the establishment, viz. hymnals, Bibles, and prayer books. It wasn't enough to preach, teach, and counsel about these matters, one needed authenticity and get involved! In fact, turn on, tune in, drop out! (For more about this, see above p 158.) For examples of many clergy, I found a great deal about prevalent ways of behaving and praying in the books of Fr. Robert Farrar Capon, Fr. Malcolm Boyd, Bishop James Pike, even the Professor of Liturgy at Seabury Western, Fr. David Babin, who suggested getting people back to church by celebrating the Eucharist with pretzels and beer.

Now in the mid to late seventies, the era of good feelings was upon society and the Episcopal Church. Episcopal clergy began trying to sound happy, warm, personable, chatty, one of the gang (call me Bob!), friendly, and huggy. Everything had to do with showing feeling! To help clergy know more about the importance of their feelings, there was group therapy or primal scream or Cursillo. And no priest was considered fixed at Cursillo unless they cried, hugged, sang dreadful music with guitars, and changed from being a cold fish into a leader passing the Peace on Sundays, talking about one's own experiences, becoming a congregational booster and cheerleader. (Shortly before I came to Nashotah the rector of Zion Episcopal Church in Oconomowoc—a church about 5 miles away—was dismissed for nudism in the rectory's hot tub, whose behavior occasionally reached the point of frolicking, or "the funny business" as Episcopalians in the Midwest said.)

For the most part engaging in these trendy behaviors was not Nashotah's way of forming men, and now, women, for the priesthood. And with all the secularism of the fifties, sixties, and seventies, affecting both Jesus and the church itself, what did the Church have to say?

Nashotah House was established in 1842 to form a priest as an *alter Christus,* as the one who through celebrating the Eucharist, baptizing individuals, visiting the suffering, pastoring the people God entrusted to a priest's care under the authority of the bishop, preaching and teaching the Lord Jesus and His Church, about the permanent things of Christian belief, and hearing confessions, a man and woman would be formed after three years in such a Benedictine life, to lead a Community of Faith. This began with prayer. Many other seminaries in mainline Protestantism, seemed to have general amnesia about the Church being *ecclesia*, those "called out" of the world by God, (cf *First Corinthians* 11:18) and *kuriakon*, (the root word for Church, or Kirk) that which is "the Lord's", (*First Corinthians* 11:20).

At five O'clock, the evening of my first being part of the large community, we heard the Angelus, and prayed quietly in the chapel in our brand new (for juniors) cassocks and surplices, in our assigned places. Then Evensong began. An entire community of about 125 joined in the prayers said and sung, as well as the prayers we knew as hymns, standing, sitting, bowing, genuflecting, crossing ourselves, listening to the two readings from the entire Bible, i.e. including the apocrypha, and I had my first experience in this Nashotah way of formation. The chapel always strikes me as a holy place.

All the juniors sat in the "Court of the Gentiles" or the Nave to the rear of the Rood Screen of carved dark wood, depicting the Crucifix and the figures of Our Lady and St. John the Evangelist. Rood screens were used from medieval times onward to separate the Chancel or Choir from the Nave. We sat in the Nave. In addition, all Juniors were assigned to a particular seat. The Dean took attendance every day at Morning Prayer at 7:30 am and Evensong at 5:00 pm. He kept his little list in his stall. Most of us had our Books of Common Prayer, Hymnals, supplemental music books, favorite devotional books in our own seats or stalls. I had from the first day my Anglo-Catholic *St. Augustine's Prayer Book*, which had all sorts of prayers for preparing for Eucharist, or for making one's confession, or for various litanies, laments, praying the Rosary, the Stations of the Cross, blessings, and so forth; a so—so translation of St. Augustine's *Confessions* by Pine-Coffin, (much improved by Henry Chadwick's translation; and then again by Garry Wills' luminous translation and commentary). I always kept Thomas a Kempis' *The Imitation of Christ*, Archbishop Michael Ramsey's *The Christian Priest Today*, easily the most important and influential book I have read on the nature of the vocation, and just for fun, Pascal's *Pensees*. Following the Evensong, we all filed into the vesting room, to remove our church clothes, and thence home on that first Friday.

Fr. Arthur Kephart offered me $30 a week to become Trinity, Baraboo's seminarian, to assist him on Sundays with anything liturgical, and he had thrown in a new English style surplice with huge bell sleeves and a Roman style cassock with buttons down the center of this black garment.

On Sunday mornings, we attended a quaint English style stone Episcopal Church, the same church in which we had gotten married. Fr. Kephart was a pleasant and cultured gentleman, a devout Anglo-Catholic priest, with a style of formality towards any lay persons. It was off putting to any parishioners born after 1945. He was always proper in his "eastward position" of celebrating Mass, with a stilted 15–18 minute sermon, which I found very dry. He was not disposed to any kind of "informality" during the Mass, and after being pressured by several parishioners to allow the passing of the peace, he finally succumbed, but insisted on all congregants using a contrived form, of the one offering the peace holding their hands in a "v" shape with the heels of the hand touching and fingers extended. The recipient of the greeting would place their hands clasped into the "v". I considered this lunacy. I wondered if it went back to the priest's potty training days. He was invariably kind and gracious to my wife and me, and invited us after each Sunday Mass to the rectory next door to the church. There he treated us with sherry, and relaxed. Like many of the traditional Anglo-Catholic clergy of the diocese, his political views, which he felt free to share, were mostly liberal. And as with most Anglo-Catholic clergy, his liberality did not extend to bringing down the wall of hostility around an all-male priesthood.

On Sunday afternoons, we ate drove back to Nashotah to begin our week. On Monday morning at 6:45 am and every day after that, I would drive with several seminarians from the Watertown apartments to Nashotah. We dressed in cassocks, and entered the short Nave, or "Court of the Gentiles". We then sang Morning Prayer, either Rite I or Rite II. This was followed by low Mass, except on Thursdays, when we had a late afternoon Solemn High Mass at 5:00 pm, this designation meaning sung, with smells and bells. Every other afternoon we gathered at 5:00pm for Evensong. We were a Benedictine style Episcopal seminary as noted above. We were a community at prayer as the center of our priestly formation. And it was also monastic in that the Dean, would check all of us off as we entered. If you missed once or twice, he would indicate to you in the vesting room right after announcements, you were to stay after for him to offer a "word". I don't know about others, but I got the treatment several times, when he would "blow". He had an uncontrollable temper. Imagine Truman Capote stark raving mad.

Once I learned the forms of prayer, and the Nashotah way of worship, I thoroughly enjoyed it. Now over 38 years since leaving seminary, I know the catholic ways of singing the Mass, swinging the thurible, reading and preaching, and communicating the faithful. Without slippers or biretta. I also know how to officiate for Evensong, something that seems now lost among clergy from some other seminaries. Our daily pattern of prayer formed us as priests in Christ's church.

As a first year or Junior student, once a month I was on the dish detail for a week, of receiving plates, and glasses, and silverware, scraping and rinsing and lining them for washing, removing them, and putting them away. We wiped down the kitchen, the refectory, and made everything spotless. While this was a job for Juniors, all students spent much of Friday mornings and early afternoons with their own work detail. I was assigned all three years to clean the bathrooms in the Library. My partner was a delightful, droll, Middler student, Alan Herbst, from Iowa. He had grown up in the United Methodist Church which his father served as pastor, and he and I would serenade the Library staff while we scrubbed toilets. "Bringing in the Sheep", with carefully placed "baaaa . . . ing", or "Gladly the Cross-eyed Bear", sung with verve, or a falsetto version of "Love Lifted Me", were included in our vast repertoire. (And we never left out George Beverly Shea.) Singing as Michael Ramsey with bushy eyebrows moving up and down, with his continual habit of yes, yes, yes, yessing, while using a tune from some awful contemporary worship song—or as Fr. Joe Hunt with deep gasps and a barrel sound, or as Dean Ruef-my personal favorite, or as Bishop Charles Gaskell singing "Wild Thing" by the Troggs, kept us happy.

The "Let there be Peace on Earth", or "They'll Know We are Christians By Our Love" folk music, was what we called, "That Shit". It was narcissism run amuck. It is. In Thomas Day's delightful book, *Why Catholics Can't Sing*, 1990, he notes how all this junk, now including "Be Not Afraid", and "On Eagle's Wings", and "Shine Jesus Shine"—which I sing as "G. David Schine", and "Lord I lift Your Name on High", is all part of a revolution in worship, bringing in the emotional need of egos to be front and center. He observes about this music:

> The singers, especially the soloists, are not really proclaiming the word of God; instead, they are *feeling* the drama in the text and acting out cozy tableaux, charming theatrical episodes, in which "I"—regardless of the text—play the leading role; God belongs in the supporting cast.
>
> In the song, *On Eagle's Wings*, and similar compositions, the Icon or the mosaic of Christ in Majesty, is replaced with the glossy poster of the male Hollywood heartthrob, the latest take-your-breath-away movie star. Perhaps *On Eagle's Wings*, and *Be Not Afraid*, and countless other "contemporary" sweet songs are just another product of the Great Hollywood Factory of Dreams and Romance. Certainly, this kind of music tries very hard to imitate the sound track of a three-hanky romantic film starring Greta Garbo or Bette Davis. You know the scene:
>
> HE: I love you forever, Samantha.
>
> SHE: We can't go on like this, Rodney. [The melody rises in the background. Violins soar.]
>
> HE: You are beautiful by moonlight. [Waves crashing against the cliffs below.]
>
> SHE: Oh, Rodney! [Globs of sound from the orchestra. Fadeout.]
>
> And the music sounds like *On Eagle's Wings*.[1] (Italics in original.)

Day also points out this isn't only bad taste, the lyrics themselves have individuals singing as God, about God's happiness with everyone, and the congregation singing back also as happy with God. It boils down to the congregation singing to itself, a kind of children's Barney theme song; or in Day's words, "Indecent Narcisscism".[2]

---

1. Day, *Why Catholics Can't Sing*, 63
2. Day, *Why Catholics Can't Sing*, 60

In his great liturgical book, *The Shape of the Liturgy*, 1945, Dom Gregory Dix makes a point about this matter in the context of describing the fundamental importance of the corporate nature of the Eucharist affecting all the *laos*, the people of God, from deep conviction, not because of "emotional experiences". He writes:

> For my own part I have long found it difficult to understand exactly how the eucharist ever became to be supposed by serious scholars at all closely comparable with the rites of the pagan mysteries. The *approach* is so different. In the mysteries there is always the attempt to arouse and play upon religious emotion, by long preparation and fasts, and (often) by elaborate ceremonies, or by alternations of light and darkness, by mystical symbols and impressive surroundings, and pageantry; or sometimes by the weird and repulsive or horrible. But always there is the attempt to impress, to arouse emotion of some kind, and so to put the initiate into a receptive frame of mind. As Aristotle said, men came to these rites 'not to learn something but to experience something'.[3]

Dix then contrasts these attempts to get emotional highs by the pagans with the attitudes of the men, women, and children who came to the *leitourgos,* the corporate nature of the Eucharist to which all the people of God played their part:

> The christian eucharist in practice was the reverse of all this. All was homely and unemotional to a degree. The christian came to the eucharist, not indeed "to learn something", for faith was presupposed, but certainly not to seek a psychological thrill. He came simply to *do* something, which he conceived he had an overwhelming personal duty to do, come what might.

Dix then puts his finger on why Christians came to the Eucharist:

> What brought him was an intense belief that in the Eucharistic action of the Body of Christ, as in no other way, he himself took a part in that act of sacrificial obedience to the will of God which was consummated on Calvary and which had redeemed the world, including himself. [4]

This is not a matter of artistic or musical taste as to why we called this contemporary music "That shit", but because it was and is destructive of the affective and aesthetic sense we have in offering to God our praise. This also affects us intellectually. C.S. Lewis once remarked that when he hears extemporaneous prayers, his mind cannot pray until he judges whether what he is hearing is true to Christian doctrine. The *Book of Common Prayer* has collects, prayers, and liturgical forms, which have been tested over time and space by millions of Christians. Recently, Bishop N. T. Wright (in many ways a modern day C. S. Lewis) wrote about this in his marvelous *Simply Christian*:

3. Dix, *The Shape of the Liturgy*, 153
4. Dix, *The Shape of the Liturgy*, 153

When Jesus's followers asked him to teach them to pray, he didn't tell them to divide into focus groups and look deep within their own hearts. He didn't begin by getting them to think slowly through their life experiences to discover what types of personality each of them had, to spend time getting in touch with their buried feelings. He and they both understood the question they had asked: they wanted and needed *a form of words, which they could learn and use.* [5](italics in the original.)

Alan and I both thought this way. For two years we worked side by side in the toilets, cleaning them, as our part in the Benedictine fashion of praying, studying, and working. All seminarians were responsible for making the entire area of Nashotah House clean.

Thank God we didn't have to wear cassocks in class, although some did. It probably came down to what was said in the Episcopal Church about making one's private confession: "All may, none must, some should".

5. Wright, *Simply Christian*, 165

XXVI

EVERY MORNING FIVE OR six of us made the drive from Watertown, to arrive at Nashotah leaving at 6:45 and arriving about 7:20. For three years I was stuck with four guys, almost all of whom were unhappy with various professors, or texts, or the traditional form of worship, or the music, or what they considered not the kind of Christianity they each wanted *sui generis*. This went beyond expected human daily bitching, in my mind, and would turn toxic. There were innumerable judgments made about the "spiritual" states of the faculty, or the clergy of the Diocese, or Episcopal nuns and monks, any theologians in the Episcopal Church, or about each other. We damned more folks to Hell than were ever considered excommunicated and damned by the early Eastern and Western Church fathers, who engaged in this frequently, through the time of everyone being damned by the mutual hurling of anathemas by the Pope and the Patriarch of Constantinople, which split the Church into Western (Catholic) and Eastern (Eastern Orthodox) Churches in 1054, causing the great Schism (pronounced "skizem", not "shizem" nor even "shazam") in the Christian Church with dire repercussions to this day. Fundamentalists of course are gifted in this minute by minute, their stock in trade, and keeping their reputations as very, very angry Evangelicals, who wish to do this apocalyptically, being inspired by *Revelation*. I did my share of this, of course, but never to a point of hating the whole damn Episcopal Church.

Later, I read of effective calumniating of other Christians by an Eastern Orthodox monk, in fact the Guest Master of the ancient Mar Saba monastery in the Judean wilderness (not far from the ruins of Qumran, about seven miles east of Jerusalem, close to the place of Bishop Pike's horrifying death.) The travel writer William Dalrymple tells the story in his *From the Holy Mountain*, 1997, of retracing a sixth century monk's pilgrimage of Christian holy places, written down as the *Spiritual Meadow of John Moschos*. Dalrymple's writing is delightfully engaging as he records the people and scenes he encounters around the Eastern Mediterranean. When finally arriving at Mar Saba, Fr. Theophanes greets him and points at the rocky gorge beneath below:

> 'Look at it!' said Fr. Theophanes . . . waving a hand . . . 'There it is: the Valley of Doom. The Valley of Dreadful Judgement' [sic].
> Below us the monastic buildings of Mar Saba fell away in a ripple of chapels, cells and oratories, each successive layer hanging like a wasps' nest from a

ledge on the rockface. Opposite, the top of the cliff wall had turned an almost unnatural shade of red in the last of the evening light. The rock was pitted with caves, each formerly the cell of a Byzantine monk. All were now deserted.

'It's very beautiful', I said.

'Beautiful?' said Fr. Theophanes, rustling his robes in horror. 'Beautiful? See down at the bottom? The river? Nowadays it's just the sewage from Jerusalem. But on Judgement Day that's where the River of Blood is going to flow. It's going to be full Freemasons, whores and heretics: Protestants, Schismatics, Jews, Catholics . . . More ouzo?'

'Please.'

The monk paused to pour another thimbleful of spirit into a small glass. When I gulped it down, he continued with his Apocalypse. 'At the head of the damned will be a troop composed of all the Popes of Rome, followed by their deputies, the Vice-Presidents of the Freemasons . . . '

'You're saying the Pope is a Freemason?'

'A Freemason? He is the Presidents of the Freemasons. Everyone knows this. Each morning he worships the Devil in the form of a naked woman with the head of a goat.'

'Actually, I'm a Catholic.'

'Then,' said Theophanes, 'unless you convert to Orthodoxy, you too will follow your Pope down that valley, through the scorching fire. We will watch you from this balcony,' he added, 'but of course it will then be too late to save you.'

I smiled, but Fr. Theophanes was in full swing and clearly in no mood for joking. 'No one can truly know what that day will be like'. He shook his head gravely. 'But some of our Orthodox fathers have had visions. Fire—fire that will never end, terrible, terrible fire—will come from the throne of Christ, just like it does on the icons. The saints—those who are to be saved, in other words the Orthodox Church-will fly in the air to meet Christ. But sinners and all non-Orthodox will be separated from the Elect. The damned will be pushed and prodded by devils down through the fire, down from the Valley of Joshephat, past here—in fact exactly the route those Israeli hikers took today—down, down to the Mouth of Hell.'

'Is that nearby?'

'Certainly,' said Theophanes, stroking his beard. 'The Mouth of Hell will open up to the Dead Sea.'

'That is in the Bible?'

'Of course', said Theophanes. 'Everything I am telling you is true.'[1].

---

1. Dalrymple, *From the Holy Mountain*, 280–1

Excursus on the Church Militant

I KEEP IN MIND that we are the Church "Militant", which so thrilled Sir Arthur Sullivan to write the music to the Rev. Sabine Baring-Gould's "Onward Christian Soldiers", written in fifteen minutes by the young Anglican Curate, at age 30, to force sad little crying tots from St. Peter's Church, Horbury Bridge, near Wakefield, in West Riding, Yorkshire, to march and march and march. The children were finally spared more of this fiendish cruel insanity, when 12 year old Grace Taylor, a lively youngster with no learning or manners, daughter of a mill hand, distracted him by succumbing to the famous Anglican divine's obvious charms, leading to their marriage when she was 16, and he was 34. That is, not, of course, before Baring-Gould had placed very young Grace in the home of a wealthy squire, lasting two years, for her to learn to speak and behave as a gentle lady, while he moved to the village of Dalton near Thirsk, the latter town named after one of two words of our Lord's while he hung on the cross. (This is right out of my favorite faux-Brit musical, Lerner and Loewe's *My Fair Lady*, based on that . . . I'm stopping there because I don't wish to mention that Nazi vegetarian and horribly preachy and prudish Irish playwright. You know whom I mean. Loewe, real Christian name Friedrich, born in Berlin to Austrian Jewish parents, ghosted several of George Beverly Shea's Nazi marching songs when they were lovers together and owned a goat farm. But I digress.) Baring-Gould treated his wife terribly, and screamed at her one time so uncontrollably that she fled back to the vicar who had officiated at their wedding to ask if she could "unwed" the turbulent priest. He said no. (She then bore Baring-Gould fifteen children. Not the record. John and Charles Wesley's parents had eighteen. Their father was also an Anglican divine.) Sometime after that, when at a church large enough for him to have a Curate, the younger man preached over the allotted ten minutes, commanded by the Christian soldier, and had to duck several times while the Rev. Baring-Gould threw hymnals at him. I actually feel like doing this when I have to sing "Onward Christian Soldiers", the favorite of the Salvation Army. (Later, Baring-Gould's own reputation was made by publishing a collection of Were-Wolf stories, which he had edited.)

My favorite lyrics from this hymn are:

Like a Mighty Tortoise, Moves the Church of God;

Brothers we are treading, where we've always trod.

Sullivan wrote his music in 1871, age 29, right at the time of his first collaboration with Gilbert, *Thespis*. He may very well have been ecstatic at this time, because of jettisoning two lovers, actually sisters, Rachel Scott Russell, two years older than Sullivan, and Louise Scott Russell, three years younger. Between the two of them, unknown to each other as a Sullivan paramour, they flooded Sullivan with over two hundred love letters in the late 1860s. After promising to forsake brothels, he bonded with a new inamorata, the highborn and married Mary Frances Ronalds, known as Fanny, a fine soloist, charming, three years Sullivan's elder, originally from Boston. She had married and then separated from her husband, whom she never divorced, meeting Sullivan in Paris in 1867. Their light flirtation turned into a more permanent and intimate relationship when she arrived in London four years later. Despite Sullivan's continual straying, they remained together until his death in 1900. (After writing "The Lost Chord" music, an utterly funny, mawkish, tawdry, bilious song—made fun of by James Joyce in *Ulysses*—by which the composer attempted to honor the poem seriously, and offer to his dying brother in 1877, said to have killed him five days later, this became Fanny's signature piece, quite often with Sullivan accompanying her. He gave her the original manuscript in his will. King Edward VII, a rake, was said to have promised to travel all over Europe just to hear Fanny sing this. Unless he was with Lady Randolph Churchill, or Lily Langtry, or Lady Warwick-the last of whom was the inspiration for "Daisy Bell" about a bicycle built for two. "The Lost Chord" reaches its height of expression sung by Dame Clara Butt. It is loved by those who find Disney composer Albert Hay Malotte's "The Lord's Prayer" high art, and weep. Malotte famously wrote the music for Disney's "Ferdinand the Bull".)

Sullivan, by his music, was known as a man for the "people"; (the favorite composer of Winston Churchill, hardly known as a discerning music critic). I have to admit I love Gilbert and Sullivan's operettas. All of this is presented—i.e. Gilbert, Sullivan, Fanny, "The Lost Chord", and Paris—with historical accuracy in director Mike Leigh's 1999 wonderful film "Topsy Turvy", set in 1884 leading to the creation of "The Mikado".

XXVII

Morning Prayer, with its versicles and responses, collects, the daily praying of the *Venite*, (pronounced the English way, ve-nigh-tee, accent on second syllable)

> O come, let us sing unto the Lord;*
>
> let us heartily rejoice in the strength of our salvation.
>
> Let us come before His presence with thanksgiving,*
>
> and show ourselves glad in him with psalms.
>
> For the Lord is a great God,*
>
> and a great King above all gods.
>
> In his hand are all the corners of the earth,*
>
> and the strength of the hills is his also.
>
> The sea is his and he made it,*
>
> And his hands prepared the dry land.
>
> O come let us worship and fall down*
>
> and kneel before the Lord our Maker.
>
> For he is the Lord our God,*
>
> and we are the people of his pasture
>
> and the sheep of his hand.
>
> O worship the Lord in the beauty of holiness;*
>
> let the whole world stand in awe of him.
>
> For he cometh, for he cometh to judge the earth,*
>
> and with righteousness to judge the world
>
> and the peoples with his truth. (BCP 44–45)

I can hardly type these words without emotion, which I, of course, still pray. They are from *Psalms* 95:1–7; 96: 9, 13. I remember the smells and sights of that lovely chapel, the frangrance of flowers, and incense (always a pungent scent), the carved wood, all of us saying or chanting this responsively, pulpit side, then lectern side, facing one another, praying with these marvelous words about the "strength" of the Lord God, who has created everything the entire world around, and everything, and now governs, sustains, brings everything to be, out of His love and sheer delight. All of us prayed this. There we were dressed in cassocks and surplices, from our own puny selves, with all of our silliness's, and sins, and frailties, now entreating God Almighty, the Holy Trinity, to be our God, as we are His people, for He made us, and redeemed by His son's "most precious blood" as we pray in the Great Litany. At the words "O come and let us worship and fall down and kneel before the Lord our Maker", you would look around and see all of the company (word from Latin from *com*-together or with, and *panis*—bread) bow, or kneel, or genuflect, with one or two prostrating-right down on the floor.

This "company" or those with whom you break bread, those companions with whom you share our Lord's very Body and Blood, those who respond to Jesus' command "Do this", and not a lot of other things; or even more strongly in St. John's Eucharistic teaching found repeatedly in the Sixth Chapter, about God's very Wisdom Incarnate in Jesus who pronounces in His solemn way *Amen, Amen* I say unto you: Unless you eat my flesh (Greek word *sarx*) the word for this meat! This *carne* in Latin! As in *chile con carne*! Jesus is the Incarnate Son of God. And eat (v.54) could be better translated "feed "here the Greek word *trogein* for what referred to animals tearing into their prey until the time of Herodotus, when he used this about how crudely people without manners and of fierce hunger acted like animals in "gnawing" or "munching" on their food. This is not for the light hearted. No don't chew the baby Jesus here! Jesus stated "Unless you feed on my flesh, and drink of my blood, you have no life in you". St. John, considered for a time in New Testament scholarship as a "spiritualist" or even a little "gnostic", shows himself to use realism, with Jesus's command to receive life from his own Body and Blood in the Eucharist. He calls himself the very Bread of Life which came from God, from heaven. (In this I am following Archbishop Michael Ramsey's teaching as well as Fr. Louis Weil, Fr. Wayne Smith, and Fr. Raymond Brown's trenchant Commentary. Well actually, I am following the teaching of Christ Himself in *The Bible*!) This is what caused wonderful, tremendous, courageous German Martin Luther to pound the table in his "colloquy" with the flighty kind of believer, humanist, Swiss, Zwingli—in 1529 the other major reformer, Calvin was later—and pronounce, " *Hoc est corpus meum*", "*This is my Body!*". It was in the Bible, God said it, that settled it!

We would pray the preces, with the suffrages, said at Morning Prayer, sung at Evensong. These would be led by a senior seminarian, all kneeling in choir:

V. O Lord, show thy mercy upon us;

R. And grant us thy salvation.

V. Endue thy ministers with righteousness;

R. And make thy chosen people joyful.

V. Give peace, O Lord, in all the world;

R. For only in thee can we live in safety. (Fr. Cooper would snort.)[1]

V. Lord, keep this nation under thy care;

R. And guide us in the way of justice and truth.

V. Let thy way be known upon earth;

R. Thy saving health among all nations.

V. Let not the needy, O Lord, be forgotten;

R. Nor the hope of the poor be taken away.

V. Create in us clean hearts, O God;

R. And sustain us with thy Holy Spirit.

Particular Collects would strike me as so true, and lovely, and felicitously phrased:

A Collect for Peace

O God, from whom all holy desires, all good counsels, and

all just works do proceed: Give unto thy servants that peace

which the world cannot give, that our hearts may be set to

obey thy commandments, and also that by thee, we, being

defended from the fear of all enemies, may pass our time in

rest and quietness; through the merits of Jesus Christ our

Savior. *Amen.* BCP p.69.

A Collect for the Presence of Christ

Lord Jesus, stay with us, for evening is at hand and the day

is past; be our companion in the in the way, kindle our hearts, and

awaken hope, that we may know thee as thou art revealed in Scripture and the

breaking of bread. Grant this for the sake of thy love. *Amen.*

One of the Collects for mission

O God, who dost manifest in thy servants the signs of thy

presence; Send forth upon us the Spirit of love, that in

companionship with one another thine abounding grace may

increase among us; through Jesus Christ our Lord. *Amen.*

---

1. Cooper snorted because he hated the change of "dwell" to "live".

These prayers shaped us day by day. They were in accord with our two thousand year old faith of the Church of Jesus Christ, of which we were a part. And, our faith was in accord with how we prayed. The old maxim is *Lex Orandi, Lex Credendi*. I smile as I recall on many occasions Archbishop Michael Ramsey clapping his hands together and speaking loudly, "How we pray is what we believe! Do you want to know what we Anglicans believe? We don't just say here is a formulary, here is a Confession! No! We say 'Come and pray with us! Come and celebrate the Eucharist with us!'". This is ingrained in me. It was so weirdly naïve for me at first to imagine that Seminary teaching would be like a secular institution's graduate study in religion. We would sit and listen to informational lectures about the Bible, and dates, and what various academicians from graduate universities thought about various problems. We would choose our classes in accord with our particular tastes and prejudices, and join in the grad school way with our credentials nicely framed on the wall. I would study Tillich to my heart's content, learn German, and know a lot of stuff, which would bowl people away. I would pick and choose what I wanted from some cafeteria line. (There is a word for this in Christian tradition, heresy.) I go with what makes sense to me. And I get up in the pulpit and preach like Dean and then Bishop James Pike, and say "this is what makes sense to me, and to let you know how clever I am, here are some clever jokes to please you and make you feel you are in on the whole thing in the 'know' and clever yourself". And then I would say something shocking, like" St. Paul was a self loathing gay man, or the Blessed Virgin was raped by a Roman soldier, or Jesus never made any claims he was God, or the whole teaching of the Atonement was unconscious bloody child abuse projected onto the crucifixion". A bishop in the Episcopal Church actually said these flippant shallow lumpen things, both from the pulpit, and in his writing, and got his applause. This form of caustically opposing central tenets of the faith we have in Christ, was part of attacks by the "cultured despisers" of the Church. Having lost any faith in the intellectually considered doctrines of the Church, and forsaking philosophy and history (as N.T. Wright lays out in his soon to be published Gifford Lectures) to assist theologians and pastors to communicate the Gospel with confidence, I noted above the approach of Schleiermacher of turning to "feeling". This made the attacks by rationalist skeptics such as Feuerbach and Marx from this new Enlightenment approach to rational truth relatively simple. A. N. Wilson begins his excellent study of the 19th century's loss of faith epitomized by Thomas Hardy's poem "God's Funeral" , the title of his book, with a rehearsal of the explosive bombshells in the 18th century thrown by David Hume and Edward Gibbon. Both used the style of 6th Formers. This is Wilson's comment about their devastating style:

> The generation who lapped up Hume's *History of England* (he eventually covered the whole story, from Julius Caesar to the Stuarts) enjoyed it on the same level that they could savour (*sic*—he's a Brit) Gibbon on the *Decline and Fall of the Roman Empire*. Both authors were incapable of dullness. They were

urbane, vigorous and, above all funny. It required a generation devoid of humour (*sic* see above) perhaps to make them dangerous.[2]

I have followed Wilson's career for a long time, enjoying his writing immensely, especially with a telling illustration, clever quotation, and having read just about everything for his subject matter. And he writes with drollery, wit, even whimsy. He has written about Archbishop Michael Ramsey, who mattered greatly to his peregrinating spiritual journey, from Anglican to Roman Catholic to Atheist (more so a Seventh Day Horizontalist) and back to Anglican. He wrote at length in his third volume of his trilogy-*Our Times*, as noted above—about the fascinations of this 100th Archbishop of Canterbury.[3] In his article published in the *New Statesman*, of April 2, 2009, concerning his return to Christianity from his "conversion" to atheism, he mentions while as an atheist, he engaged in a lunchtime dialogue sermon with the Rev. Victor Stock, rector of St. Mary-le-Bow in London. After lambasting C. S. Lewis's "muscular defense of religious belief", he said much more to his "taste" had been the "approach" of the late Archbishop of Canterbury, Michael Ramsey, whose biography—I assume by Owen Chadwick-—he had just read. Wilson recalled a particular anecdote about Ramsey in the book:

> A young priest (Wilson writes) had been to see [Ramsey] in great distress, saying that he had lost his faith in God. Ramsey's reply was a long silence followed by a repetition of the mantra 'It doesn't matter, it doesn't matter'. He told the priest to continue to worship Jesus in the Sacraments and that faith would return. 'But!' exclaimed Fr. Stock. 'That priest was me!' Like many things said by this amusing man, it brought the house down. But something had taken a grip of me, and I was thinking (did I say it out loud?): "It bloody well does matter. Just struggling on like Lord Tennyson ('and faintly trust the larger hope') is no good at all . . ."[4]

Wilson had trained for the priesthood at St. Stephen's, the Anglican seminary near Oxford, he writes, "passionately wanting to be a priest". He fled after one year. He is quoted as saying, "It was a madhouse . . . a homosexual world of a particularly high-camp kind—a girls' names and feather dusters sort of world . . . It was beyond belief".[5] I can't help adding from the same article:

> By the mid-80's, Wilson's polemical style had made him a very public figure in England. He was widely assumed to be 'Lucy Fer', the pseudonymous columnist in Private Eye who delivers scabrous attacks on the Church of England establishment: One of his more notorious columns was a diatribe against Robert

2. Wilson, *God's Funeral*, 199

3. Wilson, *Our Times*, especially 117–121

4. Wilson," Why I Believe Again," on line

5. Atlas, "The Busy, Busy Wasp", on line

Runcie, then Archbishop of Canterbury, 'a nasty tenth-rate figure' who Wilson insisted on referring to as Agatha Runcieballs.[6]

I had exactly the same thought about Runcie when I heard him speak. He could be extremely charming for the first ten to fifteen minutes with hilarious Oxbridge "donnish" wit. But then when he would shift to speaking about why the Christian faith mattered, he was shockingly shallow. I believe he was a humbug. And not just a humbug, but in the words of Peter Cook's marvelous parody of the judge's instructions to the jury in the Jeremy Thorpe attempted murder case, the judge a boot licker to the English establishment, called chief prosecution witness Bex Bissell, "a man who by his own admission is a liar, a humbug, a hypocrite, a vagabond, a loathsome spotted reptile and a self—confessed chicken strangler, a man who by his own admission, chews pillows. You may choose if you wish to believe the transparent tissue of odious lies which streamed on and on from his disgusting, reedy, slavering lips. That is entirely a matter for you . . ." [7] Doesn't this ring a bell to all those who remember Archbishop Runcie? Perhaps I go too far . . . I rest my case. And this is totally objective. Is objectivity necessarily malicious?

I have a great affinity for Wilson, as a writer, and talker, and intellectual, and coming back to the Christian faith, in part because of Archbishop Ramsey. When he wrote of Hume (especially in his *Dialogues Concerning Natural Religion*) attempting to destroy the Christian faith almost insouciantly, he was also referring to how it had affected him. The mindsets of Hume and Gibbon have left Western culture in a particular paralysis. And yet this is the way our secular culture has been taught to think and understand since the Enlightenment, with everyone on their own, believing whatever they want in accord with what they can understand, with one's own autonomy. What have been the consequences?

Walker Percy wrote in his perceptive and imaginative *Lost in the Cosmos*, "You live in a deranged age, more deranged than usual, because in spite of great technological and scientific advances, man has not the faintest idea of who he is or what he is doing".[8]

Nearly a hundred and fifty years ago, Dostoyevsky noted this:

> In truth, we do observe a great number of suicides (their abundance is also a mystery *sui generis*) strange and mysterious, committed not by reason of poverty or some affront, without any apparent reasons and not at all because of material need, unrequited love, jealousy, ill-health, hypochondria or insanity-but God only knows why. In our day, such cases constitute a great temptation, and since it is impossible to deny that they have assumed the proportions of an epidemic, they arise in the minds of many people as a most disturbing

6. Atlas, "The Busy, Busy Wasp", on line

7. Cook, "The Secret Policeman's Ball" on YouTube

8. Percy, *Lost in the Cosmos*, 76

question. Of course, I am not venturing to explain all these suicides-this I cannot do-but I am firmly convinced that the majority of suicides *in toto*, directly or indirectly, were committed as a result of one and the same spiritual illness—the absence in the souls of these men of the sublime idea of existence.[9]

Wilson himself, in explaining why atheism is unconvincing, and itself can be exhibited as such, by noting "purely materialist 'explanations' for our mysterious human existence simply won't do—on an intellectual level", which he came to after he had witnessed the deaths of friends and then his own mother. He continues, "The phenomenon of language alone should give us pause. A materialist Darwinian was having dinner with me a few years ago and we laughingly alluded to how, as the years go by, one forgets names. Eager, as committed Darwinians often are, to testify on any occasion, my friend asserted: 'It is because when we were simply anthropoid apes, there was no need to distinguish between one another by giving names' ". Wilson's reaction to this was quick, "This credal confession struck me as just as superstitious as believing in the historicity of Noah's Ark. More so, really". [10]At this point, Wilson queries:

> Do materialists really think that language just 'evolved', like finches' beaks, or have they simply never thought about the matter rationally? Where's the evidence? How could it come about that human beings all agreed that particular grunts carried particular connotations? How could it have come about that groups of anthropoid apes developed the amazing morphological complexity of a single sentence, let alone the whole grammatical mystery which has engaged Chomsky and others in our lifetime and linguists for time out of mind? No, the existence of language is one of the many phenomena—of which love and music are the two strongest—which suggest that human beings are very much more than collections of meat. They convince me that we are spiritual beings, and that the religion of the Incarnation, asserting that God made humanity in His image, and continually restores humanity in His image, is simply true. As a working blueprint for life, as a template against which to measure experience, it fits. [11]

With only the use of empiricism for "true" results, and then the thinking that knowledge is to look at the world as something to "manage" or to "control" and organize what one knows in this way and "classify" it, one may actually think one is knowledgeable, educated, intelligent. This is the mystery of life reduced to taxonomy. In *Moby Dick*, Melville has a way of presenting this:

> [The American fisherman] have provided [a whaling code] which for terse comprehensiveness surpasses Justinian's Pandects and the By-Laws of the Chinese Society for the Suppression of Meddling in other People's Business.

9. Quoted in Wilson, *God's Funeral*, 11
10. Wilson, "Why I Believe Again", *New Statesman*
11. Wilson, "Why I believe Again", *New Statesman*

Yes; these laws might be engraven on a Queen Anne's farthing, or the barb of a harpoon, and worn round the neck, so small are they.

A Fast-Fish belongs to the party fast to it.

A Loose-Fish is fair game for anybody who can soonest catch it.

But what plays the mischief with this masterly code is the admirable brevity of it, which necessitates a vast volume of commentaries to expound it.

First: What is a Fast-Fish? . . .[12]

Seminarians came to Nashotah House first to pray, to join in the prayers of Christians from around the world (the meaning of Catholic, the Church Militant),And those who are the faithful departed, the souls of Christians throughout the Church's life (the Church Expectant), and those whom the Church has recognized as reigning with Christ in Heaven, the saints led by Jesus' Mother, as noted in the New Testament, (the Church Triumphant). The Blessed Virgin is praised by the Angel of God in *St. Luke* 1 states this, and she responds with the supreme word of faith, as the true prophet who will literally birth the Word of God into the world, "Be it unto me according to thy word". We prayed with the One we asked to lead us, as the Church, which is her role, as we prayed in the *Angelus* including the *Ave Maria*. It was in *St. John* 2 in which Jesus' mother is asked to intercede at the wedding reception at Cana, and she asks, Jesus responds (by saying to Mary he as the Word of God Incarnate will not allow anyone human even family, to determine his carrying out His Father's plan for salvation) and she turns to the servants and says, "Do what he tells you". There is the invocation to the Mother of God, to ask for her intercession. Note there is not a hint of doubt in what she says. In *Revelation* 12, a Woman in Heaven who is among the sun and moon and the stars, gives birth to the child who is spared of destruction by being snatched back by God, while the woman remains as it says in the wilderness, sustained by God. She is given wings to fly to God, while her other children must contend with the Accuser, Satan, and his minions. In these highly poetic terms, including a look back to the *Book of Daniel* 7:13, which our Lord did in his calling himself Son of Man thereby establishing his fulfilling Scripture in his very being, the vision of St. John the Divine provides a glimpse into the mystery of God's work to save his people. Mary is the Mother of God, *Theotokos*, which was proclaimed at the Fourth Council of the Church at Chalcedon, 451, and intended to declare who Jesus really is. As part of the Anglican Communion, which looks back to the Apostolic Church, and the generations after Christ's apostles, with their successors, to our own day, Episcopalians believe and pray this. In keeping with *Lex Orandi, Lex Credendi,* we pray this in our prayers, Feast days, the Season of Advent and Christmas, Easter, and in hymns. We entreat the Blessed Mother to lead our praises in the hymn *Ye Watchers and Ye Holy Ones*. In this glorious hymn, the entire Church is called upon to join with seraphs, cherubim, and angels in

12. Melville, *Moby Dick*, chap.89

praising the Holy Trinity. This version of the ancient hymn the *Te Deum* (pronounced by Nashotah's seminarians as tedium) includes the invocation to the Blessed Mother:

> O higher than the cherubim, more glorious than the seraphim, lead their praises, Alleluia! Thou bearer of the eternal Word, most gracious, magnify the Lord, Alleuia. (1982 Hymnal, 618)

I can't imagine not being part of so great a cloud of witnesses, nor of considering myself a "solo Christian". Fr. Smith would rail, "There are no such things as solo Christians! Do you think the Heavenly Banquet will be eating alone? Do you think Heaven will be solitary confinement?" A major theme for Archbishop Ramsey was the Communion of Saints.

Evensong was the opportunity to chant plainsong, which I've always loved. When the last Supper was over, the Disciples sang Psalms. From what I have studied, the *Our Father* was always sung, from the first century AD on. Obviously first in Syriac. Where did the doxology come from for *St. Matthew's* version? Bishop N. T. Wright has argued strongly that this is Jewish tradition in prayer, and especially from Syria, the provenance of the Gospel. However, most ancient codices do not include it, as *St. Luke's Gospel* does not. A fine scholar, Joachim Jeremias, in his *New Testament Theology*, 1971, believes from very early on, both/and that after singing the Lord's Prayer, the priest alone would intone the doxology.[13] Evensong as I mentioned above was the Divine Office, which affected me so strongly at Madison.

13. Davies, *Commentary on St.Matthew*, I, 615

XXVIII

I HAVE NOTED FOUR of the faculty above, without saying much about two of them, the deeply learned scholarly and devout Fr. Joseph Ignatius Hunt. He spoke six languages and read a number of ancient Middle Eastern tongues that were extinct, e.g. Hurrian, Parthian, Akkadian, Ugaritic, Sumerian. He was a gentleman, and had the humility to think every one of us was as knowledgeable as he. Fr. Hunt was showing us the volumes upon volumes of Patristic writings in a special area of Library shelves. They were all in Latin and Greek, except for a couple volumes in the Syriac language (fourth century St. Ephrem the Syrian, and seventh century Mar Isaac of Nineveh). When, I think, Pat Ward jokingly suggested that perhaps there were a couple jocks here who couldn't read those languages, Fr. Hunt smiled very kindly and said, "That's no problem, Paddy. Here they are all translated into French", which received a burst of applause and laughter. Hunt had meant it to be a helpful comment. He loved scholarship to the help of the Church Catholic, in honor of our Blessed Mother, to the Glory of God. He also believed fiercely in the freedom God has given us to use our minds, and follow facts wherever they may lead. This honesty was a moral duty to him. He had been born to a Roman Catholic couple in 1920 in Spokane, Washington, and fully intended on being an attorney and work in his father's Title Insurance business. However, he received the vocation to the religious life, and after three years at Gonzaga University, he completed his undergraduate studies, and in 1942, entered the novitiate-taking Ignatius as his religious name , and began his training for the priesthood, at the Mount Angel Abbey. This is a scene of great beauty, on a rural hill, in Oregon. Benedictines do more than pour B & B down their gullets. In 526 AD St. Benedict had founded his Order and establshed it at Monte Casino, Italy, a former site of a chapel of Apollo. This was to be the center of Christian mission and civilization following the collapse of the Roman Empire.

Ignatius Hunt was ordained a priest in 1946, and in 1948 professed his formal vows as a Benedictine monk. (I'm relying on Fr. Jack Knight's "Appreciation" from the *Festshrift* , 1990). He was shortly after that sent by his Order to the University of Ottawa, where he received his doctorate in Sacred Theology. Thenceforth he began his teaching and scholarly career at the Benedictine Westminster Abbey and Seminary of Christ the King just outside of Vancouver, British Columbia, where he worked for nine years. He then became Professor of Old Testament at Conception Abbey, Conception, Missouri in 1958. One may see what kind of scholar he was by the article he was asked to write for the work of outstanding Biblical scholarship, *The Jerome Biblical Commentary*, edited by Fr. Raymond Brown, S.S., Fr. Roland Murphy, O. Carm., and Fr. Joseph Fitzmyer, S. J., in 1968. (This emerged on the heels of another Roman Catholic scholarly achievement, *The Jerusalem Bible*.) To read the list of contributors is to marvel at the extraordinary talent marshalled by these editors of such a high quality of scholarship, and how far Roman Catholic efforts had moved since Vatican II.

The great name for Old Testament and Hebrew, especially in English, was Oxford scholar and Anglican cleric Samuel Rolles Driver. He had followed the sad, old cautious to a fault, Tractarian Edward Bouverie Pusey as Regius Professor of Hebrew, and in 1900 wrote the classic *Introduction to the Literature of the Old Testament*, which remained crucial to this subject for fifty years, as well as becoming the driving force to produce the Brown-Driver-Briggs Hebrew/ English Lexicon, 1906, and the article "Bible" for the 11th edition of the *Encyclopaedia Britannica* in 1911.

Fr. Ignatius Hunt imbued all of this knowledge of various subjects relating to the History of Israel and the Hebrew Bible. He had shelves and shelves of books, journals, articles, several shelves standing free as in a library to house his books. In addition to commentaries, general surveys, histories of ancient peoples around Mesopotamia and Egypt, he was involved in many archaeological digs which provided him a far more rich understanding of the ancient near East and its various cultures. He was under constant pressure from being asked to write book reviews for a huge array of Biblical and Old Testament journals, and when he put his mind to it, he could produce them rapidly. He read day to night. He knew everything there was to know about Gerhad von Rad, or Bruce Vawter, or Sigmund Mowinkle, or Claus Westermann. He told me that he considered Edouard Dhorme's *A Commentary on the Book of Job*, the best single commentary he knew. It was written 1926, in French, and only translated into English in 1967. I should read the French, he said. (Oh, right.) He was known for being fair, even judicious, with nary a known axe to grind. To any question he was easily able to answer with a wealth of knowledge at his fingertips. One may glimpse his scholarship in the excellent article "Excursus: Israel and Her Neighbors", in the *Jerome Biblical Commentary*, published just as he was experiencing the upheaval of leaving the Benedictine Order, Roman Catholic priesthood, and the world he knew, and entering the Episcopal Church in 1969–70.

Fr. Hunt's scholarship, evenhandedness, and perspicacity about the Torah, or Pentateuch (he knew everything about the Hebrew Bible, and the *LXX Septuagint* in Greek) led him to suggest gently in two books, *Understanding the Bible*, 1962, and *The World of the Patriarchs*, 1967, evenhanded and clear written introductions for Catholic laity, that the devout consider broadly held understandings of the study of the Bible within Roman Catholic scholarship. This was completely vindicated by the Vatican II document on the study of Scripture, *Dei Verbum*, chapters III and IV. This did not halt increasing suspicion by "The Supreme Sacred Congregation of the Holy

Office"-before 1965: "The Supreme Congregation for the Doctrine of the Faith", i.e. the Inquisition, "The Inquisitors of Heretical Depravity", to haul this dear scholar and priest before them several times in the Fifties and then Sixties, to question, harry, disturb this saintly man. He said to me once, when he was shaken by the truculent way several of my Fundamentalist classmates had sullenly questioned him, on his views about Mosaic authorship of the Torah, employing the same obstreperous and disputatious tones and words used by the Catholic inquisitors in the fifties, that he had been ordered to Rome to answer charges about his spoken views. He said to me, that for a couple hours they had harangued him about what he had said about Our Lord's statements concerning Jonah. When they required him to speak, he responded, "I have no doubt that our Lord was a sound exegete of the Hebrew Scriptures". (At other times he would simply say what is ancient in the Fathers, "Jesus Christ interprets the Scriptures".)This did not satisfy them, and he was ordered not to publish anything. For a man who had given his life to the Church, and prayed constantly, and was totally devout, and had written two highly received books, and hundreds of articles and book reviews, he began praying about becoming an Episcopalian.

Father Hunt was a large man, strongly built. He was balding and always smoking a pipe. His demeanor was kind, gentle, empathic. He left the Benedictine Order in 1968, and was directed by the Bishop of West Missouri, Edward Welles, to reside with a friendly couple, Julian and Margaret Rymar. (I know this, because they told me while I was their priest at Holy Faith, Santa Fe.) The Rymars told me that Fr. Joe ate with his large arms encircling his plate, a habit from the refectory at the Monastery. A biretta of Fr. Hunt's came to me from the Rymars. Fr. Hunt was received into the Episcopal Church rather than confirmed, because of Anglican Sacramental Theology, as the Anglican Communion's Churches accept the Apostolic Order of Bishops in the Roman Catholic Church, while not having their own Orders recognized. (Archbishop Ramsey and Paul VI had a very congenial series of public meetings in 1966, and promised to work on restoring Communion, beginning with the Roman acceptance of Anglican Orders. Paul VI's promise was backed by slipping his Papal ring onto Ramsey's finger, which Ramsey always wore. He said showing this to seminarians, "You don't give this ring to a layman!". Ramsey is depicted holding this ring on the cover of his book *Be Still and Know*. Ramsey would note the sentence in the Vatican document *Unitatis Redintegratio* , "Among those in which some Catholic traditions and institutions continue to exist, the Anglican Communion occupies a special place".[1]) Fr. Hunt was then received in 1970 as a priest in the Episcopal Church. That same year he and a former nun, Carolyn were married, and he received the appointment to become Professor of Old Testament at Nashotah House.

What I remember threatening a number of seminarians about Fr. Hunt's teaching, was his insistence on using James Pritchard's remarkable books of texts and photographs of a wide variety of mythic tales and stories, with obvious similarities to the

1. Ramsey, *The Anglican Spirit*, 121

Creation and Flood narratives in Genesis, as well as statues, figurines, and a great many other archaeological material discovered during the vast number of digs taking place, entitled *The Ancient Near East: An Anthology of Texts and Pictures, Volume I*, 1958; And *Volume II*, with what had been discovered between 1958 and 1973. Fr. Hunt would point out myths coinciding or a little older than the accepted dates for the various strands of traditions found in Genesis, and discuss their similarities and dissimilarities. He never failed to state what was clearly different and revelatory found especially in *Genesis* 1, that is, the uniqueness of God creating everything out of love, and then God's revealing Himself as YHWH, or LORD after the Theophany in Moses' presence, at the burning bush. Simply bringing all this to the fore would anger these fundamentalists, especially a couple guys from Wheaton, who had studied ultra conservative and unchallenging R. K. Harrison, *Introduction to the Old Testament*, 1969, with his axe grinding away, allowing his doctrine of a single pure text for the Old Testament, with no evidence whatsoever, which was "inerrant", to control his scholarship. This is utter nonsense. This view dispenses with any human or historical process engaged in receiving this imaginary pure text. An Old Testament scholar Hunt highly regarded was James Barr, who had recently authored *Fundamentalism* in 1977, about how Conservative Evangelicals were mangling even destroying the human element in their interpretations of Scripture. Commenting on this book, which was *verboten* and taboo to my classmates, caused a hardness in their attitudes towards this outstanding and fine teacher and priest. Barr describes Fundamentalism thus:

> Fundamentalism begins when people begin to say that the doctrinal and authority of Scripture is necessarily tied to its infallibility, and in particular its historical inerrancy, when they maintain that its doctrinal and practical authority will stand up *only* if it is in general without error, and this means in particular only if it is without error in its apparently historical remarks. The center of fundamentalism is the insistence that the control of doctrine and practice by Scripture is dependent on something like a general perfection of Scripture, and there on its historical inerrancy; and this in turn involves the repudiation of the results of modern critical modes of reading the Bible.[2]

Barr was an ordained minister in the Church of Scotland, a highly regarded student of the Bible, who taught in Scotland, Princeton, Oxford, Vanderbilt. He was one of only a very few Biblical scholars invited to give the prestigious Gifford Lectures at the University of Edinburgh in 1991 (now also N. T. Wright), and shared with Fr. Hunt an aspersion to the sellout of the mind to this ideology. Four of my classmates hounded Hunt unmercifully, even studying carefully the extreme conservative Jewish scholar, Umberto Cassuto, who denied any traditions whatsoever in Torah, with a single author around 1000 BC. They would then come to class loaded for bear. Fr. Hunt bore this with grace. I would regularly see him after class and encourage him. He said to me

2. Barr, *The Scope and Authority*, 65–6

that he was praying for all these men, and chanting extra loudly (as he did Benedictine chant) to get God's attention. He did enjoy finding an Episcopal seminary, where the community chanted plainsong, or Gregorian chant, including the Psalms.

We had two glaring *lacunae* the three years I was at Nashotah. We had no New Testament professor, with the possible exception of Dean Ruef, a Pauline scholar, and we had no faculty member assigned for preaching. Ruef, or librarian James Dunkly, and for one term, visiting professor Lamar Cope, from nearby Carroll College, co-taught us, and they were dreadful. Ruef would march in in jackboots, look around, actually glare, then say a prayer as Truman Capote. He was a Bultmannian. He didn't believe in much. He didn't publish much. A reader of one of his two books published, *The Gospels and the Teachings of Jesus*, (1967), and *Paul's First Letter to Corinth*, (1971) would note that first of all they were remarkably thin, 144 pages and 198 pages, and both Unitarian, if not Gnostic. (Keep in mind that in his *Theology of the New Testament*, Bultmann has a paltry 29 pages out of 630 pages on the historical Jesus.) Ruef had weighed Jesus in the balance, and found him wanting. He wrote as he taught and preached, there was no empty tomb. Jesus was a Pharisee, with the Pharisaic view of a general Resurrection at the end of time. *Jesus died* was the essence of Ruef's belief. The Resurrection was the depth of understanding the crucifixion-this right out of Bultmann, who followed Schleiermacher and D. F. Strauss. [3] The book in which this is shone in a steady light, and in which Karl Jaspers, who knew philosophy, and accused Bultmann of being ignorant of philosophy, except reading *Being and Time* by Heidegger, and misunderstanding that work, must be read to understand this demythologizing fraud. Jaspers cornered Bultmann and the latter has nowhere to turn.[4] Ruef believed in the Real Absence. Every day was Good Friday to him, and time for the deposition of the corpse. He once while preaching said loudly, "What is there to believe?" He placed his hands over his eyes, paused and said, "There is nothing". His view, again stated in his books, the first on the Resurrection, the second found in Paul's statements in the fifteenth chapter of *First Corinthians*-in which Paul makes it plain: Jesus had been raised from the dead, and then appeared, with a long list of witnesses, this only 18 to 20 years after the Resurrection—that this is not historical. For those evasive Christians, clergy and writers, who say Jesus only appeared to those who already believed, so they already had faith-this flat out contradicts the statements of every single Gospel and *First Corinthians*, as well as Paul's own startling faith and witness, making an about face after he encountered the Crucified and Risen Lord on the road to persecute Christians in Damascus, I simply don't know how they can claim to be Christians. At most they would say there was a "feeling" among the faithful of Jesus' "presence". Ruef was not the only one to evince a thin veneer of piety based on nothing. So was Jim Griffiss, as certainly was John Macquarrie. They were all of them deist on their bad days, and pantheists on their good. By deism I mean god (Heidegger's

3. Jaspers and Bultmann, *Myth and Christianity*, 60

4. Jaspers and Bultmann, *Myth and Christianity*, 1–11, 57–69

Being-*Sein*) has emanated not created the world (Let Be, Paul McCartney comes to mind) and the height of this emanation—the Let Bees, the little *Daseins*—and then gotten tired of his little *Daseins* and wandered off. The Deist God gets tired of his toy and wanders off. It (not personal) is way down there in depths somewhere and not to be bothered. By pantheism, I mean, god is everywhere and in everything like the Star Wars' Force. There is no need to pray because this god is unknown, not revelatory, not personal. Bishop John A. T. Robinson, in his book *Honest to God* of 1963, writes of worship without ever naming this God as one to whom we may pray. It is Woolwich woolly-mindedness. There was only for these men a kind of hoped for gaseous vibe. (This would be emanated especially on Thursday evenings in the Refectory when German food was served.) Everything written about in the primitive and silly New Testament, is not really about the historical Jesus at all, but complete myths constructing some Christ avatar by the New Testament communities. To John Ruef, and especially to John Macquarrie, both Bultmannians, the job of the trained priests of Nashotah House was to go into their churches, and boldly demythologize, dehistoricize—remove all the language about Jesus using various terms and metaphors, including all spatial language which would leave their people with nothing but something vaguely existentialist, certainly not historical, maybe like *Billy Budd, a la* Thomas Jefferson's cut and paste Gospels. Karl Barth was a joke. Michael Ramsey was ignored by John Macquarrie, who later, when it suited him, spread word that he was Ramsey's favorite Anglican theologian. This was drivel, clap-trap, and now I will say it again, humbug. (See above under Robert Runcie.) These men's beliefs were for them to co-exist with Christians, use the language of Credal and Traditional Christianity, without believing it, pretty much dissemble, or dissimulate, write their books, get the applause from undergraduates, especially sophomores, and wait for your pension. These men thought of themselves as being so above all the other clueless devout Christians, they viewed it as child's play to pretend they believed in the myth of Christ. With Ruef and Griffiss and Macquarrie, the last two knowing next to nothing about the New Testament, and Ruef not believing it, it should not have been a shock at the lack of interest to find a good, devout, and knowledgeable scholar to teach New Testament.

Heidegger was Macquarrie's idol. (So also Bultmann's idol. Actually Bultmann was Macquarrie's second idol, a demiurge). Because of Heidegger, and especially his big book *Being and Time*, (*Sein und Zeit*), 1927, translated as noted above by Macquarrie, 1962, providing what Macquarrie and Bultmann wanted, he was the only philosopher for either man. Heidegger puts forward his thinking about ontology or metaphysics, meaning what is real? What is reality? Heidegger believes that all of Western philosophy has taken a wrong turn since Descartes put forward what he considered absolutely true: I think therefore I am. On this truth, Descartes imagined everything else about reality could be tested, and from it, all true thoughts about reality could be constructed. Heidegger said Descartes was totally wrong to begin with a rationalism, which was false about reality, and humanity; and actually the same with much Western philosophy going back to Plato. (I will address this further below.) So philosophy had to find another starting point: Heidegger posited *"Das Seiende"*, or "The Essent". *Das Seiende* throws off or lets be *Dasein*. This has been translated by Macquarrie and others as "Being there", or "Thrownness". A human being discovers he or she is "thrown" into the world, into everyday reality. Those *Daseins* who reflect truly on existing (*Existenz*), realize there is Being (*Seiende*) which lets be *Daseins*. This is essential to Heidegger. One must "grasp" this pantheism, that everything, rocks, trees, frogs, mountains, oceans, human beings, aardvarks, bungholes, are all "let be" by Being. Heidegger here untethers himself from "epistemology", which is one of three or four essential parts of philosophy, going back to Aristotle—depending on logic. The others are metaphysics (see above) and ethics. I read Aristotle as metaphysics— what is real, what is there, (actually strictly speaking ontology, but called metaphysics because in the First century BC Andronicus of Rhodes, arranger of the catalogue of Aristotle's books , placed ontology "after" physics, or metaphysics); epistemology—or how can I be certain, what warrants this understanding of reality, how can I justify this as true; and therefore with what rules of logic, and logical argument; and ethics—how therefore ought I to live.

Heidegger throws off all epistemology. (This is how we ensure rationality in any philosophy or theology.) He states-as a kind of guru, like Wittgenstein, or Joseph Smith, or William Booth (angels singing)-only he knows this, his "Grand Unified Theory", which is neither religious nor scientific. But it sure sounds like a religion to me. There are all these beings, but only human beings matter, because they "care" about being themselves, and alone of all *Dasein* know they will die. And thus we "take a stand" on what it means to exist. (This is actually the meaning of exist-we stand out.) But we *Care*! This is what truth is for Heidegger, with all the myriads of things going on at any particular time, we care about this X. Otherwise X remains concealed. This is truth for Heidegger. There is no self-consciousness in his theorizing, and no God. There is *Dasein*, being in the world, being there. "Authenticity" for Heidegger is for *Dasein* to take responsibility for one's "Daseinness"—if Heidegger can make up his own vocabulary, so can I-and note we are going to die. Truth boils down to this caring and acting. Evil or untruth consists in losing one's nature and existing inauthentically in the rampant consumerism of the West, and the technologies which enable this, and careful calculation, which can take us over. This is Heidegger's Satan. E.g. the Jews, he wrote.

Now, comes the tricky part for any Heideggerian, who actually thinks this *Scheiss* is important. And I mean both Bultmann and Macquarrie, as well as Ruef and Griffiss, and how this has played out in the Episcopal Church for fifty years or more, entrusting their clergy to be "Macquarrieized" in Systematic Theology through the study of various editions of *Principles of Christian Theology*. And I mean *Scheiss*. This is entirely gnostic, not based on anything at all. No one knows what Heidegger means by *Sein*. And then here comes the Nazi. In 1987, a former Heideggerian disciple, taught by

Heidegger, Victor Farias, from Chile, published a book, *Heidegger and Nazism*. With ample evidence, and affirmed by Hugo Ott's *Martin Heidegger: A Political Life* , (1988, Eng. Edition 1993), and Thomas Sheehan's numerous articles, beginning in the *New York Review of Books*, June 16, 1988, and especially now his 2014 study *Making Sense of Heidegger: A Paradigm Shift*, a stellar work, Heidegger was a convinced Nazi from the beginning. Heidegger thought as a Nazi, spoke as a Nazi, reasoned as a Nazi. And when he got older, his Nazi views became even more extreme.

In a fine review article on Heidegger's *Black Notebooks*, now being published, Peter F. Gordon in the *New York Review of Books* writes: "[Heidegger] warns of a new phenomenon: 'the gigantic', or, more typically, 'machination' (*Machenschaft*)".[5] This is how to view the Jews. Heidegger especially latches on to this idea after becoming a Nazi in 1933, and a *Rektor* for the Nazi government at the University of Freiburg, until he left in 1934. Well, he made a serious mistake, and got out of Nazidom say his apologists, including Hannah Arendt. [6]

The first three volumes, comprising the first fifteen of The *Black Notebooks*, written between 1931–41, beginning when Heidegger started recording his private thoughts, were published in 2014. These were edited by a philosopher, Peter Trawny, who also happens to be the director of the Martin Heidegger Institute of Wuppertal, Germany. In these, Gordon and another reviewer, Joshua Rothman in the *New Yorker*, have brought to light the repeated times Heidegger references the Jews as somehow outside "authentic being", that is to say, the politics of Nazism was not a sidebar, or hobby for him, but essential to his thought.[7] In 1933 he wrote, "The metaphysics of *Dasein* must deepen itself into its innermost structure and broaden into a metapolitics of the historical people". [8] Gordon then comments:

> A bit later [Heidegger] writes, that Being has a 'groundplan' but it is 'not Idea, but mission'. The ground plan 'does not detach itself into pure Spirit, but rather first opens and binds Blood and Soil [Blut and Boden] to a readiness for action and a capacity for realization and work'. [9]

Gordon spells out what Heidegger meant by "mission":

> The emphasis here is on effect, concreteness, and action. While refining his plans for the rectorship [of Freiburg] he reminds himself that 'the intellectual National Socialism is not "theoretical"'. Such statements are consonant with what we already knew about Heidegger's political commitments. In a notorious speech from November 3, 1933, he admonished students: 'Let not

5. Gordon, "Heidegger in Black", 28

6. Rothman, "Is Heidegger Contaminated by Nazism?", *New Yorker;* also Gordon, 26

7. Rothman, "Is Heidegger Contaminated by Nazism?"

8. Gordon, "Heidegger in Black", 27

9. Gordon, "Heidegger in Black", 27

propositions and ideas be the rules of your Being [Sein]. The Fuehrer alone is the present and future German reality its law'. [10]

From here on Heidegger only gets more hysterical. He showed his enthusiasm by wearing a Hitler moustache, and from an entry in 1939, Gordon writes, "[Heidegger] denounces liberalism, pacifism, and the 'rising power of Jewry." Gordon notes, " The ascendancy of the Jews belonged to [here quoting Heidegger] 'the metaphysics of the West', that helped to spread both ' empty rationality' and 'a capacity for calculation'. Gordon then adds to this, quoting Heidegger, "one of the most hidden forms of the gigantic and perhaps the oldest is the tenacious aptitude for calculating and profiteering and intermingling, upon which the worldlessness of Jewry is founded".[11] When I read this several years ago, I wrote in "Yikes!".

Heidegger had insisted in a public debate in 1929 with Ernst Cassirer, adds Gordon, "that a valid philosophy would demand 'the destruction of the former foundation of Western metaphysics' in spirit, *logos*, [and] reason". And in 1941, Heidegger warned "the question concerning the role of world Jewry is not a racial but a metaphysical question". [12] Later that same year in the summer, Heidegger spoke of an entire world conspiracy:

> "World Jewry, spurred on by the emigrants who have been let out of Germany, is ungraspable everywhere and doesn't need to get involved in military action while continuing to unfurl its influence, whereas we are left to sacrifice the best blood of the best of our people". [13]

Finally, Heidegger notoriously commented in a 1949 speech: "the manufacture of corpses in the gas chambers and the death camps" and "the motorized food industry" are "in essence the same". [14] This is Heidegger's *Zug*! (Fall). This is nihilism. And fascism.

I find it of great importance that this is the philosopher both Rudolph Bultmann and John Macquarrie relied on to assist them with their projects. And Macquarrie was instrumental in introducing both of these *dummkopfs* to the Anglophone world. His first book derived from his doctoral dissertation at the University of Glasgow, entitled *An Existentialist Theology: A Comparison of Heidegger and Bultmann*, 1955. His second book, based on lectures at Union Theological Seminary in 1957, was *The Scope of Demythologizing: Bultmann and His Critics*, published in 1960. All of his thinking and writing was founded on Heidegger. He ended his career from 1996 on as the "Martin Heidegger Professor of Philosophical Theology" at the Graduate Theological Foundation, a continuing educational center for active clergy, in Mishawaka, Indiana.

10. Gordon, "Heidegger in Black", 27
11. Gordon, "Heidegger in Black", 28
12. Gordon, "Heidegger in Black", 28
13. Gordon, "Heidegger in Black", 28
14. Gordon, "Heidegger in Black", 28

Heidegger ended his career totally withdrawn from society, in a hut on the edge of *Todtnau* in the *Schwarzwald* (Black Forest). There he sang hits from "Sound of Music", and viciously hunted little *daseins*. George Beverly Shea would show up from time to time, and yodel. Then they would sit by the campfire and sing old Nazi ditties.

I am contending that Macquarrie's theological work was a fraud, based on a Nazi guru, Martin Heidegger, who himself as a philosopher had no epistemology, unless solipsistic, indeed no ontology, either from Western philosophy, or from a Christian standpoint. In Joshua Rothman's review of the first Black Notebooks published, entitled "Is Heidegger Contaminated by Nazism", concludes that yes, Heidegger is contaminated. Indeed, " . . . Heidegger never truly apologized for being a Nazi; even worse, he never directly and publically addressed the reality of the Holocaust before he died, in 1976".[15] In quoting Peter Trawny's public talk, whom I mentioned above as the director of the Martin Heidegger Institute at the University of Wuppertal, Germany, Rothman adds this from the same speech:

> The problem is not just that I'm morally shocked-it's also a problem that [Heidegger] is so dumb . . . Observe what he is writing there. You see that, like all the others [Nazis] he was not better. You thought it, actually; for long years, you thought he was very clever, but he is not. This is something that requires a certain distance . . . You shouldn't be too much in love with what you are reading, or you will be disappointed, like always.[16]

All this matters to me deeply. For the following reasons:

1. Christian theologians and Christian clergy do have an epistemology. It is stated in Scripture and in our liturgies. The fact of the Resurrection of our Lord is our *arche*, our true starting point for understanding everything in the Cosmos, including ourselves. *St. John's Gospel* spells this out:

   > In the beginning (*arche*) was the Word, and the Word was with God, and the Word was God. He was in the beginning (*arche*) with God. All things came into being through him; and without him not one thing was made. What has come into being in him was life, and the life was the light of all people (*anthropon*-all humanity-note women and men). The light shines in the darkness, and the darkness did not overcome it . . . And the Word became flesh and dwelt among us, and we have seen his glory, as of a father's only son, full of grace and truth . . . No one has ever seen God. It is God the only Son, who is close to the Father's bosom, who has made him known. *St. John's Gospel*, 1:1-4,14,18.)

   St. Athanasius in his great book *On the Incarnation*, observes this as well after showing the obvious about various views of other religions, e.g. the Epicureans

15. Rothman,"Is Heidegger Contaminated by Nazism?"
16. Rothman, "Is Heidegger Contaminated by Nazism?"

who deny there is any Mind behind the universe at all, "This view is contrary to all the facts of experience, their own existence included"; the view of Plato who claimed God made all things out of pre-existent and uncreated matter, which limits God to using matter from another cause; or the Gnostics who "have invented for themselves an Artificer of all things other than the Father of our Lord Jesus Christ".[17] Then, he writes that we know now for sure how everything came to be because it is, " . . . declared in the Divine teaching of the Christian faith. From it we know, because there is Mind behind the universe, it did not originate itself . . . He made all things out of nothing through his own Word, our Lord Jesus Christ . . ." [18] St. Athanasius proclaims the Incarnate Lord is our foundation, our *arche*.

St. Augustine notes in a famous passage from his *Confessions* that it is God's revelation that gives us the knowledge of Jesus Christ, and not any other source:

> . . . you brought under my eye some books of the Platonists, translated from Greek into Latin. There I read, not of course in these words, but with entirely the same sense and supported by numerous and varied reasons, "In the beginning was the Word and the Word was with God and the Word was God . . . Again I read there that the Word, God, is 'born not of the flesh, nor of blood, nor of the will of man nor of the will of the flesh, but of God. But that 'the word became flesh and dwelt among us' (John 1:13–14), I did not read there. [19]

2. Heidegger and Macquarrie attempt to cut themselves off from any epistemology used in Western philosophy, which since the time of Plato and Aristotle has been observance of ourselves and the world around us, test, experiment, and draw conclusions. Macquarrie, wrote in his inaugural lecture, "How is Theology Possible?", at Union Theological Seminary in New York City in 1962, "For a long time men did try to account for many happenings in terms of supernatural agencies. With the rise of science, however, we have learned to look for our explanations in terms of factors immanent in the natural process itself".[20] And then he states, "The famous remark of Laplace to Napoleon, 'I have no need of that hypothesis', simply expresses our modern attitude to the world as a self-regulating entity".[21] Finally he appeals to no reason but Revelation. And he means Heidegger's Revelation. He writes,

---

17. St. Athanasius, *On the Incarnation*, I,2
18. St. Athanasius, *On the Incarnation*, I,3
19. St. Augustine, Confessions, VII, ix,13,14
20. Macquarrie, "How is Theology Possible?", 188
21. Macquarrie, "How is Theology Possible ?", 188

It is clear that I have already cut myself off from the rationalistic natural theology by which so many theologians in the past sought to ground their subject and establish the reality of its matter. Apart from the fact that their arguments have been discredited by modern criticism [i.e. by Heidegger], I have tried to show that their speculative approach was a mistaken one, and that their leading question about the existence of God involved a logical defect in its formulation. In any case, all those who tried to prove the existence of God already believed in him, and must have had a more primordial source for their conviction, than their own arguments. Where then are we to look? [22]

I find this puerile pablum. This is how Macquarrie sets up his claim that Heidegger knows best. That stupid Nazi. Alasdair MacIntyre, in his review of this kind of nonsense, which he found in Bishop John Robinson's *Honest to God*, and then reprinted in the same *The Honest to God Debate*, begins with the crushing words, "What is striking about Dr. Robinson's book is first and foremost that he is an atheist".[23] And Robinson is open to Nazi propaganda. As is Macquarrie. Why? That was Heidegger's bent as I argued above. And he has no basis for rational thought, only his farrago of solipsistic nonsensical assertions. The scientologists have that. In philosophy if one wishes to be taken seriously, one must put forward some kind of epistemological basis for what one argues. It must include a theory of correspondence or coherence between our minds and the world around us. Otherwise, why is there speech between humans? Why is anything sensible in what one states to humans about the world? Christians have such a theory. God created through the Word, or *Logos*. This was standard in much classical philosophy. Christians further argued that this Logos, through whom everything was made became man, *Anthropos*. There is rationality in the universe, which has been made by God through the Word, which is also the rationality in human beings. That Heidegger or Macquarrie or Ruef evades this shows complete ignorance of basic rationality at all. David Bentley Hart recently in his *The Experience of God*, lays all this out so masterfully that his book should be basic prolegomena to all future theology and philosophy. He notes, "It is an old maxim-one that infuriates unbelievers, but that happens to be true nonetheless—that one cannot meaningfully reject belief in the God of classical theism". [24] I recall Archbishop J. Augustine Di Noia, when he was theologian for what was at the time called the National Conference of Catholic Bishops, at a Conference on the Nicene Creed at Christ Cathedral in Charleston, January, 2001, saying to me over a glass of a single malt scotch, that His Holiness John Paul II, had asked him to define this strange New Age prevalent in the United States. Di Noia said to the Pope, "It is the attempt to cultivate spirituality in a closed system". Later he said that it had been instructive to him of John Paul's recent reminiscing that at the

22. Macquarrie, "How is Theology Possible?", 190
23. MacIntyre, "God and the Theologians", 215
24. Hart, *The Experience of God*, 250

beginning of his papacy he was affirming holding together faith and reason, and that in 2001 he was reduced to fighting for reason. I couldn't describe *mutatis mutandis* Macquarrie's theology better than what Di Noia said.

My thought now about the work of Heidegger and Bultmann and Macquarrie, is *Scheiss*. And nonsense. And as Professor Saul Lieberman said (about Gershom Scholem's love of Kabbalism): "Nonsense is nonsense. But the history of nonsense is scholarship". Or Burton Dreben (not Frank) an exotic Philosopher of Logic at Harvard, said "Philosophy is garbage, but the history of garbage is scholarship".

Three last quotations, first from two of my favorite contemporary Christian theologians, Stanley Hauerwas and William Willimon, both United Methodists, both of whose work and sermons I have been reading since the early 1980's. In their provocative book *Resident Aliens*, they write:

> Nazi Germany was the supreme test for modern theology. There we experienced the 'modern world', which we had so labored to understand and to become credible to, as the world, not only of the Copernican world view, computers, and the dynamo, but also of the Nazis. Barth was horrified that his church lacked the theological resources to stand against Hitler. It was the theological liberals, those who had spent their theological careers translating the faith into terms that could be understood by modern people, and used in the creation of modern civilization, who were unable to say no. Some, like Emanuel Hirsch, even said yes to Hitler. [25]

Karl Barth was the leading preacher of opposition to the Nazis' attempt to take hold of the German Church in 1934. He was the chief drafter of the Confessing Church's "Barmen Declaration", which stated foremost what the Christian Church is about:

> Jesus Christ, as he is attested for us in Holy Scripture, is the one Word of God which we have to hear and which we have to trust and obey in life and in death. We reject the false teaching, that the church could and should acknowledge any other events and powers, figures and truths, as God's revelation, or as a source of its proclamation, apart from and besides this one Word of God . . . The Christian church is the congregation of brothers and sisters in which Jesus Christ acts presently as the Lord in Word and Sacrament, through the Holy Spirit. As the church of forgiven sinners, it has to bear witness in the midst of a sinful world, with both its faith and its obedience, with its proclamation as well as its order, that it is the possession of him alone, and that it lives and wills to live only from his comfort and guidance in the expectation of his appearance. We reject the false teaching, that the church is free to abandon the form of its proclamation and order in favor of anything it pleases, or in response to prevailing ideological or political beliefs. [26]

25. Hauerwas, *Resident Aliens*, 24–25
26. McGrath, *A Passion for Truth*, 35

Third, I have thought for a long time a quotation by Lincoln about the arguments Douglas was using in their 1858 debates about slavery as they competed for the United States Senate, particularly apposite about Macquarrie's (and Ruef's and Griffiss's) writing about Jesus, about whom he switches from Jesus to Christ when he compares the historicity of the crucifixion to the Resurrection. Macquarrie does not believe in the Resurrection. He denies the empty tomb.[27] His view is entirely Gnostic! (His *Dasein* principle governs how he writes about the Transfiguration as well.) Lincoln said: Douglas' argument,". . . is as thin as homeopathic soup that was made by boiling the shadow of a pigeon that had starved to death". [28]So Macquarrie's belief in our Lord.

27. Macquarrie, *Principles of Christian Theology*, 288–90

28. Lincoln, Sixth Debate of 1858

XXVIII

I MYSELF CAME TO know New Testament scholarship, having studied, at Archbishop Ramsey's urging, himself a New Testament scholar, the unprecedented Cambridge New Testament scholarship of the late 19th century, spearheaded by Brook Foss Westcott, Joseph Barber Lightfoot, and F. J. A. Hort, the first two successive Bishops of Durham. They brought historical criticism combined with devotion to the inspiration of Scripture as witness to the Incarnation, in the creative way described by Bishop Stephen Neill's profound study, *The Interpretation of the New Testament, 1861–1961*, in 1964. This book was expanded by Neill's protégé, and brilliant scholar himself, N. T. Wright, to cover the years 1961–1986, and published in 1988. Hort and Westcott revolutionized New Testament study with their New Testament in Greek, a text which could be trusted, from the intricate careful necessary concentration needed to assemble from the mountain of papyri fragments (dating as far back as the 1st century AD) and scrolls, and later the codices or books, which were invented by Christians around 300 AD, for the sacred writings in Greek of the Bible, then improved in 600 AD by separating the words, heretofore all run together, and finally set in paragraphs with the Carolingian Renaissance of 800 AD.[1]

Ramsey himself had a *comme ci comme ca* attitude about Macquarrie. While noting briefly in various books and addresses, that Macquarrie had produced the only "systematic theology", by an Anglican, and complimenting him on that, he would also say that none of it was in any way Anglican. As I argued above, the method of *Principles of Christian Theology,* was a hybrid of Heidegger's ontology and Bultmann's existentialist theology. Ramsey once praised Macquarrie's attempt at writing about the Trinity in his big book ,and then was studiously silent or yes, yes, yessed, as he would (his record twenty two) about the obvious lack of any kind of genuine Christology found in it. And for Anglicans, the Incarnation is central to our identity.

For all my time at Nashotah House, a traditional Episcopal seminary, from 1977 to 1980, I was under some fog as to what was being taught, specifically and especially about the center of the Christian faith: Jesus Christ. I didn't know why throughout my time nothing was said in Systematic Theology, and New Testament classes about the reality of this unique revelation of God in Jesus, and whether it was true. Throughout John Macquarrie's writing, and especially in his *Principles of Christian Theology*, he

---

1. Brown, *The Rise of Western Christendom*, 23, 62–3,

fudged nearly every doctrine with his code language taken from Heidegger and Bultmann. His view was that of Bishop John Robinson, that the language about Jesus in the New Testament is so suffused with myth that all these statements are taken from somewhere else in mythology or primitive religion and then projected onto Jesus. As I found this befuddling, I turned more and more to Archbishop Ramsey, who was at Nashotah all three years I was there, except for a time when I went St. James by the Sea, La Jolla California, for my participation in the "Teaching Parishes Program", that is, follow a priest around, take assignments, and do some ministry. Otherwise, I took long daily walks with this deeply faithful priest, and talked about much to do with the church and the God we serve. It was during my senior year, that he asked me what I thought about Stephen Sykes book, *The Integrity of Anglicanism*, (1978). Sykes wrote this as a *cris de coeur* asking where were the systematic theologians faithfully and coherently presenting the Christian faith? Why did we have none at present? Ramsey was at his most candid, he was in complete agreement, and without this, bishops and priests, and therefore the church at large would not have the confidence they needed to proclaim the Gospel to the Church, and beyond, to the world. When I said the obvious, well, there's John Macquarrie, to which Ramsey exclaimed, "he is so tied to Heidegger, and Heidegger is a Trojan horse. He was not a theist, and yet with that philosophy, Macquarrie believes he's saying something Christian. That is all *passe* anyway, who reads and even knows what on earth Heidegger means? Only a couple old cranks in Paris". I then said I liked John Austin Baker's *The Foolishness of God*, and how he portrays Jesus as Savior. Ramsey agreed and he knew and respected Baker, who later became Bishop of Salisbury. Ramsey said who else? I mentioned Bishop Michael Marshall, the sometime bishop of Woolwich, a charming and engaging preacher and teacher. Here Ramsey exploded in impatience, "Yes, yes, dear Michael. Everyone thinks he will save the Church! And he won't you know, because he can't. Only God can save the Church! He's not God no matter what some of his close friends think. He's not a systematic theologian. Try again!". And luckily I didn't mention Bishop Stephen Neill, with whom Ramsey had a trying relationship. Both had been considered for the Regius Chair of Divinity at Cambridge in 1950, which went to Ramsey. If he had lived, Ramsey would have loved N. T. Wright's assertion of history, and faith in the Holy Trinity in his work, especially the necessity of studying the historical Jesus, and his obliterating Bultmann's skepticism and entire project. Wright's greatest book, is I think, *The Resurrection of the Son of God*, a masterpiece. This is volume three in his *Christian Origins and the Question of God*, now nearing volume five. (Four is on Paul.) Ramsey would have loved the theological work of Archbishop Rowan Williams, his protégé. Williams has incorporated much from Eastern Orthodoxy into his thought, very much like Ramsey. And a third fine theologian is Fr. Anthony Thiselton, with his massive work on Hermenuetics, and showing his scholarship with the magisterial commentary, *The First Epistle to the Corinthians*. Compare this to Ruef's.

Archbishop Ramsey did give his thoughts about Macquarrie in his second series of Hale Lectures, *Jesus and the Living Past*, 1980. Commenting on the Catholic Modernist movement epitomized by Tyrell and Loisy, who attempted to ground their ritualistic Roman Catholic faith on ideas, on symbols, not Scripture, nor history, he wrote:

> Lately an extreme application of the Catholic Modernist method has appeared in attempts to combine Catholic piety and sacramental rite with scepticism concerning both the historical origin of Christianity and the pattern of Christian doctrine. While there have been some who can sustain this *tour de force*, the spiritual casualties amongst those who followed this method can be numerous. Worship and Spirituality may indeed tide over crises of faith, and the worship may express the quest for God while the mind wrestles with its doubts. But . . . the heart of Christian spirituality through the ages has been the response to the divine gift in Jesus. In Jesus the gift is given to us and in Jesus the response is made; and the Jesus is one who died and rose again.[2]

Yes, he said. This was what he thought of Macquarrie's theology. And others. Ramsey's devotion to our Lord is seen his *The Resurrection of Christ*, 1945, and especially in his wonderful *The Glory of God and the Transfiguration of Christ*, 1949.

2. Ramsey, *Jesus and the Living Past*, 56

XXIX

MY PARENTS WERE COMING to Dawn's house in Milton, Wisconsin, for Christmas, and bringing Robin and Bill. Bill had been honorably discharged by the Marines for hardship, as my Dad was now at the University of Kansas Medical Center, in Kansas City, and at 5'7", down from 175 pounds to 80 or so. Mother called on the way to prepare Dawn and me for Dad's condition. Bill and Robin experienced seeing Dad on a daily basis, and he was going in and out of consciousness. Robin had become Dad's primary caregiver, and was suffering for it. In December of 1977, she was 19. We stayed with Dawn and her husband Jim for a couple days, and went to see my wife's family. I thought at the time, this is not my dad. He had always been vibrant and at times weird around me, we never learned how to communicate, unless it was about baseball. At least we had that. He was completely clueless about my Christian faith. But I had not yet learned how to express my faith, especially when I would hear priests, including when they preached, say "Christians used to express themselves in the ways of supernatural language, but we "know" that it is best understood in our modern world as "poetry", which we say but don't believe literally". Bishop John Shelby Spong was now gaining a great deal of publicity for the way in which he expressed his unbelief about core doctrines of the Trinity and Jesus as the Son of God.

And his cleverness of expression swayed a number of us, in part because so much of the teaching and preaching we heard was boring. Spong was not boring. While at first I was attracted to his style, and I had thought like him when I was a teenager, but now I was older and I was putting away childish thoughts. To Archbishop Ramsey he was a charlatan. And he shared with Dean Ruef the belief that Spong was vulgar. Ha! If you have ever seen Anthony Hopkins on you tube as John Gielgud deliver this judgment about Laurence Olivier, you'll know how they said it. Well, Ruef was always doing Truman Capote. Spong had gone on to say that since we are expressing the inexpressible, we sing it!

At one point I went into see my dad in bed, to say good bye, and he asked me if I believed in the Resurrection. I responded in complete skepticism, and showed him what were all the differences in the four Gospels. (Leander Keck, a Methodist professor at Vanderbilt, and then Dean at Yale, noted that seminaries in the mainline churches, teach their students to field strip their weapons but not put them back together again.) I felt ashamed. I hid behind this kind of pseudo-intellectualism. I went into my head, which has always been my escape when facing something too painful for me. Thank God, I got to know Fr. Wayne Smith, Archbishop Michael Ramsey, Fr. Joe Hunt, Fr. Louis Weil, Fr. Robert Cooper, because they were all believing Christian priests, who would defend the Faith at the drop of a hat. And every single one of them preached the Gospel. I saw my dad one more time before he died in late January, 1978. This was at the Medical Center at Kansas City. I saw several of his doctors march in and coldly look him over, and one of them said, well we're trying to make him comfortable, and then all marched out. He died at age 46.

My dad's funeral was at the Royal Oak Corps (as the Salvation Army calls their church). I have kept the small sheet I got from my Uncle Bill who led the service. I gave the tribute from the family. I spoke about dad's athletic ability, and love of music, and a good father to us. I noted that his favorite Salvation Army song was sung, number 51 in the old *Salvation Army Songbook*.

> There is a name I love to hear, I love to sing its;
>
> It sounds like music in mine ear, the sweetest name on earth.
>
> O how I love the Saviour's name! The sweetest name on earth.
>
> It tells me of the Saviour's love Who gave his life for me,
>
> That I, and all who come to him, From sin may be set free.

I stayed stoic, and would not show emotion. I was in the Episcopal Church now. Stiff upper lip. There is an old silly joke about a man in church becoming fervent in his faith during the sermon. After yelling Amen! Hallelujah! Praise the Lord!-two quiet and dignified ushers walk up to him and ask him what's wrong. He says,"I've got religion!". They respond in unison: Sir this is the Episcopal Church and no place to get religion. I said it was silly. I have always felt embarrassed when I cry in church. One time when I was singing loudly, in choir, at St. Mary the Virgin Chapel, Dean Ruef looked over at me, and with hands signaled that I sing quieter. He then said out loud, "Well you can take the boy out of the Salvation Army, but you can't take the Salvation Army out of the boy".

My dad's old Coleman/Dunkle quartet members sang "This World is not my Home". A cousin sang with them. I was disappointed, because I had always had a hankering to sing with them. I remember the emotion all around me. I remember we drove to the Salvation Army part of the cemetery. There was far too much talking. I love the burial rite in the Book of Common Prayer. It speaks so eloquently and precisely what the Christian hope is for Resurrection and eternal life for those who love God, which we know to be true in our Savior.

> I am the resurrection and the life, saith the Lord;
>
> he that believeth in me, though he were dead, yet shall he live;
>
> and whosoever liveth and believeth in me shall never die.

I know that my Redeemer liveth,

And that he shall stand at the latter day upon the earth;

And though this body be destroyed, yet shall I see God;

Whom I shall see for myself and mine eyes shall behold,

And not as a stranger.

For none of us liveth to himself,

And no man dieth to himself.

For if we live, we live unto the Lord;

And if we die, we die unto the Lord.

So whether we live, or die, we are the Lord's.

Blessed are the dead who die in the Lord;

Even so saith the Spirit, for they rest from their labors.

O God, whose mercies cannot be numbered: Accept our

Prayers on behalf of thy servant Dale, and grant *him* an

Entrance into the land of light and joy, in the fellowship of

Thy saints; through Jesus Christ thy Son our Lord, who liveth

And reigneth with thee and the Holy Spirit, one God, now

And for ever. Amen.

I find the prayers and *Psalms*—42—"Like as the hart desireth the water-brooks,* so longeth my soul after thee, O God"; 46—"God is our hope and strength* a very present help in trouble . . . Be still then and know that I am God"; 90—" Lord, thou hast been our refuge,* from one generation to another . . . Thou hast set our misdeeds before thee,* and our secret sins in the light of thy countenance . . . The days of our age are threescore and ten; and though men be so strong that they come to fourscore years,* yet is their strength then but labor and sorrow, so soon it passeth it away, and we are gone . . . So teach us to number our days,* that we may apply our hearts to wisdom"; 130—"Out of the deep have I called unto thee, O Lord;* Lord, hear my voice . . . If thou, Lord, wilt be extreme to mark what is done amiss,* O Lord, who may abide it? . . . For there is mercy with thee,* therefore shalt thou be feared . . . I look for the Lord; my soul doth wait for him;* in his word is my trust"; I find these ancient prayers and Psalms so well stated with deep trust in God who is addressed knowing that he hears us and responds lovingly, very comforting and consoling. The *Gospel of St. John* 14:1–6 states this also. Jesus takes care of our anxiety in the face of death and nothingness, by assuring his apostles, and us, that he is preparing "way stations" for us. His invitation to those whom he called was, "Come and see". Throughout the Fourth Gospel are the promises of Jesus that he dwells, abides with us, and we with him. And this action is the gracious work of Jesus. He promises to take us with him throughout our lives, and we are with God the Father. His promise is not one of force or "imperialism". It is one of invitation into God's life through him, because he is offering companionship, relationship, love. This will be the work of the Holy Spirit, the Comforter. This is the way of truth and life. The way of Jesus is truth and life. We see the world and ourselves truly in Jesus, we see God truly in Jesus. Our lives come alive in Him, because his way is life, indeed the very life of God.

Jesus takes us deeply into the heart of God the Father in the Holy Spirit. Andrei Rublev's 15th century Icon shows the Holy Trinity together seated as the three angels visiting Abraham, from *Genesis* 18:8. There is a place open, which is to be filled by anyone who accepts the invitation. The Icon is the beauty of Russian Orthodoxy's great tradition of loving the Holy Trinity, and showing the mystery of the life of the Trinity's life by the way each of the persons is depicted: The Son in the center blessing the chalice to give his blood; he looks and gestures to the Father on his right; who breathes the life of the Spirit on his right. The circular lines and the eyes and hands (always laden with symbolism in iconography) show us the mystery of the Trinity's love for one another, "infinitely co-dependent", in the words of Lutheran theologian Robert Jenson.[1] We are all invited into this life through the Son. We all have a place at the table. Christians are therefore part of a Communion by virtue of Baptism.

I cannot remember Rublev's great Icon without also having it in mind Rachmaninoff's choral masterpiece "The All Night Vespers", especially his "Now Lettest Thou Thy Servant Depart in Peace", which the composer asked to have sung at his funeral, at the Russian Orthodox Church in upstate New York. They take me into prayer, and the veil between this world and Paradise is lifted, just as in the Eucharist.

The French Jewish writer, philosopher and mystic Simone Weil wrote to a friend about the poem "Love III" by Anglican George Herbert, "I enclose the English poem, Love, which I recited to you. It has played a big role in my life, because I was repeating it to myself at the moment when Christ came to take possession of me for the first time. I thought I was only reciting a beautiful poem but, unknown to me it was a prayer"[2]:

> Love bade me welcome: yet my soul drew back,
>
> Guiltie of dust and sinne.
>
> But quick-ey'd Love, observing me grow slack
>
> From my first entrance in,
>
> Drew nearer to me, sweetly questioning,

---

1. Jenson, "The Trinity and Church Structure", 19
2. Sykes, *Unashamed Anglicanism*, 50–51

244

If I lack'd any thing.

A guest, I answer'd , worthy to be here:

Love said, You shall be he.

I the unkinde, ungratefull? Ah my deare,

I cannot look on thee.

Love took my hand, and smiling did reply,

Who made the eyes but I?

Truth Lord, but I have marr'd them: let me shame

Go where it doth deserve.

And know you not, says Love, who bore the blame?

My deare, then I will serve.

You must sit down, says Love, and taste my meat:

So I did sit and eat.[3]

3. Herbert, " Love" , 262

XXX

I RETURNED TO NASHOTAH with my dad's death affecting me. What did I believe? Fr. Wayne Smith was very supportive, and I was grateful for his asking me about dad. It never occurred to me that he was only a few years younger. My classes became much more interesting to me with learning the basics of Greek and Hebrew, taught by Fr. Hunt, at least enough to enable us to read the letters, and possibly more. I took an advanced class with Jim Dunkly in Greek, and I aced both. I learned how to read Greek, and memorize most important New Testament terms. This has remained for me a real help in reading the New Testament, use Lexicons, and check out what is being said in the *Koine* usage, as I prepare adult classes and sermons.

Second, I entered class for the first time with Fr. Robert Marsh Cooper, a dazzling character, originally from North Carolina, same age as Fr Wayne, 43 in 1978. I stopped by his office, which had this taped to his door, "*Homo sum, humani nihil a me alienum puto*" Terence. (Meaning: I am a man. Nothing human alienates me.) My first question was to request entrance, to which he responded did I understand about autoeroticism? Cooper, pronounced more like kupper, was ready to needle any one in my class, to find out who was squeamish about anything scatological, and uptight, priggish, prissy, goody goody, and sanctimonious. He was irritated that some of my fundamentalist classmates had continually provoked Fr. Hunt, and he was loaded for bear. His language was both elegant and coarse. He was one of the most articulate people I have known, very much like Stan Henning, or Fr. Smith. He had a ready smile, especially in the midst of a heated argument, mostly because he had well-honed debating skills, with quick as a flash rapier wit. As with the teachers I found myself liking, he would not back down. He had a physical and mental toughness, which he showed any time he was challenged. Which was often. He liked goading evangelicals and fundies and dumb jocks and swishy, brain dead Anglo-Catholics. (He hated Yankees, particularly if they were deceived by his Southern drawl or anyone's accent from the South, of which there were an amazing plethora of zoological beastie speech patterns and sounds, Texas itself with four thousand or more goofy dialects, sometimes within one inbred family, sometimes variations within one Hee Haw Junior Samples type—I hate Minnie Pearl. He imagined Yankees thought Southerners had fun on Friday nights by joining a crammed roomful of maniacal crackers, knuckle draggers to a man, all schizzo, tatted and drunk , all deranged and yee hawing over Bocephus singing "Family Tradition", proudly stupid, screaming out high decibel inane responses naming their favorite poisons of choice. Cooper thought that was how "Yankee boys" saw the South. Which was pretty close to the truth.) To North Carolina born and raised Bob Cooper, Yankees had no idea how clever and skilled Southerners could be when they wanted to hide that or anything behind their various drawls. I met this tall (6'3") lanky Southern gentleman, who could be courteous, chivalrous, kind. He wore a brown and white striped dress shirt with a red tie, and light brown corduroy jacket with blue jeans and cowboy boots. He waved me in. I noted on his end table a volume of Karl Barth's *Church Dogmatics*, and Stanley Jaki's *The Road of Science and the Ways to God*, an advance copy of the latter because he had been asked to review it. I had heard of Barth, everyone had heard of Barth, and I recognized Jaki's name, a scientist and Christian. Cooper informed me this Roman Catholic from Hungary, held both theological and science doctorates. He was a Benedictine priest and physicist, with strong views about modern science, which only could come from a Christian metaphysics and epistemology. Jaki's view was stated in this book from his 1974 and 1975 Gifford Lectures:

> Science found its only viable birth within a cultural matrix permeated by a firm conviction about the mind's ability to find in the realm of things and persons a pointer to their Creator. All great creative advances of science have been made in terms of an epistemology germane to that conviction, and whenever that epistemology was resisted with vigorous consistency, the pursuit of science invariably appears to have been deprived of its solid foundation. [1]

This is the theme of this thoughtful and capable physicist and priest. He says this even more clearly in this excellent book:

> Metaphysics is founded in the doctrine of creation-It was this belief, as cultivated especially with a Christian matrix, which supported the view for which the world was an objective and orderly entity investigable by the mind because the mind too was an orderly and objective product of the same rational, that is, perfectly consistent Creator. [2]

Finally, Jaki notes this about Isaac Newton:

> He [Newton] insisted on the need of a nonmechanical ultimate cause of mechanical patterns.[3]

1. Jaki, *The Road of Science and the Ways to God*, vii
2. Jaki, *The Road of Science*, 242
3. Jaki, *The Road of Science*, 83

Cooper loved this kind of thinking about science within the confines of metaphysics alone. The scientific method is designed to establish facts about the physical world. It is not a metaphysic. Materialism as David Bentley Hart comments, is a deeply confused metaphysic. Turning a method for reaching knowledge about the physical world, into a metaphysic, such as materialism or nihilism, is just plain stupid. It is in philosophy (because that is the area in which this must be discussed) incoherent, a category error, a howler. And Hart adds, the scientific method does not entail materialism.[4]

What about Barth? Cooper said he was the most brilliant theologian of the twentieth century. Why don't Americans read him? Because they're not educated enough and patient enough to work through Barth step by step. Stupid people have difficulty with someone who thinks the way this genius does. Barth's theological writing moves in a constant spiraling way, like Paul in *Romans*. And Barth had an advantage many Episcopal priests don't have. "Which is?", I asked. "He knows that his Redeemer lives". There it was from this teacher. He loved language and had published poetry. When I saw the film "August: Osage County", with Sam Shepard playing a poet, and pulling down T. S. Eliot poems for the young Cheyenne woman, his way of moving and talking reminded me immediately of Fr. Cooper. Cooper published poetry throughout his life, and was an editor for a poetry journal. His field at Nashotah was Professor of Morals and Ethics. His first assignment for our class was the George Steiner book I had admired, *Nostalgia for the Absolute*. (See above.)

On the first day of class, everyone was keyed up to hear the infamous Fr. Cooper. He came in light brown jacket and tie, looked around all of us, and paused for about ten seconds. The he said in a quiet, questioning voice, "What d'y'all think about free fuckin'?" Not a soul moved. I began laughing, and Al Kimel and Pat Ward joined in. The fundies were sputtering and shocked, shocked, Rick. One of the swishers fell off his chair. Pat Ward asked, "What do you think Fr. Cooper? You get paid to tell us what's moral". I loved this! Cooper launched into a poem by a Roman writer, about a married woman having an affair. "Is she justified?" he asked. Many of us began to talk as though Joseph Fletcher's situational ethics was a legitimate choice for any Christian. Others took a legalistic approach. Cooper said we are looking at a pagan; one who has not the Holy Spirit of Jesus himself. "How can Fletcher say *love*, without explaining much about the repentance all must go through because of the Sin! In our lives! Don't any of you know about sin? St. Paul warns us about not trusting our own feelings. Fletcher writes about choice in love, without anything about sin. *First Corinthians* 13 means nothing without the context of Jesus dying on a cross. What's wrong with you dumb asses? Without a strategy, love is little more than fleeting feelings." (This was one of Cooper's favorite lines.) "Jesus was tortured for hours by the best torturers in the world. They were expert. They flayed his entire back with whips. Then he died horribly on a cross, and suffocated to death when his lungs gave out and filled with fluid.

---

4. Hart, *The Experience of God*, 296

That is what Jesus did to beat sin. And you will either say some legalism or anything is fine if you feel good about it is your norm for decision making?".

Well, that was day one.

One day Cooper told us about what happened when a young twenty three year old Russian poet was arrested by the Leningrad KGB in 1964, a quiet dignified young man (my age at the time I heard this). He was charged with "malicious parasitism", with not doing necessary work, and writing doggerel. Josef Brodsky was brought before the Soviet court, and was noted to have written pornography, anti–Soviet poetry, and he wore "velvet pants". A journalist, Frida Vigdorova, 39, took notes at the trial and wrote the trial record, which became, in David Remnick's later article in the *New Yorker*, "the most famous legal exchange in Russia since Stalin's show trials . . ." Vigdorova got this hand written "samizdat"—smuggled to the West. She wrote:

> Judge: And what is your profession?
> Brodsky: Poet. Poet and translator.
> Judge: And who told you that you were a poet? Who assigned you that rank?
> Brodsky: No one. (*Non-confrontationally.*) Who assigned me to the human race?
> Judge: And did you study for this?
> Brodsky: For what?
> Judge: To become a poet? Did you try to attend school where they train [poets] . . . where they teach . . .
> Brodsky: I don't think it comes from education.
> Judge: From what then?
> Brodsky: I think it's . . . (*at a loss*) . . . from God.[5]

I remember suddenly being hit by the thought that that was how I knew I would be a priest. This is deeply mysterious to me, except that I have never desired doing, or, better, *being* anything else. Cooper was amazing at bringing just the right quotations or poems, or Scriptural passages to class. He taught me the most from my professors at Nashotah what it might mean to have a Christian vocation and mindset as we were formed to be priests. I also recall how much this quotation from Brodsky stayed with me about who a priest is and what he or she "is". If one does not have this vocation, one has no idea about this calling. And in all my years as a priest, various parishioners have almost the same ignorance about this as the Soviets. They want to know about a priest's "job description" as though this is functional and positivist. The questions and discussions I have been involved with, lead me to think a great many of the laity-perhaps lacking much faith and understanding of God, as we know Him in Jesus—are functionally atheists, like the dominant culture around us. William Butler Yeats hints at this mystery in his poem about being a poet, or even a beautiful woman, entitled *Adam's Curse*:

5. Remnick, "Gulag Lite", 39

We sat together at one summer's end,

That beautiful mild woman, your close friend,

And you and I, and talked of poetry.

I said, "A line will take us hours maybe;

Yet if it does not seem a moment's thought,

Our stitching and unstitching has been naught.

Better go down upon your marrow-bones

And scrub a kitchen pavement, or break stones

Like an old pauper, in all kinds of weather;

For to articulate sweet sounds together

Is to work harder than all these, and yet

Be thought an idler by the noisy set

Of bankers, schoolmasters, and clergymen

The martyrs call the world.

And thereupon

That beautiful mild woman for whose sake

There's many a one shall find all heartache

On finding that her voice is sweet and low

Replied, "To be born woman is to know-

Although they do not talk of it at school-

That we must labour to be beautiful."

I said, "It's certain there is no fine thing

Since Adam's fall but needs much laboring.

There have been lovers who thought love should be

So much compounded of high courtesy

That they would sigh and quote with learned looks

Precedents out of beautiful old books;

Yet now it seems an idle trade enough."

We sat grown quiet at the name of love;

We saw the last embers of the daylight die,

And in the trembling blue-green of the sky

A moon, worn as if it had been a shell

Washed by time's waters as they rose and fell

About the stars and broke in days and years.

I had a thought for no one's but your ears:

That you were beautiful, and that I strove

To love you in the old high way of love;

That it had all seemed happy, and yet we'd grown

As weary-hearted as that hollow moon.[6]

Cooper told us about a recent book written by a Southerner about racism as it exists in the South. The author was Will Campbell, a Southern Baptist preacher, who in 1977 published this memoir entitled *Brother to a Dragonfly*. If *To Kill a Mockingbird* was my favorite fictional account depicting Blacks and Whites in the South, and the entire United States, this book has by far been the most important to me for understanding racism, sin, bearing witness to Christ, how people live in terrible conditions with some integrity, how Christian folk can be some of the worst sorts of blood thirsty low down mean hypocrites and bigots, how everybody is caught in some sort of sinful web they help spin, and avoid looking at themselves, while they sanctimoniously run down anyone else. Preacher Will's book is by far one of the wisest human stories I've ever read. It's about growing up, learning about one's family, one's kin, loving deeply one's people, even the most fiercely dumb ones, and allowing them to love you back. And unlike Samuel Beckett's narrator in *Malone Dies*, who says, "Let me say before I go any further, I forgive nobody. I wish them all an atrocious life and the fires and ice of hell . . ."; Campbell learns to forgive everyone. Even Thomas Coleman, who blasted and killed 26 year old Episcopal Seminarian Jonathan Daniels in the grocery store in Haynesville, Alabama, 1965, while Daniels was attempting to shield Ruby Sales, age 17.

Campbell was born in 1924 to a dirt poor Baptist farm family in Amite County, Mississippi. His story is being part of a family with a history, and becoming close to his brother, Joe. They experience so much including love, violence, murder, deception, and betrayal, and getting saved by Jesus, and taking their first steps to understanding and experiencing the mystery of sex. They hear about a hanging, and then witness the death of a young handsome Black man, one of his daddy's field hands, killed in front of a strangely very popular two room house owned by two unmarried sisters, shot clean through the heart by an older Black man, whose story of self-defense is immediately believed by the white sheriff, because black on black violence is lower than white on white, or even worse black on white.

Campbell was ordained a Southern Baptist minister at 17, went to Louisiana College in Pineville, Louisiana, served as a medic in World War Two, and then got himself really educated at Wake Forest, Tulane, and Yale. He describes all this with constant wry observations, along with his coming back to the South, due to his dislike

6. Yeats, "Adam's Curse", 78—9

of Yankees. And their chickenshit ways-his word. Especially the upper elitist liberals. From early on, he knew to follow Jesus was to lead him to fight everything racist, and become a civil rights activist. So he did. He was called to pastor a small Baptist church in Taylor, Louisiana, from 1952–4, just down the road from where I would serve at St. Matthias', Shreveport in the 90's. Before long he was leading the Civil Rights work of the National Conference of Churches, involved with the Black High School students integrating the Little Rock public schools in 1957, the only White assisting Dr. Martin Luther King in the founding of the Southern Christian Leadership Conference, engaging in the Freedom Rides (to integrate the interstate bus system), and receiving death threats everywhere he went. He was his own man, and hated any political organizations which might affect his independence and ability to respond to human beings rather than with political labels or strait jackets; e.g., his insistence that Jesus loves bigots, James Earl Ray, and the Klan. He became the inspiration for Doug Marlette's *Kudzu* cartoon's Preacher Will.

Brother to a Dragonfly is one of the most stirring stories I've ever read, especially as a memoir of what a central actor in the struggle for racial equality went through to help bring the beginnings of civil and political rights to America's Blacks. He became involved totally in this Christian work in the aftermath of the Supreme Court's *Brown vs. Board of Education*, a 5–4 decision in 1954. An enormous backlash occurred all over the South, with Campbell noting this was led by the White Citizen's Councils of Mississippi and the South. These White racists, energized by a well-spoken, educated lawyer and circuit judge, Thomas P. Brady, who gave an incendiary speech to the Sons of the American Revolution in Greenwood, which was later published in book form, the title referring to the day *Brown vs Board* was announced, *Black Monday*, included quotations such as these two:

> You can dress a chimpanzee, house break him, and teach him to use a knife and a fork, but it will take countless generations of evolutionary development, if ever, before you can convince him that a caterpillar or a cockroach is not a delicacy.[7]

Or this showing he was a learned vicious racist:

> The decision, which you handed down on, Black Monday has arrested and retarded the economic and political, and yes, the social status of the negro in the South for at least one hundred years . . . .One rudimentary truth, which is apparently unknown and unappreciated by the high priests [i.e. in this case the majority of Supreme Court justices] is simply this: A law is never paramount to mores. Habits and customs produce folkways which in turn evolve in mores. Laws limp behind and reflect as a mirror the essence of mores . . . .Sacred mores are invulnerable to the dagger of Brutus. When a law transgresses the

---

7. Campbell, *Brother to a Dragonfly*, 110

moral and ethical sanctions and standards of the mores, invariably strife, bloodshed and revolution follow in the wake of its attempted enforcement. [8]

There are numerous times when Campbell is at pains to educate Northerners about their naiveté concerning who were key players among these racist organizations, an ignorance which stretched as far as the Attorney General's office, Robert Kennedy, and the Department of Justice. Repeatedly Campbell urged the FBI and others from Washington not to share information on what the agents and others were planning with local law officials in the South, because of the police and sheriff's departments and States' Attorneys very much active and leading some of the more horrific forms of harassment, intimidation, maiming and murder of Blacks in the South. All forms of State and local governmental power were implicated in the resistance to civil rights and political equality in the South. One of several places where Campbell makes this observation:

> With [Brady's] prose as a backdrop, a small group of Delta aristocrats met in Indianola that summer to discuss the possibility of an organization such as the judge had suggested. A Harvard-educated attorney, a prominent banker, and the manager of the well-known Indianola Cotton Compress were among those present. Later the group was expanded to include fourteen of the most substantial civic and business leaders in the area, none of whom could be called ignorant rednecks or any of the other names which have so often been used to identify southern racists. They were not only leaders in business and commerce, they were leaders in culture and learning. Intelligentsia. Not just in Indianola, Mississippi. Intelligentsia in any circles. And their circle encompassed the world, no part of which would have considered them uncouth.[9]

Will Campbell has the finest story I have come across about why anyone would become a minister. It is told in his simple homespun way, and deeply ironic, while conveying great insight into the meaning of responding to God for his church. He sets this up by relating a few stories about the most significant Baptist preacher in his life, called Thad Garner, from Granny White, Louisiana. The man is so memorable, so well-drawn, that I asked Will in 1993 at a conference at Kanuga, an Episcopal Camp in Western North Carolina, who Thad was. The town was Jonesville, which in the 1950's was then thriving with a textile mill, now closed. I have now forgotten the name of the preacher. I spent four nights with Campbell, as he allowed me to talk with him as long as I brought a quart of Jack Daniels. I pointed to the huge bottle of Evan Williams next to him, and asked if that wasn't his favorite. No, he replied. That bottle was now five years old. He had kept it full with Jack, a subterfuge, because his "little lady" Brenda, "mightily disapproved of Mr. Daniels". So I did as asked. We spoke about his mentor, and he read this all over again from the book I brought to have autographed:

8. Campbell, *Brother to a Dragonfly*, 110
9. Campbell, *Brother to a Dragonfly*, 111

Thad Garner was, I suppose, the most profane man I have ever met. And, I suppose, in a way he was also the most profound. Whatever he was, he made a deep impression on me at the time.[10]

Campbell notes all the successes Garner achieved and how bright his light shone as one of the most popular and sought after preachers he was, looking and sounding as pure as driven snow. Then he comes to know reality about his hero:

Then I discovered that Thad had once worn white bucks and a tweed cap, still smoked a pipe, conducted revival meetings for money, had gone to the Holy Land because his congregation had lifted a surprise love offering for that purpose, and had bought the set of color slides he showed to youth groups in the Tel Aviv Airport, even really disliked teenagers, drank a lot of wine-though he had but one kidney and couldn't handle it very well—and cussed a lot.[11]

At this, Campbell adds somewhat sanctimoniously (remembering his younger self), even judgmentally:

Learning those things made it easy for me to think of myself as a Southern Baptist preacher and increasingly difficult to think of Thad as one. I believed somewhat definite things about the Faith while Thad would not admit to believing anything. Yet somehow you did not get the feeling that you were in the presence of a fraudulent or deceitful person. You didn't think of Elmer Gantry . . . There was just a fascination that you had not met anyone quite like this before.[12]

Finally, he tells what for him was the key story of what occurred between them that is masterful to me about the personal meaning of responding in faith to our Lord's call to the ordained ministry while hunting. After a time of great frustration, and finding no quail flushed, the hounds finally, suddenly, pointed:

This time Thad got off three quick shots, each BOOM! blending with and echoing the last. As his last shot was dying away I jerked the trigger and waited for the jolt against my shoulder and the ringing in my ears. But nothing happened. The thing was not even loaded. Despite the three volleys in such rapid succession nothing lay dead for the dogs to retrieve. Thad had missed as surely as I had with an empty gun (or piece, as he liked to call any weapon). Though I had not led what one would call a sheltered existence during my life, and my own language did not always measure up to garden party standards, I was not familiar with some of Thad's words. For a full sixty seconds the big Louisiana field was filled with his expletives. At the dogs, at the birds, at me, at the gun, at the manufacturer of the shells, at the Almighty—all were profaned and reviled

10. Campbell, *Brother to a Dragonfly*, 172
11. Campbell, *Brother to a Dragonfly*, 172
12. Campbell, *Brother to a Dragonfly*,172

because of this misfortune. When he had quieted down he sank backward onto an eroded levee. I sat on the ground not far away. It was an occasion for a question I had wanted to ask him for some time.

"Thad, why did you ever decide to be a Baptist preacher?" He looked puzzled and not a little hurt. He pondered my question for a long time, sighting and squinting down the barrel of his shotgun. Finally he looked me straight in the eye and answered my question: "Cause I was *called*, you goddam fool!"

I have met a lot of preachers since then. But none of them could preach with such assuring certainty, claimed to believe so little, or was as convinced that he was *called* to do exactly what Thad was doing.[13] (Italics in the original.)

Will Campbell's entire book is marvelous to ponder (using his word). He tells later about Thad's mental breakdown, something which all too often happens with clergy doing too much as though everything on earth and in God's church depends only on them, this called pelagianism, everywhere alive in American churches. Everything is up to us, including saving ourselves. Of course breakdowns can also occur because we are used up as clergy, and forget prayer, and even taking care of ourselves. We become too important in our own eyes, or in the eyes of others, or both. It is the sin of pride, which is allowed to run rampant in America, coinciding with the business model of success by what we do, rather than who we are.

Will also charts in his book the slow illness of his pharmacist brother who uses drugs to take care of his emotional support. Nothing in Campbell's life and training as a pastor, nor his experience of working with people, can halt his brother's slide into severe illness, loss of jobs, two marriages, his children's love, his sense of purpose and dignity, and finally his life. This is hinted at with the quotation from Gerard Manley Hopkins used as the book's epigraph: "As kingfishers catch fire, dragonflies draw flame . . ." Almost all clergy I have known as gifted devoted caring leaders, have drawn fire. And their suffering becomes unbearable for those who have not allowed themselves to be revealed to God, or to intimacy in their lives. Clergy hide in plain view.

I am never far from Will Campbell's book since reading it first forty years ago. His summary of the Gospel was simple: We're all bastards, but God loves us anyway.

There are two other quotations which I believe are insightful in discerning whether one has a call to the priesthood or pastorate. The late Michael Novak, a former Roman Catholic priest before he was laicized, quoted the fastidious grammarian Logan Pearsall Smith's brief description: "The test of a vocation is the love of drudgery it involves." Novak then added his own belief: "Long hours, frustrations, small steps forward, struggles: unless these too are welcomed with a center joy, the claim to being called has a hollow ring to it."

13. Campbell, *Brother to a Dragonfly*, 172–3

XXXI

NEAR THE END OF our spring semester, Fr. Kephart finally let me preach. The Sunday he chose for me to preach was Trinity Sunday. He warned me what a Nashotah professor had said to him twenty years or more before: If you preach beyond three minutes you are in heresy. I preached that Sunday at both eight and ten o'clock Eucharists, about our knowing the names of the Holy Trinity by revelation from the Son. Jesus declares God's name as Father. He calls us into relationship with God the Father through himself, whom he reveals as Son. This is accomplished through the Holy Spirit, all the names of the persons of the Trinity. Therefore we do not believe that God's "job descriptions" of Creator, Redeemer, Sustainer, name God. As I am named Dale at baptism, and known by that name to God, so I come to know God as Father, Son, and Holy Spirit. This was right at the time in which various theologians and liturgists and those susceptible to current political ideas currently in vogue, were suggesting changing God's name to something other than what we have received by "Revelation" by the Son, something less "sexist". My argument always is that of the faithful Catholic and Apostolic Church—we have not been given God's permission to re-name God, after the revelation of and by the Son. If we do so, we are making ourselves equal to our Lord himself, who taught us when we pray to say, "Our Father . . ." St. Paul talks about this matter of factly in his great chapter of *Romans* 8. This chapter lays out who we are as adopted children of God, who have come to know the Father of Jesus as "Abba, Father!", as Paul reminds us when we pray, and he continues, "it is that very Spirit of God bearing witness with our spirit that we are children of God, and if children, then heirs, heirs of God and joint heirs with Christ-if, in fact, we suffer with him so that we may be glorified with him." (*Romans* 8:15b-17.) It is through relationship with the Son, that we know and pray to the Lord and Father of our Lord Jesus Christ, in the Spirit. This to me is an amazing gift God the Holy Trinity bestows upon us. Bishop N. T. Wright brilliantly "unpacks" this chapter in *Romans* to show that Paul's analogy is of the Children of Israel being led out of slavery in Egypt, to come into the Promised Land. Now Jesus leads us out of the slavery of the "flesh", with no hope of knowing our identities as children of God, nor any hope of any meaning in life, to coming to know God as our Father, through our "Brother" Jesus, through the Spirit, to the Kingdom of God. (See for example N. T. Wright's brief two volume commentary, *Paul for Everyone*, *Romans*, especially chapter 8 . Wright is known as "Tom" Wright in this series of books. Also in his marvelous commentary on *Romans* in the *New Interpreter's Bible*, again chapter 8. Wright has commented that readers of these books will say how much they like "Tom Wright", but "N. T. Wright" puts them off. This is a metaphysical problem.) I once responded to the silliness of a major Mainline Church in the US, requesting the help of anyone to assist these folks "rename" God for non-sexist reasons. I sent in the following suggestions, "Moe, Larry, Curley", and "Rock, Scissors, Paper". I never heard back.

Near the end of the semester, my classmates and I were introduced to various clergy who were also therapists on the staffs of several hospitals in the Waukesha and Milwaukee areas, for our seven week Clinical Pastoral Education to take place in the summer. This was established as a check on any of us, who were unaware of our own "agendas" for desiring ordination, and being unleashed on unsuspecting congregations, for our nasty little power plays. Or worse.[1] My friend Al Kimel and I were both chosen to spend our summer vacation doing CPE at St. Joseph's Hospital in Milwaukee, where we would be under the supervision of Fr. Arnaldo Pangrazzi, one of the liveliest minds I have known.

The entire build up for Clinical Pastoral Education caused a number of my classmates to become "skeered", as Fr. Cooper said in his hillbilly imitation, which gave him great pleasure. He incorporated skeery comments in his presentations, along with anecdotes of what kinds of knowledge these therapists will gleam just from how we dress, or eat, or treat one another especially the "wimmen foke" in group therapy. What a hoot! "They'll discover so fast you are a strange easily intimidated fuss budget, and then talk about your sexual proclivities as occupying a niche clear off the grid! Whooee! You cain't hide nuffin." The fundies were peeing their pants at this. By the time-a Saturday—when we met with the various psychologists and therapists, all ordained, the anxiety levels of these folks had passed into the stratosphere. I distinctly remember Thad and Hal looking like they had seen ghosts, when they caught up with me and Al to tell us the horrors of what they witnessed and heard. *"He took notes!"* "This shrink asked about my fidgeting! Was I always anxious?" And a favorite: "Did you hear what was the very first question to Hope? She was asked if she masturbated!!!" And a lot more along these lines. All this got back to Cooper, which was his plan for "funnin'" with us all along. He began quoting from the film "High Anxiety", especially from Nurse Diesel (played by Cloris Leachman and directed by Mel Brooks.) "If you're tardy, you'll get no fruitcup". Cooper warned everyone not to say that they were into bondage and discipline. Why? Asked Jerry Anderson. Not the brightest star in the belt of Orion. (cf. *Job* 38:31.) Cooper continued quoting. "Nurse Diesel: Oh, get off it. I know you better than you know yourself. Bondage and discipline. Dr. Montague: Too much bondage. Too much bondage and not enough discipline." Fr. Cooper shared with us that whatever happened, blame your mother. Duh. He was jocular about a recent book on homosexuality by the guy who had filmed many of Kinsey's sexual

---

1. See above, 6

couplings and other configurations, named Clarence A. Tripp, entitled *The Homo-sexual Matrix*, which Latin word derived from *mater*, the womb of the mother.

So over the summer, Al Kimel (feigning illness most days, which Archbishop Ramsey had already diagnosed as "obsessing on extreme Barthianism"), Rob Lord—a very soft spoken fundie, and I, drove to St. Joseph's Hospital. There we met up with another twelve or thirteen folks, a couple United Methodists, and a number of Catholics, meaning women religious, and sordid others. The United Church of Christ guy and Methodists worked at appearing the nicest and most caring. Monday through Friday we met in group in the morning, and then we were assigned floors to meet with patients, and once a week we would take one conversation with one patient, and write up the dialogue we remembered having with them. This would produce a "verbatim". In addition, we were each take turns, once every fortnight to remain at the hospital as chaplain overnight, to be available for any emergency. And after that assignment, we would be responsible for a report, again for the group. From the start, the three sixty-ish aged nuns began crying in group session if they were up for their verbatims. (We also had a couple Roman Catholic seminarians, who hadn't had enough experience to have their break downs.) I was bewildered. I had not lived long enough to have my regrets. Fr. Arnaldo was outstanding at offering pastoral support, while encouraging the sisters to talk about what they were experiencing. He could be piercingly intense.

And then he facilitated our group discussions as we began responding to one another's verbatims. It amazed me how we could each be revealed to have certain agendas about ourselves and our fantasies about our own understandings of ministry, by our choosing a particular person to write about, and how we wrote it. Within a couple weeks we were all overly confident in our diagnoses of one another, naming sexual identity problems, asexual nun, vaguely interested in zebras, alcoholic, narcissism (every one of us), homophobia, hemophobia (these had to be distinguished carefully), off the charts weirdo, flashers, fixated on girl scout cookies, chocoholics, oral compulsives, and anal retentives, (this last also known as phlegmatism—or just about every Junior or Senior Warden we knew. Add Treasurers to that. And the severe maladjustment type known as Canon lawyers. Bishops. I need to stop now.) I had developed a diagnosis for both my friends from Nashotah, viz. Developmentally Arrested Infantile Dysfunctional Narcissists. I felt healthier because I was mostly a functional one. One of our number admitted excessive fear of flying. I noted that I hated Erica Jong. I think her name was Marie, a United Methodist seminarian. She was happy all the time. Except when talking about her phobia. She said that there were three reasons: 1) The wings might fall off; 2) There might be a sudden loss of oxygen; 3) And then there's the (I thought she said) "flatulence", which I immediately supported. Airplanes easily become filled with gaseous smells, and have nowhere to go. It then came over me that one of the older women religious was looking much less doleful then she had in a while, and that there was a distinct "wind" smell in the room. Marie said no, she had said "turbulence". Two or three of my "friends" derided me for thinking otherwise. And then the smell overcame us, a distinct smell of rotten eggs, and I said someone has a "rumbly in the tumbly". Fr. Arnaldo suggested we push on. He said that. I shuddered. I have only smelled that much sulfur at the waste treatment plant down Portage road at Sault Ste. Marie, Michigan, or at Yellowstone. Come to think of it, or at Cursillo which I attended in Beloit, located next to a paper plant. The name Beloit comes from dropping a half dollar in a toilet.

The work we all did together, and I learned to gain empathy for my group, as diverse as we were. Except for the religious, we wore collars with a black "skunk stripe" on them to indicate we were seminarians. This never made sense to me, because skunks are black with white stripes. It was often when at this Roman Catholic hospital that one of us would be treated very hatefully by a patient, and this and other ways of interacting with patients gave us the opportunities to work this through with one another and Fr. Arnaldo's skilled ways of leading the group. Near the end of our weeks, each of us met individually with this priest to look over what each of us made of the program, and what growth we found ourselves experiencing. It had been seven months since my dad had died, and in some immature stupidity, I had prided myself on not crying.

I had been feeling something, because a week or so before the end Easter term, an oncologist on Nashotah's Board of Trustees had addressed the student body about what to expect from medical doctors. Dr. Conlon had coldly and severely asserted that the desire for doctors to have a warm bedside manner was old fashioned. "A patient is a patient, not your best buddy. That's why you have friends and family." I lost my temper and angrily countered Conlon by stating what had occurred the last time I was with my dad shortly before he died, and how unfeelingly the doctors were in announcing his impending death. I had no understanding of emotional states of the bereaved for months after the death of someone like a parent. None of the faculty, from what I could tell, at seminary, had much pastoral sense. In fact, a couple classmates and two of the priests, came up to me and criticized my behavior. I remember blushing, and feeling intense shame. I hurriedly left the gathering. I wrote Doctor Conlon and apologized. His note in response was a gruff "no need to apologize".

Here I will add that our pastoral care Professor was Fr. Richard Greatwood, also my faculty advisor, who was immersed in the silly fad of "feelings" psychology of "Transactional Analysis". Developed by Eric Berne, the bestseller, *I'm OK, You're OK*, by Thomas Harris, resonated with the late sixties and seventies "feelings and warm fuzzies" people. It was one more self-help, human potential movement. Berne postulated that Freud's id, ego, superego, could easily be changed to "child, adult, parent". Our troubles with interactive communication came about because we communicate out of different roles than the other. We "play games" and don't learn how to "stroke" and compliment each other in communication. We need to learn how to "stroke" each other, and play out of our child, or adult, depending on circumstances. Parent was a no no. We need to remember we're "all OK!". Greatwood was from Florida, a trained lawyer, who had been ordained a priest for a few years. His teaching of this shit, and his manner, "Hey! How are you? That's OK! Where's the pool?", created in members of my class the need for primal screaming. During finals week every year the seminarians enjoyed a spring banquet, and had the opportunity to parody faculty. I got about six to take part in an "OK Chorale" mass. "God is OK in the highest", the "we're not OK" general confession, with the absolution said in the very exaggerated "fer sure" way of Greatwood, "Stop that! You're all OK!!!! Yes you are!". Then we would pass the peace called "stroke one another". I once drew on a blackboard, a large picture of Jesus on the cross. Inside a balloon linked to his mouth I wrote, "If I'm OK, and you're OK, what the hell am I doing on this cross?" Greatwood came into the classroom, looked and said, "That OK!".

In my session with Fr. Arnaldo, he asked me about dad. I began crying, which continued for a few moments. I came to realize how self-deluded I could be about my own emotional state. I miss my dad. He has been dead for over forty years now.

> He found his father alone in the well-ordered orchard
>
> Digging round a plant: he was wearing a dirty tunic,
>
> Patched and unseemly, and round his shins he had bound
>
> Sewn leather leg-guards keeping off scratches,
>
> And he had gloves on his hands because of the thorns.
>
> On his head he wore a goatskin cap, increasing his air of sorrow,
>
> When noble enduring Odysseus saw him
>
> Worn by old age with great sorrow in his heart,
>
> He stood beneath a pear-tree and shed tears.[2]

---

2. Homer, *Odyssey*, 24:226–334

XXXII

I STARTED THE "MICHAELMAS Term" that fall as a middler student. The new Junior Class was about the complete opposite from mine. They were moderate quiet scholars, and possibly only two Fundamentalists. These last two came out of Cursillo. On the day before classes would start, while playing mixed-up doubles, having just come through "shrinkage" with group therapy, I twisted my ankle something awful, and watched my foot fill with blood. While writhing, thrashing, contorting on the ground near the court, and pulling grass out in intense pain, my companions assumed I was pantomiming, because my side had just lost the point, and laughed and applauded. Back in Watertown, my doctor put a cast on, and gave me crutches. In a day or two, Fr. Wayne Smith at Trinity, Janesville, informed me I would be preaching my first Sunday back to Seminary, since I was now serving my home church as Seminarian. Over the phone in the Book store, I said I must decline due to my injury. Everyone in the store then heard this man of God yell at me, hollering, "Would St. Paul have neglected ever to preach the Gospel to the stupid-ass sodomites or hermaphrodites or stalactites or shittites, because he had an owie?" This at about ear rupturing three hundred thousand decibels, or some thousand times your garbage disposal grind. "And which of those tites do you think corresponds with your congregation?", I inquired innocently. "Hematites", he snapped back. "They're dumb as rocks." So, I did as St. Paul would do to the hermaphrodites. I preached at Trinity at both the 8:00 and 10:00 am Sunday Eucharists. During announcements at the later service, Fr. Smith said to the congregation of 175 or so, "Today was a big day in the life of this Junior Birdman from the Salvation Army. He preached without a drum. But with a crutch. And on a scale from one to ten, that sermon was at least a one". Tepid, obligatory applause. I lie. Great applause and laughter by these horrid people of Janesville. I thought of the line of a similar congregation in Handel's Messiah: "All they that see him; laugh him to scorn. They shoot out their lips, and shake their heads saying . . ." Try saying something while laughing, shaking your head and shooting out your lips. It would be a happy Mussolini.

It was an hour and a half drive southwest from Watertown to get to Trinity Episcopal Church in Janesville. I had coffee but tried to follow the Anglo-Catholic custom of putting no food in my stomach until I had received Holy Communion. On that first Sunday, I had eaten nothing, except perhaps a sweet roll during the Adult Forum at 9:15, between the Eucharists. I was beginning to feel queasy. With a painful headache coming on. While tasting vomit in my mouth during the later Eucharist, I was determined to get through. However while starting to leave the coffee hour to get some crackers and ginger ale for the drive back, I was caught by the Thills (I was on crutches) to inform me they had signed up for this first Sunday's "Take a Seminarian Out to Lunch", a sign-up sheet I knew nothing about. They showed me the horrid sheet, and it dawned on me I would be stuck with these lip shooters for the next two school years. So, I followed them to their bungalow. They had other guests there to meet me. Great.

I was plied with gin and tonics, and proceeded to wait another hour, until 1:20 pm. Then "brunch" was announced. Mrs. Thill took me to view "brunch" while still in a large cast iron Dutch oven. I hobbled over. She opened the lid, and what I saw was the most terrifying sight of bubbly greasy eggy pork product offal chum! I had that gag pressure building fast and yelled "Excuuuuuuuuuse meeeeeee!!", and I somehow got on crutches raced for the nearest toilet, while soliciting God for help. God answered this prayer, and I let loose of everything possible right down to the green colored stuff. I gave a courtesy flush, and wiped up what hadn't landed in the toilet. Then I wiped most of what had gotten on my shirt and tie. After a final face and mouth rinsing I went back for the "brunch". The Thills were most solicitous, and hoped I hadn't drunk too much gin. "Oh, no. I'm just fine." I lied. I was ushered to my place, with the children and a couple adults trying to suppress laughter. The bubbly greasy offal was then plopped onto our plates, and I was requested to return thanks. At that moment all I could think of was, "Mother Mary full of grace; watch us while we stuff our face". That was part of my anti-Catholic phase, now past. But there it was. I came up with, "Bless, O Lord, this house; those who live here and those fortunate to be their guests. And, bless this food to our use and us to thy service. Through Jesus Christ. Amen". I no sooner croaked that out then the gagging hit me once again, and I yelled, "Excuuuuuuuuuse meeeeeee!", and made a mad crutch assisted dash to the toilet. *Ohhh Noooo!* Someone was in there! And making noises! Jesus told me to stuff the cloth napkin in my mouth, and I lurched past the dinner table and poor people shoveling down their "brunch"—which didn't help—and found the small lavatory near the living room. I obeyed. This time, my heaves were louder and dryer. This summed up my first pastoral involvement at my home parish.

XXXIII

SEVERAL CLASSES IN THE fall of 1978 were dull. Awful. Mediocre. Fr. Greatwood led a class on important church meetings, how to plan, work with lay leaders, put forward an agenda, stick to it, contact key leaders ahead of time, and basically run the business of the church as a business. In no way was this administrative necessity integrated or even have any organic connection with what the seminarians were being formed to be and do as priests in the Church of God. The teaching was shallow, wasteful, entirely secular. Nothing was taught with regard to "building up the Church" as St. Paul addresses in his *First Epistle to the Corinthians* 3:9, and chapters 12–14; *Colossians* 1; *Ephesians* 5. And still more fundamental to *ecclesiology*, which has been the hallmark of the Anglican heritage through the years, our Lord's own presence and teaching with the Apostles, carefully forming them to be His own people as in *St Mark* 3:13–19. I remember throughout the late seventies and eighties, attending Diocesan and National Church gatherings, with no prayer at all invoking God's grace and guidance for what we believed we needed to do as God's people. Fr. Arlin Rothauge had become the new member ministry guru after publishing *Sizing Up the Congregation For New Member Ministry*, in 1983. At a Province V seminar, incorporating the mid-western dioceses, Rothauge led, with mostly clergy present, this sociological approach, taught without a single corporate prayer over a two and a half day period. There was no Biblical or theological foundation provided whatsoever, so it could have been a gathering of the Oddfellows, or the Flat Earth Society, or the Swedenborgians, or even a new kind of Lions' Club led by some chromosomally aberrant, freakish tail twister. It was all completely secularized sociological theory. It was not (as Episcopalians began claiming) "Evangelism". Rothauge taught that in the Episcopal Church (later Mainline Protestant Churches) everything depended on size. This from a man who was a dwarf. If that didn't "float your boat", the rumored title he originally wanted, you could go to an Episcopal brand Meyers/Briggs testing, again without prayer (and why would you?) to find your personality type as the indicator for everything. "Personality testing" begun by Katherine Briggs in 1917 to show her daughter Isabel that her future son-in-law Clarence Meyers was "weird", and totally unlike the Briggs' master race, and without any psychological training whatsoever, only some agricultural classes, she began to develop her personality type indicator. This didn't stop Isabel from screaming and yelling, and marrying Clarence. Then after Isabel's college schooling, again not in psychology, mother and daughter read Carl Jung in 1923 and his experiments with personality types (some, as Jung said, based on anecdote), and developed the mother's theories further. They did this after dumbing down Jung. They changed Jung from five factors to four, and came up with their all-inclusive sixteen personality types. This is their Grand United Theory. MBTI was brought to the attention of the OSS war bureaucrats during WWII, scrambling to deal with a great need for spies with the right personalities, by determining for which jobs each tested applicant was suitable. For a psychologically based testing, there was nothing at all about a clinical psychologist or medical doctor screening those individuals for personality disorders, neuroses, or psychoses. In fact everything one identifies about himself or herself is entirely one's own judgment. I did in the late 1970s, and I still do now, consider this the Episcopal Church's version of astrology. This has today become the main cult for corporate America. In an article Lillian Cunningham, has written, "Does it Pay to know Your Type", *Washington Post*, December 14, 2012, she points out that no psychologist has ever published test results or any kind of academic or professional paper about MBTI.[1] This includes three eminent psychologists on MBTI's Board. We are back to the cults of unreason.[2] It is now a growing popular fad to note that all ESTJ 's are Republicans, and all INFP's are Democrats. And recently in a review in the *New York Review of Books* of a book by Merve Emre, entitled *The Personality Brokers: The Strange History of Myers-Briggs and the Birth of Personality Testing*, Anne Diebel notes, "The MBTI is wildly unempirical, but the need it answers is not fundamentally about knowledge. Like astrology (which is newly trendy and lacks the MBTI's Boomer corporatism), or even the Hogwarts houses . . . typology need not be believed to be found useful or diverting. Diebel also offers this observation on MBTI and other comparable personality tests, "[they] depend on self-reporting, so their accuracy may be undermined by subjects' self-deception, lack of self-awareness, or varying abilities to comprehend the questions themselves and the possible intent behind them-a Keynesian beauty contest of gaming out the psychological significance of selecting one answer over another."[3] Diebel explains this, for those such as myself who didn't know this, "Keynes described a theoretical contest in which the participants base their choices not on their true preferences but on what they perceive to be the underlying consensus about the best selections." [4]

I simply didn't get all these fads being promoted in the Episcopal Church. Why do this when there were the spiritual resources of the Book of Common Prayer, the Bible, and the outstanding Hymnal? The Hymnal (the 1940 one that I first used, then the 1982) is filled with corporate and devotional prayer treasures. For my own taste, theological and literary, as well as musical, several stand out. "St. Patrick's Breastplate", or "St. Patrick's Lorica" refers to the protective Prayer of the Saint in pagan Ireland, in the early fifth century. This exorcism (verse 6 of Episcopal Hymn 370) translated by the Victorian Church of Ireland poet Cecil Frances Alexander, wife of the Bishop

---

1. Cunningham, "Does it Pay to Know Your Type?",
2. See above, 104-5
3. Diebel, "Simple Answers", 59
4. Diebel, Simple Answers, 59

of Derry, and a prolific hymn writer, was deployed by none other than Bishop James Pike, who got frightened several times in and out of churches from early on in his priestly vocation, and believed something demonic was always right around the corner plaguing him. In the big historic Christ Church in Poughkeepsie, New York, he became convinced that the ghost of his Low Church predecessor, Dr. Cummins, was hounding him. He heard Cummins daily upstairs in the rectory shuffling, and shifting boxes of his books around. And once when he went to the Church to fetch the Reserved Sacrament to take to a dying man, he was sure Cummins was blowing out the candles on the altar, and sending a strong cold wind to intimidate Pike and keep him from practicing his moderate high Church rituals. Then, as he later told and re-told, a famous supernatural incident, after removing the Sacrament from the Tabernacle, and getting his stole from the Sacristy, he stepped into a narrow hall and out from nowhere a giant bat came at him, swooping all around the poor priest with Low Church viciousness. Pike said he decided to go low, and the bat did also! He whipped around and got back to the sacristy just in time, to save his life! He went for a brass alms basin to protect himself, and then thought to call his assistant Dick Corney to rush to the church with a tennis racket! But the phone line suddenly went dead! He then remembered by God's help (not the Holy Spirit-Pike would read the Trinity out of his Christian faith), the "charm" or *Lorica*, or Breastplate of St. Patrick! It is very probably St. Patrick's own prayer.

> Christ be with me, Christ within me, Christ behind me,
>
> Christ before me, Christ beside me, Christ to win me,
>
> Christ to comfort and restore me.
>
> Christ beneath me, Christ above me, Christ in quiet,
>
> Christ in danger, Christ in hearts of all that love me,
>
> Christ in mouth of friend, and stranger. (Hymn 370.)

And the giant bat vanished! I found this story, charmingly written in *The Death and Life of Bishop Pike* by William Stringfellow and Anthony Towne.[5] Stringfellow was an eloquent speaker and writer, a lawyer-particularly for the indigent and very poor of Harlem, a lay theologian who influenced Rowan Williams, and Stanley Hauerwas, as well as Will Campbell. Stringfellow and Towne became fast friends of Pike's, through the few years while Pike's star rose very high, before the spectacular flame out in 1966, and death in the wilderness of Israel in 1969. As Dean of St. John's Cathedral in New York City from 1952–1958, Pike bluntly challenged and derided many of the Church's central doctrines. He found a large audience at the cathedral, and then expanded his influence on television. He was the equal of Bishop Fulton Sheen, Norman Vincent Peale, and Billy Graham as a media celebrity. Incidentally, after pursuing assiduously

---

5. Stringfellow, *The Death and Life of Bishop Pike*, 122–3

his celebrity status, first at St. John the Divine-with his own television program, and then from 1958 as Bishop Co-adjutor, and Bishop of California in San Francisco, fueled by alcohol, cigarettes, and hallucinogenic drugs, destroying his mental, physical, and spiritual health, witnessing his son's suicide, the breakdown of his second marriage, the attempted suicide of his daughter, he was censured by his fellow bishops in 1966. Then his mistress, whose apartment was paid through the bishop's discretionary fund, committed suicide. He thereupon resigned his orders, sought out mediums or "spiritualists "or necromancers, communicated with his son and Paul Tillich (died 1965), married for a third time, to Diane Kennedy, and went to the Israeli wilderness in 1969, near Qumran, as noted above, without water or food, taking two cokes for his young wife and himself. There he died the gruesome death his wife described in *Search: The Personal Story of a Wilderness Journey*, and retold in the Stringfellow and Towne biography.[6] He was the first bishop in the Episcopal Church to have three wives at his funeral. (I am pleased to note that both books, as well as the last book Pike wrote, *The Other Side: An Account of My Experiences with Psychic Phenomena*, are all available at Wipf and Stock. I get no cut for this information.)

I know a great deal about Pike's time as Bishop in California, from several bishops I talked with at length: a nutty water witcher who dug up the grounds of Nashotah House when I was there, Chandler Sterling, bishop of Montana, 1957–68; a former vaudeville actor, Richard Watson, bishop of Utah, 1951–71; and Reginald Heber Gooden, a loveable character, son of a bishop, born in 1910, Dean of the Episcopal Church's Cathedral in Havana, Cuba, 1939–45, Bishop of much Central America from 1945–72. All three said to me Pike went to the desert to die.

6. Stringfellow, *The Death and Life*, 3–29

XXXIV

BUT I WAS TALKING about hymns. There are lovely Celtic hymns: "Be Thou My Vision O Lord of My Heart", "Lord of all Hopefulness, Lord of all Joy". There are some outstanding Easter hymns: "The Strife is o'er, the Battle Done", "Hail Thee Festival Day", "Welcome Happy Morning"—the first from the 17th century, with music by Palestrina; the latter two late 6th century hymns, and the music of Ralph Vaughn Williams, and Arthur Sullivan. (OK, I know, I like it.) "Morning Has Broken", is a 1931 hymn by a fascinating children's poetry writer set to a Scottish tune. "Christ Whose Glory Fills the Skies", and the many by Charles Wesley, including a smattering of hymns for Christmas, Easter, and the Eucharist are present. There are borrowings from liturgies of many centuries, and music by Mozart, Bach, Beethoven, African-American spirituals, even one from Ghana. Hymn 10 is by John Keble, "New every Morning is the love, our Wakening and Uprising prove, through sleep and Darkness safely brought, restored to life, and power and thought", which continues about how God gives us grace to be loving witnesses of Christ in our domestic day to day lives, and throughout our lives. The Eucharistic Hymns are my favorites, "And Now O Father Mindful of the Love", with Tractarian William Bright clear about the Atonement: "Look Father, look on his anointed face, and only look at us as found in him; look not on our misusings of thy grace, our prayer so languid, and our faith so dim: for lo! Between our sins and their reward, we set the passion of thy Son our Lord". St. Thomas Aquinas' hymn "Humbly I adore thee" with its marvelous statement of Real Presence in the Eucharist is number 314:

Humbly I adore thee, Verity unseen,

Who thy glory hidest 'neath these shadows mean;

Lo, to thee surrendered, my whole heart is bowed,

Tranced as it beholds thee, shrined within the cloud.

Taste and touch and vision to discern thee fail;

Faith, that comes by hearing, pierces through the veil.

I believe whate'er the Son of God hath told;

What the Truth hath spoken, that for truth I hold.

O memorial wondrous of the Lord's own death;

Living Bread that givest all thy creatures breath,

Grant my spirit ever by thy life may live,

To my taste thy sweetness never failing give.

Jesus, whom now hidden, I by faith behold,

What my soul doth long for, that thy word foretold;

Face to face thy splendor, I at last shall see,

In the glorious vision, blessed Lord, of thee.

This is to me one of the finest expressions of Sacramental truth, I know of. It is the highest theological statement, combined with strong but chaste devotion, in poetic form. This is one of many reasons I am so grateful to the Episcopal Church, embedded in Anglican Tradition, putting forward such a wide array of fine poetry, set at times to glorious music. The same is true of *Schmueche Dich*, "Deck thyself my soul with gladness", a Eucharistic hymn of Johann Franck's set to Johann Cruger's music. The Choral Prelude of the Cantata by Bach, especially played by Ton Koopman, a Dutch organist and Professor at the Royal Conservatory at the Hague, is one of the marvels of Baroque Sacred Music. (I also like Koopman's refusal to play or record music after Mozart, except Poulenc of the early to mid—twentieth century.) Koopman 's recording is sublime, and sweet. I listen to this several times a week as it always brings my soul to contemplation and prayer. The Hymn is in the Episcopal Church's 1982 Hymnal. It is brilliant and glorious, truly "orthodox" which means proper worship of Almighty God. Right doctrine assists the meaning, but this is an example of the Early Church's understanding of one's attendance at the Holy Eucharist, something so lost in today's secular culture, with the worst kind of philistinism found in the vast wastelands of Fundamentalist, Left Behind, Prosperity Gospel, happy clappers. One may turn on television's zoo channels like TBN and find this brand of hucksterism, 24/7. Take Jimmy Swaggert. Please.

A thought I have had for a long time is that one does not go to church to be entertained. One attends and takes part in Christian community shown fully in the celebration of the Holy Eucharist, in the presence of the Holy Trinity. One then is tutored over time to become what one is: a full participant in the Body of Christ, according to St. Paul and quoted in the traditional rite of the consecratory prayer, "And here we offer and present unto thee, O Lord, ourselves, our souls and bodies, to be a *reasonable, holy, and living sacrifice unto thee*; humbly beseeching thee that we, and all others who shall be partakers of this Holy Communion, may worthily receive the most precious Body and Blood of thy Son Jesus Christ, be filled with thy grace and heavenly benediction, and made one body with him, that he may dwell with us, and we in him."[1] (italics added.) This is found in St. Paul's counsel to his readers of *Romans*, 12:1–2. N. T. Wright notes that these two verses are some of St. Paul's most

1. BCP, 336

densely packed with meaning about what life we are offering to God, which gives God "pleasure".[2] Paul writes: Therefore, that is based on all that has gone before, laying out who we now are as a new creation, and fulfilling the living, reasonable, entire selves-nothing held back—that God demands through this sacrifice. We offer to God our "reasonable" selves, *ten logiken* , not *ton pneumatikon*. This entire giving of bodies and minds means we give all of ourselves, allowed by God's mercy, and we worship, *latreia*. To reduce this to our emotions, with tacky manipulative music and blather, even with a "holy tone", is so far apart from St. Paul's meaning as to be risible, preposterous. St. Augustine says somewhere that the first few times he went to Christian worship, he was struck by the moans and groans of the worshipers. He loved hearing the chants and hymns.[3] I have come across Christians who think as the Manichees St. Augustine writes about those who thought what God wanted was their "spirit", or their "minds" (as in Christian Science), which is Gnosticism. They therefore despise "fleshly" things especially the Dominically commanded Baptism and Holy Communion. St. Augustine states that these errant folks were so obviously ill, but would refuse God's "remedies", of the Sacraments. These Sacraments alone would make them well.[4] We use our bodies in worship. The physical is the medium of the spiritual.

There are poems and hymns about the Presence of Christ in the Eucharist, which I have found a great joy to me devotionally. Episcopalians and Anglicans sometimes state their great but restrained fervor in our love in God through his life giving Son through Holy Communion. The gargantuan controversy before and during and after the 16th century over the scope of Papal authority, apart from Scripture or Conciliar affirmation, particularly the Papal formulation of the definition of Christ's Presence in the Eucharist called "Transubstantiation", and declared as *De Fide*, brought the gravest controversy centered on the Eucharist itself. Queen Elisabeth I used a very quiet way declaring her faith in the Real Presence, and in her trust in Jesus' own words of promise:

> Christ was the Word who spake it,
>
> Christ took the bread and brake it,
>
> And what his word doth make it,
>
> That I believe and take it.
>
> (*Attributed to Elizabeth I.*)

I loved hearing this. Or Archbishop Ramsey's quoting the marvelous words of the great theologian of 16th century Anglicans, from Richard Hooker on the assurance we may have in Christ's living Sacrament of His Body and Blood:

2. Wright, *Romans*, 703

3. St. Augustine, *Confessions*, IX.vi.14

4. St. Augustine, *Confessions*, IX. iv. 8

Let it therefore be sufficient for me presenting myself at the Lord's table to know what there I receive from him, without searching or inquiring of the manner of how Christ performeth His promise . . . Let curious and sharp-witted men beat their heads about what questions themselves will, the very letter of the word of Christ giveth plain security that these mysteries do as nails fasten us to his very cross, that by them we draw out, as touching efficacy, force, and virtue, even the blood of his pierced side, in the wounds of our Redeemer we there dip our tongues, we are dyed red both within and without, our hunger is satisfied, and our thirst forever quenched; they are things wonderful which he feeleth, great which he seeth, and unheard of which he uttereth, whose soul is possessed of this paschal lamb, and made joyful in the strength of this new wine . . . What these elements are in themselves it skilleth not, it is enough that to me which take them they are the body and blood of Christ, his promise in witness sufficeth, his word he knoweth which way to accomplish; why should any cogitation possess the mind of a faithful communicant but this, *O my God thou art true, O my soul thou art happy?* [5]

John Betjeman, Poet Laureate of Britain, whose recent biographer is the writer A. N. Wilson, much praised repeatedly throughout this memoir, used the expression about someone he imagined might be gay: "I say, he looks rather unmarried, wouldn't you say?" This lively poet, a tad indelicate, but devoted High Church Anglican, has several poems about his Christian faith, and particularly the Real Presence of Christ in the Sacrament, as e.g. in his poem, *Christmas*:

> And is it true? And is it true,
>
> This most tremendous tale of all,
>
> Seen in a stained-glass window's hue,
>
> A Baby in an ox's stall?
>
> The Maker of the stars and sea
>
> Become a Child on earth for me?
>
> No love that in a family dwells,
>
> No caroling in frosty air,
>
> Nor all the steeple-shaking bells
>
> Can with this single Truth compare
>
> That God was man in Palestine
>
> And lives today in Bread and Wine. [6]

---

5. Hooker, *Of the Laws of Ecclesiastical Polity*, V.67.12

6. Betjeman, "Christmas", 189, 190

His poem, *House of Rest*, imagines an elderly widow of an Anglican vicar, alone, "Now all the world she knew is dead/ In this small room she lives her days", with dead sons, and "daughters far away", in reverie about all their lives many years before, especially remembering the delight of them waiting to eat porridge together while her husband says Grace. Then she hears the Sunday Church bells:

Now when the bells for Eucharist

Sound in the Market Square,

With sunshine struggling through the mist

And Sunday in the air,

The veil between her and her dead

Dissolves and shows them clear,

The Consecration Prayer is said

And all of them are near.[7]

This is true Catholic teaching, and why a great many Christians attend the Eucharist, and pray for those close and loved family members, friends, clergy, who have died, during Prayers of the People or at the Offertory, name them, and know that the faithful departed are joining in the Eucharist, alive in God.

The words that I found particularly memorable and touching, were those of Dom Gregory Dix, which I first heard in a Liturgy class from Fr. Louis Weil forty years ago, about the command of our Lord to "Do this in Remembrance of me", and He will show Himself present, the meaning of *anamnesis*:

Was there ever another command so obeyed? For century after century, spreading slowly to every continent and country and among every race on earth, this action has been done, in every conceivable human circumstance, for every conceivable human need from infancy and before it to extreme old age and after it, from the pinnacles of earthly greatness to the refuge of fugitives in the caves and dens of the earth. Men have found no better thing than to do this for kings at their crowning and for criminals going to the scaffold; for armies in triumph or for a bride and bridegroom in a little country church; for the proclamation of a dogma or for a good crop of wheat; for the wisdom of the Parliament of a mighty nation or for a sick old woman afraid to die. For a schoolboy sitting an examination or for Columbus setting out to discover America; for the famine of whole provinces or for the soul of a dead lover; in thankfulness because my father did not die of pneumonia; for a village headman much tempted to return to fetich because the yams had failed; because the Turk was at the gates of Vienna; for the repentance of Margaret; for the settlement of a strike; for a son for a barren woman; for Captain so-and-so,

7. Betjeman," House of Rest", 202–3

wounded and prisoner of war; while the lions roared in the nearby amphitheater; on the beach at Dunkirk; while the hiss of scythes in the thick June grass came faintly through the windows of the church; tremulously, by an old monk on the fiftieth anniversary of his vows; furtively, by an exiled bishop who had hewn timber in a prison camp near Murmansk; gorgeously, for the canonization of S. Joan of Arc—one could fill many pages for the reasons why men have done this, and not tell a hundredth part of them. And best of all, week by week, month by month, on a hundred thousand successive Sundays, faithfully, unfailingly, across all the parishes of christendom, the pastors have done this to make the *plebs sancta Dei*—the holy common people of God.[8]

8. Dix, *The Shape of the Liturgy*, 744

XXXV

WITH THE 1978 CLASS, so different from mine, we became friends with the (get this) Wayne Smiths, Wayne and Debi, from Northwest Texas. In fact, he had been ordained a Baptist minister, before converting to the Episcopal Church, and confirmed by Bishop Willis Henton, called "Bugs", because of his uncanny resemblance to the cartoon character. Bishop Henton's wife, Martha, ran their show, and on visitations to churches in Northwest Texas, and later in Western Louisiana, she would wear purple or magenta, fuchsia, incarnadine, purplish-crimson, to show she ran the show, not Bugs. And why not? Her maiden name was "Bishop". She was Martha Bishop Henton. He was Bugs. Bugs B. Henton. (I got this from a weisenheimer priest and theologian, Fr. Ralph McMichael, Jr, who was also in Wayne Smith's class.) Since there already was a Fr. Wayne Smith, Wayne Smith began using his first name, George. We became good friends, whom I saw more often than Al Kimel, who was always in Barthian blues, obsessing on his guilt, speaking through clenched teeth. For the longest time this Baptist was a theological liberal, which I understood, because of suffering from fundamentalist PTSD. I was interested in Tillich, he was interested in heresy. Same difference. (Who doesn't like oxymorons?) Except I came out of it, and he reveled in it. Just like Spong-which also sounds like a *sanctus* gong, only for Spong it would be because nothing happens. Reminds me of the country song, "When the phone doesn't ring, I'll know it's you". George Wayne introduced me to Willie Nelson's "Red Headed Stranger". I introduced George Wayne to Monty Python's "Life of Brian", during the showing of which, at a movie theater in Oconomowoc, he huffed and puffed and walked out! This today I find very ironic, because he has announced his retirement from the episcopate as Bishop of Missouri, and has not ever been called a conservative by anyone. We remain friends. And now he can laugh. David Hayden said once you let go of your morals, everything becomes funny. But enough about him.

Two incidents occurred that winter. Both involved my "ministry" of watching over 30 or so junior high kids. Fr. Smith and the Vestry had moved Church School from Sundays to Wednesday afternoons, which ran from 5:00pm to 7:15 pm. Everyone gathered and we all ate together. At 6:00 everyone moved to their classrooms. Between 75 and 125 would be on hand every Wednesday. Finally at 7 we would close with prayers. I would meet with 25-30 of the youngsters, who were very active and high spirited, in a room designed for about 14 with two long tables down the center. Everyone packed in, with four or five boys hiding under the tables and making loud raspberry noises, or anything that they thought was funny. Imitating farm animals while I said prayers for them was especially effective to disrupt the seminarian. It took me about eight weeks to learn how to take control, beginning with learning their names, to get past simply babysitting. I am in awe of Junior High teachers. This age would have kept Hitler edgy, and add to his stress. Then Father Smith came to my class (he taught 5th and 6th graders—about twenty five or so) and informed me in front of the young people that he had great news. I was to oversee the Christmas pageant and include the little devils as part of my "team". First, I had no idea what a Christmas Pageant was, except the one in Charlie Brown. Second, how was I to find a script and get a pageant organized? Smith ordered me to "just do it", a little like Lucy. The weeks rolled by with my anxieties having anxieties. What was I going to do? And when? I had not the slightest clue about this. The parishioners treated me as though I was a knowledgeable young priest, or curate. I hadn't even learned how to tie a cincture around my alb when I wore that with an amice during the Holy Eucharist. (At Nashotah we always wore a cassock and surplice , both for the Daily Offices, and for the Holy Eucharist. The alb, amice, and cincture were worn over a cassock, for those assisting in the big smells and bells Solemn High Eucharist at Nashotah on Thursdays, along with a "sub-deacon's" tunicle, a long outer "tunic" style vestment with one horizontal orphrey, or stripe. A deacon wore a deacon's stole over the left shoulder along with a dalmatic, a similar garment with two orphreys. The celebrant wore a priest's stole, around his neck, signifying as stoles do, the office of the holder; then a cope for the liturgy of the Word, before changing into a chasuble at the offertory for the celebration of the Eucharist. Some "precious" Anglo-Catholics (mostly men-like people) went spikey high with lots of goofy *frou—frou*, specifically *zucchettos* (skull cap), *birettas* (with their three peaks, or better "horns", and a bouncy little pom pom or poofy thing or tuft), lace, even white gloves and various colored little prancy slippers, all part of their costumes.(There is a photo of mean as hell Cardinal Burke dressed to the you know what, with this kind of lacy loopy get up, resembling an old deranged dowager. He would holler about *girls and women* destroying the Church!)You got to see even more little rituals of lifting the biretta several times during the Mass and changing costumes, to show off their bright pink leather shoes (Obviously a Rose Sunday.) The once, twice, three times of the celebrant in cope censing the altar, including deacon and sub-deacon sort of mincing while holding the edges of the vestment was simply divine! Then the organ music would sound, the hits of Judy Garland or Bette Midler. There is the well-known story of Tallulah Bankhead, who loved high camp Episcopal liturgy, attending Mass at St. Mary the Virgin Church near Times Square. As the thurifer passed by her, she was quoted as saying, "Dahling I love your dress, but your purse is on fire". She was referring to all the incense, so constitutive of the Eucharist worship there that the Church is called Smoky Mary's. These priests and bishops were called BDACS by most of us. This meant brain damaged Anglo-Catholics. But I digress. Someone is reported to have seen an elderly Cardinal Newman walking down the Street close to his oratory in Birmingham, England. The story goes the observer thought he was seeing a little old lady. ,[1]

Newman was buried in the same grave as his longtime friend, Fr. Ambrose St. John in Rednal, at the country house of the Birmingham Oratory. When the grave was exhumed in 2008 for bones and relics and what not, and to be moved to the Birmingham Oratory for extravagant piety, with green Italian marble, it was discovered the corpses had completely disintegrated due to Newman's insistence that a soft mulch be placed in the coffin.[2] That Newman ever had saintly reluctance, Owen Chadwick says, is mawkish pish posh. This is a nice upper crust Brit way of saying Bullshit. He believes Newman had been engaged in a total power trip, first as an Anglican, and then as a Roman Catholic.(Chadwick's article about *The Oxford Movement, 1833–1845*, Dean Church's classic 1892 history of Newman and his followers, in "The Oxford Movement and its Historian", [3]). I take delight in noting Chadwick's article in support of what Archbishop Michael Ramsey said about Newman, that he never had an Anglican vocation. He had Peter envy. I am paraphrasing.[4] The late John Woolverton haughtily said about Ramsey's opinion, pish posh. Oh, really, John? This eminent Church Historian, a low-churchman, hear screams from "Psycho", and author of a book I like very much, *Colonial Anglicanism in North America,* was reported to have made that remark, and now is finding out about the company he must keep in Purgatory, while listening to Billy Graham harangue the faithless. Before "Bev" starts singing.

But I digress. My first incident involved what must I do to organize a "team" of junior high demons, and then put on a Christmas Pageant? I prayed to our Lord, who threw his blessed hands up in the air. No one helped. A week before the Pageant was scheduled, I managed to inform Fr. Smith of this calamity. He blew up at my misfortune, this was just before prayers on a Wednesday night, and asked an elementary school principal and Deacon, George McKilligan, to throw one together. Fr. Smith then told me he had a special role for me in the play. So the following Wednesday the special costumes I had not known existed were all sized and tried on by the children, and everyone was happy that finally someone had taken charge. Fr. Smith then announced that the new seminarian would also have a starring role, which caused deep concern showing on children and adult faces. I wondered what the hell? On Sunday, the Fourth Sunday of Advent, I found out. Fr. Smith introduced the director and actors. Then he asked me to meet him behind the altar. He told me to crouch down and stay there while preparing for my scene. He then gave me a long pole with fishing line, and a large garish golden star on the end of it. "Put that up when the star is mentioned, and this will be your starring role. You think you can do that?" When at the end of the

---

1. Wilson, *Eminent Victorians*, 158,177

2. Duffy, "A Hero of the Church", 62

3. Chadwick, "The Oxford Movement"83–106

4. Ramsey, *The Anglican Spirit*, 60

show, he thanked everyone, and last mentioned my name after all the kids, I was the star. This became a tradition at Trinity Church, Janesville.

The second incident which startled me was my naïve assumption that Junior High students would change their behaviors and everything would be happy and peaceful in my working with them if we had a lockdown. They were all invited to our apartment in Watertown for a Friday night all-nighter. They needed to bring their Bibles, not just any Bibles, but preferably the *Revised Standard Version*, with Apocrypha. We would feed them with pizza and soda, they would all behave, and the girls would sleep with sleeping bags in the living room, and the boys in the spare bedroom. What could go wrong? We prayed together, I spoke about being Christian in a growing secular world, and how we were all called to be grateful witnesses using Jesus' Parable of the Prodigal Son, and what Conversion to Jesus meant for those already in Him as baptized Christians. St. Augustine said God has some, which the Church has not; and the Church has some, which God has not. For those in Junior High, it is obviously the latter of these groups. So, about 16 kids were part of this experiment. Everything was hopping and noisy, and we separated the sheep from the goats. The next morning their parents showed up, and praised our courage. See? It could be done to have those hellions get saved overnight. Praise Jesus! Parishioners who had been standoffish now signed up in droves for taking the Seminarian out for brunch. Great.

About three weeks later we got our AT&T bill. It was for approximately $450. We didn't have that kind of money. There were phone calls to China, Japan, Britain. A couple numbers were in Mexico. And then New York City, Chicago, Omaha. I put everything aside and called Ma Bell. I explained I was a seminarian, my wife worked, we barely got through financially month by month. The woman who took my call apologized and said she would check this out with her boss. Five minutes later, her boss called to say they had made a terrible mistake, and we had monthly bills of $30 to $40, nothing like this. He apologized and said our bill would be zero for the month. I told my wife. Something nagged at me, and a few hours later I checked the dates for the calls. They had all been made during the evening and early hours of the morning of the night Jesus had saved the kids. Martin Luther said we were *simul justus et peccator*, at the same time justified in our faith and yet we go on sinning. Tell me about it.

In November, my classmates and I began finding out about needing to get assigned to a rector, to follow him around for weeks and see what he did. Then our eyes would be opened and we would grasp reality! The priest overseeing this was a strange little man with continual facial tics from both sides of his visage. He was a former Roman Catholic, who had seen the light and moved into the Episcopal Church. His name was Fr. Barton DeMerchant, a Michigander, and he was clever and of good humor, a wag in fact. He had coined the phrase that "an Episcopalian was Calvinist in theology, Pelagian in *modus operandi*, and Catholic in haberdashery".

I liked him, and found him an enjoyable conversationalist and preacher. He was very well educated in theology, having degrees from Notre Dame, and advanced degrees from Marquette University. He was 43 or so when we became friends with a Pete Rose style haircut. His wife, Joan, was taller, more angular, severe, who looked like an English Setter on her good days, and a Doberman otherwise. Bart was into Bichons. Awww. He was in charge of Nashotah House's "Teaching Parishes Program", for the Winter term each year involving Middlers. We all made appointments to see him, with most seminarians going to churches around the area. He told me he had arranged for me to go to St. James By-the-Sea, La Jolla. He added that the rector, Benjamin Verdier Lavey, a Michigander, but now an Anglophile, was eccentric, and addressed one in the third person. "Would father care for some more port?" That sounded promising, and fun. In what turned out to be a very cold winter, in January, 1979, I found myself on my way to San Diego International Airport, and the experience of witnessing conspicuous consumption on a grand scale. Once or twice in communicating with Fr. Lavey, I had concerns about what the next six weeks would bring. He never seemed at all interested in what I said, that this would be nothing but a chore for him.

I had provided Fr. Lavey with my airline details, then I saw no one when I arrived about 10:00 in the morning. After twenty minutes, I called the church, and when he finally answered—going through about five lesser staff members to provide him with a buffer-as I soon found out. He did not like people. He liked Fr. Lavey. And very rich people at his church. Which was about all with whom he wished to converse. St. James by-the-Sea was some 25 minutes away, and in an hour's time I saw him. He was well dressed in a black tailored suit, from London he noted; black satin or silk clerical shirt, high collar, luxurious cuff links, black leather Italian shoes (he told me all this with costs), and what did I think of his silk stockings? Would I care for luncheon? Of course, I said, if you're buying. He was, and at the La Jolla Beach and Tennis Club. Everything I now saw was *chichi*. Oh, the clergy shirt came from Asia. He was around 50, and proud of how high he had reached in life, actually in church. His face was round, smooth and shiny. Very shiny. Kevin Spacey shiny. He wore glasses, expensive ones. Duh. His hair was well-coiffed. He was unctuous, ingratiating, oozing charm. I noticed during his deliberate walk to the pulpit one Sunday, he left a trail of ooze. I remember his telling me two maxims about himself: 1) a true Episcopal priest keeps his collar very white, and his dress shoes very black, and 2) he knew he was on a tangent to become a bishop. Then his life would have meaning. The English bishop I thought of when he said these things was Cosmo Gordon Lang, Archbishop of Canterbury following Randall Davidson, from 1928–1942. Lang while a vicar wrote his name with the Canterbury Latin, "Cosmo Cantuar".[5] He never spoke or spent time with any but the highest classes, the nobility. Then when the *arriviste* arrived, he was bored as archbishop. He was the humbug who attacked Edward VIII following the abdication. He made sure the last act of his as Archbishop would be to confirm Princess Elizabeth, this in 1942.

5. Edwards, *Leaders of the Church of England*, 306

When we got to St. James by-the-Sea, on Prospect, just a couple blocks from the La Jolla Cove and beach, we walked past a receptionist, then his private secretary's office-her own room complete with sign that read, "No man cometh unto the Father, but by me", then his own spacious, luxurious sitting room, with all leather chairs and couch, a few books, expensive Persian rug, numerous green Elephant ear plants, very dramatic looking, which when I identified them, he informed me that at this church, they were known as "colocasia", and would I please use that proper word. The same sort of reproval greeted me a few weeks later when I led the Prayers of the People. Fr. Lavey allowed the praying for the President, but not the Governor, who was Jerry Brown, seen all over La Jolla with his then companion, Linda Ronstadt. Fr. Lavey disapproved their arrangement. I prayed that Sunday for Jimmy our President. Following the Eucharist, the late one, in the ornate vesting room, he lit into me something fierce, and said *the President* is only named in liturgical prayers as "James". "I suppose", he said in a carefully slow admonishing tone, " if you had prayed for the Governor, it would be "Jerry". Then we would have Jimmy and Jerry. Do you see? Do you understand now what is proper?" Oh, dear. (My response was to point at his lavalier mike, with chord going into his pants, and say he spoke *ex catheter*. I really said that.) The horrible trials through which I put this man. Father was a very strict moralist. I'm unsure how he would ground his morals in Scripture. I never heard him quote the Bible at all. Even his sermons were about the triumphs of the rich and the famous.

I found where I was to stay. A few blocks south was The Bishop's School, the private Episcopal school for the rich and famous' daughters and sons. (Originally a boarding school for girls only, it went co-ed in 1971.) I enjoyed a very large room with double bed, private bathroom, a sitting area. I would eat all my meals with the students. And convert them. I enjoyed their company when I ate there. I was an adult sponsor on a trip to the J. Paul Getty Museum, referred to as simply *the Getty*, said through clenched teeth, then much smaller than now, but housed inside and outside the spacious First Century Roman Villa reproduction. This is just north of Santa Monica, close to the Malibu beach area. We left at six in the morning for the nearly three-hour trip. For a huge display of ancient artifacts, this was delightful. This was two years or so after the death of the richest man in the world, billionaire J. Paul Getty, oil mogul. His daughter-in-law, Gail, managed to expand the famed museum begun in 1953. She was of course the mother of John Paul Getty III, who in 1973, at age 16, had been kidnapped in Rome by Mafiosi, and held for months, due to his grandfather's miserly ways. Gail was heroic in achieving her son's freedom. She saved most of him. Not his right ear.

Every day, I was in the graces of Fr. MacDonald Wilhite, curate. He was kind hearted, and we became friends. He told me story after story about Lavey. Including his tippling. According to Don, Lavey was a determined world class dipsomaniac. The spirits guided him. Every waking moment. He put gin on his Captain Crunch. He insisted on preparing the altar for any mass, so that he could add extra wine, which then after the communicating of the people, he would slurp up. Altar wine was continually low. Don told me this and many other priestly things at lunch with a Bacardi Cocktail, at a restaurant either on Girard or Prospect. I could handle one. I think Don liked having Fr. Lavey as boss, because his two or three cocktails seemed abstemious in comparison. He was wonderful company. His job was to keep me occupied. And he was a knowledgeable Anglo-Catholic priest. We discussed women's ordination, and the blessings of gays, and ordination of gay men already in a sexual relationship. He supported the gay change. But he opposed women's ordination. I saw this the other way around. Of course if one was gay, and not in a sexual relationship, as a large number of Anglo-Catholics were, and a number of my friends, both classmates and priests, one already could be ordained. The Bishop of Chicago, much respected, considered compassionate, devout, a gentleman, almost saintly was Bishop James Montgomery, widely known as a gay man. And no one delved deeply into anyone's personal details, unless one "Scared the horses". (This was the figurative way Episcopalians had for what the Salvation Army would call "The Funny Business". Methodists said "Get caught with your hand in the cookie jar".)

Every Sunday I met the rich and the famous. My first Sunday I was introduced to Major General Lemuel Shepherd, former U.S Marine Commandant, first Commandant to be part of the Joint Chiefs of Staff under Eisenhower. He was from the previous century, born in the 1890's, and a decorated hero from WWI, WWII, and Korea. He distinguished himself at Belleau Wood in the first; Guam and Okinawa in the second; Inchon in the third. Then I met Dr. Jonas Salk, a quiet, kindhearted man, the famous discoverer of the polio vaccine, using "dead" polio virus. It was tested on children in 1954, my birth year, and won approval to be used in 1955. Salk did not seek to patent or make money off his discovery. He wanted to save children from the disease that had so affected the greatest President of the twentieth century, Franklin Delano Roosevelt. And one of his finest biographers, Geoffrey Ward. Ward wrote two books on Roosevelt, which I treasure, especially *A First Class Temperament: The Emergence of Franklin Roosevelt*, 1989. He wrote the scripts for Ken Burns' magnificent *The Civil War, The Roosevelts: An Intimate History*, and *Vietnam*. His second volume on Franklin Roosevelt includes a number of deeply moving references to this Episcopalian's Christian faith, and how it bolstered him after he experienced "the Terror" in 1921. Ward contracted polio at age nine in 1949.

Salk was quiet and unassuming. I asked him questions about his life and schooling. Then I asked him about his equally famous wife, the painter and writer Francoise Gilot. This scientist and this artist somehow found each other, and married in 1970. And it was due to their mutual love for modern architecture. Salk's top assistant was despised by Gilot for referring to her as Picasso's ex. Which he thought darkly humorous. Dark because she, and of all Picasso's women, was the only one to have had the strength to leave him, after years of verbal and physical abuse. She left with their two children. She wrote her fascinating *Life With Picasso* in 1964. She had endured ten years with the man, from 1943–1953. Besides being a major influence on Picasso, she was also a muse for Matisse. Both credited her painting and art criticism as affecting their styles. In 1990 she wrote a book about both of them, *Matisse and Picasso: A Friendship in Art.*

I met lots of people, some kind and pleasant, Mrs. Putney, an Englishwoman and expat, who invited me to lunch for her favorite leek soup. I went. I ate. I loved it! I met Bishop Richard Watson, mentioned above, delightful, with smiling eyes, courteous, "You must come for dinner. When?" Mrs. Figgy, a proper lady, in the worst way, a big woman, really big, unsmiling, late 60s, who actually snorted at me. She looked, honest to God, porcine. Big porcine. Huge face, large wide nostrils into which you could see these black caves. The kind Injun Joe would hide in. She did not want me to come to lunch. And then a couple of big, fat people, with two big, fat kids in tow, the kind who are all on scooters at Walmart. I can't remember their names for the life of me. They did want me to come to dinner. "How does tonight sound?" Yikes. He was "King of the Ponderosa", so-called because of a large franchise he owned of this questionable mystery meat restaurant, somewhere in San Diego. All I remember of the evening was everyone talking at the same time, and at a high decibel, plastic on the furniture, which always surprises me: Why do this? (Paul Fussell has some droll comments on this in his book I've mentioned above, *Class: A Guide Through the American Status System.*) And when the "horsedurvs" *sic* were presented, of the cheese whiz and little weenies wrapped in bacon variety, they were almost immediately gobbled up by the kids. I had wanted some. I was hungry. And too much alcohol was served. I am not above any of what I have just described. I simply found it hilarious. But these folks wanted to please me, share their home, and feel comfortable with me. I hope they considered me a good guest. But it was what it was. I even enjoyed the liver and onions. And six pack.

It was the opposite at the Laveys. They were kind enough to invite me to dine. I was to arrive at six, with dinner served at seven fifteen. Cigars and brandy afterwards. I dressed as nicely as I could, and arrived right on time. I greeted both Anne and Father, and was ushered into Father's study. Actually, Father's special bar. With not one but two liquor cabinets. Cabinets made of teak wood. And Father's special material was in abundance. Leather. He told me how much he appreciated how "durable" it was. Father had jumped the gun on imbibing. Father was bright red and perspiring. He had a tumbler next to him, which I knew to be of the juniper berry kind. "Would our guest care for a highball this evening?" "I don't mind if I do", I replied trying like mad to remember how conversations like this go in Cary Grant movies. (If you remember "North by Northwest", you'll remember how the alcohol was poured down the hero's gullet. Father would have taken much longer to become inebriated.) This message was relayed to Anne. Anne was the spitting image of Sian Phillips, the Welsh actress who played the evil Livia in "I, Claudius", and George Smiley's Lady Ann in "Tinker Tailor, Soldier, Spy", and later as Clementine opposite Robert Hardy, in "Winston Churchill: The Wilderness Years", (which I find mostly accurate historically, and riveting to watch. The best bits are based on Robert Rhodes James, *Churchill: A Study in Failure, 1905–1939*, a subtle, nuanced masterpiece, published in 1970.) Both were heavy smokers. I received my gin and tonic with lime. There was one ice cube in the tumbler. At my first sip, I nearly gagged. There was no tonic! I gasped, "I need a little more ice, please". Anne brought the ice bucket to me, and plopped one more in. "Perhaps Mr. Coleman appreciates this fine Gin? It's Tanqueray." Oh. Well, Mr. Coleman doubted it, and became anxious lest he slur his words and fall into his salmon at dinner. At least I didn't check to see if they had cheese whiz. It was over two hours before dinner was announced. I may have had one more drink, this time with tonic. I don't remember much else that evening. I think it was amusing. This time I did not have to heave.

Next day was Wednesday when at 9:30 am was the weekly staff meeting. Don Wilhite warned me the Rector was in a "pinchy" mood. Steer clear of him. I didn't think I had to worry at all. Lavey had his favorite. At several of the meetings Lavey flirted openly with the Organist/ Music Director, Jared Jacobsen. Jared mostly avoided gracefully getting pinched. He was lively, and excellent musician who could inspire a great many parishioners to sing for the Eucharistic worship. The treasurer, whose name I only remember as Charles, was from Atlanta, and fixed delicious scrambled eggs for the twenty or so staff. The Rector announced that I would begin giving a series of five talks on "What Every Episcopalian Ought to Know". They would occur between the mid and late Eucharist on Sundays. I had no idea. I freaked. Then I came up with using clergy and clergy types in the arts, to show similarities and dissimilarities among clergy and extrapolate from that to say how Episcopalians are "different" from other churches. I used Anthony Trollope's *Barchester Towers*, and a passage about the Bishop's Chaplain, Mr. Obadiah Slope, who attacks church music and deeply upsets the saintly Mr. Septimus Harding; The Rector in Clarence Day's *Life with Father*; Willa Cather's *Death Comes For the Archbishop*, set in nineteenth century New Mexico; and Canon Chasuble, so stuffy and sententious, from Oscar Wilde's *The Importance of Being Earnest*. But I began with what I have always enjoyed as my favorite musical, Meredith Willson's *The Music Man*, which I suggested is the quintessential American preacher/huckster story. This 1962 film has been my favorite from the opening number of the salesmen on a train heading for River City, Iowa. The opening number with the "whadya talk, whadya talk, whadya talk, whatdya talk, whadya talk", and the "what's the fella's line?", "doesn't worry about his line", and changes to the way and how to sell, because of the rise of credit, and the "Model T Ford" changing everything these guys knew. "Things are different than it was", "No it aint, no it ain't, but ya gotta know the territory!", with the voices and singing imitating a train's sounds. "Onomatopoeia." Every time I watch this, I find it amazing that this is how every clergy gathering strikes me, with bewildered priests, stunned by the changes in the world, the *stupidor mundi*, as Terry Holmes described this phenomenon in his *The Future Shape of Ministry* in 1970, and continuing right up to the present. What then do we do to deal with our anxieties as stunned clergy? In fact, what's the answer that many people in various professions, even nations gravitate to?

Simple! Bring in the magnetic personality, someone who sells him or herself! Someone with a proven track record! Professor Harold Hill will know just how to do this! Nearly every rector I met with a growing and thriving church, considered successful in American terms, was a personality cult figure. There were exceptions: Archbishop Michael Ramsey, Fr. Robert Matthews at Trinity, Lawrence, Kansas. The priest or bishop who was by far the largest personality, who would always fill up a room when present, was my bishop in the Diocese of Milwaukee, from 1984 until 2003, Bishop Roger White. All these men eventually had a fall, a "Come to Jesus Moment". One cannot sustain the priestly vocation, or episcopal vocation, on personality or charisma alone. And then the moment comes for us to recognize we will either sink into the waves of the sea, as Peter faced this, or we will be saved by asking, pleading for help from one outside ourselves as Peter did. All clergy, as human beings, have feet of clay. Dust thou art, and unto dust shalt thou return. *Romans* 8: 1–4 is always where I turn:

> There is therefore now no condemnation for those who are in Christ Jesus. For the law of the Spirit of life in Christ Jesus has set you free from the law of sin and death. For God has done what the law, weakened by the flesh, could not do: by sending his own Son in the likeness of sinful flesh, and to deal with sin, he condemned sin in the flesh, so that the just requirement of the law might be fulfilled in us, who walk not according to the flesh but according to the Spirit.

Fr. John Claypool shares his own personal experience about coming to crisis with his vocation, and learning to trust our Lord in his remarkable memoir, *Opening Blind Eyes*, published in 1983. I have loved his wisdom and deep knowledge of faith in Jesus, in all his books. For those who have been deeply hurt, especially by the church, which means all of us who love the church, his book *Mending the Heart* is wonderful. For those who are feeling hopeless, *The Hopeful Heart*, will help. His books are deeply prayerful as Archbishop Ramsey's are. St. Ambrose wrote:

> In Christ, then, are all things, And He is everything to us;
>
> If you have wounds to be healed, He is your physician;
>
> If fever inflames you, He is a fountain;
>
> If you seek to correct evil doing, He is justice.
>
> Do you need help? He is strength.
>
> Do you fear death? He is life.
>
> Do you long for heaven? He is the way.
>
> Do you flee from darkness? He is light.
>
> Do you hunger? He is food.

It was while offering my thoughts on why I loved "The Music Man", and how feelings or charisma, or logic chopping not only will not save us, but cannot save us, that I realized I was converted to Christ, and thought as a Christian. It was about time. I was already in seminary. I read this in St. Augustine's *Confessions*:

> Late have I loved you, beauty so old and so new: late have I loved you. And see, you were within and I was in the external world and sought you there, and in my unlovely state I plunged into those lovely created things which you made. You were with me, and I was not with you. The lovely things kept me far from you, though if they did not have their existence in you, they had no existence at all. You called and cried out loud and shattered my deafness. You were radiant and resplendent, you put to flight my blindness. You were fragrant, and I drew in my breath and now pant after you. I tasted you, and I feel but hunger and thirst for you. You touched me, and I am set on fire to attain the peace which is yours.[6]

I learned step by step to love John Henry Newman, who in a famous passage of his *Apologia Pro Vita Sua*, has these words to say about conversion, of receiving Revelation from God:

> And then I felt altogether the force of the maxim of St. Ambrose,"*Non in dialectica complacuit Deo salvam facere populum suum*";-(It did not please God to save the world through logic.)I had a great dislike for paper logic. For myself, it was not logic that carried me on; as well might one say that the quicksilver in the barometer changes the weather. It is the concrete being that reasons; pass a number of years, and I find my mind in a new place; how? The whole man moves; paper logic is but the record of it. All the logic in the world would not have made me move faster towards Rome than I did; as well might you say that I have arrived at the end of my journey, because I see the village church before me, as venture to asset that the miles, over which my soul had to pass before it got to Rome, could be annihilated, even though I had been in possession of some far clearer view than I then had, that Rome was my ultimate destination. Great acts take time. At least this is what I felt in my own case; and therefore to come to me with methods of logic, had in it the nature of a provocation, and, though I do not think I ever showed it made me somewhat indifferent how I met them, made me somewhat indifferent how I met them, and perhaps led me, as a means of relieving my impatience, to be mysterious or irrelevant, or to give in because I could not meet them to my satisfaction. And I greater trouble still than these logical mazes, was the introduction of logic into every subject whatever, so far, that is, as this was done. Before I was at Oriel (Newman's College at Oxford), I recollect an acquaintance saying to me that "the

---

6. St. Augustine, *Confessions*, X xxvii.38

Oriel Common Room stank of Logic." One is not at all pleased when poetry, or eloquence, or devotion, is considered intended to feed syllogisms.[7]

I keep in mind when reading about Newman's "conversion" to Rome, what Schleiermacher said in his distinction between Catholics and Protestants: " In so far as the Reformation was not simply a purification and reaction from abuses which had crept in, but was the origination of a distinctive form of Christian communion, the antithesis between Protestantism and Catholicism may provisionally be conceived thus: the former makes the individual's relation to the Church dependent on his relation to Christ, while the latter contrariwise makes the individual's relation to Christ dependent on his relation to the Church".[8]

7. Newman, *Apologia Pro Vita Sua*, 169–70

8. Schleiermacher, *The Christian Faith*, 24, 103

XXXVI

As an Episcopalian, and Anglican, I am an inheritor of the ancient Church, the Patristic Church, the Church before the divisions between East and West in 1054, and then the Reformation of 1517. So, neither of Schleiermacher's categories works for me. In fact, from a Catholic point of view, coming out of the first thousand years of the undivided Church, Rome strikes me as the first Protestant Church. And what Roman pontiffs did in making unilateral decisions, simply by assertion, I think that Rome has caused more damage to the Church Catholic, and to the entire Western philosophical and epistemological foundation for reason and theology, which has finally led Western philosophy to the sorry pathetic dead end in which we find it. Christ did not die for the world to give us logical analysis, or deconstruction, or whatever that led to Sartre or finally the giving up of philosophy in Heidegger.

This has been the underpinning of my understanding of Catholic and Apostolic, Credal Christianity. Now, I show my hand. Various abbots and bishops of the Western Church even before 800 AD, allowed or inserted into the Ecumenical Creed (the Niceno-Constantinopolitan, Nicene for short) the phrase "And the Son", or *Filioque*, to the language concerning the procession of the Holy Spirit, sent through the Son, though issues from God the Father, changing the Creed, and making everybody mad. And this comes down to interpretation of *St. John* 15: 16, "When the Advocate comes, whom I (Jesus) will send to you from the Father, the Spirit of truth who comes from the Father, he will testify on my behalf."

The Orthodox, and later Magisterial Reformation theologians, recognized the problem in the economy of God. The Romans went ahead with the change. The change is called the double procession of the Holy Spirit. Then Charlemagne insisted, for political reasons, to make the bishops in the Frankish empire, and the Pope, Leo III, (d.814) to permit this, and require that it become part of the Eucharistic liturgy, with this *innovation* intact. Leo III, basically said, the theology was not heresy, but he wasn't happy about the way this *innovation* was being handled. Now Leo III was a saint, not a good decider. (George W) Over the next two centuries in the West, this *innovation* was allowed by the various Popes , though not officially until c. 1000. Along with a number of other political matters (like who has Episcopal authority over the Slavs, still a contentious matter), this addition by the Pope in the West, became the rallying cry for opponents in the East. Not only was there the Scriptural interpretation to resolve, but by whose authority was the Great Ecumenical Creed of 325 AD, being changed? This was the question. Popes had the ready answer: We do! (Royal we.) How in God's name was this in keeping with the Credal Church? And no one could use our Lord's words from *St. Matthew* 16:18, "I tell you are Peter, and on this rock I will build my Church, and the gates of hell will not prevail against it", to say what was repeatedly asserted by Popes as their own authority, indeed over the Ecumenical Creed of the Church. (They add that it was Rome where Peter was martyred.) Our Lord never says this to St. Peter, who it may be noted got a lot of important things wrong. Agreed? Jesus told this not terribly bright man, who comes up right next to his Lord and rebukes Jesus about the plan of Salvation, *that he was not infallible*. About suffering and the death on the cross, Peter does not stay behind his Lord, as disciples did, knowing their place, but claims equality with him. So again in *St. Matthew* 16:22–3, Christ rebukes Peter, "Get behind me Satan, for you are a scandal to me. You are setting your mind not on things of God, but on things of man". Duh! Peter is the rock, but he bounces like a rubber ball. Still, there must be human authority in the Church, unless you're a Gnostic, and human beings sin and err. (Pronounced uhr. Not heir. Look it up. And it's mischievous, three syllables, not four. Accent on the first. Jeez.) And don't forget, Peter is publically rebuked by Paul, for acting like a coward. See *Galatians* 2: 11–14. Peter was publically rebuked both by our Lord, and by St. Paul! Being Jewish, that meant a lot more years of analysis. A lot. Can you see him telling his psychoanalyst, while whining, "He didn't have to yell at me! Sob, sob". The analyst would ask which one? Peter, "Ohhhhhhh Noooooo . . ." Peter is a classic victim of a Jewish mother.

Anyway, Pope Innocent III, called the Fourth Lateran Council in 1215, to get agreement on what he already infallibly knew, which was to declare the very philosophical ontological way the Sacrament on the Altar was changed from bread and wine into the very Body and Blood of Christ. The philosophy for "Transubstantiation" was that of Aristotle. Imagine that. And why did the Eucharistic Sacrament need this careful definition? Because the Pope said so. And this particular decision was proclaimed to be *De Fide*, of the essence of the Faith, equal to the Ecumenical Creed, which had already been tampered with by popes. By the time we get to 1854, with the Immaculate Conception of the Blessed Virgin, defined by the authority of Pius IX, "*Pio Nono*", again with no scriptural authority, in fact inconsistent with the plain meaning of how Blessed Mary is portrayed in *St. Mark*, and that Jesus states that not his family, but those who hear the Word of God are his family, the Pope once again has moved outside the realm of what the Apostlic Church and the Patristic Church believed and taught in continuity with our Lord's Apostles. (So much for St. Vincent of Lerins' fifth century *Commonitorium*: We are sure as catholics when we hold fast to what has been believed everywhere, always, by all—*quod ubique quod semper quod ab omnibus creditum est*. (Chapter 2, section 6.) There is development, and there is development. Newman wrote his great book about this in *The Development of Christian Doctrine* in 1845. He privately held mental reservation about what Pius IX was up to.

This was certainly true for Newman when in 1870, at Vatican I, the doctrine of Papal Infallibility was defined, and held to be *De Fide*. This authority had been utilized many times already, obviously, but now it was defined.

> When the Roman Pontiff speaks *ex cathedra* . . . he defines a doctrine . . . to be held by the whole church, he possesses . . . that infallibility which the divine Redeemer willed his church to enjoy . . . Therefore such definitions of the Roman Pontiff are irreformable in their own right and not by the consent of the church.[1]

This is tremendously disconcerting to non-Catholics, and many Catholics, and especially to those with a Patristic or Orthodox sensibility. Robert Jenson, who recently died, was a greatly respected Lutheran theologian as well as shrewd Ecumenical observer and commentator, noted that this surely cannot mean what it says, witness the obvious problem of Honorius I solemnly defining "monotheletism" as part of the Faith! This was overturned by the Sixth Ecumenical Council, which declared monotheletism as heresy, and denounced Honorius I as a heretic! Jenson goes on to note that Boniface VIII, ". . . used every conceivable formula of final definition, 'we declare, teach, and define ' in proclaiming that political submission to the papacy is 'necessarily' a condition of salvation, yet no one, including the Pope, seems now to believe this".[2] Jenson points out that key sticking problem began in the middle ages with the separation in the papal office of "sacrament and jurisdiction", using the then Pope's (Benedict XVI) words, alluded to in *Called to Communion: Understanding the Church Today*.[3]

Furthermore, Jenson states that this has been identified as the "chief false development in the West's understanding of churchly office".[4] With Vatican II's unclarity about this serious conundrum, both for non-Catholics as well as Catholics, and the last several popes seeming deafness to concerns about their use of this office in an autocratic way, no wonder there are continued suspicions about the papacy including for those Anglicans and others who would otherwise support the need for Rome's universal pastorate.

Now I will get to my Grand Unified Theory. The papal assertion of infallibility right up to the time it was defined, and since then, was false. It caused the division between East and West in 1054 AD. It caused the Reformation. It broke down a universal system of Canons, Scriptural authority and Doctrinal authority included. The Church now being split led to the epistemological crises from the 11th century on, and particularly in the 16th century. The papal church added to Scripture and Doctrine something completely false, something alien, including its assertion used

---

1. Jenson, *Systematic Theology* II, 243–4
2. Jenson, *Systematic Theology* II, 244
3. Ratzinger, *Called to Communion*, 93.
4. Jenson, *Systematic Theology* II, 248

against Protestants who said the Truth can be found in Scripture, as seen through the lenses of the Ecumenical Creed, and in the Holy Spirit, and Roman Catholics answered and said No, the Pope alone has a special conduit to God the Holy Spirit, and decides what is Truth, and can add to it. This shoves aside reason as part of faith, in this new attempt to claim certainty, for what was before, probability. The unity of theology and philosophy came apart in the West. No longer could one argue from Scripture and the Church's tradition, using reason, what was true, because both sides argued from the same Bible. This led to *Skepticism* among all thinking people, meaning, one will never find Truth: one simply has to believe. (And torture and kill the heretics.) There falls away at that point any sense of reason completed by faith, as St. Thomas had argued. How than can we find truth? This epistemological matter, took over as the first central need for philosophy, and it has plagued the West ever since. In a time of complete skepticism, in which clever French priests, could argue both sides of a question, including proving and disproving the existence of God, one no longer had essentials of Unity and Holiness in the Church, without Truth. The unity of the Truth was completely shattered. Richard H. Popkin has carefully argued what was at stake in his brilliant *History of Skepticism from Erasmus to Spinoza*, published in 1979. This is the background to the French Roman Catholic Rene Descartes, writing in his *Second Meditation* in 1637, to the Theological Faculty of the University of Paris, looking for a new foundation of truth, to bring about Christian Peace, in his discovery of "I think, therefore I am". Actually, "I think, I am". Later there was the Christian attempt to argue the Five Ways to God of St. Thomas as providing a faithful answer.[5] They will not stand the test of the arguments rationally, outside of the *faith* context of what St. Thomas actually wrote. Based on assenting to Christian Doctrine, which is by true faith, and known through Revelation, here are five ways to show that belief in God is coherent. Remove the Five Ways from St. Thomas' *Summa Theologiae*, and one is left with an entire misreading of Thomas. These are not proofs standing alone, and Thomas states we cannot reach God through reason alone. Hume and Kant showed this with their arguments exhibiting the weakness of these arguments proved through reason alone, and not on the grounds Thomas was actually putting forward. Kant went so far as to say one must accept God, Freedom, and Immortality, and not attempt to prove them. He knew that one couldn't live on reason alone. One could not reach certainty using the new instrument of reason as understood by the Enlightenment philosophes. Schleiermacher then attempted to find a basis for Christian Faith in "feeling", which cannot bear that weight. And yet feeling has taken over in the Mainline Protestant Churches, and the adverse consequences resulting due to this approach. One's epistemology becomes, " I know because I am so sincere". That has led to guitars leading Christian worship. And God awful emotional preaching. And the philosophical and theological searching for truth in Church have come to a standstill. Alasdair MacIntyre describes how these attempts have led to a fissiparous scatter-

5. St. Thomas Aquinas, *Summa Theologiae*, I, ii, art.3

ing of seeking truth in a secular age, beginning with his seminal work *After Virtue: A Study in Moral Theory* in 1981. Charles Taylor's brilliant *A Secular Age*, 2006, has looked at the breakdown of seeking truth in the last five hundred years of the Western world, and how it has led to this sour toxicity in secular Western Culture. For myself, I think Wolfhart Pannenberg has been most successful in his project of achieving a foundation for truth, beginning with his careful deployment of philosophy, especially epistemology, unified with theology, begun and completed in the Christian God in his various books culminating in his *Systematic Theology*. I also think N. T. Wright's new Gifford Lectures will evince an historical approach to belief in the Triune God, and will be the touchstone for demonstrating right reason in his *Discerning the Dawn: History, Eschatology and New Creation*. How ironic to note that it was an assertion of truth by the Roman Catholic Popes that started this breakdown in Western thought. Not atheists. For a lucid and marvelous book on this, see William J. Abraham, *Canon and Criterion in Christian Theology*, 1998. He is a fascinating Methodist theologian and philosopher of religion from Northern Ireland, St. Patrick country. Leslie Newbiggin's *Proper Confidence* is a basic primer on tackling the epistemological question for Christian witness.

Truth is the central question for Wolfhart Pannenberg, and he states this clearly in his *Introduction to Systematic Theology*: "If theology does not properly face its particular task regarding truth claims of the Christian tradition, then it easily happens that the clergy of the church are the first to become insecure and evasive about the message they are supposed to preach."[6]

6. Pannenberg, *Introduction to Systematic Theology*, 6

XXXVII

ONE EVENING I SPENT with Bishop Richard Watson. His wife had left dinner for us, and I found his company delightful. He had enjoyed a delightful and colorful life, and enjoyed talking about it, including what Gypsy Rose Lee and Bishop James Pike were like. He had a twinkle in his eyes, and we both talked endlessly. I asked him about any number of matters and people he had known, and then he hooked me with Archbishop William Temple. Temple was garrulous and outgoing, and a Christian socialist, and philosopher. I had read Temple's Gifford Lectures, *Nature, Man and God*, published in 1934. He was a happy man, who exuded charm and Christian love. He was known as being unpompous, genial, generous, able to talk with anyone, and at the same time an extremely learned man, who according to Adrian Hastings in *A History of English Christianity 1920–1990*, was the towering Christian leader for the first half of the twentieth century.[1] Both Hastings and A. N. Wilson in *After the Victorians: The Decline of Britain in the World*, focus on the Oxford Mission Temple led, and the many conversions to Christ that took place among the intelligent and educated. This mission of 1931 changed the direction of Christian faith among the thoughtful for generations. [2]Temple had met the acquaintance of Michael Ramsey following the latter's publishing his first book, the monumental *The Gospel and the Catholic Church*, in 1936. Ramsey notes this in *The Anglican Spirit*.[3] That was a wonderful evening, and Watson was like Ramsey at ease with his faith, and talked about it openly, gracefully, and movingly. As the night wore on, and while he was describing the effect Temple's *Readings in St. John's Gospel* had on him, he went into his study and brought out his F. E. Iremonger's biography of Temple, inscribed it to me, and presented it to me. Bishop Watson, born in 1902, died in 1987. The next day Fr. Wilhite was chuckling about hearing from Bishop Watson's evening that he had enjoyed a pleasant time with the "loquacious" seminarian. I struggle to think that's a better word than verbose.

Those weeks saw the Presiding Bishop of the Episcopal Church, John Maury Allin, come and preach at the Diocesan Convention at St. James-By-The-Sea. He was an entrancing preacher, with a treasury of stories, of a variety I've never found in anyone else. The bishop, Robert Wolterstorff, chaired and moved the business of the church along briskly. Someone would stand to speak, be recognized and begin with some

---

1. Hastings, *History of English Christianity*, 254–7
2. Wilson, *After the Victorians*, 305–7
3. Ramsey, *The Anglican Spirit*, 97

bilge, as we clergy are bound to do, and the Bishop would interrupt and say, "Would Fr. Harrison (or whomever), please let us know if he is addressing the question? If so, is he for it or against it?" Quite often, the speaker didn't know, and Bishop Wolterstorff would say, "then please take your seat, so that someone may be recognized who is understanding of the question, and not wasting our time".

Musicians were brought to this musical loving church. A Dutch family of various pianists, flutists, and a harpist, by the name of Naute came and stayed for some time. They were delightful. A famed young organist, who thought of herself as the next Virgil Fox, who wanted to be flashing, and exciting, with her looks and theatrical skills on display as well as her musicianship, Jane Parker-Smith, 29, long hair cut all around her face in a 1920's flapper sort of way, played all French Romantic music of the Saint—Saens, Vierne, Francke school, if you like that, and all showy, and fortissimo! She was a virtuoso! All of her materials said so.

It was time to head back.to Nashotah House just in time for Ash Wednesday.

XXXVIII

I ARRIVED BACK FROM sunny Southern California to the real world. The real world was freezing, in fact one of the coldest winters for Wisconsin. It was time for the Lenten retreat, which we participated in at DeKoven. This was in Racine, Wisconsin, where an order of Anglican women religious (nuns) ran the retreat center. They were the Order of the Community of St. Mary, who ran the Center like Captain Bligh, and produced some of the worst tasting vegetarian food anyone could imagine. The smell of onions, limburger cheese, boiled cabbage, spoiled eggs, could be forcing itself on the guests of DeKoven at almost any time, day or night, and there was no getting away from it. During Lent, one could swear that the smell was from unwashed, reclusive clergy, whose feet were producing something nasty, a new life form perhaps. That cheese was the worst smell possible, the cheese from Gloustershire, using juices from a prickly pear, the horrible Stinking Bishop cheese. Or, so the rumor went. I found out the truth. The cat began to emerge from the stinking bishop bag. The stench always occurred when "Sherry", the sanctimonious bishop of Northern Indiana, William Sheridan, was present. He loved DeKoven. (He was once asked why he adored Dekoven. His response, "Because that is where De witches are". I kid you not.) He was so covered in lace you would have thought he was the original Indiana Jones, fleeing the cave caught in spider webs. He used secret Gnostic prayers during every Eucharist, and held his hands together so strangely that many of us seminarians wondered if he had received irregular orders from the Illuminati associated (secretly) with the Bilderberg. There was a lot of irregularity about him. He was the stinking bishop.

DeKoven was originally Racine College begun in 1852 and lasted as an Episcopal preparatory school and college until 1933. Its fame was brought to the college by Fr. James DeKoven, a lightening rod of wit, oratory and wisdom, a saintly man who followed the Tractarian ideals of John Keble and Edward Pusey. He was born in Middleton, Connecticut, and educated at Columbia College, and then at General Theological Seminary in New York. He was ordained a deacon at his home parish, and accepted an invitation to become Professor of Ecclesiastical History at Nashotah House. After Bishop Kemper ordained him a priest, in 1855, he added Rector of St. John's, Delevan to his responsibilities. He was a fervent educator, always summoning young men to hear about the joys of Scripture, Church History, the full belief of the Real Presence of Christ, in fact the leader in the Church of ritualism, those in the second generation of

Tractarians who favored colored vestments, bowing and genuflecting, incense, bells, candles on the altar, and the reservation of the Sacrament, and Gothic architecture. He then became professor at St. John's Hall, a preparatory school for young men wishing to attend Nashotah House. It didn't last long due to a major economic depression in the country in 1857, and St. John's Hall and Racine College decided to merge. DeKoven went there and became Warden of the College. Within a short period of time, he had built the college into the major educational institution, with 225 students in attendance. His influence made the college take on High Church ideals. Racine College in the 1860's and 70's was considered the finest college in the West (of the Alleghenies), the equivalent of their sister school at Sewanee. It was said that Mary Todd Lincoln in 1870, took Tad with her to visit for possible future education.

DeKoven gave well received addresses at General Convention in 1868 and 1871 in favor of toleration for these ritualistic practices, noting what mattered most was belief in Christ's Real Presence, which was all important, not the ritual or devotion as first, and for church members to respect and love each other. However, he was elected Bishop of Wisconsin in 1874, and Bishop of Illinois in 1875, but failed to get consents from the Bishops and the Standing Committees. He fell on an icy street in Milwaukee, in 1879, and broke his ankle, but was not rescued for some time. He died of a Heart Attack four weeks later, on March 18, 1879, at age 47. I should imagine he and William Porcher Dubose of Sewanee, were the most attractive, intellectual and devout Episcopalians in the latter part of the 19th century. And add Bishop Charles Todd Quintard, a Northern born first elected Bishop in the South, after the Civil War, in Tennessee, who also was a high churchman. He was Vice Chancellor and then Chancellor at the University of the South. Dubose shared with Quintard the honor of being chaplains during the War, both for the Confederate armies, and of both teaching at Sewanee.

I deeply respect these men, and find DeKoven in particular a hero of mine. I was ordained to the Diaconate on March 22, 1980, the day set aside to remember James DeKoven, the day of his funeral in 1879. The St. John's Chapel at DeKoven was constructed in 1864. DeKoven's grave is on the chapel grounds.(I am indebted to a friend, Prof. Thomas Reeves' small book, *James DeKoven: Anglican Saint*, 1978.)

But I hated the cooking of the Sisters. The Racine College closed in 1933, and the Sisters of St. Mary bought the place. They turned the college into the DeKoven Retreat Center in 1934. It was eventually sold to the Diocese of Milwaukee in 1983. There are famous people who attended Racine College during its heyday.

Mary Todd Lincoln, experiencing severe emotional difficulties, and living in Chicago, took Tad to check out Racine College. Tad died shortly thereafter in 1871. She had some ups and downs. She was institutionalized at Bellevue Place in Batavia, Illinois, after a public trial (Illinois loves drama), in 1875. It was known then the food prepared for her there was of a much better variety and taste then the food of DeKoven run by the Community of St. Mary. There is no evidence at all of the smell of a stinking bishop. Mary Todd Lincoln was an Episcopalian.

Francis Joseph "Daddy" Hall went to Racine College. He was ordained a priest, and after a couple degrees he taught Dogmatic Theology at Western Seminary, after 1933 Seabury Western. He went nuts, and continued teaching while hiding in a box in the middle of the classroom. Seabury seminarians didn't notice any change in teaching quality. While in the box, he wrote the most awful theology in thick volumes you could imagine. This tells you all you need to know about Seabury Western.

General Mark Clark went there. Look up Italian Campaign in World War Two. Look up letting Nazi soldiers get away while Clark races to Rome, to be first for no particular strategic reason. Got it? Check out the totally unnecessary bombing of Monte Cassino, the ancient and beautiful Abbey of the Benedictines. Note that Clark was a low church Episcopalian, and a Mason. Note that he was ordered to bomb Monte Cassino by British Field Marshall Sir Harold Alexander, also low church, snake belly low, an Ulster-Scot from County Tyrone. For this action, he was named Governor General of Canada. King George VI thought this was funny. I like Canadians. Their National Anthem states they stand on cars and freeze. I am sorry.

General Billy Mitchell attended Racine College. He yelled and yelled and got mad and madder. He drove everyone including his first wife nuts. I like him. He was an eccentric flyboy. He got court-martialed. He was born in West Allis, Wisconsin, and buried in Forest Lawn, Milwaukee.

Finally, my favorite. Earl Winfield Spencer, Jr., attended Racine College. He was a Navy guy. He was first commander of the Naval Air Station North Island in San Diego. He married Bessie Wallis Warfield, in 1916. They were both Episcopalians. They did not get along. They got divorced. He married four more times. He never got it right. Bessie Wallis married Ernest Aldrich Simpson. Then she met Edward, Prince of Wales, in 1934. He got rid of his mistresses. He became besotted with Wallis and champagne. They married in 1937. They were both Anglicans.

So much for the real world.

XXXIX

I THOROUGHLY LOVED LENT my second or Middler year at Nashotah. Fr. Cooper's classes discussing an epistemological basis for Christian ethics centered on a fascinating book about the subject entitled *Ethical Values in the Age of Science* by a man born in 1898 in Prague to Jewish parents, Paul Roubiczek. He was highly educated, and fought for Austria in the First World War. His tragic experiences with how he saw science and technology being used to destroy human life, based on the scientific method, led him to a time of deep reflection on faith in God as the only foundation for human decision-making. He foresaw, as many reflective men and women did after WWI, a new epoch in human history obsessed with death. If governments of highly civilized Christian nations employing scientists, biologists, chemists, could produce and utilize weapons including poison gases, first by Germans then by all the warring nations in Europe, without any means of check or control, what hope was there for a future for any human and all other forms of life. Germany began using tear gas, which would be an irritant especially in eyes, but not disabling nor fatal. Then on April 22, 1915, Germany used chlorine, which did horrible harm to a man's eyes, nose, throat, and lungs, causing extreme damage and pain before death. The chlorine when entering water in the lungs became hydrochloric and hypochlorous acids destroying lung tissue. The Entente powers, France and Britain and their allies immediately called foul, and appealed to the Hague Declaration Concerning Asphyxiating Gases of 1899. The Treaty prohibited as "War Crimes" the use of these gases as weapons launched through shells. But they could be brought to a locale in tanks, syphoned as liquid chlorine, and projected releasing enormous grey-green clouds of gas. Wind did the rest, if it were moving in the enemy's direction. The British responded with the use of Chlorine at the Battle of Loos, September 25, 1915, but the winds were not favorable. Then the French created phosgene gas, colorless and hard to spot, but more deadly than chlorine, with a delaying effect. Austrians used a combination of Phosgene and Chlorine gas. The Germans produced mustard gas which left large watery blisters on the soldiers, and affected their mucous membranes and eyes. This became the favored gas by the combatant armies. The Americans entered the war having produced large quantities of Lewisite. This blistered the skin and throat as did mustard gas. Americans had no hesitancy whatever to join in with the use of gas. By the last two years of the war, the Allies were producing and delivering higher quantities of poison gas than the Germans.

The entire experience of the civilized highly developed Christian nations, using their scientific know how to destroy human life affected Roubiczek, among a great others, greatly. Of the total 40 million casualties in WWI, 20 million died. Almost exactly half were civilians. The United States suffered approximately 120 thousand deaths, and 200 thousand causalities, of the four million mobilized. These include deaths by influenza, the epidemic that hit worldwide in 1918. Fifty million were later killed by influenza. In comparison, during the Civil War, the seven hundred thousand died, due in part to scientific advance, especially of armament, the use of rifles and minie balls. It's hard to remind oneself these were Americans killing Americans, over America's evil of slavery.

Nearly 60 million died in World War Two. This doesn't include (I think) the 10 million Chinese, Koreans, Malaysians and others Japan killed, before 1939. The Allied bombings of German cities during and especially near the end of the War caused as many as 600,000 civilian casualties. The fire bombings of Tokyo and many other Japanese cities, killing significant numbers of civilians was twice the number of the two atomic bombs dropped on Hiroshima and Nagasaki. Nearly 240, 000 died in the bombings of cities. One hundred and twenty thousand died from the two Atomic bombs. These were all civilian casualties. Estimates vary widely on Korean and Vietnam War deaths. As many as one million and a half civilian casualities were inflicted on North and South Korea. All told with all nations including a half million Chinese deaths, 3 million died in the Korean war. Another 3 million died in the Vietnamese War. The Turks killed 2 million Armenians. Hitler killed 25 million or so. Under the Soviet Regimes the low would be 25 million also to as high as 60 million. Mao killed 40 million.

When I hear that science is the future, and we can all hope for peace, I wonder what planet the person is from. More advanced science and technology meant deaths on a scale in the murderous 20th century than can be imaginable. Please note I am not a Luddite.

Paul Roubiczek looked at the World after World War One and realized everything would only get darker and more evil. *The horrible visions of terror and death revealed to St. John the Divine in his Apocalypse, or Revelation, have all been witnessed as never before in the Twentieth Century.* Roubiczek wrote this book on ethical values as an experiment in whether an epistemological basis could be established so that human beings could say there is this probability for making sound human decisions based on right and wrong. Roubiczek had converted to Christianity after his war time experience. In his book, he thought that Kant and the modern west could never establish such a basis philosophically. He laid out that there is not any basis whatsoever in the scientific method used as a metaphysical understanding of the world at all to claim any humanistic ethic or absolute morality he thought obviously needed in the twentieth century. That it was referred to as "objective" was shown by him to be false.

He then turned to Kierkegaard and found Kierkegaard's leap into the unknown to find certainty offered the kind of undergirding for such moral decision making.

Today, I find Roubiczek's thinking an approximation of searching in the right way, especially his rejecting the scientific "objective" method to find truth. John Lukacs recently wrote about this in his thoughtful book *At the End of an Age*. Written by this wise old man, which I find masterful, readable, exhilarating, he notes the failures of modernity to live up to the early hopes of offering the world peace and healing. He sees in 2002, the end of the 500 year epoch of the Modern Age, dead but not yet buried. Lukacs comments on the growing ugliness in the arts and culture, and the breakdown of language in the sciences, with scientists employing language in strange metaphorical and figurative ways, which are laughable. E. g. in Physics, supposedly the most objective of the sciences, we observe scientists providing us the laws of physics which they say should be true at anytime and anywhere, true even before man appeared on earth, which is completely naïve and arrogant. (Even without employing Heisenberg's Uncertainty/Indeterminacy principle.) He quotes a theoretical physicist, David Lindley, also an astrophysicist, a senior editor of *Science*, from his 1993 book, *The End of Physics: The Myth of a Unified Theory*, to state that for the last one hundred years, the search by physicists for the Holy Grail of modern science, is nonsense:

> . . . the most recent speculation of the theoretical physicists is that the elementary particles are not particles at all but vibrations of tiny loops of quantum-mechanical string, wriggling around in twenty-six-dimensional space . . . To the outsider, it may seem that the theoretical physicists of today are in the grip of a collective mathematical zaniness, inventing twenty-six-dimensional spaces and filling them with strings out of obfuscatory glee . . . Each speaks in a private gobbledygook understandable only to those similarly initiated.
>
> In one sense, such criticism of modern theoretical physics is philistine . . . [but] the inexorable progress of physics from the world we can see and touch into a world made accessible by huge and expensive experimental equipment, and on into a world illuminated by the intellect alone, is a genuine cause for alarm. [When] the trend toward increasing abstraction is turning theoretical physics into recreational mathematics, endlessly amusing to those who can master the technique and join the game, [it becomes] ultimately meaningless because the objects of mathematical manipulation are forever beyond the access of experiment and measurement . . . [Is that] another milestone on the road to the end of physics? . . . What is the use of a theory that looks attractive but contains no additional power of prediction, and makes no statement that can be tested? Does physics then become a branch of aesthetics? [1]

Listening one Sunday to National Public Radio, I caught a show pretentiously called, "On Being with Krista Tippett", she of the "On Being Project", this educated woman talking about religion and "spirituality" in the gummy, watery way a number of

---

1. Lukacs, *At the End of an Age*, 106–7

educated people do these days, without any referent to anything but themselves. Everything she said had no intellectual content whatsoever. She is the epitome of today's solipsistic pseudo-intellectual. On this particular Sunday, she had as her guest, astrophysicist Brian Greene, who is a celebrity somewhat in the way Carl Sagan used to be. His language as he spun his strange esoteric half-baked ideas, not even reaching mythology, was childlike self-authenticating speculations of string theory, and multidimensional worlds, and (once again) reaching for the Grand United Theory—he actually said that—which would "save humanity". How a physicist or astrophysicist can ever imagine reaching such an idea, from a scientific method of studying the physical world is beyond me. Richard Feynman, the Theoretical Physicist, once said: "I believe that a scientist looking at nonscientific problems is just as dumb as the next guy . . . and when he talks about a nonscientific matter, he will sound as naïve as anyone untrained in the matter." [2] And Ms. Tippett seemed to have no grasp at all for basic philosophy, or linguistics, or, God help me, logic. It was like listening to two children running around enthusiastically with their butterfly nets laughing and jumping to catch butterflies only they could see.

Lent is the season developed in the Christian Calendar, to allow the church to remember that we are as dust of the earth, and nothing without God. Lent calls the church as church to repentance, and as at private confession individually, and the General Confession generally, to recognize that we all sin, individually and corporately. The church does not do this to accord with every individual's own journey as a Christian. It declares the Church sins. The Church is the Church as it looks toward the one who has paid the price for us to gain what all these other voices with their messages of salvation promise but cannot deliver. And it comes with the message, Christ or nihilism.

Ash Wednesday began in silence. The ministers entered the chancel, and prostrated themselves. Then we heard the solemn word of the Lord and Gospel warning us not to be hypocrites, "play-actors" as those who are always seeking to impress others around them with their piety, and tone of voice. Our Lord impresses on us to seek out God in the still small voice of God's in secret. This is calling us to individual repentance, different from corporate liturgy. However, after receiving the ash cross, for all who attend church, I insist on washing it off. In the very Gospel of the day Jesus reminds us to wash our faces, and not look dismal, as the play actors do. This is one of two fast days in the church, so we had hot crossed buns after.

The Weekday and Sunday liturgies are penitential, particularly Rite One. The prayer of humble access thus:

> We do not presume to come to thy Table, O merciful Lord, trusting in our own righteousness, but in thy manifold and great mercies. We are not worthy so much as to gather up the crumbs under thy Table. But thou art the same Lord

2. Feynman, "The Value of Science"

whose property is always to have mercy. Grant us therefore, gracious Lord, so
to eat the flesh of thy dear Son Jesus Christ, and to drink his blood, that we
may evermore dwell in him, and he in us. *Amen.*

For the First Sunday in Lent, I stayed at Nashotah on the Sundays, and began the
Sunday Mass with the Great Litany, the first series of prayers Cranmer translated into
English. The Litany is deeply expressive of the sorrow we hold in the Church, and
the firm trust knowing that God hears us and responds in Love and forgiveness. The
Gospel readings in Year A from *St. John's Gospel* embody the readings used in the
Western Church from the 4th century and later for Catechumens, making their way
Sunday by Sunday to Baptism during the Easter Vigil. In so doing they remind the
church of who we are: *St John* 3:1-22, Jesus' dialogue with Nicodemus, and Jesus'
dismissal of following any other way except the One who was sent by God into the
world to save the world. Jesus saying you must be born from above, means of God,
sweeping away any other form of religion or salvation. "Water and the Spirit" means
real water, and the gift of the Holy Spirit. This is the Lord's Sacrament of Baptism. The
following Sunday's Gospel narrates Jesus' encounter with the woman at the well. Jesus
offers her living water and tells her all about herself, and she believes in this Savior and
is converted to Him. She goes and evangelizes the town, and brings them to Jesus. The
Gospel from *St. John* 9 follows, with the religious elders seeing Jesus but not seeing
him, and the man born blind receiving the Light from the Light of the world. Finally,
the raising of Lazarus, shows the authority of Jesus to give life to the dead, for Jesus is
Life. Finally we came to Holy Week. Palm/Passion Sunday includes all the elements of
the Passion of Jesus, with the reading of the Passion by members of the laity. And quiet
and solemnity is observed. Then there are daily readings for Masses on Holy Monday,
Tuesday and Wednesday.

On Maundy Thursday, the themes of the Passover, and our Lord's Mandatum
or command to wash one another's feet to show servanthood was before us. (We all
took part in having our feet washed. Some of us were careful to remove our hose.)
In the Liturgy this is presented with the Institution of the Eucharist; sung in Franck's
Panis Angelicus, and in Mozart's 1791 composition *Ave Verum Corpus,* the praise for
the Real Presence of Christ in the consecrated Bread and Wine, the words from the
Hymn of St. Thomas Aquinas for the feast of Corpus Christi, the Body of Christ in
the Eucharist.

Following the Communion was the procession of the Reserved Sacrament, the
Pre-Sanctified Elements of Christ's Body and Blood, taken to the Chapel of Repose
for devotions overnight. Then the Liturgy ended in silence, and the Sanctuary-I mean
the Sanctuary—was stripped bare and the Sanctuary lamp put out. The Officiant then
washed the altar.

Maundy Thursday begins the holiest three days in the Church calendar called
the Triduum. On Good Friday, the solemn narrative of Jesus' Passion from *St. John's*

Gospel was proclaimed, and Jesus' walking God's way of Love takes him to the Cross. It was at Nashotah that I heard the plainsong *Passion of St. John*, intending to be somber and meditative. I loved the reproaches, and the Hymn from St. John of Portugal, "Faithful Cross above all other, one and only noble tree". The Crucifix was brought through the Nave and Choir, and placed on the Sanctuary steps for veneration. We came up without shoes, genuflected three times on the way, and kissed the foot of the Christ figure. To me, this is the strongest form of liturgical devotion and faith to the Crucified one. The Liturgy continued with the bringing of the Pre-Sanctified Elements back to the altar, for the communicating and nourishment of God's people. A quotation from John Henry Newman on the true meaning of the Crucifixion and Atonement has stayed with me since I first came across it forty years ago. It is about the love of the One who died for the world:

> Let us suppose that some aged and venerable person whom we have known as long as we can recollect anything, and loved and reverenced, suppose such a one, who had done us kindnesses, who taught us, who had given us good advice, who had encouraged us, smiled on us, comforted us in trouble, whom we knew to be very good and religious, very holy, full of wisdom, full of heaven, with grey hairs and awful countenance, waiting for Almighty God's summons to leave this world for a better place; suppose, I say such a one whom we have ourselves known, and whose memory is dear to us, rudely seized by fierce men, stripped naked in public, insulted, driven about here and there, made a laughing-stock, struck, spit upon, dressed up in other clothes in ridicule, then severely scourged on the back, then laden with some heavy load till he could carry it no longer, pulled and dragged about, and at last exposed with all his wounds to the gaze of a rude multitude who came and jeered him, what would be our feelings? Let us in our mind think of this person or that and consider how we should we be overwhelmed and pierced through and through by such a hideous occurrence. But what is all this to the suffering of holy Jesus, which we bear to read of as a matter of course? Only think of Him, when in His wounded state, and without a garment on , He to creep up a ladder, as He could, which led Him on the Cross high enough for His murderers to nail Him to it; and consider who it was in that misery. Now I bid you that Face, so ruthlessly smitten, was the Face of God himself.[3]

The Saturday night Easter Vigil, Baptisms, and Solemn Eucharist of Easter was deeply impressive to me. We began in darkness and the lighting of the Paschal Candle and the Light of Christ sung by the deacon and congregation. Then the Exultet was sung, this ancient hymn of praise to God for Christ's Passover. This was followed by the seminal readings from the Old Testament of God and God alone giving life and salvation, healing to His people. Everything placed around the altar, and in the sanctuary, was covered with light veils. After the readings, we sang the ancient Catholic litany

---

3. Wilson, "Newman the Writer", 129, 139. I originally came across this in an article by J. M. Cameron.

of saints, including a number of Eastern Fathers, Western Fathers, martyrs, confessors, Anglican saints, very much surrounding us with the great cloud of witnesses as noted in the *Epistle to the Hebrews*. We noted various holy men and women associated with the founding and sustaining of the "House". Then Dean Ruef, or Archbishop Ramsey baptized those brought forward. And then, the celebrant shouted, "Alleuia, Christ is risen!", With the response roared, "The Lord is risen indeed, Alleluia!". On would come the lights, the veils were removed, candles were lit, bells were rung, and the great procession to the altar for the first High Solemn, or Pontifical High Solemn Mass of Easter would take place. We sang my favorite Easter Hymn, "The Strife is o'er, the Battle done":

> Alleluia, Alleluia, Alleluia!
>
> The Strife is o'er, the battle done, the victory of life is won;
>
> The song of triumph has begun. Alleluia!
>
> The powers of death have done their worst, but Christ their legions hath dispersed: Let shout of holy joy outburst. Alleluia!
>
> The three sad days are quickly sped, he rises glorious from the dead:
>
> All glory to our risen Head! Alleluia!
>
> He closed the yawning gates of hell, the bars from heavens high portals fell; let hymns of praise his triumphs tell! Alleluia!
>
> Lord! By the stripes which wounded thee, from death's dread sting thy servants free, that we may live and sing to thee. Alleluia!
>
> Alleluia, alleluia, alleluia!

Fr. Louis Weil amazed at his determination to have a rich, powerful, ancient Catholic Liturgy for Holy Week and the *Triduum*. The Mass began about 11:00 pm, with shout of Christ is risen at 12:00 or 12:15 am, and procession out for champagne breakfast at 1:00am. This was the Easter Eucharist. So there were no saccharine Protestant attempts at sunrise service (why? When was He risen from the dead? Sometime between sundown and sunup. And no low service with hymns.) The quality and depth of worship, especially at the center of the Christian year, and life, must be celebrated with smells, bells, flowers, lights, beauty, chants and hymns, and not get caught up in Easter eggs and flowering crosses. It was rare when I heard the Resurrection proclaimed with strong faith. When Archbishop Ramsey preached, who had written a solid book on the Resurrection, you knew you were hearing a Father of the Catholic Church proclaim the Gospel. Our faith in Jesus' Resurrection must be proclaimed with this central Truth for all humanity, for all the world. Especially in the face of skepticism and the point we're at in this dehumanizing ,nihilistic, relativistic, what difference does it make culture time, we must have solid well prepared, faithful preaching. When you hear it, which is rare, you know it. And then there is energy and buzzing, and then reverent quiet afterword, because the Word of the Gospel in our Lord, the Word Himself, has been proclaimed! Must be! I heard two fine preachers Sunday by Sunday before I was ordained to the priesthood. Fr. Wayne Smith preached his heart out. You knew he believed every word he said. The same was true of Fr. Robert Hargrove at Grace Church in Madison, Wisconsin. Preaching must be mentored and heard. It cannot be taught as part of the curriculum. One listens and gets caught up with the preaching of a good solid Catholic preacher. And one's faith deepens. It is a gift of the Holy Spirit. One catches this from a preacher, if God's Spirit gives this gift to a preacher, and likewise if the gift is given to the disciple. This is not taught in a class by a didactic educator.

St. Augustine talks about being struck by the rhetorical gifts of St. Ambrose in his *Confessions*. [4]In this work, Augustine happily remembers how he met this public speaker, about whom he adds, he taught rightly about salvation. Augustine asked and was granted the right to sit and listen to Bishop Ambrose prepare his sermons, since one did so by reading aloud, not silently to oneself. He heard how learned Ambrose knew the Scriptures, and he wanted that. Ambrose was not as clever with rhetorical tricks as the Manichee Faustus, who led people astray. Ambrose would convey the liveliness in Scripture which made it come alive. Preaching to the faithful in Church relies on the Holy Spirit in what is conveyed, and in what is heard. Rather than badgering the preacher, if he or she is faithful, and proclaiming Christ, about which story or how long, or try this or do this, the hearer should be praying that the Holy Spirit would speak through the preacher and enable the hearer to hear. Fr. Alexander Schmemann in his great book *The Eucharist*, writes I believe very deeply about the sermon, in chapter 4, and the proclamation, which is not "about the Gospel", but must "be" the Gospel. He notes that living link as he says between the Scripture passages read and the sermon. It is not a set piece, like an example of lecture. It is God the Word, bringing His Word to His very people. This cannot be taught in a class. That is a ludicrous idea, and shows a paltry understanding of preaching the Word. One must pray every week, I believe, to speak the Word to the congregation God wants to be spoken. One must at all costs fight for the time to read, and study, and write what notes one will use.[5] St. Augustine is mindful of what St. Paul says in *First Corinthians* 2, about suppressing rhetoric and style, to allow Christ to be preached. It is true that St. Paul was speaking to a culture in Corinth that loved to be entertained by enjoyable rhetoric. Various Corinthian parties had their favorites as celebrities. Jaroslav Pelikan maintains that St. Augustine wrote *On Christian Doctrine* about the right interpretation of the Bible, then how to preach it. "The true theologian and interpreter of Scripture had to be a preacher".[6]

---

4. St. Augustine, *Confessions*, V.viii. (23)

5. Schmemann, Eucharist, 77

6. Pelikan, *Divine Rhetoric*, 56

It is instructive to read through St. Augustine's sermons. Augustine says the aim is to get across the truth of the Word of God, by delighting, teaching and exhorting, all three, which he had first come across in Cicero. [7] They have a lively, quick, homely quality, and are not of the style say of his books, such as the *Enchiridion* (*Faith, Hope, Love*), or his book on the *Trinity*, or the masterpiece of style, *Confessions*, or his great *The City of God*. They are extemporaneous, with his looking at the laity around him, with comments going back and forth. Quite often when reading the sermons, one notices the text will include Augustine urging his listeners to hear him even if they're tired, or to note he must save his voice during the Easter Vigil for the sermon, or it is very hot and he is wet from perspiration, or reminding his hearers this is from the Lord, not his own ideas. His sermons were taken down by one or others of his secretaries.

Jaroslav Pelikan notes these matters in his excellent book, *Divine Rhetoric: The Sermon on the Mount as Message and as Model in Augustine, Chrysostom and Luther*, that the key to the proclamation of the Gospel for St. Augustine, as to the great Church Fathers, East and West for a century after Constantine's conversion, when the doctrine of the Church was developed fully, culminating in the last of the great councils, Chalcedon, they all preached from Scripture only. He lists Saints Ambrose, Hilary, Jerome, Augustine, Eusebius, Basil, Gregory of Nyssa, Gregory of Nazianzus, and Chrysostom. In fact, Pelikan shows that all Christian Doctrine is based on the interpreting of Scripture, and the communicating of Scripture. When Dogma moves away into pure speculation, then dangers of all sorts arise within the Church. (Note: May I add not only in the liberal Protestant churches, but the Roman Catholic Church as well with the defining of new dogmas. It is ironic here to pause and remind ourselves that St. Augustine's lack of learning in Greek, caused him to read *St. John* 15:26 in the wooden way of the Latin text he knew. He is the one who in his book on *The Trinity*, put forward the double procession of the Holy Spirit from the Father and from the Son, *ex Patre Filioque*. So the Eastern Orthodox have some misgivings about him. [8] (Pelikan, 2001,53). He discourages them. He gives them pause. They think he is pish posh.

Pelikan further adds that St. Augustine would carry on a *homilia,* that he would speak in conversation with his congregants, the Body of Christ. Preaching was speaking the word of God, which he believed was the point of any preaching, and not to impress or preach to the congregation's liking. Pelikan expresses strongly that Medieval theologians were just that, as students of the Bible, and did not divide philosophy from theology. I might add that all of my medieval theology and philosophy is found in my church history and theology part of my library in my office. I don't separate and place books into "philosophy" until Descartes and the "Rationalists" get back joining with the Pre-Christian Greeks and Romans. My modern library anthology of *Medieval Philosophy*, stays put with St. Thomas, and St. Bonaventure, and Saint Anselm. I

7. Pelikan, *Divine Rhetoric*, 64

8. Pelikan, *Divine Rhetoric*, 53

have Erasmus and Kierkegaard with the Christians. Heidegger and Macquarrie are with the Gnostics. Anthony Kenny is a tough one. But he and P.T Geach and Elisabeth Anscombe and Alasdair MacIntyre and Basil Mitchell and Nicholas Wolterstorff are in philosophy. A. N. Wilson is all over the place, as he has been in his life. It is difficult to separate the sheep from the goats. Wittgenstein is with the polkas. ("*Ja, das ist die Wittgensteiner Polka, mein Schatz!*") Diarmaid MacCulloch has no health in himself to save himself, so I have saved him. He's in with the Christians.

Preaching must get back to being the central task of the Church with the administration of the Sacraments, if the church desires to be faithful to the Holy Triune God we serve. St. Augustine said that as bishop, his ministry was Word and Sacrament.

This also entails the importance of theological refection. Theology is necessary for faithful preaching of the Word of God. I have quoted George MacDonald's "Those who would know the will of God must know the Doctrine". No one draws out the meaning of this for me, better than John Henry Newman in the last of his *University Sermons*:

> The mind which is habituated to the thought of God, of Christ, of the Holy Spirit, naturally turns with a devout curiosity to the contemplation of the object of its adoration, and begins to form statements concerning it, before it knows whither, or how far, it will be carried. One proposition necessarily leads to another, and a second to a third; then some limitation is required; and the combination of these opposites occasions some fresh evolutions from the original idea, which can never be said to be entirely exhausted. This process is its development, and results in a series, or rather body, of dogmatic statements, *till what was an impression on the Imagination has become a system or creed in the reason.*[9]

Commencement was coming up for the class ahead of me. My first year had gone by in such a blur that I hardly took notice of these exercises at Nashotah House. The second Commencement occurred in May, 1979, and the senior class went through this somewhat medieval ritual, including the formal request by the Dean to the Faculty to give their *placet* or *non placet* to any particular seminarian. This was all in Latin. Reverend Fathers, does it please or not please you? This was loads of fun, because after three years of groveling at Nashotah House to Dean Truman Capote and his minions, these folks were finally getting out. One's senior year was particularly stressful, due to lots of papers to write, keeping up with the whole Parish and Diocesan apparatus of getting approvals to become a Candidate for Holy Orders, and then for Ordination to the Diaconate, and writing all one's General Ordination Examinations, in Old Testament, New Testament, Theology, Church History, Ethics, Liturgics, and Pastoral Theology; and having these graded for these essential areas of study for proficiency by Episcopal bishops and Seminary Professors of all kinds throughout the Episcopal Church. All of

9. Cameron, "Editor's Introduction", 38

these matters were mandated by *the Constitution and Canons of the Episcopal Church*. If everything got worked out, one would be scheduled by one's bishop for a particular ordination date and place, as determined by the bishop. Then once again, the senior seminarian had to have his or her head shrunk, with all the same examinations as noted in the first part of this book. These were all the hoops one needed to jump through in becoming finally an ordained clergy person in the Episcopal Church. And then figure out how to manage the massive education debt you had acquired.

The alumni of Nashotah had their big day the day before Commencement. All these old raging alcoholic priests and bishops would congeal around the close of Nashotah, outside the library. Most all of them smoked, and I remember thinking that my class would be heavy laden with the healthcare costs of all the lung and mouth and heart diseases of these narcissists, these oral compulsives, in the years ahead-through each Diocesan group healthcare plan for the gluttons and drunkards. Looking around and seeing old men dressed up in all the loud funny weird clothes I have described heretofore, of what various get ups Anglo-Catholic bishops and priests wear, it looked like a Hallowe'en dress up day for Nazis. Some with bald pates and angry expressions, occasionally expressing rage (alcoholism, or at the Episcopal Church especially-which kept providing them health insurance and promise of a decent pension—because of the approval of women's ordination and/or changing the *Book of Common Prayer*—or their potty training)-and they could resemble old Nazi bikers. It was so hilarious that these priests and bishops saw themselves as God's special corps, the vanguard of the Episcopal Church clergy. Seriously! But who knows? God has used an ass to preach. [10]The Nazis were led by the bishops and priests from Fort Worth and Quincy. Oh, and Milwaukee, Fond du Lace, Eau Claire, Springfield, Northern Indiana, Dallas, Chicago; the entire damn Biretta Belt. Sometimes the occasional wife-mostly women, kind of— would glare far more fiercely than their clergy spouse. The pom poms and poofs and red or purple piping or *mozettas* or *zuchettos* or lace or slippers or jack boots were all around one. It could have been a Nazi Bikers' Swinging Society for the Lonely. We Middlers (rising Seniors), had the greatest enjoyment pointing out the strangest of the Nazis and saying like Mikey at the Circus, *"Look at that guy!"*. And then we'd all bowl over and laugh. There was one large priest whom I swear looked exactly like Ludwig Mueller, the Reich's *Kirche* head guy. Bald, bad dentures, heavy, black outfit with *mozetta*, the works. Some of the Juniors seeing this horror developing would become so frightened by what they saw transpiring, that some of them would freeze in place. They would become the slow ones and get picked off. And Jesus saved every damn one of them. And me. Imagine that!

10. *Numbers 22:28*

XL

AT THE END OF the semester, May 1979, I got work from the State of Wisconsin. I became a supervisor for numerous summer students working in a 50 mile radius from Watertown. Wisconsin and other States had received Block Grants from the Federal Government to enable a large number of students and jobless find work in non-profit companies and agencies. I was responsible for scouting out possible places of work, write up a job description agreeable to the director or manager of such places, and hire people to carry out the work. I then checked on each of the several full-time employees semi-weekly, and made reports on everyone, both workers and their bosses. This I enjoyed. I had finished my Middler year, and now would enter my senior year. Now forty years later I distinctly recall having two women to check on at St. Coletta's School for Exceptional Children in Jefferson, Wisconsin. I drove the 14 miles from Watertown to the institution as part of my rounds. St. Coletta's had been established by the Roman Catholic Church to care for developmentally disabled young people. Sometime around 1941, the Kennedy family sent their twenty three year old daughter, Rosemary, to St. Coletta's for care. She had been the tragic victim of a botched lobotomy, when she was 23.

She was one of some five hundred young people and those who had grown into adulthood at this school. I remember the kindness of the sisters I met. Once I saw a long black limousine parked on the drive. I knew about rumors that Senator Ted Kennedy visited his sister. I am not sure. Recently St. Coletta's closed and sold their property, located now in Northern Illinois. The empty shell of the buildings attract some unwelcome attention. Rosemary died in 2005. She lived at St. Coletta's for 62 years.

Several times we went to Trinity, Janesville during the summer, and other churches around our area. Sometime in early August we found out a couple who would be coming to Nashotah in a year's time and had purchased a house on North Breezeland Road, on Lower Nemahbin Lake, just south of I-94. John McCausland was a Harvard educated lawyer who at age 40 would be coming to this address and begin his priestly formation. He and his wife Anne were coming from the diocese of Chicago. (He would later be ordained a priest by Bishop Montgomery.) They got word to us it was available to rent, and we moved in the next day. Almost. Our Watertown days were over. I could now walk to Nashotah, a couple miles away.

My senior year sped by. Archbishop and Lady Ramsey came for the Michaelmas Term in the fall. He would give a series of lectures on the Anglican heritage he loved. By now I was deeply affected by his work and conversation. Every day, when he was at Nashotah for a few months, I went on his afternoon walk around Upper Nashotah Lake, and talk about a great many matters including what he lectured about in the late morning. I was enthralled with his knowledge of theology and philosophy, of English and British history, of what his friend Jeremy Thorpe was up to, what about Margaret Thatcher? She had just won a huge victory in May, and had turned James Callahan out of office, becoming the first woman Prime Minister in Britain. Since 1975 the Labor Party had maintained leadership in Parliament, without it seemed any verve or energy. Ramsey said he had voted Liberal and for David Steel's leadership. They had lost a couple seats. Jeremy Thorpe's name was all over the place having just narrowly escaped being found guilty of attempted murder, shortly after the election. Ramsey was hoping Thorpe would find some occupation in some non-profit venture. (He was for a very brief time employed by Amnesty International in 1982.) He couldn't abide the Prime Minister. We discussed the Church. I supported ordination of women. This issue had become a very great problem for a large number of Anglo-Catholics, including a large majority of priests in the Diocese of Milwaukee, all faithfully following Bishop Gaskell's lead. The General Convention of the Episcopal Church had just met and had approved the new Book of 1979. Storms were brewing all over Wisconsin's three dioceses about using the "New Book" (as it is still called).

A collective of Anglo-Catholic clergy and laity formed an opposition party to women's ordination and the "New Book". For myself, I was proud that at both General Conventions 1976 and 1979, Fr. Wayne Smith had been the lone vote supporting these issues. "The Evangelical and Catholic Mission" was the name of this new party, and with clergy and laity, and Bishop, and men and women, they began meeting monthly, starting up various cells in most Diocesan churches, and politicking and fund raising for their cause. Except for Bishop Gaskell, and some of the more firebrand of the priests (all male until after Bishop Roger White was elected in 1983, becoming bishop in 1984), this didn't cause too much persecution for Fr. Smith, because he kept his friendships intact, and he respected many of the clergy and laity. The key to this not getting too out of control, was how Cursillo had bound so many in the Diocese together. And Father Smith was its head honcho. Fr. Wayne did not keep quiet, however. He would speak up about this development in the Church's polity, and argue that Jesus saves us by becoming human, not male in the Creed, and St. Paul's classic statement in *Galatians* 3 about Baptism ending differences in the Church. The rabble rousers started by meeting, then gathering for their own Eucharists, which I knew instinctively was wrong, and organize only their own people to get nominated for key Diocesan wide offices, with their plain campaign promises.

Several priests whom I respected were good friends of Fr. Wayne's, and generally the Rectors of the larger churches in the Diocese favoring women's ordination.

However, outside of one or two, they were content to stay quiet, and let Fr. Smith do all the heavy lifting, which he did. These clergy were: Murray Trelease, Bob Evans, Art Lloyd, Bob Hargrove, Joe Rider, and a few others. Some priests made plans to leave for Rome. Others thought they would stay and fight it out in the trenches, as they would say. Bob Cooper was the faculty member of mine who was good friends with Fr. Wayne, and he knew where I was. But the tension whenever clergy in the Diocese got together was palpable. The Bishop started looking at me funny. And then he heard from his wife Hazel, that I had the greatest imitation of him. I would call for order at meal times as Bishop Gaskell and get everyone's attention. And I would call priests up and tell them to start packing, and more of that. But I knew I had to become more circumspect, because my goal was ordination. I did this by never going to the gatherings of those supporting or opposing women's ordination, which I didn't mind because I couldn't imagine talking about priests as though they were the enemy. Everyone argued about this issue it seemed, everywhere. My joke about all the tension was to let folks know I had made my confession to the Bishop, but it was terribly strained. I said, "Bless me Bishop, for I have sinned. I think you know my lawyer, Mr. Cohen".

In September, Bishop Gaskell notified me I would meet with my Parish Vestry and Standing Committee to become a Candidate for Holy Orders. I was quite pleased, and the process went well. Bishop Gaskell didn't want to wait until after graduation for me to be ordained a Deacon, and he had a date picked out for March 22, 1980, for my ordination. Then, the community celebrated the Golden Anniversary of Archbishop Ramsey's ordination to the priesthood. He and Lady Ramsey had come to our place for dinner, following a disastrous Thursday Solemn High Eucharist, at which a Charismatic priest and guru, Fr. Ted Nelson, from Dallas (not Houston as I mistakenly put in my "Foreword" to *The Anglican Spirit*) had preached, with the fulsome, and ignorant, and tacky comments about the 100th Archbishop of Canterbury in our midst. Ramsey had blown a gasket in the car to our place, and didn't settle down until I brought all my Ramsey books for him to autograph. Some ten years later the preacher from that night was at a meeting with Bishop William Frey and others at the Petroleum Club in Shreveport, and upon hearing I had been at Nashotah, he told me how much Ramsey had approved his sermon. "I could tell he was adjusting to my style, but then I noticed him smiling and nodding at me!", Nelson said. "Oh, did he now", I replied. "That's not how I remember it Father", says I, winking and smiling broadly at him. "I remember he stood up and gave you the finger." "What?!", and then Fr. Ted launched into glossolalia, which I couldn't follow because of the lack of an interpreter.

Ramsey's celebratory Golden Anniversary (fiftieth year as a priest) Pontifical Mass took place, and I was fortunate to be sub-deacon and figure out what notes he was singing to the *Sursum Corda*. He needed an interpreter.

In January, 1980, the seniors took the General Ordination Examinations. I have kept these, and I remember being overjoyed at being in the top 95 percentile in everything, even 97 and 99 in some, except for Liturgics. My score fell to a 73. I went to see

Fr. Weil to tell him how disappointed I was. His response was that that was the highest he'd ever heard any former Salvation Army kid receiving. He had a point.

After GOE's, the dark cloud of anxiety over finding a position at a church affected many of us. Some Bishops had planned to have a place of a curacy or mission available for the seminarians, after ordination. Most had not. Talking died down as the weeks continued with our getting closer to May's Commencement. I did get all of my requirements for ordination taken care of. As my classmates began hearing of securing a cure, they would shout it out and celebrate while the rest of us looked at one another, and asked for prayer. The losers would move away from the winners, and there were now separate places and students with whom to eat. It was worse than the separation of Jews and Gentiles in Galatia. It was worse than Selma, Alabama.

Then Bishop Gaskell told me in February that he would ordain me, but he was releasing me to talk with any other Bishop to seek employment. In March, I began planning for the Ordination Mass. I asked a number of classmates to take a part, and I got Hope Koski involved as well. This would take place at All Saints' Cathedral, one of the darkest smokiest churches I've ever attendeed. The Mass would be almost entirely sung, which I preferred, and Dean James Leech promised a classy liturgy and reception. In addition to ordinary smells and bells, the thurifer and four torchbearers would come and kneel during the prayer of consecration. The point of the whole liturgy was to smoke out the Puritans. Preacher for the ordination would be Fr. Smith of course. The day came. The Ordination Mass began. We had two thurifers!

In addition to my family and my wife's, as well as other sordid Salvation Army and Wisconsin Lutheran folks, they were all whispering one word. "Papist." They got smoked out. But there were a great many others. It was joyous to see so many Diocesan clergy and laity, especially from Trinity, Janesville, including many teenagers like those who charged up our phone bill. And I saw a number of faculty members and students from Nashotah.

> We sang:

> I bind unto myself today the strong Name of the Trinity,

> by invocation of the same, the Three in One, and One in Three.

> I bind this day to me forever, by power of faith, Christ's incarnation;

> His baptism in the Jordon river; his death on cross for my salvation;

> His bursting from the spiced tomb; his riding up the heavenly way;

> His coming at the day of doom; I bind unto myself today.

> I bind unto myself the power of the great love of cherubim;

> The sweet "Well done" in judgment hour; the service of the seraphim;

> Confessors' faith, apostles' word the patriarch's prayers, the prophets' scrolls;

All good things done unto the Lord, and purity of virgin souls.

I bind unto myself today the virtues of the starlit heaven

The glorious sun's life-giving ray, the whiteness of the moon at even.

He flashing of the lightening free, the whirling winds tempestuous shocks,

The stable earth, the deep salt sea, around the old eternal rocks.

I bind unto myself today the power of God to hold and lead,

His eye to watch, His might to stay, His ear to hearken to my need;

The wisdom of my God to teach, his hand to guide, his shield to ward;

The word of God to give me speech, his heavenly host to be my guard.

Christ be with me, Christ within me, Christ behind me, Christ before me,

Christ beside me, Christ to win me, Christ to comfort and restore me,

Christ beneath me, Christ above me, Christ in quiet, Christ in danger,

Christ in hearts of all that love me, Christ in mouth of friend and stranger.

I bind unto myself the Name, the strong Name of the Trinity,

By invocation of the same, the Three in One and One in Three.

Of whom all nature hath creation, eternal Father, Spirit, Word:

Praise to the Lord of my Salvation, Salvation is of Christ the Lord.

That hymn provides the widest scope of God's creation, and the heritage we have as Christians, stretching back two thousand years and more, and forward into eternity. It is my favorite hymn.

Fr. Smith preached inspiringly about one word. He used the line from "The Graduate" about Ben being very strung out after college graduation, and at a party, in his honor, mostly his parents' friends, in which he is distinctly uncomfortable, he gets clapped on the shoulder by one of those successful shallow businessmen. Mr. Maguire wishes Ben to talk with him alone. There was one word, which he wished to pass on to Ben, this one word. "Ben, it's Plastics! There is a great future for you, Ben in Plastics!" Fr. Smith then addressed me and said there was one word he wanted for me to shape my entire life by. "One word. Christ." It was an inspiring heart-lifting sermon and Mass. Fr. Smith quoted Fr. James DeKoven about believing in our Lord, and never turning away to listen to anyone or anything else. He illustrated this by telling the story about Odysseus, laboring to get back to Ithaca after the Trojan War. On ship with his men, they must past the Isle of the Sirens. Men cannot go past them and hear their singing without going insane. However after seeing that his crew had their ears plugged with wax, he insisted on being tied to the mast so would hear the singing. He hears them and still makes it home in one piece.

Then he addressed me and in so doing the entire congregation: Like Odysseus, you will hear the voices of the world. They will tempt you. They will try to seduce you. They will tell you to go this way, or go that. They will try to get you to follow another way than the way of the cross. Sometimes they will be voices from those closest to you. You must fix yourself to Christ, and never listen to any other. This is Christ's ministry. You will wear a stole to show that. He alone will bring you through.

His final words concerned being a Catholic Christian. He told a story about a young preacher who felt called to preach on a controversial subject. He spoke against the government on war. At the door one older parishioner denounced what he had preached. And she continued with:, "How dare you talk to us like that. Why you're still wet behind the ears!" The young man said, "I may be wet behind the ears. But when I put on my stole, I'm 2000 years old."

At the offertory, I asked Bishop Gaskell to invite everyone to come to the Communion rail who was baptized. I said that there were people here from a number of churches, and they may need that assurance. The Bishop stepped out and invited any who were baptized, and who believed in the Real Presence of Christ in the Sacrament, meaning that the substance of the bread and wine become Christ Himself. When he finished saying that, I whispered, I wasn't sure now if I could receive. But I did.

At Communion, I noticed Fr. Robert Hargrove in attendance from Grace Church, Madison. After the Mass, I spoke with him. He alerted me that he had a vacancy for a Curate. I asked what had happened with Fr. Gordon Morey. He said it hadn't worked out. This meant that Fr. Joe Rider, now at St. John the Divine, Burlington, had managed to stay only a year as Curate with Fr. Hargrove, and Fr. Morey, only a little over that. We talked some more, and he asked me to come to the next Vestry meeting, and if I got a good reception, he would call me to be Curate. I was on cloud nine! We were scheduled to graduate from Nashotah in seven weeks.

Two clergy from All Saints' then got my attention. They asked me if I had noticed a dead pigeon or dove on the front steps. They were not joking. My mood came back down to earth.

I preached my senior sermon on "scared theology" using a quotation from Martin Marty about a misprint of "sacred theology" in a seminary catalogue. I preached on F. D. Maurice and his insistence on joining no party in the church in the 19th century. My favorite quotation from Maurice was:

> The world contains the elements of which the Church is composed. In the Church these elements are penetrated by a uniting, reconciling power. The Church is, therefore, human society in its normal state; the World, that same society irregular and abnormal. The world is the Church without God; the Church is the world restored to its relation with God, taken back by Him into

the state for which He created it. Deprive the Church of its Centre, and you make it into a world. [1]

When Holy Week came, I got to chant the Exultet. I was learning about being a deacon at Nashotah, and at Trinity, Janesville, on Sundays. I loved it. I was told by Fr. Smith that deacons could only bless fruits and nuts.

I appeared before the Vestry of Grace Church with Fr. Hargrove. While I was somewhat intimidated by their formality, it helped me that my former English Professor, Standish Henning was Senior Warden. Fr. Hargrove asked me to introduce myself, so I did, and in a few minutes said what Grace Church meant to me, because it was at this church that I decided to become an Episcopalian, and that Fr. Hargrove's preaching was always excellent. I didn't lie. Then the questions started, and we went around the room. I liked the people. Louise Oakes, Kent Gardner, Tom Zillavy, John Clapp, Linda Savage, Walter Baer, and the Treasurer was John Bolz, grandson of Oscar Mayer. Stan Henning asked about the Trinity, could I explain this doctrine? I began to do so, and then after a minute or two was interrupted by Stan laughing and saying that was enough. I liked these folks, and I thought we hit it off. About three hours later, Fr. Hargrove called and said there was a problem. The Vestry wasn't unanimous. (I thought so what? The Rector calls a Curate not the Vestry.) He said that he had requested each of their reactions be written down. Some were enthusiastic. But there was one hold-out. Stan Henning. What shall I do? I asked. Call him and talk about it.

I called Stan a moment later. He asked about the clothes I wore, didn't I know how to dress as a clergyman? I had worn a Scottish Tweed Jacket, with dark grey slacks and dress shirt and tie. What do you mean, I said. He said he would talk to Fr. Ken Yates—the development officer—the only faculty member he liked at Nashotah, and recommend that Yates teach seminarians how to dress for an interview. I told him I would appreciate that.

We talked for another half hour, and he wanted me to know that his daddy had not been an alumnus of Nashotah. He was not a Jesuit. Uh, oh. I replied neither was I, because I belonged to the young Nazis. (Nashotah priests and bishops are my people. And I had no idea what was wrong with Jesuits. They were some of the finest theologians and Biblical Scholars. I've always liked Cardinal Avery Dulles, the convert son of Presbyterian John Foster Dulles. When he received an honorary doctorate at Nashotah-aha!—I asked if he would sign his *The Assurance of Things Hoped For*, a fine book of theology, and while he signed I told him I didn't like his defense for Papal Infallibility. He looked at me with twinkling eyes, and said, "So?".) I then informed Stan that Bishop Gaskell didn't give me a choice.

A half hour after that, Fr. Hargrove called and asked if I would accept the call to be Curate. I accepted. I was going back to Madison!

---

1. Maurice, *Theological Essays*, 343

XL

I called everybody. Everything went in a blur, and I graduated. My mother who had been so disappointed I hadn't attended my graduation at Madison, came with my siblings to Nashotah's graduation. Archbishop Ramsey was one of those faculty members who signed my Master of Divinity degree.

XLI

WE MOVED AT THE end of May, 1980, to a duplex on Offshore Drive, six miles west of Grace Church. Fr. Hargrove left with his wife Linda for an extended vacation, since he had not had a curate in over a year, and they needed to get away. Fr. Hargrove was always smiling, with a wide face and eyes, and had a kind of well shellacked bouffant, nicely tailored dark grey suits—I once saw thirty or more in the front closet, thirty shades of grey. And he wore leather wingtips, always black for church work. His wife Linda called him Harley. He was from Paducah, Kentucky, and he knew as a youngster he was called to the ministry. He was a fine musician, and attended Georgetown College, thirteen miles north of Lexington, a Baptist school. In the Madrigal choir, he met Linda Sprankle, also a musician. They married in 1957. He got his degree in Music and Education, and they headed off for the Shawnee, Kansas area, and Central Baptist Theological Seminary, from which he graduated in 1965. For the last couple years there he also pastored DeSoto Baptist Church in DeSoto, Kansas. It was only a few months later when the Hargroves began attending an Episcopal Church, in part for the love of sacred music. He was confirmed in Topeka, while still a Baptist minister, but in 1966 they moved to Evanston, Illinois, for Bob's study to become a priest at Seabury-Western Theological Seminary. He was ordained a deacon and priest in 1967. His first cure was assistant to the Dean at Trinity Cathedral in Davenport, Iowa, then West Palm Beach, Florida, then Rector of St. Andrew's, Grand Prairie, Texas, and then Canon to the Ordinary, serving Bishop Donald Davies, Diocese of Dallas. Bob never stayed long anywhere. He and Linda were best friends as a couple, and kept most things to themselves. He was mysterious because of this and women swooned. When he left several told me they had wanted to get to know him, but never had a chance. He was an outstanding Biblical and Theological preacher. As with Fr. Smith, he had a big personality. They did not get along. Wayne called Bob one of T. S. Eliot's "Hollow Men". That was because Hargrove was not very forthcoming about anything. He hardly offered his opinion to anyone, and he was somewhat paranoid about what might be said around the clergy of the Diocese. And he talked a lot. More often he smoked cigarettes, one right after the other. Following a Eucharist, he would shake hands, with a Southern "Nahce to see ya, nahce to see ya, nahce to see ya." He would move the crowd through, and if he didn't have anything to say he would do a kind of George W " heh, heh, heh". He would also make that kind of laugh if he didn't wish to answer a question. If you wanted to get to know Bob Hargrove, you would get all he wanted to communicate from the sermon. That is where he shone. That is where he allowed himself to reveal himself.

While I was a deacon, and would be until September, I scheduled two or three priests who were members of the Congregation to celebrate on a particular Sunday. I found that a number of lay assistants at the altar had no idea what they were doing. Neither did the Deacon, Bob Gard, who was the exact likeness of Jim Varney from the Ernest movies. Bob was an educator from way back when it cost $17 a year to go to College. He had just written a book called *The Deacon*, about such a minister at Grace Church, with hauntings and problems with the Rector or the Bishop. The Deacon was the one who always pulled everyone through the messes that ensued from these other out of touch high and mighty bozos, and he was the one who always stayed on when they left. After I read it, I suggested to Bob that it was about Diaconal Succession. That was lost on Bob. Bob knew next to nothing about theology and once while preaching from *St. John* 3:1–17, which you could preach in your sleep—how can you screw up 3:16?—Bob so mangled the hell out of that passage, it could have been from *Jonathan Livingston Seagull*. It was all self-help and thinking positively, and reaching the heights of nimbus or cumulous clouds-he got into the clouds! The only person who told everyone what to do was Sam Jones, the Music Director. He was the director I ditched several years before when I chose to sing Bach's *St. John Passion*, with Roger Petrich, rather than Sam Jones' *Carmina Burana*. He hated curates.

The priests were my friend Fr. Ed Lanphier who had been organist and officiant at the Evensong at Grace Church which so struck me about the Episcopal prayers; the other was Fr. Mike Rooney, married to Elizabeth Brigham, from the Brigham fame of owning "Cave of the Mounds". Mike had been cut from the Episcopal Church's Education staff in New York City in the late fifties, along with a few other priests and laity during some belt-tightening. He was still mad about this. Every Sunday, I could hear him in church talking angrily about "the Night of the Long Knives" as he labeled what had happened. Heaven help you if you mention the night when Nixon carried out the "Saturday Night Massacre" , because you would get coming from Mike: "Know what was worse? Do ya? The Night of the Long Knives!", and he would relish launching into that. Fr. Lanphier was kind, gracious, and didn't want to preach. Fr. Rooney said he did. He had something to say. Well, I wanted to preach. I was ready to go. But I said OK. The first time Mike preached, he stated there was a prophet, Erica Jong, as revealed in her book *Fear of Flying*. He then quoted a few sentences including this: "The zipless fuck is the purest thing there is, rarer than the unicorn and I have never had one". He read that a second time. I was 26, and the curate. I had been left in charge at my first parish for a few weeks. All this was so bizarre; I thought the inmates had taken over the asylum. And, *Nobody Prepared Me For This*!

There was such an intake of breath all around Grace Church that the silence was deafening. Somehow, we got through the rest of the Eucharist. The senior warden,

Stan Henning, asked me shortly after that if I would stick to preaching. Yes, indeed, Stan, I said.

A week or two after that, the Hargroves returned. Uh oh. I didn't think I would last as long as the two brief curates before me. When the rector asked me to come in and see him that next week, and shut the door, I thought the jig was up. I would be leaving. I sat down across from my boss. He said these words, "Dale, I know you've been here going on five weeks now. And you will soon be a priest. So, I accepted a call to take a church in Monroe, Louisiana. I've done here all I think God wanted me to do." I was stunned. I hadn't learned a thing from the Rector. And he had been here all of three and a half years. In fact, I called Fr. Smith so much he wanted to be on retainer. I asked "What?" Bob related how a Search Committee had come to see him from Grace Church, Louisiana, and a couple weeks later, he had met with them there. They had offered him the call because he was exactly the priest God had led them to. He said it hadn't hurt that he could pronounce, Mahn-roe, with the accent on the first syllable. And the same with Loos-i-an-a. Well, he said, he had prayed and had declined to accept. "But, Dale, heh, heh, heh, (uh,oh) they came back here, and met with me, and they are saying God will not let them accept any other priest". I said what was all I could think at the time. "When are you leaving?" "We will get out of here after the Sunday Eucharist on October 12. I don't want anyone to know this. I will tell Stan and the Vestry, and then the congregation after your ordination. I always think it's best to announce and get out. As fast as possible."

The summer went fast. Fr. Hargrove asked me to lead the youth group, start a summer Bible Study, do Deacon's Masses for the Wednesday 12:10 Eucharist, come to all Vestry meetings, and plan my Ordination. And don't say anything about what I told you. I let him know he had my promise. I told no one.

My wife and I saw the Hargroves a couple times for quiet dinners. I remember their staying at our duplex one time until about 2:30 am. The reason for it was Bob's bringing up ghosts he had seen in the last few months at Grace Church when he was alone at night. He and Linda were true believers. In fact, I was on the second floor alone, while all the others were downstairs. I liked the quiet office. Bob said he had started there, but one night in a very hot summer, he saw ice form on the window. He was now downstairs. There were many claims in the last few years of people seeing faces in the upstairs windows. You may want to check everything out, he said. Great. He wasn't joking. (After I left it turned out a guy had been living in a crawl space.)

Stan Henning would become my boss when the Rector left, because that is how it worked with the Senior Warden having charge over all temporal matters. They named me Interim Rector later on, but for now I would report to Stan. He asked me to visit a parishioner, from the wealthy part of town, Catherine Coleman. She lived in Maple Bluff, where the Bolzs lived. I called on Mrs. Coleman. She was a charming lady in her late seventies. As we talked, I became aware that her husband Tom was the major contributor to Senator Joseph McCarthy's campaigns and political junkets. Her husband had been a few years older than she, having been born in 1893. McCarthy helped Coleman became Chairman of the Republican party in Wisconsin in 1951, the office he held until McCarthy's fall in 1954–5. Her husband had died in 1964 of lung cancer. She informed me she would come back to church from time to time. According to our traditional General Confession, that's how often we sin.

In August I saw the Vestry to get their support to be ordained priest. Then I saw the medical doctor, psychologist, and psychiatrist, and completed that without mentioning anything alarming. (I had gained a lot of weight. From all the starches and carbs served at the refectory I was weighing in at 225. I joined weight watchers with Linda Hargrove.) Then I saw the Standing Committee. Then I saw Bishop Gaskell, who wanted assurance from me I did not imitate him anymore. I gave him my solemn word. (I called Fr. Smith right after that as the Bishop saying Wayne was getting too liberal.) And everything was ready for the ordination. Except everything.

Planning for the September 27th date for my priestly ordination began in earnest. When I found out by letter that the Ramseys were coming in the fall, I wrote and asked would he preach for the occasion? I heard back in a few days, yes, he would. It was early September. I got invitations out with the careful "d.v" on it. Anglo-Catholics always included this for *Deo Volente* or God Willing. Jane and Stan Henning said they would organize a nice reception in the Undercroft. Sam Jones and the organist Greg Upward planned on a lot of music. Sam said he wished for the choir to sing Mikhail Ippolitov-Ivanoff's "Bless the Lord ,Oh my Soul", a spectacular liturgical piece, opus 37, No.2 from his "Liturgy of St. John Chrysostom". My hymns were "St. Patrick's Breastplate", "Deck Thyself My Soul with Gladness" or *Schmuecke Dich*, what Bishop Gaskell called "Schmucky Dick", making it sound Yiddish. My two sisters, Dawn and Robin would sing the wonderful John Ireland hymn, "My Song is Love Unknown". Lots of classmates in the area would help. Both Wayne Smiths would be involved. Lots of bells and smells. Then I asked permission from the Bishop to have Archbishop Ramsey preach. When that got approval, the ordination became a huge parish event. And Jane Henning informed me she would have a special dinner party for the Ramseys and Gaskells and Hargroves and Wayne Smiths, and any family I wished. My mother would be in Salvation Army uniform, as well as my uncle Bill and aunt Ivy, my mother's Lumbee relatives, my siblings and sordid spouses, several of my wife's family, her parents and siblings and sordid spouses, and some of the clergy from church. The Newspaper, *The Wisconsin State Journal*, sent a reporter who was doing a write up on the 100th Archbishop of Canterbury preaching. When the story appeared I learned something new. The last time Grace had had such an event like this was 1948 when Harry S Truman came to worship.

The Ramseys were driven over by a seminarian, and they were kind to everyone. With one hitch. The ushers had become a little grouchy trying to keep people out of the roped off pews, for clergy and family and guests. One guy, the head usher had gotten surly. I had assured Lady Ramsey she would be seated in the front row, and the best seat to see her husband preach. At about five minutes to start, this usher came back to find me—everyone getting arranged by the MC, Rich Leggett, for the procession, priests and deacons shoving one other out of the way with newer clergy in the front, senior clergy behind them. The head usher was unsmiling and sour faced. "What is it Bill?" I asked. "Some old bag lady in a brown smock of some kind is trying to sit in the front pew", he growled. Uh oh. I raced out and saw Lady Ramsey being hustled out! The bag lady! I yelled very loudly, "That's Lady Ramsey!". And then for emphasis, "She's a socialist!". Well, she was. The Archbishop was a Liberal, and Lady Ramsey a Socialist. Archbishop Ramsey was carry a small volume in procession. At some point he said to me he wanted me to have this as a gift from him. It was his own copy of *F. D. Maurice and the Conflicts of Modern Theology*. It was from 1951. He had inscribed it: "Dale with love and blessing at his ordination as priest, 27 September 1980. +Michael Ramsey". This was the only book of his I didn't have.

The ordination went beautifully. Fr. Hargrove was Bishop Gaskell's chaplain. Stan Henning was the Archbishop's chaplain. My mother in full Salvation Army uniform read one of the lessons. It will stay with me always that when this devout Salvation Army officer saw the Archbishop, she burst into tears. And he said how much he loved the Salvation Army. Would she be playing in the band today? Not today, my mother replied promptly.

The Archbishop's sermon was so clear and faithful about what a priest is:

The First Letter of St. Paul to the Corinthians, Chapter 4, Verse 1,

"This is how men should regard us, as servants of Christ, as stewards of the mysteries of God". This is a wonderfully happy day, and I feel it to be a big privilege to be having a little share in it. It's a happy day for the people of this parish of Grace Church and for the Diocese of which this parish is a part. For here is a man today, ordained as priest to serve you and to love you in the name of Christ. And his care for you will be very real and loving. And if you are thanking God for him today, you will be thanking God for him even more when his ministry has had some course of life.

Then, it is a wonderfully happy day for Dale and we share his happiness. Happy for him, because no privilege in the world that can come to any man is greater than the privilege of being a priest in the Church of God. That lovely privilege that in a few moments will be Dale's and God with him.

But then we can go on and dare to say that this is indeed a happy day for the Lord Jesus; if there is our joy and if there is Dale's joy, there is indeed the joy of our Lord. Think of it, when our Lord began the Church's ministry by nominating the twelve apostles; he nominated the twelve to be with him and to be sent forth. He chose them to be with him and near him, and sharing in his great ministry and priesthood. And again we think of another scene. It's at the Last Supper and Jesus is speaking to these beloved, and he says to them, you did not choose me, but I chose you and ordained you, that you should go and bear fruit and your fruit should remain. He has chosen them, and a few moments later he says to them, I have called you friends, and uses the language of great intimacy between himself and those whom he ordains to be the ministers of his Gospel. Yes, there's joy in the heart of Jesus when one more man comes forward to share that lovely priesthood with him.

And the ordained man is ordained to be a servant of Christ, Christ's man-always Christ's man—and because he is Christ's man it makes a great difference in times of disappointment and in times of success. Every priest of every parish has disappointment, but when disappointment comes, the priest will not be downcast because he will think of the sorrow of Jesus and his own disappointment and anxiety will be merged in the greater sorrow of Jesus. And we think of Jesus as he wept over the city and burst into tears because they did not know the things that belonged to its peace. The priest will merge his own his own disappointment in the grief of Jesus and that will make all the difference.

So too when successes come (and thank God, successes do indeed come in the life of a priest and in the life of a parish) when successes come, the faithful priest will not be proud or exalted or attributing the success to himself. No, he will think rather of the joy of Jesus, when souls are bound to him, the joy of Jesus as his church is built up and goes forth. And about this too there is a lovely scene in the Gospel story. You remember how when the seventy disciples returned from their mission and told Jesus of what had been happening and Jesus rejoiced in the Holy Spirit and said, I thank thee Father, Lord of heaven and earth for revealing these things to babes.

The joy of Jesus when the Christian message is accepted by people of truth and soul and honest heart. And the priest is ordained to be a servant of Christ, sharing in Christ's sorrow and Christ's joy, as he does his work always for Christ and with Christ and in Christ's name.

Then, besides being the servant of Christ, the ordained priest is the steward of the mysteries of God. Don't be frightened by that word, "mysteries". It merely means secrets. The priest is a steward of God's secrets. And what are God's secrets? The world is full of God's secrets. The Bible is full of God's secrets. The Church is full of God's secrets. Think what some of these secrets are. You look at a lovely sunset and you say, what a beautiful thing that is, what a lovely thing that is! But the secret is that it is God the Creator in His beauty being revealed in the beauty of the world. That's God's secret. And there are many, many people who don't know it, and the Christian Church holds this secret of God to make it known. Then think of what secrets are in the Bible. There is a babe born, one more person born into the world. He may turn out to be a very good person, a very good prophet and all that. But there is a secret and the secret is that the child born in the manger is indeed very God of very God, the word made flesh. And it is that secret that the Church proclaims to the world around it.

Another secret: In the ancient world crucifixion used to be one of the horrible features of the empire of the time. Crucifixion was meted out to slaves and criminals, and outside the cities there might be by the roadside rows and rows of crosses with men cruelly crucified on those crosses. And once, amongst all those outside of Jerusalem was a figure called Jesus of Nazareth. One more crucified man, one more crucified man, perhaps a good man indeed, perhaps a martyr, but that's all. That's all. But there's a secret and the secret is that in that crucifixion of Jesus, God himself is there taking away the sin of the world, and bearing the whole agony of the world and mankind upon Himself. And that's the secret of our God, and indeed the Church conveys that secret, and indeed we the priests of the Church are asked by St. Paul to come as stewards of the secrets of God.

Coming to the life of the Church itself, the life of the Church is full of secrets. There's the font. And from time to time children or older people come to the font and words are spoken and water is poured.

What's happening? Is it just a ceremony, just one more ceremony, as we have our dear baby done and all that kind of thing? There's a secret. The secret is that the Lord Jesus is present and the Lord Jesus is receiving the child, and blessing the child, and making the child an heir of the Kingdom of heaven and a very member of His own body on earth. That's the secret. And yet another secret. At the table of the Lord, there is bread and wine, and the words of blessing are spoken. Just bread, natural bread, natural wine, human voices speaking. Is that all? No. there's a secret. And the secret is in that Jesus himself, crucified and risen, is there to be in the food of those who propose to come. Or again, one more secret. From time to time, we sin. We do indeed sin and when we sin and go and confess our sins, though it may be the words of the priest who says, "Go in peace and sin no more", it is the Lord Jesus who is there, and the Lord Jesus himself is speaking words of forgiveness as truly as he spoke to those who came to him with their troubled consciences.

We live in a world full of secrets, we have the Bible full of secrets, we have the family of the Christian Church full of secrets, and while all of us who are Christians share in those secrets, the ordained priest was born to be a steward of those secrets, to make them his own, to live by them, and to share them with all of you, so that you in turn may be sharing those secrets in a world that needs them so very much. This being so, on this day of the ordination of a priest, what specially can the lay people be doing in response to take their part? The lay people can , I am sure, be resolving two things: The first is to resolve to help your priest by having the right expectation about him, and the second is to help your priest by praying for him. Help your priest by having the right expectations. Don't just expect him to be so nice, and so friendly, and so kind, and so agreeable. I am sure he will be so nice, and so friendly, and so agreeable. But a man does not go through the great sacrificial operation of being ordained a priest just for that. So, have expectations of your priest that he will be Christ's servant, that he will be a man of prayer to help you to be the men and women of prayer, and that he will be a true steward of the mysteries of Christ. And expect him also to be brave where there is evil to be met. Where there is wrong to be met, expect your priest to be brave and support him in his courage, as he witnesses against anything that is wrong alongside of the righteousness of Christ.

And beside having made true expectations of your priest, pray, pray: and when I say pray, I don't mean just pray for him sometimes, or pray for him when you come to church, or pray for him on Tuesday afternoon or Thursday morning. No, I mean pray for him every day. He needs your prayers every single day, and you need to be called upon as Christian people to be praying for him every day. And let that be the great resolve that all of us every day will be praying for our priests, praying for the priests of the Church of God, and our prayers will be helping them to be true servants of Christ, and stewards of the secrets of God in a world that needs that service and a world that so desperately needs the secrets of God Himself.

Amen.

The Archbishop gave me that sermon. Then the Creed was recited, followed by the examination of the ordinand by the bishop, so the ordinand will publically bear witness to the Church's belief in the Triune God, and he/she will be shaped by the Scriptures, which contain all things necessary for Salvation. The ordinand had already stated this earlier in the Rite, and had signed a document stating this. This was followed by the great weight of the bishops and all priests present laying hands on my head. I had no idea how heavy this would be. My favorite Professor at Nashotah gave me this poem which he had published in 1971, and inscribed it,

"Dear Fodder, Every warm good wish, and hands of mercy on you laid. As ever, Bob Cooper".

I close this memoir with Bob Cooper's poem:

LAYING ON OF HANDS

Shekinah:

The weight of glory

Of Yahweh on Israel.

Moses sees the hindparts

Of God's glory

As he passes him,

Rock-hidden,

Hidden to bear

The grumbling squally sack

Of Hebrews.

I was ready for most of that

But not for brute gross flesh-weight

Of all those hands

Laid on my head

When God shifted his bag of worlds

To ease his walking

Cosmos-wide: some

Old-new part now

Is mine—less heavy

Though than

Green cross—wood.

I bend

Praise Him!

Bibliography

Anastaplo, George. *The Constitutionalist: Notes on the First Amendment*. Dallas: SMU Press, 1971

Anselm, St. *Cur Deus Homo*, translated by S. N. Deane. LaSalle, Illinois: Open Court, 1990.

————. *Proslogium*, translated by S. N. Deane. LaSalle, Illinois: Open Court, 1990.

Aquinas, St. Thomas. See under Thomas.

Athanasius, St. *On the Incarnation of the Word of God*, translated by a Religious of CSMV. London: Mowbray, 1953.

Atlas, James. "The Busy, Busy Wasp", in *The New York Times Magazine*, (October 18, 1992) https://www.nytimes.com/1992/10/18/magazine/the-busy-busy-wasp.html

Augustine, St. *Confessions*, translated by Henry Chadwick. Oxford: Oxford University Press, 1991.

————. *The Trinity*, translated by Edward Hill, OP. Brooklyn: New City Press, 1997.

Ashcraft, Kent. "An Open Letter to Dr. Laura". July, 2001. www.users.york.ac.uk.

Barr, James. *The Scope and Authority of the Bible*. Philadelphia: Westminster Press, 1980.

Barth, Karl. *The Epistle to the Romans*, translated by Edwyn C. Hoskyns. London: Oxford University Press, 1953.

————. *Protestant Theology in the Nineteenth Century: Its Background and History*. Valley Forge: Judson Press, 1973.

Betjeman, John. "Christmas". In *John Betjeman's Collected Poems*, compiled by Lord Birkenhead. London: John Murray, 1967.

————. "House of Rest". In *John Betjeman's Collected Poems*, compiled by Lord Birkenhead. London: John Murray, 1967.

Blythe, Ronald. In *The Penguin Companion to Literature 1*, ed. David Daiches. London: Penguin, 1971.

Brown, Peter. *The Rise of Western Christendom: Triumph and Diversity, A.D. 200—1000*. Second Edition. Oxford, Blackwell, 2003.

Browning, Robert. "A Grammarian's Funeral". In *Browning's Poetical Works*. New York: Houghton, Mifflin, 1895.

Buckley, Christopher. *But Enough About You*. New York, NY: Simon & Schuster, 2014.

Buckley, William F., " Introduction: Did You Ever See a Dream Walking?" In *Did You Ever See a Dream Walking? : American Conservative Thought in the Twentieth Century*, ed. William F. Buckley. Indianapolis: Bobbs—Merrill, 1970.

Buruma, Ian. "The War Over the Bomb". *New York Review of Books*. (September 21,1995) https://www.nybooks.com/articles/1995/09/21/the--war--over--the--bomb/

Cameron, J. M. "Editor's Introduction", to *An Essay on the Development of Christian Doctrine* by John Henry Newman. Baltimore: Penguin Books Ltd., 1974.

Campbell, Will. *Brother to a Dragonfly*. New York: Seabury Press, 1977.

Caro, Robert. *The Passage of Power: The Years of Lyndon Johnson*. New York: Knopf, 2012.

Chadwick, Owen. "The Oxford Movement and its Historian." In *The Anglican Tradition*, ed. Richard Holloway. Oxford: Mowbrays, 1984.

Chambers, Whittaker. *Witness*. New York: Random House, 1952.

Chaucer, Geoffrey. *Canterbury Tales*. "General Prologue". In Norton Anthology of English Literature, Volume 1, M. H. Abrams, General Editor. New York: Norton, 1993.

Chesterfield, Lord. *Letters of Lord Chesterfield to his Son*. London: J. M. Dent and Sons. 1929.

Clark, Kenneth. *Civilisation*. New York: Harper and Row, 1970.

Coffin, William Sloane. *Letters to a Young Doubter*. Louisville, Kentucky: Westminster John Knox Press, 2012.

Cohen, Morton. *Lewis Carroll: A Biography*. New York: Vintage, 1996.

Cory, William Johnson. *Heraclitus*. In the New Oxford Book of English Verse, ed. Helen Gardner. New York: Oxford University Press. 1972.

Cunningham, Lillian. "Does it Pay to Know Your Type?", in the *Washington Post*, December 14, 2012. Online: https://www.washingtonpost.com/national/on-leadership/meyers-briggs-does-it-pay-to-know-your-type/2012/12/14

Dalrymple, William. *From the Holy Mountain: A Journey among the Christians of the Middle East*. New York: Holt, 1999.

Davies, W. D. and Dale C. Allison Jr. *A Critical and Exegetical Commentary on The Gospel According to Saint Matthew*, Volume I, Introduction and Commentary on Matthew I—VII. Edinburgh: T & T Clark, 1988.

DaVinci, Leonardo. *The Notebooks of Leonardo DaVinci*, translated by Edward MacCurdy. New York: Reynal & Hitchcock, 1939.

Day, Peter. *Why Catholics Can't Sing: The Culture of Catholicism and the Triumph of Bad Taste*. New York: Crossroad, 1994.

Diebel, Anne. "Simple Answers to Profound Questions." In *The New York Review of Books*, December 20, 2018. Online: https://www.nybooks.com/articles/2018/12/20/meyers-briggs-test-simple-answers-profound-questions/

Dix, Dom Gregory. *The Shape of the Liturgy*. London: Dacre Press, 1978.

Duffy, Eamon. "A Hero of the Church." In *New York Review of Books*,(December 23, 2010) 62–4.

Edwards, David L. *Leaders of the Church of England: 1828—1944*. London: Oxford University Press, 1971.

Eiseley, Loren. *The Immense Journey: An Imaginative Naturalist Explores the Mysteries of Man and Nature*. New York: Vintage, 1959.

Eliot, T. S. "Little Gidding". In *T. S. Eliot: The Complete Poems and Plays 1909—1950*. New York: Harcourt, Brace & World, 1962.

Eusebius. *Ecclesiastical History*. III, 39. My own translation.

Feuerbach, Ludwig. *The Essence of Christianity*, translated by George Eliot. New York: Harper and Row, 1957.

Frost, Robert. "Revelation", in *Robert Frost: All Eleven of His Books—Complete*. New York: Holt, Rinehart and Winston.

Feynman, Richard. "The Value of Science". A Public Address. 1955.

Gibbon, Edward. *The History of the Decline and Fall of the Roman Empire*. Boston: AMS Press, 1974.

St. Gregory of Nazianzus. *First Letter to Cledonius Presbyter: Against Apollinarius*, translated by Charles Gordon Browne, and James Edward Swallow. In *The Nicene and Post—Nicene Fathers of the Christian Church*, ed. Philip Schaff, and Henry Wace. Grand Rapids: Eerdmans, 1978.

Grier, Peter. "The Chappie James Way". Air Force Magazine (October—November 2018) 70—73.

Gordon, Peter E. "Heidegger in Black" in the *New York Review of Books*, Oct. 9, 2014, 26–28.

Harrington, Michael. *Cacotopias and Utopias*. Santa Barbara: The Center for the Study of Democratic Institutions, 1965.

Hart, David Bentley. *The Experience of God: Being, Consciousness, Bliss*. New Haven: Yale University Press, 2013.

Hauerwas, Stanley, and William Willimon. *Resident Aliens: Life in the Christian Colony*. Nashville: Abingdon, 1989.

Herbert, George. "The Collar". In New Oxford Book of English Verse, ed. Helen Gardner, 272. New York: Oxford University Press, 1972.

———. "Love". In *The New Oxford Book of English Verse*, ed. Helen Gardner, 277. New York: Oxford University Press, 1972.

Hilton, Timothy. *John Ruskin: The Early Years*. New Haven, CT: Yale University Press, 1985.

Homer. *Odyssey*. Translated by Robert Fagles. New York: Viking Penguin, 1996.

Hooker, Richard. *Of the Laws of Ecclesiastical Polity*, Volumes I and II. Edited by W. Speed Hill. Cambridge: Belknap Press of Harvard University Press, 1977.

Irenaeus, St. *Against the Heresies*, Three Volumes, translated by Matthew C Steenberg and Dominic J. Unger OFM Cap. (Ancient Christian Writers). Matwah, New Jersey: Paulist Press, 2012.

Jaki, Stanley. *The Road to Science and the Ways to God*. Chicago: University of Chicago Press, 1978.

James, Bill. "The Man Who Invented Winning Ugly". *In The New Bill James Historical Baseball Abstract*, 245—6. New York: Free Press, 2001.

James, Robert Rhodes. *Lord Randolph Churchill*. London: Penguin Books, 1986.

Jaspers, Karl and Rudolph Bultmann. *Myth and Christianity: An Inquiry Into the Possibility of Religion Without Myth*. New York: The Noonday Press, 1969.

Jefferson, Thomas. *The Jefferson Bible, Smithsonian Edition: The Life and Morals of Jesus of Nazareth Extracted Textually from the Gospels*. Washington, D. C.: Smithsonian Books, 2011.

Jenson, Robert. *Systematic Theology, Volume 2: The Works of God*. New York: Oxford University Press, 1999.

———. "The Trinity and Church Structure", in *Shaping Our Future*, 15—26, ed. J. Stephen Freeman. Boston: Cowley Publications, 1994.

Josephus. *The Antiquities of the Jews*, translated by William Whiston. Grand Rapids: Kregel Publications, 1978.

Kennedy, John F. *Profiles in Courage*. New York: Harper and Brothers, 1956.

Keynes, John Maynard. *Essays in Biography*. Eastford, Connecticut: Martino Fine Books, 2012.

Lee, Harper. *To Kill a Mockingbird*. Philadelphia: J. B. Lippincott, 1960.

Levy, Paul. *Moore: G. E. Moore and the Cambridge Apostles*. New York: Holt Rinehart and Winston, 1979.

Lewis, C. S. *God in the Dock*, edited by Walter Hooper. Grand Rapids, Michigan: Eerdmans, 1970.

———. *The Problem of Pain*. London: Geoffrey Bles, 1943

———. *Surprised By Joy: The Shape of my Early Life*. London: Macmillan, 1955.

Lukacs, John. *At the End of an Age*. New Haven: Yale University Press. 2003.

"Lumbee Indians Break Up KKK Rally". *Life Magazine*. January 18, 1958.

MacIntyre, Alasdair. "God and the Theologians". In *The Honest to God Debate*, edited by David L. Edwards, 215—228. Philadelphia: Westminster Press, 1963.

Macquarrie, John. "How is Theology Possible". In *The Honest to God Debate*, edited by David L. Edwards, 187—193. Philadelphia: Westminster Press, 1963.

———. *Principles of Christian Theology*. New York: Scribner's, 1977.

Mann, Robert. *A Grand Delusion: America's Descent into Vietnam*. New York: Basic Books, 2001.

Maurice, Frederick Denison. *Theological Essays*. London: Macmillan, 1891.

McConnadine, John. "The Teachings of Karl Barth: A Positive Movement in German Theology." In *The Hibbert Journal* 23 (April 1927) 385–386.

McGrath, Alister. *A Passion for Truth: The Intellectual Coherence of Evangelicanism*. Downers Grove, Illinois: Intervarsity Press, 1989.

Melville, Herman. *Moby Dick: Or the Whale*. Norwalk, Connecticut :Easton Press, 1975.

Monk, Ray. *Ludwig Wittgenstein: The Duty of Genius*. London: Penguin, 1991.

Newman, John Henry Cardinal. *Apologia Pro Vita Sua: Being a History of His Religious Opinions*. London: Longmans, Green, 1895.

———. *The Idea of a University: Defined and Illustrated*. London: Longmans, Green, 1929.

Neill, Stephen. "Jesus and Myth". In *The Truth of God Incarnate*, ed. Michael Green. Grand Rapids: Eerdmans, 1977.

Niebuhr, H. R. *The Kingdom of God in America*. New York: Harper, 1937.

Palamas, St. Gregory. *The Triads*. Mahwah, New Jersey: Paulist Press, 1981.

Pannenberg, Wolfhart. *An Introduction to Systematic Theology*. Grand Rapids: Eerdmans, 1991.

Pelikan, Jaroslav. *Divine Rhetoric: The Sermon on the Mount as Message and as Model in Augustine, Chrysostom, and Luther*. Crestwood, New York: St. Vladimir's Seminary Press, 2001.

———. *Jesus Through the Centuries: His Place in the History of Culture*. New Haven: Yale University Press, 1985.

———. *What Has Athens to Do with Jerusalem?: Timaeus and Genesis in Counterpoint*. Ann Arbor: University of Michigan Press, 1997.

Percy, Walker. *Lost in the Cosmos: the last Self Help Book*. New York: Picador/Macmillan, 2000.

Piozzi, Hester Lynch. *Anecdotes of the Late Samuel Johnson, LLD.: During the Last Twenty Years of his Life*. Westport, Connecticut: Praeger, 1971.

Plato. " Laches", translated by Benjamin Jowett. In *The Collected Dialogues of Plato: Including the Letters*, ed. Edith Hamilton and Huntington Cairns. Princeton: Princeton University Press, 1961.

———. " Republic", translated by Paul Shorey. In *The Collected Dialogues of Plato: Including the Letters*, ed. Edith Hamilton and Huntington Cairns. Princeton: Princeton University Press, 1961.

———. " Timaeus,"translated by Benjamin Jowett. In *The Collected Dialogues of Plato: Including the Letters*, ed. Edith Hamilton and Huntington Cairns. Princeton: Princeton University Press, 1961.

Pliny the Younger. *Complete Letters (Oxford World's Classics)*, translated by P. G. Walsh. Oxford: Oxford University, 2009.

Rahner, Karl. *Theological Investigations: Volume IV More Recent Writings*, translated by Kevin Smyth. Baltimore: Helicon Press, 1966.

Ramsey, Michael. *The Anglican Spirit*, edited by Dale Coleman. New York: Church Publishing, 2004.

———. *Jesus and the Living Past*. Oxford: Oxford University Press, 1980.

Ratzinger, Joseph Cardinal. *Called to Communion: Understanding the Church Today*. San Francisco: Ignatius Press, 1996.

Reeves, Thomas. *Life and Times of Joe McCarthy: A Biography*. London: Blond & Briggs, 1982.

Remnick, David. "Gulag Lite". In *The New Yorker*, December 20, 2010. Online: https://www.newyorker.com/magazine/2010/12/20/gulag-lite

Roethke, Theodore. "The Waking," in *Words for the Wind*. Bloomington, Indiana: Indiana University Press, 1971.

Rosebery, Lord. *Lord Randolph Churchill*. New York: Harper and Brothers, 1906.

Rothman, Joshua. "Is Heidegger Contaminated by Nazism?", *The New Yorker* April 28, 2014. Online:https://www.newyorker.com/books/page-turner/is-heidegger-contaminated – by-nazism?

Schiller, Friedrich. *An die Freude*, Beethoven-Schiller nach "Urtext" von Max Unger. Leipzig: Ernst Eulenburg, c. 1925.

Schleiermacher, Friedrich. *The Christian Faith*, translated by H. R. Macintosh and James S. Stewart. Philadelphia: Fortress, 1976.

Schmemann, Alexander. *The Eucharist*. Crestwood, New York: St. Vladimir's Press, 1987.

Schurz, Carl. *Abraham Lincoln: A Biographical Essay*. New York: Houghton Mifflin, 1942.

Schweitzer, Albert. *The Quest of the Historical Jesus: A Critical Study of its Progress From Reimarus to Wrede*, translated by W. Montgomery. London: Adam and Charles Black, 1911.

Sittler, Joseph. *Essays on Nature and Grace*. Philadelphia: Fortress, 1972.

Steiner, George. *Nostalgia for the Absolute (CBC Massey Lecture)* . Toronto: House of Asansi Press, 1974.

Strauss, Leo. "A Giving of Accounts." In *Jewish Philosophy and the Crisis of Modernity: Essays and Lectures in Modern Jewish Thought*, ed. Kenneth Hart Green, 457–466. Albany: SUNY Press, 1997.

Stringfellow, William and Anthony Towne. *The Death and Life of Bishop Pike*. Garden City, New York: Doubleday, 1976.

Sykes, Stephen. *Unashamed Anglicanism*. Nashville: Abingdon, 1995.

Tacitus. *The Annals (Penguin Classics)* translated by Cynthia Damon. London: Penguin, 2012.

The Telegraph Obituary. "John Grigg". 2 January 2002. London.

St. Thomas Aquinas. *Summa Contra Gentiles*: Book I God, Chapter 3.2, translated by A. C. Pegis. In *Medieval Philosophy*, ed. Herman Shapiro. New York: Random House, 1964.

———. *Summa Theologiae*, translated by Anton C. Pegis. New York: Random House, 1945.

Tillich, Hannah. *From Time to Time*. New York: Stein and Day, 1973.

Tillich, Rene. "My Father, Paul Tillich". In *Spurensuche: Lebens---und Denkwege Paul Tillichs*, ed. Ilona Nord and Yorick Spiegel. Muenster: Lit Verlag, 2001.

Tillich, Paul. *A History of Christian Thought: From Its Judaic and Hellenistic Origins to Existentialism*. New York: Simon and Schuster, 1972.

———. *Systematic Theology* III. Chicago: University of Chicago Press, 1967.

Twain, Mark. *Letters from the Earth: New Uncensored Writings by Mark Twain*. New York: Fawcett Crest, 1962.

Tyrrell, George. *Christianity at the Crossroads*. Whitefish, Montana: Kessinger Publishing, 2010.

Waugh, Auberon. *Will This Do?: An Autobiography* . Boston: Da Capo, 1998.

Waugh, Evelyn. *The Loved One*. Columbus, Georgia: Little, Brown, and Company, 1965.

Weinstein, Allen. *The Haunted Wood: Soviet Espionage in America—The Stalin Era*. New York: Random House, 1998.

———. *Perjury: The Hiss—Chambers Case*. New York: Random House, 1985, 1997.

Williams, Rowan. *Anglican Identities*. Boston: Cowley Publications, 2003.

Wills, Garry. *Nixon Agonistes: The Triumph of the Self—Made Man*. Boston: Houghton Mifflin, 1970.

Wilson, A. N. *After the Victorians: The Decline of Britain in the World*. New York: Farrar, Straus, and Giroux, 2005.

———. *C. S. Lewis: A Biography*. New York: Random House, 1991.

———. *Eminent Victorians*. New York: Norton, 1989.

———. *God's Funeral: The Decline of Faith in Western Civilization*. New York: Norton, 1999.

———. *Our Times: The Age of Elizabeth II*. Farrar, Straus, and Giroux, 2009.

———. *The Victorians*. New York: Norton, 2003.

———. "Why I Believe Again" in *New Statesman*, 2 April 2009. http://www.newstatesman.com/print/node/163530

———. "Newman the Writer", in *Newman a Man For Our Time*, ed. David Brown. Wilton CT: Morehouse Press.

Wilson, Paul. "The Road to Rejection". *New York Review of Books*. (April 24, 2014) 28—30.

Wordsworth, William. "The Prelude: Book Eleventh, France, Conclusion". In *The Complete Poetical Works by William Wordsworth*. London: Macmillan, 1888.

Wright, N. T. *Paul and His Recent Interpreters: Some Contemporary Debates*. Philadelphia: Fortress, 2015.

———. *The Letter to the Romans: Introduction, Commentary, and Reflections*. In *The New Interpreter's Bible, Volume Ten*. Nashville, Abingdon, 2002.

———. *Simply Christian: Why Christianity Makes Sense*. San Francisco: Harper One, 2010.

Yeats, W. B . "Adam's Curse". In *The Collected Poems of W. B. Yeats*. New York: Macmillan, 1956.

CPSIA information can be obtained
at www.ICGtesting.com
Printed in the USA
BVHW011510010419
544230BV00023B/1307/P